REREADING THE STONE

REREADING THE STONE

DESIRE AND THE MAKING OF FICTION IN
DREAM OF THE RED CHAMBER

Anthony C. Yu

PRINCETON UNIVERSITY PRESS   PRINCETON, NEW JERSEY

Copyright © 1997 by Princeton University Press
Published by Princeton University Press, 41 William Street,
Princeton, New Jersey 08540
In the United Kingdom: Princeton University Press, Chichester, West
Sussex

Library of Congress Cataloging-in-Publication Data

Yu, Anthony C., 1938–
Rereading the stone : desire and the making of fiction in Dream of
the red chamber / Anthony C. Yu.
p. cm.
Includes bibliographical references (p.   ) and index.
ISBN 0-691-01561-9 (cl : alk. paper)
1. Ts'ao Hsüeh-ch'in, ca. 1717–1763. Hung lou meng. 2. Chinese
fiction—History and criticism. I. Title.
PL2727.S2Y6 1997
895'.1348—dc21 97-2207 CIP

This book has been composed in Times Roman

Princeton University Press books are printed on acid-free paper and meet
the guidelines for permanence and durability of the Committee of
Production Guidelines for Book Longevity of the Council on Library
Resources

Printed in the United States of America

1 3 5 7 9 10 8 6 4 2

For my students at
the University of Chicago
and *in memoriam*
the Dead at Tiananmen Square
June 4, 1989

Mi avvedevo ora che si possono sognare
anche dei libri, e dunque si possono sognare dei
sogni . . .
Un sogno è una scrittura, e molte scritture
non sono altro che sogni.
(Umberto Eco, *Il nome della rosa*)

Contents

Abbreviations

CLEAR	*Chinese Literature: Essays, Articles, Review*s
CWLM	*Chung Wai Literary Monthly* (Zhongwai wenxue 中外文學)
GDWXLLYJ	*Gudai wenxue lilun yanjiu* 古代文學理論研究
HCJ	*Historians of China and Japan*. Edited by W. G. Beasley and E. G. Pulleyblank. London: Oxford University Press, 1961.
HJAS	*Harvard Journal of Asiatic Studies*
HLM	*Hongloumeng* 紅樓夢. By Cao Xueqin and Gao E 曹雪芹, 高鶚. 3 vols. Beijing: Renmin wenxue, 1982. Citations refer only to this edition.
HLMJ	*Hongloumeng juan* 紅樓夢卷. Compiled by Yi Su 一粟. 2 vols. Shanghai: Zhonghua, 1963.
HLMXK	*Hongloumeng xuekan* 紅樓夢學刊
HLMYJJK	*Hongloumeng yanjiu jikan* 紅樓夢研究集刊
HLMZP	*Hongloumeng zhuping* 紅樓夢注評. Edited and compiled by Mao Debiao 毛德彪 et al. Nanning: Guangxi renmin, 1981.
HSWC	*Hu Shi(h) wencun* 胡適文存. By Hu Shi(h). 4 vols. Taipei: Yuandong, 1961.
Itō	Itō Sōhei 伊藤漱平, trans. *Kōrōmu* 紅樓夢. 3 vols. In *Chūgoku koten bungaku taikei* 中國古典文學大系. Tokyo: Heibonsha, 1969.
JAAR	*Journal of the American Academy of Religion*
JAS	*Journal of Asian Studies*
JCP	*Journal of Chinese Philosophy*
JW	*The Journey to the West*. Translated by Anthony C. Yu. 4 vols. Chicago: University of Chicago Press, 1977-1984.
Leningrad	*Shitouji* 石頭記. Facsimile edition of a handwritten manuscript kept in the Leningrad branch of the Institute of Oriental Studies, Soviet Academy of Sciences. 6 vols. Beijing: Zhonghua, 1986.
NLH	*New Literary History*
Pingyu	*Xinbian Shitouji Zhiyanzhai pingyu jijiao* 新編石頭記脂硯齋評語輯校. Edited by Chan Hingho (Chen Qinghao) 陳慶浩. Revised edition. Taipei: Lianjing, 1986.
PR	*La rêve dans le pavillon rouge*. Translated by Li Tche-houa and Jacqueline Alézaïs. 2 vols. Paris: Gallimard, 1981.
Qianlong	*Qianlong chaoben bainian hui Hongloumeng gao* 乾隆抄本百廿回紅樓夢稿. Reprint of 1963 facsimile edition. Shanghai: Guji, 1984.

QSC   *Quan Song ci* 全宋詞. Edited by Tang Guizhang 唐圭璋. 5 vols. Beijing: Zhonghua, 1965; Tainan: Minglun, 1975.

QTS   *Quan Tang shi* 全唐詩. 12 vols. Beijing: Zhonghua, 1960; Tainan: Minglun, 1974.

Sanjia   *Hongloumeng sanjia pingben* 紅樓夢三家評本. 4 vols. Shanghai: Guji, 1988.

SBBY   *Sibu beiyao* 四部備要

SBCK   *Sibu congkan* 四部叢刊

SCC   *Science and Civilisation in China*. By Joseph Needham. 13 vols. Cambridge: Cambridge University Press, 1954–.

SGLCW   *Quan shanggu sandai Qin Han Sanguo liuchao wen* 全上古三代秦漢三國六朝文. Compiled by Yan Kejun 嚴可均. 5 vols. Shanghai: Zhonghua, 1965.

SS   *The Story of the Stone*. By Cao Xueqin and Gao E; translated by David Hawkes and John Minford. 5 vols. Harmondsworth: Penguin, 1973-1986.

1754   *Qianlong Jiaxuben Zhiyanzhai chongping Shitouji* 乾隆甲戌本脂硯齋重評石頭記. Taipei: Hu Shi(h) jinianguan, 1961.

1759   *Zhiyanzhai chongping Shitouji* 脂硯齋重評石頭記. Facsimile edition of the Jimao (1759) manuscript kept in Beijing Library. 2 vols. Shanghai: Guji, 1981.

1760   *Gengchen chaoben Shitouji* 庚辰抄本石頭記. Reprint of 1955 edition by Beijing wenxue guji kanxingshe. 6 vols. Taipei: Guangwen, 1977.

T.   *Taishō shinshū dai-zōkyō* (The Tripitaka) 大正新脩大藏經. 85 vols. Edited by Takakusu Junjirō 高楠順次郎 and Watanabe Kaikyoku 渡邉海旭. Tokyo: Daizō shuppan kabushiki gaisha, 1934.

TPYL   *Taiping yulan* 太平御覽. Compiled by Li Fang 李昉 et al. 4 vols. Beijing: Zhonghua, 1960.

WSTY   *Wenshi tongyi* 文史通義. By Zhang Xuecheng 章學誠. Beijing: Zhonghua, 1975.

Yang   *A Dream of Red Mansions*. By Tsao Hsueh-chin and Kao Ngo; translated by Yang Hsien-yi and Gladys Yang. 3 vols. Beijing: Foreign Languages Press, 1978.

References to all Standard Histories, unless otherwise indicated, are to the *SBCK Bona* 百衲 edition.

THIS STUDY attempts to go beyond the customary verdict on the virtue of the eighteenth-century Chinese masterpiece of prose fiction, *Hongloumeng* (*Dream of the Red Chamber*, or alternatively, *Dream of Red Mansions* and *The Story of the Stone*), as that of the most vivid and comprehensive reflection of late imperial culture and social institutions. Instead, *Rereading the Stone* argues a thesis that has hitherto received little systematic treatment: that the narrative's merit as verbal art lies in its reflexive and innovative insistence, made through myriad occasions and devices, that it is a work of fiction. The novel, in other words, is as much a story about fictive representation as it is about human life.

Stated simply and directly, my thesis may be susceptible to the charge of pandering to critical notions currently fashionable in the Western academy. In my own defense, I should like to make two points clear. First, in talking this way about this particular literary text of premodern China, I am not making a general claim, as is the wont among certain literary theorists these days, that all literary texts are by definition reflexive and self-referential, that the reigning impulse of literature is the display of its own rhetoricity, and that in their most basic mode of existence texts cannot help miming themselves. The "prison-house of language," so goes the story, is also a hall of mirrors. This totalizing claim may or may not be true, depending on how one views the nature of language and literature, though I suspect that its uncritical acceptance may lead to a rather dull picture of the literary world and a predictable mode of criticism. Nonetheless, I do want to claim that *Hongloumeng* happens to be one text which places peculiar emphasis on its own nature and being and makes its own fictionality a subject of sustained exploration and dramatization. It does this by structuring literally the origin, genesis, production, and reception of the tale into the plot of the tale itself. If such an emphasis and such a technique are commonplace phenomena in Western literatures (from, say, the *Odyssey*, through *Hamlet* and *Don Quixote,* to *Ulysses* and *The Auroras of Autumn*), they constitute a rare—perhaps even unique—achievement in the history of Chinese literature. This achievement, therefore, deserves to be studied in some detail.

My second claim about what I am doing is consequent upon my first. Although this particular aspect of *Hongloumeng* was already evident to some extent to its very first readers (the Red Inkstone group of commentators), few modern students of the novel have examined the novel's achievement in this respect and its self-imposed challenge to the readers in a focused manner. The vast majority of critical studies of the work undertaken by Chinese scholars are dominated by the overriding concerns of various forms of historicism.

Since the dawn of the twentieth century, to be sure, these studies have vastly improved our knowledge of the novel's textual history, the author's family background, part of the process of the story's genesis, and China's social and cultural history that must serve as the interpretive contexts for the novel. The problem, however, lies in what I call the aesthetics of misplaced historicism that more often than not pervades these studies: namely, the assumption that the novel's acclaimed excellence as art is to be defined solely by the work's faithful reflection and representation of historical and social reality. In this sense, the attitude of the earliest readers of the narrative (the Red Inkstone circle) and that of many of the latest remains essentially the same: they praise the work because they always come away from their reading with the feeling that "there truly was such a person, truly such an event (*zhen you qi ren, zhen you qi shi*)."

One can run through the scholia of Red Inkstone and tabulate how many times remarks of such or similar sentiments occur, in contrast to how few times (or perhaps even none at all) those early readers have remarked: "this is totally false. What a nice fabrication!" At most the scholiasts would praise the author for his "cunning," but this commendation arguably has more to do with narrative technique than with fictionality as such. The way that Chinese readers tend to emphasize mimetic fidelity to history—in the form of authorial experience and family background, or in the form of social and cultural milieu, or a combination thereof—as a praiseworthy aesthetic criterion is thus not merely a decisive revelation of Chinese cultural value, namely, the privileged status of history as a bearer of meaning. Just as significantly, their silence with respect to *Hongloumeng*'s most noteworthy feature may indicate both their uneasiness with something that "happens" only in language and imagination, and their failure to comprehend the seriousness wherewith the narrative challenges sacrosanct history by its insistent and many-faceted query, posed in both plot and rhetoric of the work, about what is real and what is false—in sum, the *zhenjia* dialectic that confronts every reader in the very first pages of the tale.

To examine some of those devices in rhetoric, language, and emplotment, this study engages in close readings of selected episodes of the text, contextualized by different themes and topics. Chapter I discusses the artifice of reading by distinguishing the first scholiasts from more recent practitioners, and by differentiating the obligations of reading imposed by traditional Chinese historiography and fiction. Chapter II sketches a partial genealogy of subjectivity or desire (*qing*) that attempts to show not only the concept's centrality in Chinese intellectual and literary history but also how its Confucian formulation functions as agent of both control and conflict in the novelistic world. Chapter III concentrates on major Buddhist themes (monastic vocation, sentient wood and stone, obdurate stone, dream, mirror, and enlightenment) and analyzes how they are deployed by the text to aid in its assertion of fictionality. After canvasing briefly the interlocking issues of education, examination, vocation, marriage, and literary censorship, Chapter IV discusses *Hongloumeng*'s own view of imaginative literature as potent medium for the dissemination of desire. Chapter V, considering Lin Dai-yu as tragic protagonist, seeks to explore how this work of literary tragedy is built on the confluence of impersonal forces and the conflict of irreconcilable desires.[1]

Echoing a recurrent motif descending from ancient Chinese thought, the tale regards desire as both the defining trait and distinctive problem of the human. In narrating desire (*tan qing*), however, the novelistic text challenges the propensity of its traditional culture to contain desire through politics and ethics or to promise deliverance through religion. This focalizing treatment of desire and how it shapes literary invention and effect, I have sought to demonstrate, may well be *Hongloumeng*'s most enduring and distinctive accomplishment.

The book began in the classroom. In 1984–1985, Leo Ou-fan Lee and I finally realized our hope of jointly teaching a two-quarter sequence on the novel. The assembly of graduate and undergraduate students for more than half a year provided an unforgettable experience of intense and sustained reflection. We read this magnificent narrative in its full-length version from cover to cover, and we extended the discussion of its many aspects to spaces and times quite beyond the formal confines of the classroom.[2] Although I had already published one essay on the narrative prior to the class, I knew that the excitement I received from teaching the work would have to find further expression in writing.

The essays that eventually appeared in print were: "History, Fiction, and the Reading of Chinese Narrative," *CLEAR* 10 (1988): 1–19; "The Quest of Brother Amor: Buddhist Intimations in *The Story of the Stone*," *HJAS* 49/1 (June 1989): 55–92; and "The Stone of Fiction and the Fiction of Stone: Reflexivity and Religious Symbolism in *Hongloumeng*," *Studies in Language and Literature* (Taiwan) 4 (October 1990): 1–30. Along with my first essay, "Self and Family

---

[1] For all characters of the novel, I follow the practice of David Hawkes in segregating the given names.

[2] The current study also makes use of the full-length version of the novel because I share C. T. Hsia's high regard for the artistic merit of the last forty chapters (see *The Classic Chinese Novel*, pp. 250–57) and agree with John Minford's judgment in the Preface to vol. 4 of *SS* (pp. 22ff.) that Gao E and Cheng Weiyuan, the self-proclaimed editors and redactors of the full-length version, essentially told the truth. Those who accept the skeptical queries of the last third of the novel posed by such early authorities as Wu Shi-chang and Yu Pingbo may want to consult Minford's painstaking and meticulous study, "The Last Forty Chapters of *The Story of the Stone*." For a balanced assessment of the four early printed editions of *Hongloumeng*, see Xü Rencun and Xü Youwei, *Cheng keben Hongloumeng xinkao*. One recent study that also affirms the merit of the Cheng-Gao version is Chow Tse-chung, "*Honglou sanwen*." For two innovative studies that seek through computerized statistical analyses to question the argument for the separation of the first eighty chapters from the last forty on the bases of diction, style, and vocabulary, see the titles listed under Bing C. Chan in the selected bibliography.

in the *Hung-lou meng*: A New Look at Lin Tai-yü as Tragic Heroine," *CLEAR* 2 (1980): 199–223, they appear in revised form as portions of Chapters I, III, and V of the book. I thank the editors of the journals for their permission to use the materials.

A senior fellowship from the American Council of Learned Societies (1985–1986) gave me the needed time for moving forward the initial phase of research. During the years thereafter, faculty and student colleagues both in America and abroad have indulged my "ancient marinerlike" obsession with *Hongloumeng* by providing me with an occasional forum to try out my ideas and interpretations. The institutions that thus bestowed on me their generous hospitaity and an enabling context of discussion include Princeton University, Indiana University, University of British Columbia, University of Washington, Hong Kong University, University of Pittsburgh, University of Puget Sound, Yale University, University of California at San Diego, University of California at Los Angeles, Washington University, University of California at Irvine, University of Utah, University of Alberta, University of California at Berkeley, Stanford University, and Columbia University.

Over the years, my deans at the University of Chicago (Franklin Gamwell and Clark Gilpin of the Divinity School; Stuart Tave and Philip Gossett of the Division of Humanities) have given me unstinting support, which continues to facilitate my work. Tai-loi Ma, Wen-pai Tai, and Eizaburo Okuizumi of our East Asian Library have my deep gratitude for indulging, with kindness and good humor, my compulsive requests for books, articles, microfilms, and other materials. Colleagues who have read various portions of the manuscript at different times and offered their instructive response include C. T. Hsia, Patrick Hanan, Andrew Plaks, Barbara Stoler Miller, Whalen Lai, Robert Hegel, Zhang Longxi, K'ang-i Sun Chang, Nathan Sivin, Wang Jing, Haun Saussy, Victor Mair, Edward Shaughnessy, and Wai-yee Li. Two Press readers for Princeton have also provided discerning critiques and comments for improving the study, though its faults and shortcomings remain my own.

At the final stages of preparing the manuscript, Richard G. Wang, Xu Dongfeng, Hajime Nakatani, and Wallace Sher-shiueh Li—all doctoral students at Chicago—have lent me invaluable assistance in proofreading a long and unwieldy text. Mr. Li, especially, has accelerated the book's production by compiling the glossary, bibliography, and index. With immense generosity, Professor Michael Puett of Harvard University also helped in proofreading.

Discussions of literatures and literary studies with our son Christopher, now having just completed his own graduate training, have occasioned immense pleasure and inspiration. I express abiding gratitude to my wife Priscilla for urging me to discover for myself the seemingly inexhaustible gratification that the reading of *Hongloumeng* can yield. As always, she has proven to be the most patient listener, the sternest critic, and the most ardent believer.

The completion of this book also marks the end of twenty-nine years of teaching at the University of Chicago. To the hundreds of graduate students and the smaller groups of undergraduates once enrolled in my classes, I owe a debt of the intellect and stimulation that defies any easy description. From casual remarks to the most cogent formulations, from the briefest exercises to the most elaborate dissertations, their work has never failed to present for me new vistas of thought or possibilities of inquiry. If I have grown to be a better teacher and scholar in this long stretch a time, they must claim a good share of the credit.

Even as I write to affirm my appreciation for those I have been privileged to teach, I cannot forget a less fortunate group of young people in China who some years ago sacrificed their lives for their hopes and beliefs. May the day come soon when all Chinese students can think the unthinkable, and thus can speak and write in freedom.

REREADING THE STONE

CHAPTER I.

Reading

Toute graphie, dont l'historiographie,
relève d'une théorie élargée de la lecture.
(Paul Ricoeur, *Temps et récit*)

READING THE FIRST READINGS

Truth becomes fiction when the fiction's true;
Real becomes not-real when the unreal's real.

(*SS* 1: 130; *HLM* 1: 75)

This couplet, which presides over an archway leading to the Land of Illusion mentioned in chapter 1 of *Hongloumeng* and visited by Jia Bao-yu in chapter 5, has long been regarded as one succinct summation of that narrative's ordering principle and thematic focus. In view of the history of its criticism since publication of the *Hongloumeng* in the late eighteenth century, one may argue as well that the issue of truth and fiction has preoccupied much of the scholarly investigation of this masterpiece. This tendency undoubtedly owes its genesis and continuous reinforcement to several factors.

The first is manifestly linguistic. Throughout the history of Chinese prose fiction, from the early tales of the anomalous (*zhiguai*) to the vernacular short stories and the developed novels of the Ming-Qing period, there is an unbroken tradition of word play, verbal riddle, and paronomastic rhetoric. A story on the stereotypical wicked stepmother collected in the *Yuanhunzhi* names her own son Tiechu (Iron Pestle) so that he can assume symbolic prominence over his stepbrother named Tiejiu (Iron Mortar).[1] In chapter 23 of *The Journey to the West*, where the pilgrims are tested by various deities, the goddess in the guise of a mortal widow announces, "My maiden surname is Jia (Unreal) and the surname of my husband's family is Mo (Nonexisting)."[2] In the *Jinpingmei* or *The Plum in the Golden Vase*, there are many "names of characters like Wu Tien-en ('No Trace of Benevolence') or Pu Chih-tao ('Don't Know') among Hsi-men Ch'ing's cronies, or the singing-girl Ch'i Hsiang-erh, whose surname Ch'i (literally, 'to regulate') calls up the *Ta-hsüeh* every time her brothel (*ch'i-*

---

[1] See Xu Zhen'e, *Han Wei liuchao xiaoshuo xuan*, pp. 80–81.
[2] *JW* 1: 449.

chia or 'regulate the household') is mentioned."[3] In the *Xiyoubu* or *The Tower of Myriad Mirrors* (completed 1641), Dong Yue, the putative author, breaks up the word *qing* (desire, sentiment, feeling) into its anagrammatic components to form King Little Moon, the name of one of the characters. Within such a context *Hongloumeng* is not only a highly traditional work in its deployment of paronomastic rhetoric but its exceptional achievement arguably lies in the extent to which it exploits its linguistic medium—the peculiarities of the Chinese language in both its phonetic and ideographic elements.

If there is any discernible thread of commonality running through the recorded experience of generations of readers since the novel's publication—such as that gathered in *Hongloumeng juan*, a compendium of criticism and commentary of the narrative from the eighteenth to the twentieth century—it is the delight and constant effort of those readers to decipher the hidden signification of puns, enigmas, riddles, names, anagrams, metonyms, and oracular verses that stud the text. Whether all such devices add up finally to one grand and consistent scheme of narration that can justify the nomenclature of continuous allegory is a question still subject to debate. There can be no denial, however, that this type of language game, conducted with such panache and dexterity by its author, has succeeded in arousing the curiosity of even the most lethargic reader and alerting him to the possibility of the displacement of meaning. Why does this lengthy tale resort to such insistent and elaborate word play on *zhen* and *jia*, the words translated as "truth" and "fiction" in the couplet cited at the beginning of this chapter? If a framing character at the start of the narrative is given the name Zhen Shi-yin (homonymically, true-events-concealed), and he is only one of scores of characters whose names are built on similar double entendres, are we to suppose that certain true incidents and persons have indeed been hidden in, or by, the text? If so, what and who are they? These are but a sample of the many similar and obvious questions that attentive readers of the tale may be provoked to ponder. As a scholar has written of Renaissance allegory, "that which is so ostentatiously hidden must necessarily call attention to its own hidden presence—otherwise hidden meaning might remain forever hidden."[4] The first lesson one learns from the reading of *Hongloumeng*, a lesson as profound as its expression is commonplace, is that there is more to the linguistic sign than meets the eye and ear.[5]

---

[3] Katherine Carlitz, *The Rhetoric of "Chin P'ing Mei,"* p. 78.

[4] Mindele Anne Treip, *Allegorical Poetics and the Epic*, p. 133.

[5] Hidden meaning in Chinese texts, according to David L. Rolston's analysis, may be employed because of the following factors: concern for the author's political safety, embarrassing content or details, esoteric knowledge and the need for secrecy, abstract ideas or patterns that require realistic figuration, and the reader's intellectual pleasure. See his *Reading and Writing between the Lines*, Part II, chapter 4. Such factors may all be found as well in the history of Western hermeneutics, from Augustine's examination of signs and scriptural difficulties in *De doctrina christiana*, through the development of medieval and Renaissance allegory and

The second reason for a reader's suspicion of the narrative's surface meaning is attributable to the history of this work's dissemination and reception. We know that even prior to reaching any semblance of completion, the narrative at various stages of its formation was circulated by mid-eighteenth century to a widening circle of readers largely made up of friends and possible relatives of the principal author, Cao Xueqin. At least eleven versions of manually transcribed manuscripts are now known to us, all bearing the notations by a person with the sobriquet of Zhiyanzhai or the Red Inkstone Studio Scholiast, and additional remarks by one Jihusou or Odd Tablet (as David Hawkes calls him) as well as by several other named and unnamed readers.[6] The composite scholia draws the picture that several readers would discuss at times the emergent manuscript and one person would then write down specific remarks. Calligraphic evidence of these handwritten manuscripts indicate a body of scholia written by quite a few hands, and those who had copied the narrative itself would produce an even greater number.

Neither the existence of a scholiast like Red Inkstone Studio nor the extensiveness of his remarks should in itself occasion excessive attention for, after all, the practice of fiction criticism by means of marginal and interlinear comments has a long history in China. It was a practice, moreover, common to the elucidation of philosophical, historical, and literary texts that, in turn, was based on an established pedagogical method extending from antiquity to modern times.[7] The four masterworks of fiction of the Ming period with which *Hongloumeng* has most often been compared and grouped as China's most enduring novelistic monuments, as well as many other works of drama and poetry, have come down to us often in printed versions that bear the introductory, marginal, head, and interlinear scholia of various commentators. Thus *Sanguozhi yanyi* (*The Three Kingdoms*) found its most distinguished critical spokesman in Mao Zonggang (fl. 1660), *Shuihuzhuan* (*Outlaws of the Marsh*) in Jin Shengtan (1610–1661), *Jinpingmei* (*The Plum in the Golden Vase*) in Zhang Zhupo (1670–1698?), and *Xiyouji* (*The Journey to the West*) in Li Zhi (1520–1602),

---

allegoresis, to the modern and post-modern notions of metaphor. For the purpose of this study, I use allegory for creative allegory and allegoresis as a method of exegesis or interpretation.

[6] For authoritative studies of the work's textual history, see Wang Sanqing *Hongloumeng banben yanjiu*, and Chan Hing-ho (Chen Qinghao), *Le "Hongloumeng" et les commentaires de Zhiyanzhai*.

[7] A fine survey of the subject will be found in the Introduction to David L. Rolston, ed., *How to Read the Chinese Novel*. An expanded and even more astute discussion of the related subjects of readership and commentary of traditional Chinese fiction will appear with his forthcoming *Reading and Writing between the Lines*. I use the term scholia in the strict sense of a body of notes or glosses, inscribed either in the various margins or interlineally in the texts, which expound or criticize the language or subject matter of a specific, selected passage. It is in this sense that the Red Inkstone remarks should most appropriately be understood. Chinese texts differ from those of Western antiquity in that an individual scholium would not necessarily contain a lemma.

if genuine, or Chen Shibin (fl. second half of the seventeenth century). Although Mao Zonggang along with his father must be credited with the final redaction of *Three Kingdoms*, a version that attained undiminished popularity for more than three hundred years, none of the commentators enumerated here could be said to have known the authors—real or putative—of these novels, let alone enjoyed the kind of intimate relations that apparently obtained between the circle of Red Inkstone and Cao Xueqin. Since the habit of showing and discussing one's writings, completed or not, with friends or relatives is a custom of long standing in China, the importance of the Red Inkstone scholia must be defined not merely by its revelation of how a text like *Hongloumeng* has been read by a group of readers in a specific moment of Chinese history—by itself a feature certainly no different from all other scholia or commentaries—but much more decisively by the degree to which it illumines the process of artistic creation and textual formation peculiar to this novel.[8]

In the most recent and most detailed examination of the Red Inkstone group of manuscripts that constitute the earliest layer of *Hongloumeng*'s textual stemma, the specialist Chan Hing-ho (Chen Qinghao) follows the suggestion by Hu Shi and most other students of the narrative to affirm that Cao Xueqin, in 1745, had in his possession a manuscript entitled *Fengyue baojian* or *A Bejeweled Mirror of Romantic Love.*[9] For the next ten years or so, Cao spent his time fastidiously fashioning and refashioning this emergent masterpiece by adding or deleting certain portions, dividing the narrative into chapters, and assigning them their titular headings. In all likelihood the text that Cao worked on had already by this time accrued some comments by various readers. By the year *jiaxu* (1754) during the reign of Qianlong, the text in this view could have been nearly completed. It was in this same year that Red Inkstone

---

[8] See Richard B. Matther, trans., *Shih-shuo Hsin-yü: A New Account of Tales of the World*, pp. 130–33, for some examples of discussing works in progress with one's friends.

[9] See Chan Hing-ho, *Le "Hongloumeng" et les commentaires*, pp. 298–99; see also *Pingyu*, "Introduction," pp. 110–12, and Sun Xun, *Hongloumeng zhiping chutan*, pp. 135–41. Hu Shi, "Kaozheng *Hongloumeng* di xin cailiao," p. 377, based his suggestion on the scholiast's headnote of chapter 1 found in the 1754 (*jiaxu*) version: "Formerly Xueqin had in his possession the book, *Fengyue baojian*, for which his brother Tangcun wrote a preface. Now that Tangcun is dead, the sight of the new makes me recall the old, and I thus continue to use it." See *Pingyu*, p. 12. The controversy surrounding this particular scholium has to do with the ambiguous antecedent to the terminal pronoun "it" (*zhi*): that is, whether "it" refers to the preface of the book, or the sentence in the text that elicited the scholium. For a different interpretation, see Wu Shih-ch'ang, *On "The Red Chamber Dream,"* pp. 63–72. For a critique of Wu's position, see Itō Sōhei's 1962 essay in *Tokyo Shina gaku hō*. Wu's rebuttal and further view on the "old book" and preface may be found in his *Hongloumeng tanyuan waibian*, pp. 201–50. Zhao Gang in *Hongloumeng kaozheng shiyi*, p. 180, thinks that "it" merely refers to the particular sentence of the text. For further disagreement with Wu, see Pi Shumin, *Hongloumeng kaolunji*, pp. 17–29. It may be pointed out that the pronoun is not the only word of ambiguity in the scholium, for the verb *you* can similarly mean either that Cao had owned a book or had written one. See also discussion by Yu Yingshi in "Guanyu *Hongloumeng* di zuozhe he sixiang wenti," pp. 181–96.

made a new copy of the tale and contributed a new—and much more extensive—set of commentaries. For the next four years thereafter, according to Chan, Red Inkstone would continue to add his comments, large portions of which would be copied and preserved, though sometimes rearranged, in one or another manuscript tradition, all bearing the appellation *Zhiyanzhai congping "Shitouji"* or, literally, *The Story of the Stone, again Annotated by the Studio of the Rouge Inkstone.*

Whether Chan's reconstruction of this sequence of filiation undergone by the handwritten manuscripts finds acceptance in the scholarly community remains to be seen. That the reconstruction is based more on textual scholia than on comparative study of the texts themselves, and that a didactic, cautionary tale named *Fengyue baojian* is posited as Cao Xueqin's Urtext are proposals that should stimulate further deliberation. Chan's meticulous investigation, however, serves at the very least to bring out more sharply than ever the scholiasts' peculiar relationship to the author and their passionate involvement with the narrative. In the 1760 (*gengchen*) manuscript, for example, chapter 18 (*SS* 1: 371; *HLM* 1: 257) bears the following observation by Red Inkstone on the episode of a little actress's haughty behavior during the imperial consort's homecoming:

> According to a recent proverb, "You may support a thousand soldiers but not a single show." This saying is meant to convey that good actors ought not to be supported. For if a certain individual among the troupe happens to excel in his craft, he would put on airs and use his ability to dominate the others. All kinds of detestable behavior would place his patron in a dilemma: the patron would have neither the heart to banish him nor the courage to rebuke him. . . . I've had vast experience with actors and actresses, and in each instance, the same thing occurs. I've also discussed this matter with various cousins of our noble house who were accustomed to supporting theatrical troupes. All of them were aware of this problem, but none had the talent to describe it. When I read *The Story of the Stone* and come upon such a statement as "neither [play] had a suitable part for a soubrette in it, and Charmante obdurately refused," I can see—splashed all over the page— exactly this kind of insolence borne of cocksureness in one's abilities. As for, moreover, the episode of the Pear Tree Court [chap. 36] where the deepest feelings of some characters are suddenly made known, the entire scene is as perfectly wrought as if it had been set out on a tray. Persons whom I saw thirty years ago and with whom I was intimate now appear on the page, and this compels me to declare that *The Story of the Stone* is a book of the deepest feelings and the truest words. Unless, however, one has in fact experienced such events or been deluded by such feelings, reading it is like "chewing wax" absentmindedly, never understanding the miraculous wonders of what one has witnessed. (*Pingyu*, p. 349)

This passage makes apparent that the scholiast's response to what he reads entails a deeper and, perhaps, altogether different involvement than the usual understanding of readerly identification with fictive representation. Admittedly, the scholiast also declares in chapter 20 that the reader must "put oneself in the position of Bao-yu and a Dai-yu before one could understand" certain remarks those fictive characters have made to each other (*Pingyu*, p. 402). But the fundamental assumption underlying both scholia draws on the conviction, characteristic of so much of Chinese thought, that the appreciation of fiction depends on its validation by the reader's empirical or lived experience. As we shall see in our discussion of the subject of *qing* (disposition, desire) in Chapter II, the stimulus-response (*ganying*) aesthetics that dominated the Chinese tradition from antiquity down to the present posits the author's real emotions and experiences as those finding expression in whatever medium utilized. Correspondingly, the most apposite response by reader or audience lies in the correct ascertainment of what is "really" represented. Aesthetics, like it or not, is always autobiography; herein resides as well the ultimate political and moral meaning of art. Appropriately, therefore, the scholiast bases his verdict of the tale he read as "a book of the deepest feelings and the truest words" on double ground: persons encountered thirty years ago reappear as fictive characters, and his own shared experience with the author makes him a much more discerning reader. Fiction, in such a view, seems to have no higher truth than that which has actually occurred or happened.

It is this conviction that creates the thrust of the remarks by Red Inkstone and his circle, because they focus precisely on the *privilege* of those readers as eyewitnesses to many of the events and persons represented. This is certainly the perspective wherewith Red Inkstone views himself, and this is also how he has been regarded by modern readers of the work. Throughout the scholia runs the repeated emphasis on "a ready-made composition personally experienced by the author and not fashioned by appropriate invention" (*Pingyu*, p. 710), and that "unless one had personally experienced such a setting (*qin li qi jing*) one could not have written it" (*Pingyu*, p. 707; see also p. 337). Moreover, the scholiast insists that he, too, is "a person of experience (*guolai ren, jingliguo zhe*)" (*Pingyu*, pp. 125, 131, 180–81), who has himself "seen and heard (*mudu, qinwen*)" (*Pingyu*, pp. 669, 710) and "lived through what the author had lived through" (*Pingyu*, p. 695).[10]

These assertions of Red Inkstone may not amount to a total disavowal of *Hongloumeng* as a work of fiction. In chapter 12, a comment contained in the 1760 manuscript (*Pingyu*, p. 235) has even pointed out that the mirror used in vain by Jia Rui to cure himself of illness brought on by his lechery is, in fact,

---

[10] For further enumeration and discussion of such remarks by the scholiast, see Zhao Gang and Chen Zhongyi, *Hongloumeng yanjiu xinbian*, pp. 149–47, and *Pingyu*, "Introduction," pp. 102–3. Chen Xizhong's argument that the phrase *zhen you shishi* (real, existing events) means not true incidents in the author's or the scholiast's life but merely general occurrences is not persuasive. See "Zhen you shishi," in *Hongxue sanshinian lunwen xuan* 3: 384–87.

a symbol of the novel's fabricative and illusory nature (*yan qi shu yuanshi kongxu huanshe*), for the instrument has etched on its back the words "a bejeweled mirror of romantic love," which is, of course, also a title of the narrative. In chapter 19 of the 1759 (*jimao*) manuscript (*Pingyu*, pp. 354–55), there is also the declaration that "the character of Bao-yu is the kind of person seen and known by us only through the book; actually we have never met him in person." Such disclaimers notwithstanding, the drift of the scholia as a whole is clear: specific passages and incidents in the text are found to be moving on account of their authentic repetition or replication of what the scholiasts had seen and heard years before. These segments are frequently praised precisely because the verbal representations found therein are said to be never deliberately invented. Taken literally, these remarks of Red Inkstone and others certainly highlight the hallmark of their annotations. Whereas the shared truth of an imagined reality is what unites reader and author in every act of sympathetic reading of fiction, the special bond between the circle of Red Inkstone Studio and their author is forged by a particular set of circumstances.

In another text of traditional Chinese commentary of a novel, for example, the anonymous "On the Parabolic Meaning of *Jinpingmei* (*Jinpingmei* yuyishuo)," the very opening defines the novel in terms of its parabolic or allegorical nature (*baiguan zhe, yuyan ye*: literally, that which is collected by the petty official [traditional metaphor for *xiaoshuo* or novel] is parable or allegory). It then goes on immediately to characterize it as a "discourse of wind and shadow (*fengying zhi tan*)" built on the "unreal fashioning of a person (*jia nie yi ren*) and the illusory invention of an event (*huan zao yi shi*)."[11] The Red Inkstone circle, on the other hand, would hardly subscribe to such an assessment of their favored text. Readers and author, as far as this novel is concerend, are linked not so much by empathetic understanding as they are by actual participation in allegedly the same experience. Theirs is the authority—and secret—of a shared history.

When the young Bao-yu in chapter 5 is told that no one would comprehend the wonders of the oracular songs he just heard without being also an "insider (*ge zhong ren*),"[12] the remark of the Goddess Disenchantment has elicited this interlinear scholium in the 1754 manuscript: "These three words are most important. I wonder who is an insider. Is Bao-yu an insider? But then, is the Stone also an insider? Is the author also an insider? Is the reader, too, an insider?" (*Pingyu*, p. 128)

Notwithstanding its playful tone, this observation of the scholiast touches on a serious problem of interpretation, namely, the question of identity—for

[11] See "*Jinpingmei* yuyishuo," 1.

[12] David Hawkes's translation (in *SS* 1: 139) of the passage as "you need to know what the songs are about" misses the force of the term by shifting the emphasis from the hearer to the content of the songs.

the text, and for the reader or reading community. Are Bao-yu and the Stone merely fictive entities or are they allegories of some actual, historical figures? Is special knowledge of whatever nature a requisite for the text's proper reading? By posing his questions in the manner cited, the scholiast seems to want to sharpen his reader's awareness that there are different levels of knowledge that can be distinguished and must be presupposed when we encounter an episode such as Bao-yu's tour of the Land of Illusion. What the human youth of chapter 5 knows differs greatly from what the Stone (possibly as narrator and mythical precursor of Bao-yu) knows. The meaning of the Goddess's remark also seems clear: Bao-yu cannot attain a true understanding of what he hears, sees, and reads in his dream until he has acquired experiential knowledge that would grant him such understanding. Only experience such as that both prescribed by the Goddess and intimated in the oracular songs can qualify him to be the "insider," but that denomination also does not mean quite the same thing when it is applied to either the author or the reader (in this case, presumably the scholiast). The Goddess's use of the term "insider" thus generates immense irony, made more explicit and multidimensioned by Red Inkstone's rhetorical questions that both identify and augment the chain of readings implicit in the text: Bao-yu's reading of the riddling oracles, Disenchantment's reading of Bao-yu and the family, the implied narrator's reading of the episode, the author's reading of the narrator, Red Inkstone's reading of the author, and our reading of both text and Red Inkstone.

Much of traditional *dufa* (literally, how to read) and *pingdian* (literally, commentarial and dotted) criticism in Chinese literary history purports to provide some knowledge, effective or not, whereby the benighted reader may acquire better understanding of a particular text. The Red Inkstone scholia, however, frequently diverge from this mission, because their comments scattered throughout the text intrigue and perplex as much as they enlighten and inform. More often than not, their wilful ambiguities arguably betray a desire to maintain a position of privilege over the uninformed reader.[13]

It is no small frustration to students of the novel that the identity of Red Inkstone and his circle continue to elude detection. There is no dispute, however,

---

[13] John C. Y. Wang in "The Chih-yen-chai Commentary and the *Dream of the Red Chamber*," p. 193, has asserted that "the main impression one gets from reading the Commentary is that it is meant to elucidate the meaning and fine writing in the novel for the sake of the reader with no inside knowledge of the events described." By focusing his study on the traditional terms of fiction criticism used by the scholiasts, Wang has indeed made a good case that their remarks highlight what they consider to be "fine writing" in the novel. The scholiasts' commendation of the work as innovative through constant comparison with antecedent novels is also a prominent feature noted by David Rolston in *Reading and Writing between the Lines*, Part IV, chapter 4. Whether, however, they always succeed in imparting to the reader comprehensible "inside knowledge" remains debatable.

that the scholiasts, particularly Red Inkstone and Odd Tablet, were familiar with certain aspects of the Cao family. Such remarks as the references to "the true cause of catastrophe at Nanjing" (*Pingyu*, p. 28), to "the story of West Hall" (*Pingyu*, p. 544), and to the peculiar significance of the word, "west" (see *Pingyu*, p. 45), themselves betoken more than a passing knowledge.[14] The intense feel that their comments have for the bustling life of a large aristocratic household and the pervasive sense of loss and nostalgia for bygone glory have led to the speculation that Red Inkstone and Odd Tablet might well have been descendents of Cao Yin, the grandfather of Xueqin.[15]

Added to such intimate acquaintance with the vicissitudes of the Cao family is the intimation that the scholiast may have had a hand in the actual construction of certain episodes of the tale. The most frequently cited example of such intervention is Odd Tablet's allusion to the manner of Qin Ke-qing's death at the end of chapter 13:

That "Qin Keqing dies in the Celestial Fragrance Pavilion because of her adultery" indicates the author's use of a historiographical style. The two episodes of her soul's appearance to Phoenix and her prophecy concerning the later developments of the Jia household are matters that people secure in the enjoyment of their wealth can indeed think of. Even without revealing her [incestuous?] affair, her words and their meaning can move people to deep grief and admiration. For these reasons, this old codger had left her off the hook and ordered Xueqin and Meixi to delete [the incident of incest?]. (*Pingyu*, p. 253)

Although this remark has aroused the curiosity of many readers with the veiled allusion to the cause of Qin's death (possibly suicide) and a tantalizing glimpse of one part of a suppressed plot, what is more germane to our discussion is the lilt of authorization in the scholiast's voice. Indeed, the strong sense of themselves as participants in the novel's creation has led Red Inkstone and Odd Tablet to a form of indulgence normally reserved for the author. Throughout their comments, they refer to many of the principal fictive characters as practically their own children or kin, addressing them with such hypocorisms

---

[14] The "catastrophe of Nanjing" is taken by most modern students as a reference to the imperial dismissal of Cao Fu as textile commissioner of Nanking and the confiscation of his estate in January 1728. For an authoritative account of the Cao family and its tragic decline, see Jonathan D. Spence, *Ts'ao Yin and the K'ang-hsi Emperor*, especially chapter 7. The significance of "west" seems to have derived from the fact that Cao Yin, the author's grandfather, had given himself the appellation "The Flower-Sweeping Acolyte of West Hall" (*Xitang saohua xingzhe*). So fond of the west was he that he named his garden West Garden (*Xi yuan*), his study West Hall and West Studio (*Xi tang, Xi xuan*), and his volume of collected lyrics, *Works of the Western Farmer (Xinongji)*. See Zhao Gang, *Hongloumeng kaozheng shiyi*, p. 145.

[15] See Zhao Gang and Chen Zhongyi, *Hongloumeng yanjiu xinbian*, pp. 73–138; and Chan Hing-ho in *Pingyu*, Introduction, pp. 99–111. Zhou Ruchang in *Hongloumeng xinzheng* 2: 867–68, however, advocates a female scholiast, perhaps the author's wife.

or augmentatives as Ah So-and-So, child (*er*), big brother (*xiong*), and beloved (*qing*). Thus they would have us see their intimacy with the novelistic household as a link paradoxically secured by the special knowledge of real history and the special authority of a creative artist.[16] As a result of this unusual combination, the temptation which their comments offer to all subsequent readers of the work is to submit to that authority and as much as possible to acquire that knowledge.

Even in the capacious history of Chinese literature, in which certain texts have spawned a vast quantity of annotations and commentaries, the magnitude of critical interest that *Hongloumeng*, a relatively late work of the eighteenth century, has attracted is both awesome and mind-boggling. Since the rediscovery of the Red Inkstone manuscripts early in this century, students of the novel have been swayed by the seductive rhetoric of the scholiasts to such extent that a good deal of contemporary discussion of the novel now centers on conflicting interpretations, not of the text but of the scholia themselves.

One instance of such controversy, for example, concerns the characterization of Dai-yu and Bao-chai, a problem of no mean significance since it affects one's final assessment of the novel, the eventual outcome of its plot, and even the authenticity of the last forty chapters. Certain episodes of the narrative portray these two cousins as enduring rivals for the protagonist's love. Moreover, in the 120-chapter version of the work published in 1791/92, Bao-yu is tricked into marrying Bao-chai by the schemes of his nearest kin, while his preferred Dai-yu dies a lonely, agonizing death on his wedding night. Ostensibly contradicting this line of development, however, is the episode of Bao-yu touring the Land of Illusion in chapter 5. The oracular songs and prophecies he hears and scenes he witnesses purport to sketch out individually the destiny of

---

[16] The rhetoric of the commentator that arrogates to itself authorial authority did not originate with the Red Inkstone scholiasts, nor was it unique to China, as Ellen Widmer has pointed out in her perceptive comparison of Roland Barthes and Jin Shengtan. See *The Margins of Utopia*, p. 106. Widmer remarks that "any serious comparison of Eastern and Western critical experience would have to go beyond the critic's own frame of reference. For example, Barthes may have added his voice to a Balzac story, but few readers of today would agree that only in Barthes' version could 'Sarrasine' have something to say." The problem of interpretation becomes even more vexing when and if the "reading community" upholds as its conscious belief that there is no essential difference between midrash and the "primary" text of scripture or literature. On the related issue of whether Cao Xueqin and Red Inkstone could be the same person, see also the discussion by Rolston in *Reading and Writing between the Lines*, Part VI chapter 4. On the tendency to merge author and commentator in certain moments of the history of Chinese fiction, see the shrewd analysis by Martin W. Huang in "Author(ity) and Reader in Traditional Chinese *Xiaoshuo* Commentary," 41–67. For imperial canonization of Song editions and interpretations of the Classics, see *Da Qing huidian* 51: 20a (Guangxu ed.); R. Kent Guy, *The Emperor's Four Treasuries*, pp. 18–20. On midrash and literature, see Gerald L. Bruns, "Midrash and Allegory," pp. 625–46; Daniel Boyarin, *Intertextuality and the Reading of Midrash* and "Voices in the Text: Midrash and the Inner Tension of Biblical Narrative"; Geoffrey H. Hartman and Sanford Budick, eds., *Midrash and Literature*; and Geoffrey H. Hartman, "Midrash as Law and Literature."

each of the twelve female companions dear to his young life, but Dai-yu and Bao-chai at one point seem to receive a combined treatment in a single verse (*SS* 1: 133; *HLM* 1: 78). This one peculiar feature, together with certain remarks of the scholiasts that tend to minimize any discord between the two girls, has led to the modern view that the author's intention is to fashion the two female cousins as a composite character. The scholiasts not only construe the name "Two-in-one (*Jian Mei*)" (*SS* 1: 146; *HLM* 1: 90) as a reference to both Bao-chai and Dai-yu (*Pingyu*, p. 135), but they also assert in a general prefatory comment for chapter 42 in the 1760 manuscript: "though the names of Bao-chai and Dai-yu are two, there is only one person. This is an example of imaginative writing (*huanbi*, literally the brush of deception or illusion)" (*Pingyu*, p. 606). On such bases the contemporary reader Zhao Gang can assert that "Grandmother Jia and others never plotted to force Bao-yu and Bao-chai to marry, . . . and that during the last half of the novel. Bao-chai and Dai-yu remained harmonious companions, without jealousy or rivalry.[17]

In an oracular song of chapter 5, the vision of Bao-yu's marriage seems to indicate clearly that his appreciation for his spouse Bao-chai cannot stifle his longing for his deceased beloved.

> Let others all
> Commend the marriage rites of gold and jade;
> I still recall
> The bond of old by stone and flower made;
> And while my vacant eyes behold
> Crystalline snows of beauty pure and cold,
> From my mind can not be banished
> That fairy wood forlorn that from the world has vanished.
> How true I find
> That every good some imperfection holds!
> Even a wife so courteous and so kind
> No comfort brings to my afflicted mind.
>
> (*SS* 1: 140; *HLM* 1: 85)

Despite such specific depiction by the text, the scholiast of the 1760 version seems to indicate in chapter 20 that Bao-yu and Bao-chai, after marriage, would amiably "chitchat about the old days" much as they did when they were young (*Pingyu*, p. 400), an observation eagerly expanded by Zhao to mean that the couple enjoy in marriage "complete affection and such opportunities for intimate conversations and self-disclosures that they never had prior to their union."[18] Such a view of the matter, of course, clashes with the picture of the couple found in the last forty chapters, but in the occasional circular logic of

---

[17] *Hongloumeng yanjiu xinbian*, pp. 214–15.
[18] Ibid., p. 215.

specialists on this novel, it is one more argument against those chapters' authenticity. Zhao's preference for following the scholiast's suggestion of composite characterization of the two girls, however, has in turn been severely criticized by the late Xu Fuguan. The two scholia cited, according to Xu, "can only be termed utter nonsense that demeans and degrades *Hongloumeng*."[19]

If Red Inkstone's remarks tend to condition our reading of the novel in a certain way—in sum, to treat it as more than, or other than, a tale wholly fabricated—this tendency is undeniably reinforced by certain features of the text itself. In the first chapter of the narrative, for example, we seem to have been granted unprecedented knowledge of the author's identity (that it was Cao Xueqin in the Lamentation-of-Red Studio) and the possible role he had in the tale's composition by "working" on it for ten years, making additions and deletions no fewer than five times.[20] There is, moreover, a sardonic assessment of the enigma that is both text and author set forth in the couplet:

> All men call the author fool;
> None his secret message hears.
>
> (*SS* 1: 51; *HLM* 1: 7)

More astonishingly, even before we have a chance to move into the narrative proper, we are thrust into the presence of some such strange words and sentiments as the following:

> In the opening first chapter of this book, the author himself has declared that, having undergone a dreamlike and illusory experience, he deliberately had the true events concealed, and composed instead this book, *The Story of the Stone*. That is why he speaks of Zhen Shi-yin [true-events-concealed] who by means of a dream makes acquaintance with Perfect Comprehension. But what indeed are the events recorded in this book, and what are the reasons for its composition? Listen to what he himself has to say.
>
> Having made an utter failure of my life, I found myself one day, in the midst of my poverty and wretchedness, thinking about the female companions of my youth. As I went over them one by one, examining and comparing them in my mind's eye, it suddenly came over me that those slips of girls—which is all they were then—were in every way, both morally and intellectually, superior to the

---

[19] "Zhao Gang *Hongloumeng xintan* di tupodian," p. 494; also reprinted in Zhao, *Hongloumeng lunji*, p. 186. It should be pointed out that Zhao Gang is not the first to advocate the theory of "composite characterization." Yu Pingbo's 1950 essay, "Hou sanshihui di *Hongloumeng*," p. 213, already presented not merely the view of "Two-in-one," but also the view of "Three-in-one" because of the Goddess Disenchantment's reference to Qin Keqing in the same passage. The composite theory is also endorsed by David Hawkes in "*The Story of the Stone:* A Symbolist Novel," pp. 16–17. For further criticism of the scholiasts, see Sun Xun, *Hongloumeng zhiping chutan*, pp. 262–82.

[20] "Working" is Hawkes' translation of the ambiguous *piyue*, literally "annotated and read."

"grave and mustached signior" I am now supposed to have become. The realization brought with it an overpowering sense of shame and remorse, and for a while I was plunged in the deepest despair. There and then I resolved to make a record of all the recollections of those days I could muster—those golden days when I dressed in silk and ate delicately, when we still nestled in the protecting shadow of the Ancestors and Heaven still smiled on us. I resolved to tell the world how, in defiance of my family's attempts to bring me up properly and all the warnings and advice of my friends, I had brought myself to this present wretched state, in which, having frittered away half a lifetime, I find myself without a single skill with which I could earn a decent living. I resolved that, however unsightly my own shortcomings might be, I must not, for the sake of keeping them hid, allow those wonderful girls to pass into oblivion without a memorial.

Reminders of my poverty were all about me: that thatched roof, the wicker lattices, the string beds, the crockery stove. But these did not need to be an impediment to the workings of the imagination. Indeed, the beauties of nature outside my door—the morning breeze, the evening dew, the flowers and trees of my garden—were a positive encouragement to write. I might lack learning and literary aptitude, but what was to prevent me from turning it all into a story and writing it in the vernacular? (*SS* 1: 20–21 [first para., my translation]; *HLM* 1: 1)

Because these words appear in the earliest manuscript tradition (that is, 1754) under the section titled *fanli* (statement of general principles) prior to the first chapter proper, though they were almost immediately incorporated into the main narrative as the beginning of the first chapter in later manuscripts (that is, as early as the 1760 version), they have understandably aroused questions of their authorship and whether they form part of the intended novel.[21] Most critics thus query whether Cao Xueqin, if intent on writing an autobiographical novel, would have been likely to refer to himself in the third person and announce his theme in such a matter-of-fact manner.[22] David Hawkes has surmised that the entire section might have been written as an introduction by the author's younger brother, but the last extended statement on the adverse fortunes of self and family is taken to be, most plausibly, a quotation of Cao Xueqin's own words (*SS* 1: 20).

Whatever might have been the true origin of such an introductory statement, the idea that has captured the unrelenting attention of readers from the

[21] We do not know about the 1759 version because the opening portions of that manuscript are missing.

[22] See Chen Yupi, "*Hongloumeng* shi zenyang kaitou di?" for an excellent discussion of the textual and interpretive problems. Chen considers the entry to be a product of Red Inkstone and contends that all the entries of the General Principles are designed to explain away the novel's subversive features and shield it from political censorship. Zhang Ailing in *Hongloumeng yan*, pp. 104–10, has a completely different theory about the composition of the General Principles and their relationship to the manuscripts.

beginning has been this notion of the concealment of true events. In earlier generations, allegorists of the so-called *suoyin* school (literally, exploring obscurity or concealment) have sought to interpret the work either as a veiled romance of the early Qing court or as a coded tract of Han nationalism calling for revival of the Ming. It was to combat these interpretations that Hu Shi wrote his essay of 1922 and called attention to other elements prominent in those opening remarks of the narrative. According to him, that poignant self-reference sustaining the use of the novel as a passionate apologia pro vita sua must lead to our recognition that "*Dream of the Red Chamber* is clearly an autobiographical book that has 'concealed the true events.' If the author is Cao Xueqin, then Cao is the deeply penitent 'I' of the beginning! He is the original text (*diben*) behind the Zhen and Jia [true, false], the two Bao-yus of the novel! If one understands this principle, one will realize that the Jia and Zhen mansions in the book are but reflections of Cao Xueqin's household."[23]

Not only has this assessment of the novel's essential character seemed persuasive to countless readers, but his brief injunction on how the book is to be read has also exerted enormous influence on the direction of subsequent research. Chiding the allegorist's tendency to force his interpretation of incidental details in the novel in terms of scattered, unrelated events of history, Hu Shi has pleaded instead for critical investigations of authorship, context, and textual history. In this, Hu has displayed his customary sagacity as a literary historian and critic, for the decades following the publication of his essay have witnessed important advances in the scholarship pertaining to these three areas. Nevertheless, his emphasis on the autobiographical nature of the novel has also spawned its ironic effect, for it continues to focus critical attention on dimensions of reality external to the novel, merely shifting the imperial or political referent to a familial one. If the legion of characters that inhabit the vast and complex world of *Hongloumeng* are but shadowy signifiers of real persons in a real household, then the irresistible conclusion to be drawn is that the more we know of the Cao family, the better we are able to understand what goes on in the work itself. Family history (*jiashi*) and biographical research must light our path into the world of the text.[24]

---

[23] "*Hongloumeng* kaozheng," p. 599.

[24] My remark here is meant to dispute the exclusivity in this kind of critical ideal and practice, not deny that there may well be autobiographical elements scattered throughout the text; nor do I question the escalating autobiographical impulse in Chinese prose writings that became evident in both fictional and nonfictional works since the Ming. For the latter subject, see Rodney Leon Taylor, *The Cultivation of Sagehood as a Religious Goal in Neo-Confucianism*; Andrew H. Plaks, "After the Fall"; and Wu Pei-yi, *The Confucian's Progress*. For the same impulse in traditional verse, see Stephen Owen, "The Self's Perfect Mirror." Finally, I do not question the premise developed in contemporary literary theory that the subject of any autobiography may not correspond to the author's historical self, because character and characterization in the same text may not, or even never, coincide (see, for example, John D. Barbour, *The Conscience of the Autobiographer*, especially chapter 2). For a brilliant development of the thesis that

Twentieth-century criticism of the novel, particularly that by Chinese scholars, may thus be seen as largely an effort to respond to a potent conjunction of
certain features of authorial rhetoric and part of the original audience reaction
(Red Inkstone and company). The powerful temptation imposed by this union,
for devoted students, is to accord a privileged position to the scholia and to
regard the history of the Cao family as the key to unlocking the novel's design
and plot. That these students have succumbed to such temptation is seen in the
obsessive research undertaken on the author and his family—from alleged
Han origin in antiquity (with the Cao Cao of Three Kingdoms' fame as the
author's distant ancestor!), then migration to Manchuria, to re-sinicization as
imperial banner bondservants after the Qing conquest of China (latest [1996]
identification of Cao's ancestral home places it in Liaoning Province); from
the central members of the clan and lineage to the remotest of kin and acquaintances; from important public events keenly affecting familial fortunes (such
as the southern expeditions of the emperor Kangxi and his visitations of Cao
Yin, or the dismissal of Cao Fu from office and the confiscation of his estate in
1727–1728) to the ruins of dilapidated alleys in Beijing's suburbs where the
author was thought to have lived out his final years. Who might have been a
model for Bao-yu, the male protagonist? Was it the author himself, his uncle
(as the Manchu Yurui suggested long ago), or someone else? Were Bao-yu's

---

autobiography in Chinese novels can also be read as so many "metaphors" or "fictions" of the
self, see Martin W. Huang, *Literati and Self-Re/Presentation*. The expansive chapter 3 that
Huang devotes to *The Dream of the Red Chamber* offers many perceptive and persuasive nug-
gets, but his overall thesis exacts too high a price from the novel's sympathetic reader. The
notion that fully realized characters like Bao-chai, Dai-yu, and Xi-feng are merely "displaced
selves" of a frustrated male literatus robs the females of their represented authenticity and thus
their existential impact. However cultural-bound and subject to institutional and ideological
constraints, the text, as I read it, at least attempts to show that the sufferings of women (the *nüer
bei* that serves as a constant refrain of their songs in chapter 28 of the novel) cannot easily be
equated with, or allegorized as, male anxiety. At one point (p. 87) Huang appeals to a remark
by Red Inkstone in chapter 2 (*Pingyu*, p. 50) about "the great allegorical game" of the text that
enlists "this account of the fair sex's boudoir (*guige tingwei zhi zhuan*)" to express the author's
grief over fraternal losses or deaths. Of course, such a remark decisively reveals the scholiast's
subscription to a hermeneutical ideology that, as I will argue in the following chapter, runs the
gamut of Chinese intellectual and cultural history from the Han "Great Preface" to the *Poetry
Classic* to the "Women's Learning (*Fu Xue*)" of Zhang Xuecheng in the Qing. That ideology of
meiren xiangcao would provide convenient shelter for the scholiast to shield his beloved author from political harm and moral censure, because desire and sexual passions, always a dangerous eruption of privateness (*si*), can through allegoresis quickly be translated into a manifestation concordant with the dictates of patriarchal ritualism—the filial and fraternal alle-
giances that are considered ultimately homologous to relations between ruler and subjects.
That a scholar like Wu Shih-chang endorses the scholium further validates my argument here
about the modern tendency to privilege Red Inkstone and circle as unerring spokesmen for
authorial intentionality. It proves nothing about whether this observation can indeed function
as a normative guide to the text's interpretation.

four immediate cousins a mimesis of Cao Xueqin's aunts? Did Cao Xueqin have an elder brother who died young, as was the case with Bao-yu? How could we harmonize Bao-yu's handsome features with the reputed stoutness of Cao's person and dark complexion? So intense and insatiable has been the craving for such knowledge that nothing connected with the Cao family is too trivial for the notice of the specialists known as *hongxuejia* or Redologists.[25] It is no accident that the life of Cao Xueqin himself has now become a subject for further fictionalization.

Even in the studies that eschew the emphasis on autobiography or biography, the interest in exploiting the narrative to document all kinds of historical details remains sustained and pervasive. When one surveys the endless flow of secondary literature, one encounters increasingly complex and minute reconstructions of the economic, social, intellectual, and cultural settings of the story. The variety of divergent topics treated by books, monographs, and articles encompasses land holdings, monetary policy, agricultural and horticultural customs, furniture and household accoutrements, architecture and garden design, textile production, regional dialects and colloquial speech patterns, physiognomic and divinatory practices, culinary products and techniques, and imported artifacts and consumer goods such as snuff and cold medications. Although the bulk of such lucubration does serve to confirm the encyclopedic scope of the narrative and provide illumination of isolated aspects of its copious content, it remains to be seen how this kind of scholarship can enhance our perception and enjoyment of *Hongloumeng* as verbal art beyond, say, the assurance that the drinking of imported port wine was indeed a coveted practice for aristocratic families in Qianlong's China. When one reads an essay such as that by Jian Bozan on "The Economic Nature of Chinese Society in the First Half of the Eighteenth Century: A Concurrent Study of the Socio-Economic Conditions Reflected in *Hongloumeng*,"[26] there can be little dissent over the meticulousness of the research and the magnitude of its coverage—from the planting of tobacco, mulberry, and sugar cane to the consumption levels of different species of rice wine; from the production of porcelain ware to the raising of domestic fowl and animals. Indeed, the topical range of this essay may well be construed as an extended exegesis, and more, of the list of New Year tributary gifts brought by Bailiff Wu in chapter 53 to the Jia mansion. The very nature of the study, however, must lead a student of literature to ask how we are to regard a critique which, in the final analysis, treats the novel as

---

[25] For a sober, informative account of the Cao family, see Zhao and Chen, *Hongloumeng yanjiu xinbian*, pp. 1–72. Zhou Ruchang's two volumes of *Hongloumeng xinzheng* present an exhaustive investigation of author and family that is not without some highly speculative conclusions.

[26] That is, his "Lun shiba shiji shangbanqi Zhongguo shehui jingji di xingzhi," pp. 188–252.

little different from district and regional gazettes, anthologies of court transactions and memorials, merchant account books, or the *Collected Writings on
Statecraft of the Ming Dynasty.*

It may be argued, of course, that the example used here is a deliberately
prejudicial one; that not all historical criticism directed at the novel displays
such crude and opprobrious preoccupations.[27] Even if the validity of this caveat
is acknowledged, however, our misgiving concerning much of "Redology"
remains unmitigated. For the point at issue is not whether *Hongloumeng* the
novel is reflective of Chinese society—how could it not be, as a work of fiction
wrought in a specific moment of history?—but whether the compulsive attempt
of the modern reader to go beyond the text and arrive at its real referent, posited
as either the larger world of the eighteenth century or the immediate realm of
its celebrated author's household, represents in the end a futile undertaking.
Futile, because it demands from the text a kind of knowledge or information
that it is not wholly designed to yield. Fiction is hereby confused with history,
and even in those great number of critical studies which pay routine homage
to the narrative's artistic merits, *Hongloumeng* functions essentially as one
among many other kinds of historical documents. Yu Yingshi is both succinct
and unerring when he remarks, "We certainly have here a strange, paradoxical
situation: in the eyes of the general reader, *Hongloumeng* is entirely a work of
fiction, but within the main currents of Redological research of the last century,
it has never truly assumed the place of fiction. On the contrary, it has always
been treated as an historical document."[28] This is a costly reduction, for as
Dominick LaCapra reminds us, "literature becomes redundant when it tells us
what can be gleaned from other documentary sources. In this sense, literature
is paradoxically most superfluous when it seems to provide us with the most
'useful' and 'reputable' information, for it must simply replicate or confirm
what can be found in more literal documents such as police reports."[29] Where
the crudely historical or autobiographical emphasis prevails, therefore, the
verbal, intransitive experience of a literary text is bound to be undermined,
because the concern for finding extrinsic correspondence or verification inevitably assumes a presiding role in criticism. That concern, moreover, may
seduce the reader to neglect or ignore other kinds of historical data and cultural
materials equally useful and elucidative in textual interpretation.

---

[27] Though if another example is needed, one can cite Tong Xue, *Hongloumeng zhuti lun.*

[29] *Hongloumeng di liangge shijie*, p. 5. His sentiment, interestingly, is echoed almost verbatim by Yu Pingbo, who in an interview criticized the critics who belong to the allegorical
(*suoyin*) and the autobiography schools for investigating the novel as if it were an historical
document. See *Zhong Bao* (January 7, 1987), p. 17.

[29] See his *History and Criticism*, p. 126.

READING AS HISTORY

How, then, are we to read a work like *Hongloumeng*? My answer to this question will be spelled out in successive portions of the present study. Given the drift of the discussion thus far, one would expect me to say at the beginning that I should want to answer the call of Yu Yingshi and let *Hongloumeng* "truly assume the place of fiction": to read it on the many terms the text has posed for itself. This is indeed the case, but so stated, the task I have set for myself cannot avoid the appearance of being obvious or platitudinous. I should note at once that the analysis of a novel's "fictional contract," so to speak, must by its very nature follow a dialectical process of interpretation not formally different from the thousands of readings—lengthy or brief, enlightening or obfuscating—that have already taken place with respect to this particular text. For after all, they, too, claim in one way or another that in carrying out their respective agendas they have been faithful to what they regard as the text's demands, compliant with both message and features that the text transmits. My purpose in this study, therefore, is not to repudiate the bias for history in much of *Hongloumeng* scholarship, although I must acknowledge that J. Hillis Miller's critique of a part of contemporary Western criticism seems equally applicable to that surrounding this Chinese narrative:

> even when the exact form of the relation of the text to its context has been identi-
> fied, the work of interpretation has only begun. The difficult business of actually
> reading the work and showing how the adduced historical context inheres in the
> fine grain of its language still remains to be done. Until it is done nothing has
> been done beyond making a vague claim that the context "explains" the text.[30]

The purpose of my study, rather, is to indicate a different approach expressive of a different reaction to the text at hand.

Reading *Hongloumeng*, like all literary readings, is in my judgment a partic-
ular response to the rhetoric of a literary text, and it is with this understanding that I endorse Jean-Paul Sartre's statement that "reading seems . . . to be the synthesis of perception and creation."[31] Rhetoric is understood here in its broad-
est meaning of both the verbal structures, "the words . . . like traps set for arousing our feelings and for reflecting them toward us,"[32] and the full panoply of communicative devices (generic conventions, allusions, manipulation of point of view, innovative use of traditional literary forms) embedded in the

---

[30] *The Ethics of Reading*, p. 7.

[31] "La lecture . . . semble la synthèse de la perception et de la création," in *Qu'est-ce que la littérature?*, p. 55.

[32] "Les mots . . . comme des pièges pour susciter nos sentiments et les réfléchir vers nous." Ibid., p. 58.

textual language. Taken together, the two remarks by Sartre may provide, in fact, an interesting gloss on certain salient aspects of poetics and criticism in the Chinese tradition, for "the synthesis of perception and creation" which is reading can serve to epitomize the entire practice known as *pingdian* enshrined in Chinese commentarial writings. In the first part of this binominal term, the act of *ping* (literally, to evaluate) would denote inclusively the related activities of *pi* (the addition of a judgment or disposition to a document), *zhu* (notation), *shu* (gloss or elucidation), *jie* (explanation), and *zhuan* (extended commentary).[33] The second half of the compound, on the other hand, indicates another abbreviation, alluding to *quandian* (literally, circles and dots) that betokens activities at once evaluative and reconstructive. The small circles that the traditional Chinese reader is taught to make alongside individual words (usually on the right side) of various portions of a text may signal a student's commendation of a poem's particular lines, an examiner's special appreciation of a candidate's particular columns, or an author's peculiar emphasis imposed on certain segments of his or her own writings, much as Western readers may underline a document. When used individually and regularly at the end of a linguistic unit, however, the small circle functions no differently from a dot (*dian*), a mark of punctuation. Because all premodern texts in China (whether written in the literary or vernacular language) were either printed or copied without such a device, the task of separating the units (*duan ju*), in fact, constitutes a ready-made test of the reader's literacy with each reading. The specific placement of the *dian*, by turning an endless series of graphs into coherent semantic units, measures the person's grasp of grammar, syntax, and diction. The readable text is literally created by the dot or circle. Particularly when confronting texts of literary Chinese, as every reader of chapter 1 of the received text of Laozi's *Daodejing* or the beginning of chapter 2 of the *Huainanzi* will concur, punctuation is already interpretation.[34]

Punctuation, of course, highlights only one aspect of how premodern Chinese texts have been read. In the following chapter, which studies the notion of

[33] For a thorough review of this set of terms, see David Rolston, "Sources of Traditional Chinese Fiction Criticism," in *How to Read the Chinese Novel*, pp. 3–34.

[34] Hu Shi's pioneering essay proposing the use of new punctation marks for Chinese writings, "Qing banxing xinshi biaodian fuhao yi'an," p. 126, gives as an example of how punctuation affects the meaning of a line of twelve words from the chapter on "The Rectification of Names" from *Xunzi*. Subsequent commentators have read this line either as three units of four words each or two of six words. Needless to say, the meanings of these two readings differ markedly. Texts like the manuscripts of *The Story of the Stone*, to the extent that they are written largely in the vernacular, are much easier to comprehend, but the punctuation dot seems still to be favored by some of the copyists. The 1754 version is completely unpunctuated, but continuous circles are used a few times to call attention to particular sentences or units. In the Leningrad manuscript (dated around 1759–1760) we may witness the use of both circles and dots for punctuation in the first fourteen chapters, whereas the 1760 manuscript consistently employs the circle for punctuation.

desire in premodern thought and literature, I shall refer to a familiar but paramount aim of the Confucian discourse: to legitimate both the aesthetic and the
didactic functions of the arts. Aesthetically, poetry, along with music and dance,
provides proper channels for the expression of *qing* (disposition, inward
bearing, aspiration, the affects), as long as such expression does not transgress
the boundary set by ritualism. To uphold the Confucian verdict that the three
hundred odes "think no waywardness (*si wu xie*)," a persistent method of elaborate allegoresis displaces what is considered subversive or illicit meaning. The
rectitude of content and the rectitude of the expressive subjectivity latent in
that content are thereby guaranteed further by the rectitude of perception; in
sum, of reading. To put the matter in Sartrean terms, only such warrants can
render those traplike words safe "for arousing our feelings."

Thus understood, early Chinese poetics seems to assign to the text (and its
correct reading) the decisive role in inculcating the requisite political and moral
virtues. Other instances of literary and cultural history, however, indicate that
there may have been a different, though parallel, emphasis. According to
Stephen Owen, the

> confident assumptions about the determinate affect of the *Songs* was crumbling
> in the Sung, and finally collapsed in Chu Hsi's attempt to reconcile the dubious
> morality of certain of the *Songs* with Confucius' dictum that the *Songs* have "no
> warped thoughts" [*Analects* 2. 2]. Chu Hsi's dangerous resolution was that the
> virtue embodied in an individual *Song* resided in the virtue of the reader (thus a
> virtuous reader would recognize immorality in certain of the *Songs* and have his
> moral sense sharpened by the experience). The reader is no longer "imprinted"
> by the *Song*; and there is a balanced, reflective relation between the inherent
> quality of the *Song* and the nature of the reader.[35]

Whether those assumptions did crumble and whether Zhu Xi's "resolution"
was truly that dangerous remain matters of debate,[36] but the Song philosopher's
point about reading had been anticipated as long ago as the *Great Commentary*
(*Xici zhuan*) of *The Book of Changes*. Section 5 of the treatise opens with the
following:

> That which appears alternately as Light and Dark is called the Dao. What contin-
> ues it is goodness; what completes it is nature. The benevolent sees it and calls it
> benevolent, while the intelligent sees it and calls it intelligent. The people use it
> daily without knowing it. Thus the way of the superior man is rare.[37]

This theme of the relativism of perception was picked up across the ages by
one Wen Long of late nineteenth century and incorporated into his defense of
The Plum in the Golden Vase (*Jinpingmei*).

---

[35] *Readings in Chinese Literary Thought*, pp. 454–55.
[36] A point taken up briefly in Martin W. Huang, "Author(ity) and Reader," pp. 55–56.
[37] *Zhouyi jinzhu jinyi*, pp. 392–93.

Some have called *Jinpingmei* a licentious book. That's not so. Only the licentious, when he sees it, will call it licentious. The nonlicentious, seeing it, will not call it licentious; all he sees is a group of male and female birds and beasts. Some have called *Jinpingmei* a virtuous book (*shanshu*). That's not so. The virtuous, upon seeing virtue, will call it virtuous. The nonvirtuous will call it nonvirtuous; all he feels is a life of indulgent pleasures.[38]

Pressed to its limit, this sort of readerly relativism would seem to mitigate all attempts at determinate reading through appeal to authorial intentionaltiy or original meaning, and promote instead the plurality of readings by diversified readers. The variety of moral characters in the readers would now breed a corresponding variety of readings.

To the extent that traditional Chinese fiction commentary frequently employs such terms as readers (*du zhe*) and authors (*zuo zhe*), it might seem that it had an early start in developing what is known today as "reader criticism." Actually, however, that would be too precipitous a conclusion, for as Martin Huang has observed,

due to the ultimate monological desire to "control" the meaning shared by both Zhu Xi and the *xiaoshuo* commentators, a reading theory that privileged the reader never developed. Rather, emphasis on "author" or "reader" was often predicated on the commentator's perceived need to "control the meaning of a text" and to police the readings by others (or the need to "burn the book," to use Jin Shengtan's metaphor).[39]

To put the matter even more precisely, a reading theory that did privilege the reader has always been in place, but such a theory, when carried out by its practitioners, has almost always been blind to its own assumptions and presuppositions. Huang is certainly correct about the commentator's double motivation: the need to regulate textual meaning and to police other readings, but the relativity of readings is often unrecognized because such motivation remains unacknowledged. In the history of textual interpretation—in China or in the West—I know of no one intent on reading a work of literature, of law, of philosophy, or of scripture who announces that he or she is deliberately embarked on an errant undertaking, or is out to misconstrue, misread, or mislead. All other readings may be faulty or flawed, much as all other readers may be unbenevolent or licentious; this reader alone sees "benevolence" or "intelligence" and thus remains intelligent and virtuous. Unless one fully grants this presumption of better and truer vision on the part of each critical reading, one cannot appreciate the ferocity in the conflict of interpretation dogging much of traditional commentarial literature in the world. Even in variorium editions of

[38] See "Wen Long *Jinpingmei huiping*" in *Jinpingmei zhiliao huibian, juan* 5, p. 511. I thank my colleague David Roy for calling my attention to this entry.

[39] "Author(ity) and Reader," p. 59.

literary texts, where different commentaries or interpretations exist side by side, the supervening task of the editor does not nullify the individual commentator's monological desire for authority founded on presumed rectitude in both knowledge and character.[40]

The study of *Hongloumeng* as a work of literary fiction, despite its comparatively late appearance in China's imperial history, has attained such scope and complexity that scholars today can distinguish quite a few stages in the criticism directed toward this narrative. Although a firm consensus about the overall achievement of the Red Inkstone scholia has yet to be reached, scholars reviewing Redology or *hongxue* can routinely point to such discernibly different groups of critical readers across two centuries as those belonging to the "Small Details" school (mostly of the nineteenth century), the "Hidden Meaning (*suoyin*)" school (early republican era), the "New *Hongxue*" school (begun with Hu Shi and Yu Pingbo), and so forth.[41] Although commentators of diverse and even contradictory persuasions invariably write with the assumption, declared or not, that their readings better our understanding of the text in one way or another by bringing out various aspects of "truth" embodied in the text, what the cumulative and still expanding body of scholarship actually discloses is not so much progress as its own temporality. In linear fashion we can work through the "biographical" predilections of the Red Inkstone scholia, through Zhang Xinzhi's appeal to *Yijing* symbolics and Neo-Confucian principles to expound (*yanyi*) narrative meaning and emplotment (*Sanjia* 1: 2, 4, 7), to contemporary investigations of intertextuality and gender ideology. The reception history of this narrative, like those of many other canonical classics, is thus also arguably a history that reveals the historicity of its readership.

I have already defined literary reading as a particular response to textual rhetoric. Now we may proceed to argue that the historicity of both text and reader, rooted unavoidably in the difference of cultural nurture and institutional or ideological allegiance, renders it certain that no act of critical reading, even if it is a word-for-word exegesis, can attain the condition of being complete or permanently stable. "Reading" in the sense we are using it here is not simply exposing the clash of temporalized differences of culture embodied unambiguously in text and readers, from which one may hope for an eventual resolution with "better" readings. Rather, the clash itself is represented and

---

[40] Huang, ibid., p. 61, cites the *Zengping butu Shitou ji* (The Story of the Stone with Added Commentaries and Supplemental Illustrations) as an example of such a variorum edition. This is why the emphasis on critical pluralism or the democratization of readings as a conceptual and practical ideal belongs distinctly to modernity. In the words of Frank Kermode when he discusses Roland Barthes, "our business as moderns is to read in order to maximize plurality, not in order to understand secrets. The apricot stone must go. We must not seek to discover structures but to produce structurations." See *The Art of Telling*, p. 75.

[41] For convenient summaries, see Louise P. Edwards, *Men and Women in Qing China*, pp. 10–32.

perpetuated by the production of one sign system out of another. As Paul de Man has remarked in his discussion of Charles Sanders Peirce, "the interpretation of the sign is not, for Peirce, a meaning but another sign; it is a reading, not a decodage, and this reading has, in its turn, to be interpreted into another sign, and so on *ad infinitum*."[42] This process by which "one sign gives birth to another" constitutes the very historicity of reading. Because it exists only on the treadmill of hermeneutical labor, no reading of a text can claim to be definitive for all time. The only definitive reading in the sense that it excludes all other possible readings will have to be a verbatim repetition of the text, the perfect reproduction of every sign that is recitation, not interpretation. Thus the impossibility of exact identity between text and reading, even if the latter is meant to be the most faithful kind of replicative criticism, is assured by the difference inherent in both readership and the process of reading itself.[43] For this reason as well, criticism like translation is not only "directed creation (*création dirigée*)," as Satre has pointed out, but like translation it is also perennially needed because it is always supplemental, partial, and selective.

To answer the question posed at the beginning of this section, I should therefore point out that my reading of *Hongloumeng* must also be supplemental, partial, and selective. Although this study purports to probe and analyze what seems to me to be neglected topics in much of the criticism that has been done on this work, the book in no way seeks to provide definitive readings or total solutions. The rest of this chapter continues to examine some of the issues pertaining to the reading of history and fiction, and successive chapters will take up such topics as desire, dream, reflexivity, literature (as viewed in the narrative), and tragedy. The topics reflect my interests, but they hardly exhaust

---

[42] See *Allegories of Reading*, p. 9.

[43] See Norman Holland, "Unity Identity Text Self," p. 123: "the unity we find in literary texts is impregnated with the identity that finds that unity . . . As readers, each of us will . . . have different ways of making the text into an experience with a coherence and significance that satisfies." And also Paul Ricoeur, in *Time and Narrative* 3: 169: "Every text, even a systematically fragmentary one, is revealed to be inexhaustible in terms of reading, as though through its unavoidably selective character, reading revealed an unwritten aspect in the text. It is the perogative of reading to strive to provide a figure for this unwritten side of the text." The traditional Chinese discussion of whether meaning resides beyond words (*yi zai yan wai*) or how words cannot exhaust meaning (*yan bu jin yi*) from *Yijing* commentaries through Tang-Song poetics becomes pertinent for comparison. For an important essay tracing the historical development of this discussion, see Tang Yongtong, "Yi yan zhi bian." See also Stephen Owen, *Traditional Chinese Poetry and Poetics*, pp. 58–63, for some stimulating observations about Chinese understanding of the relationship between language and world. For the meaning of *yan bu jin yi*, Owen thinks that "linguistic expression is conceived as somehow a diminution of a prior fullness." In the end Owen thinks that *yan wai* (beyond words) points to some sort of "prelinguistic experience—the ineffable." For me, however, discussions in traditional *shihua* such as those by Ouyang Xiu in "Liuyi shihua" (*Lidai shihua* 1: 267–68) and Yang Wanli in "Chengzhai shihua" (*Lidai shihua xubian* 1: 136–38) seem to indicate that the concept was understood more as inference than as ineffability.

the possibility of investigation. The topics serve as different means of con-textualizing the text of *Hongloumeng*, but the study of the topics themselves also requires further contextualization. Because "total context is unmasterable, both in principle and in practice," and because "meaning is context bound, but context is boundless," every step of every approach to text or topic involves choice and selection.[44] To plumb, for example, the significance of *qing*, an elusive and allusive term that looms so large in the narrative's linguistic horizon, I find that I must undertake philological excursions that seem to have little immediate connection with *Hongloumeng*. To bring to light what may be the narrative's reflexive view of itself as literature, I find myself prodded to consider, however briefly, the problem of literary censorship. Even as I write, I am also keenly aware of my own historicity, but such a confession does not amount to a claim of virtue. Rather, it is more of an admission that the critical choices and selections are not purely or objectively determined by the subject under investigation. They are as much dictated by my own subjectivity—my predi-lections, my preoccupations as an academic, my Gadamerian "prejudices" formed and nurtured by my cultural background no less than by my educa-tional experience. My act of (re)reading *The Stone* thus participates in what Matei Calinescu has called a form of textual visitation or "haunting."[45] The act is "double-faced" to the extent that it contains elements of both the novel and the repetitive. If the reading attempts to do what others have not done or not done as much, it strives to be innovative, to be, as it were, a "first" reading. Inasmuch as it is a rereading, it must be reckoned also a form of repetition: the reader is revisiting the text, haunted by both this and other texts. In view of the fact that the very first public name of my text already dramatizes the fact of its prevenient reading and copying—*The Story of the Stone again Annotated* (*Congping Shitouji*)—the circularity or recursiveness that inevitably pervades an attempt to read this work may seem particularly fitting. Perhaps belatedly, readers of this tale are beginning to grasp what Cao Xueqin seemed to have intimated all along, that any reading of his text is already a rereading.

READING HISTORY, READING FICTION

Past readers of *Hongloumeng* have not been completely oblivious to the textual claim to fictionality. Very few of them, it seems to me, have moved beyond such recognition to grapple with the question: how does the text claim fictionality, and why? The answer to the first part of this query would entail scrutiny of rhetorical features and their implications hitherto unexamined or

---

[44] The quotation is from Jonathan Culler, *On Deconstructionism*, p. 123.
[45] See his provocative book, *Rereading*.

little noticed, and a reply to the second part would require probing the text's peculiar and insistent emphasis on its own nature in the context of other fictive narratives of the tradition and their criticism. In the study of this context, recent Western scholarship has emphasized the difference of assumptions underlying traditional Chinese response to literary art. Craig Fisk, for example, has noted that

> among the very general differences between Chinese criticism and Western criticism, taken as a whole, the three most important concern imitation, fictionality, and genres. In China there were no concepts comparable to Aristotelian mimesis or Christian figura, both of which are bound to the representation of action in time. Rather, the object of representation is mood at a point in time and correspondences between mind and state of the surrounding world. Fictionality is not a concern for essentially similar reasons. Although the fantastical, the unreal, the impersonation all have their place in Chinese literature, the literary work is generally understood by the critic as if it were personal history.[46]

This observation by Fisk has found strong echo in Stephen Owen's study of traditional Chinese poetry and poetics. Contrasting a poem of Wordsworth with one by Du Fu, Owen declares that their

> differences shape two fiercely distinct concepts of the nature of literature and its place in the human and natural universe. For Tu Fu's reader the poem is not a fiction: it is a unique, factual account of an experience in historical time, a human consciousness encountering, interpreting, and responding to the world. And in his own turn the reader, at some later historical moment, encounters, interprets, and responds to the poem.[47]

Although the categorical nature of these assertions may invite dispute, and although the assertions concern response to poetry and not prose fiction, they nevertheless serve to highlight how the traditional Chinese reader tends to

---

[46] Craig Fisk, "Literary Criticism," p. 49.

[47] Owen, *Traditional Chinese Poetry and Poetics*, p. 15. See also Pauline Yu's comparison of Western and Chinese understanding of allegory and criticism in *The Reading of Imagery in the Chinese Poetic Tradition*, pp. 80–81, where she contrasts Western allegory, rooted in "an abstract, metaphysical dimension," with Chinese poetics, which is dictated by "the earliest Confucian doctrines on the identity of ethics and politics," and seeks in history an authoritative context for morality. "Thus, whereas didactic literature in the West commonly aims to present a vision of the world as it ought to be, Chinese didactic criticism sees literature as inferring lessons from the world as it actually was." Similarly, "the de-emphasis on such notions as creation ex nihilo and fictionality (owing perhaps to the conscipicuous lack in indigenous Chinese cosmogonic thinking of a creator-figure)" means that the genesis of a literary text is not merely indissolubly bound to the human agent, but that textual meaning will find its most decisive illumination from historical sources and references of any author's work. As we shall see, however, *Hongloumeng* may be suggesting ways of indicating fictionality other than the notion of artist as creator.

respond to literary materials.[48] That tendency, however, is still subject to modification when specific works of literature are considered. For example, *The Three Kingdoms* (*Sanguozhi yanyi*) is undoubtedly one work in the canon of classic prose fiction that affects great semblance to conventional historiography, but readers of all ages have little difficulty in seeing it for what it is. Even Jin Shengtan, a commentator who gave the book unstinting praise for "narrating established events" and thus considered it superior to both *Outlaws of the Marshes* and *The Journey to the West*, is unhesitant in referring to it as a work of prose fiction (Item 4 in "Dufa").[49] By contrast, *Hongloumeng* exults in the persistent and proud affirmation of its fictive being, but readers seem to have been led constantly to turn aside from the text's internal drama to look elsewhere for its "true" historical referent. Such has been the irony dogging the reception of *Sanguo* and *Hongloumeng*, and in this regard, the latent attitude of many readers of even vernacular fiction seems hardly different from that of those perusing classic verse: "poetry chronicled the life of an individual as naturally as it did the fate of a feudal state."[50] To appreciate more fully the radical originality of Cao Xueqin, we must make a brief detour to investigate further the how and why of this prevalent mode of reading that tends to privilege the bond of historical life and imaginative art. We need to know, in other words, the disparity and similarity in the reading of history and fiction.

In the study of traditional Chinese narrative it is customary to speak of the developmental dependence of prose fiction on history, or more precisely on historiographic writing.[51] Although the generic name of fiction is thought to be the small talk or idle discourse (*xiaoshuo*) of the streets and alleys supposedly gathered by minor officials (*baiguan*) as a kind of sociological report, according to the *Yiwenzhi* of the *Hanshu* (chap. 30),[52] its designation by the later nomenclature of "unofficial or fragmented history (*yeshi, baishi*)" points to

---

[48] My use of contemporary discussion of traditional Chinese poetry and poetics in relations to fiction criticism is not entirely arbitrary. First, the traditional critic Jin Shengtan, though well-known for his work on *Shuihuzhuan*, has also made important contributions to the criticism of both drama and poetry. Second, there is a good deal of modern scholarship that seeks to relate the text of *Hongloumeng* to the poetic tradition. For debate on whether the novel has as one of its main purposes the transmission of poetry (*chuan shi*), see Pi Shumin, *Hongloumeng kaolunji*, pp. 54–69. For discussions of the "lyric vision" in the novel and *Hongloumeng* as "lyric novel," see Wong Kam-ming, "Point of View, Norms, and Structure," Yu-kung Kao, "Lyric Vision in Chinese Narrative," and Wai-yee Li, *Enchantment and Disenchantment*, chapter 5, "Self-Reflexivity and the Lyrical Ideal in *Hung-lou meng*."

[49] *Yuanben Sanguozhi yanyi*, "Dufa" 1: 22.

[50] Pauline Yu, *The Reading of Imagery*, p. 82.

[51] See Andrew H. Plaks, "Towards a Critical Theory of Chinese Narrative," p. 311.

[52] I take this to be the *point de départ* for our discussion here, though an earlier reference to *xiaoshuo* in *Zhuangzi* (chap. 26) can also be translated as small or, even fictive, tales. See also David Rolston, *Reading and Writing between the Lines*, Part III, chapter 3, "Liberating Fiction from History."

the unmistakable ranking of the original model over the supposedly deviant nature of its imitator.

The nomenclature presumably indicates the characteristic amalgamation of the factual and the nonverifiable (according to criteria acceptable to traditional Chinese culture) in fictive narrative. Thus Y. W. Ma defines the Chinese historical novel as "a fictional work which embodies, in an artistic blending of actuality and imagination, a core of historically factual material, with allowance for inventiveness in both figures and events combined with respect for established facts."[53] This statement apparently emphasizes subject matter or what the author elsewhere has termed "the realism of substance," but it says little about the possible commonality of form for both kinds of narrative.[54] Nor does it tell us how much inventiveness is allowable before the historical takes on the appearance of the fictive and, vice versa, how great "respect for established facts" is needed before the fictive becomes the historical. This commingling of the factual and the imaginary poses not merely a problem in the definition of an historical novel, but more importantly, it may serve to highlight the reasons for both the formal affinity and the generic tension between historical and fictive narratives—in China and in the literary tradition of the West, as well.

To the extent that history is acknowledged to be a verbal account of the past, and therefore that it must be narrated (whether in an oral or written account), it has frequently been observed that historical narrative must perforce participate in certain formal characteristics common to other narratives.[55] Thus modern students of the *Zuo Commentary* have made illuminating analyses of this ancient text by focusing on plot, character, point of view, assimilated speeches and dialogues, predictive pronouncements, and dramatized incidents or anecdotes.[56] These various features of narrativity are thought to transform what would be merely a pointillistic recital of unrelated incidents into a true

---

[53] Y. W. Ma, "The Chinese Historical Novel," p. 278.

[54] Y. W. Ma, "Fact and Fantasy in T'ang Tales," p. 168.

[55] Although here I am obviously emphasizing the specifically linguistic aspect of history, I am fully aware that all elements of material culture (utensils, artifacts, buildings, ruins, the plastic and graphic arts, etc.) and natural occurences (climatic and geological changes, recession of coast lines, floods, droughts, famines, volcanic eruptions, etc.) constitute what the modern historian calls "traces" or "tracks," without which the writing of history would be immensely impoverished and incomplete, if not impossible. See Paul Ricoeur, *Temps et récit*, 3: 171–82, 268. Also Fernand Braudel, *On History*, pp. 105–19; Edward Shils, *Tradition*, especially chapters 2 and 3.

[56] See John C. Y. Wang, "Early Chinese Narrative," and Ronald C. Egan, "Narratives in *Tso Chuan*." Jacques Gernet, on the other hand, takes the less complimentary view that much of early Chinese historiography amounts to no more than a patchwork of documents (*"une marqueterie des documents"*) that lacks true semblance to historical narration. See his "Écrit et histoire." Gernet's conclusion has in turn influenced the contemporary historian Jacques Le Goff; see *History and Memory*, pp. 138–39.

narrative—that is, a unified story with its own integrity. To the extent, however, that history is acknowledged to be an account of the *factual* past, the inevitable question centers on what is to be considered historical truth, on what did or did not take place according to the developed criteria of verification, and on the ascertainment of causality. Such a concern for the actual and the verifiable demarcates the domains of the historical as against the literary or imaginary.

Although the Homeric bards and historians of Greek antiquity have long been regarded as participating in a common narrative tradition (particularly because of the use of first-person narration), scholars are also quick to point out the difference of the Greek *histor*'s narrative posture in his effort to ground his narration upon a new kind of authority. The name of this person, after all, denotes an inquirer and investigator, and not merely a recorder or recounter in the form of a singer or stitcher of songs (*aoidê, rhapsodos*) or a maker (*poiêtês*). After giving a brief summary of Persian and Phoenician accounts of the beginning of the Trojan conflict, Herodotus declares in his famous *Histories*: "As for myself, I will not say this or that story has indeed taken place, but I will name him whom I myself know to have done unprovoked injury to the Greeks, and thus to proceed with my story" (Herodotus, 1. 5). The Herodotan way of recording, in a self-consciously learned manner, the great and marvelous deeds of the Greeks and other peoples in order to preserve the memory of the past against the destructiveness of time (*to chrōnō exitêla*: Herodotus, 1. 1) finds its echo in Sima Qian (145?–90? B.C.E.), the Grand Historian of China. He had stated in his "Autobiography" that he would be guilty of the greatest crime "if he should allow the labors of the meritorious ministers, the feudal families, and the worthy officials to fall into oblivion and not be told." His famous description of his monumental enterprise as "transmitting by narrating (*shu*) past events and putting in order the genealogies and biographies, not undertaking what one might call authorship (*zuo*)" (*Shiji*, 130), seen in this light, indicates not so much his own modesty—he refused comparison of his history writing with Confucius' editing of the *Chunqiu Annals*—as his desire to emphasize the true nature of his writings. Although neither Herodotus nor Sima Qian could lay claim to practicing full-fledged historical scholarship in the modern sense of systematic citation of sources and critical sifting of evidence, documentary or otherwise, the spirit of critical inquiry is manifest throughout their respective works.[57] Theirs is an authority born first from "the authority of the historical narrative" which, as Hayden White points out, "is the authority of reality itself" and, second, from the act of memory and writing in the recording, preservation, and transmission of that reality.[58] From such a perspective, it is the mutually constitutive constraint between narrative discourse and reality

[57] Arnaldo Momigliano, "Ancient History and the Antiquarian."
[58] See White, *The Content of the Form*, p. 20.

that separates the historian from the poet. "Where the traditional poet must confine himself to one version of his story," as two modern scholars have commented on the Greek historians, "the *histor* can present conflicting versions in his search for the truth or fact."[59] Such a form of presentation can also be found in Sima Qian.[60]

If one raises the question at this juncture as to what qualifies as historical evidence, Arnaldo Momigliano's reply would be: "the evidence, to be evidence, must somehow be dated."[61] In other words, what passes for evidence must possess the characteristic of an event anchored in chronological time. This emphasis on dated occurrence as the sine qua non of the historical again may find parallel in the Chinese understanding of history first and foremost as the linguistic transcription of what had been said and of what had occurred (*jiyan, jishi*). An awareness of the treacherous potency of language is perhaps what gave rise to the characteristic opposition in ancient Chinese thought between *shishi* (real or actual event) and *kongyan*, whether the latter term refers to "empty words, vain speeches," or takes on the special meaning of "theoretical formulations" in the sense that such formulations are not self-evidently based on facts.[62] Thus Dong Zhongshu (c. 179–c. 104 B.C.E.) attributed the editing of the *Spring and Autumn Annals* to this motivation of Confucius: "To their past actions I have added the mind of a king, for I believe that the illustration by means of airy formulations is not as effective as the depth and clarity of past actions."[63] Sima Qian in turn has built on this utterance when he makes his Confucius say: "I would have liked to convey [my thoughts] through airy formulations, but that is not as effective as illustrating them through the depth and clarity of past events" (*Shiji*, 130). Again, Ban Gu (32–92) in his "Treatise on Literature" cited Confucius' stress on his need for evidence (*zheng*) to support his discourse on state rites (*Analects*, 3. 9) in order to buttress the argument that this same principle also underlay the motivation of the *Zuo Commentary*: "that the Master would not employ airy formulations to discourse on the classics" (*Hanshu*, 30). Such a need for emphatic bonding of language and thought to event has been affirmed down through the ages, as when the Qing historian, Zhang Xuecheng (1738–1801) opens his *Wenshi tongyi* (The Complementary Meaning of Literature and History) with the famous declaration: "The

[59] Robert Scholes and Robert Kellogg, *The Nature of Narrative*, p. 243.

[60] For a recent and capacious discussion of Sima Qian as a historian, see Wai-yee Li, "The Idea of Authority in the *Shih chi*." Li's study effectively redresses the imbalance of Gernet's brief essay, which focuses almost exclusively on the ritual content of such ancient documents as the *Shujing* and the *Zhouli*. The book or document (*écrit*) thus functions as "a means of communication with the divine powers"; see Gernet, "Écrit et histoire,"pp. 356–57.

[61] *Essays in Ancient and Modern Historiography*, p. 192. See also Louis O. Mink, "History as Modes of Comprehension," p. 23.

[62] For a discussion of *jiyan*, see Qian Zhongshu, *Guanzhuibian* 1: 162 ff. On the general and special meanings of *kongyan*, see Burton Watson, trans., *Ssu-ma Ch'ien*, 2: 87–89.

[63] *Chunqiu fanlu*, 6: 3a (*SBBY*).

Six Classics are all histories. . . . The ancients never abandoned events to discourse on principles."[64]

So insistent was Zhang on the indivisibility of word and event (*yan, shi*) in the proper writing of history that he did not hesitate to challenge the venerable, accepted view that there were two official agencies—the "Left" and the "Right"—in Chinese antiquity wherewith words and events were recorded, on the ground that only "later Confucians" misconstrued the nature of the *Book of Documents* and the *Chunqiu*. Because the "'Canon' and 'Counsels' chapters of the *Book of Documents* recorded events but words were also present, and because the 'Announcement' and 'Instruction' chapters recorded words but events were also seen," Zhang concludes that "the ancients illustrated events by means of words and considered words as constitutive of events. They never separated events and words into two different things."[65]

Although Zhang's expansive definition of history as inclusive of such works as the Six Classics has spurred scholarly debate on its precise meaning and rationale, the greatest contribution of his writings to the reflection on history concerns the sufficiency or limitation of evidence.[66] Granted that the ideal of the historian is that he should follow the ancients and never indulge in gratuitous theories, how much latitude does he enjoy in "abandoning the events" momentarily, when the need arises, in order to accomplish his task? How free is he in exercising his imagination to fill in the gaps, to supply here and there what is missing, so as to provide a plausible and coherent narration of the past?

Historians of the West as early as Thucydides were conscious of this fundamental problem of historical discourse, conventionally distinguished as the inevitable combination of facts (data or information) and interpretation (explanation or story told about the facts).[67] The explanatory act may begin with the interpolation of plausible utterance (what might Confucius have said when he faced famine in the State of Chen?) and the attribution of motive in the case of an individual, and extend to the larger and more complex undertaking of "reading" a longer stretch of time by discovering causality, denominating patterns or configurations, and describing "the outside and inside of an event."[68] Thus Thucydides remarked: "as for the speeches made on the eve of the war or during the course, it was hard for me, when I heard them myself, and for any others who reported them to me to recollect exactly what had been said. I have

[64] *WSTY*, p. 1.

[65] Ibid., pp. 8–9.

[66] See Jin Yifu, *Zhongguo shixue shi*, pp. 232–33; David S. Nivison, "The Philosophy of Chang Hsüeh-ch'eng," and "The Problem of 'Knowledge' and 'Action' in Chinese Thought since Wang Yang-ming"; Yu Yingshi, *Lun Dai Zhen yu Zhang Xuecheng*, pp. 202–25; and Paul Demiéville, "Chang Hsüeh-ch'eng and his Historiography."

[67] Hayden White, *Tropics of Discourse*, p. 107. For some penetrating observations on this problem in the Chinese context, see Qian Zhongshu, *Guanzhuibian* 1: 161–66.

[68] R. G. Collingwood, *The Idea of History*, p. 213.

therefore put into the mouth of each speaker the views that, in my opinion, they have been most likely to express, as the particular occasions demanded, while keeping as nearly as I could to the general purport of what was actually said" (*The Peloponnesian Wars*, 1. 22).

For the Greek historian to have an opinion on what his characters "have been most likely to express" in accordance with the demands of particular occasions is for him to think, by means of inference, deduction, or analogy, the thoughts of those persons by whose agency the events came about. This, according to Collingwood, is "the re-enactment of past thought in the historian's mind."[69] Although contemporary historians of the West would no more agree with Collingwood's emphasis on all history as the history of thought than with the Romantic bias of his hermeneutics (for example, Schleiermacher's notion of interpretation as essentially psychological divination and replication [*Nachbildung*]), they certainly acknowledge with him the necessity of the "constructive imagination" in writing history.[70] The data themselves, the welter of facts however abundant, do not add up to a coherent narrative, a history in the sense of a story and an inquiry. For that level of discourse to be reached, the critical ascertainment of fact or evidence is but the first step of a long and laborious task wherein the data are selected and assembled by the historian and the proper linkages are discerned or deviced. All this takes place not as separate steps of a linear procedure but as a synthetic, emplotting act of the historian. As Hayden White has observed, "the fact is presented where and how it is in the discourse in order to sanction the interpretation to which it is meant to contribute. And the interpretation derives its force of plausibility from the order and manner in which the facts are presented in the discourse. The discourse itself is the actual combination of facts and meaning which gives to it the aspect of a *specific* structure of meaning that permits us to identify it as a product of one kind of historical consciousness rather than another."[71] This is, in fact, how White explains Collingwood's understanding of the constructive imagination, which for the latter, "was both *a priori* (which meant that it did not act capriciously) and *structural* (which meant that it was governed by notions of formal coherency in its constitution of possible objects of thought)."[72]

Once the historian's craft is conceded to be constitutive of its object both formally (in the sense of endowing it with meaning and structure) and ontologically (in the sense of its creation through language and narration), it will not be long before one reaches the conclusion that the process of reading history is similar to that of reading fiction. And one can do this not because there is no possible distinction between historical truth and imaginative art

---

[69] Ibid., p. 215.
[70] Fr. D. E. Schleiermacher, *Hermeneutik*, pp. 108–9.
[71] White, *Tropics of Discourse*, p. 107.
[72] Ibid., p. 60.

(though certain contemporary theorists of the West might indeed so contend), but because the obligations on the reader of these two genres of writing are similar.[73] Such indeed is Paul Ricoeur's argument, which deserves a full citation.

> A history book can be read as a novel. In doing this, we enter an implicit pact of reading and share in the complicity it establishes between the narrative voice and the implied reader. By virtue of this pact, the reader's guard is lowered. Mistrust is willingly suspended. Confidence reigns. The reader is prepared to accord the historian the exorbitant right to know other minds. In the name of this right, ancient historians did not hesitate to place in the mouths of their heroes invented discourses, which the documents did not guarantee but only made plausible. Modern historians no longer permit themselves these fanciful incursions, fanciful in the strict sense of the term. They do, however, still appeal in more subtle ways to the novelistic genius when they strive to reenact, that is, to rethink, a certain weighing of means and ends. Historians, then, are not prohibited from "depicting" a situation, from "rendering" a train of thought, or from giving it the "vividness" of an internal discourse. Through this aspect we rediscover an effect of discourse stressed by Aristotle in his theory of *lexis*. "Locution"—or "diction"—according to his *Rhetoric*, has the virtue of "placing before our eyes" and so of "making visible." An additional step is thus taken, over and beyond seeing-as, which does not prohibit the marriage of metaphor, which assimilates, and irony, which creates a distance. We have entered into the realm of illusion that confuses, in the precise sense of the term, "seeing-as" with "believing we are seeing." Here, "holding as true," which defines belief, succumbs to the hallucination of presence.[74]

When we look at the testimony on the Chinese side, we find that Sima Qian himself was already caught up in this process. When, for example, he acknowledged at the end of the "Biography of Guan Zhong" in his own voice that "after having seen (*jian*) the books [Guan] had authored, I would like to look at his deeds (*guan qi xing shi*) and thus I ended up with his biography" (*Shiji*, 62), he, too, was succumbing "to the hallucination of presence" both as a writer and a reader of history. That succumbing both affirms and makes problematic the means and manner of representation.

Zhang Xuecheng was quite aware of the intimate relation between language and history. "What history prizes above all," he wrote, "is the correct meaning (*yi*), but what it presents [as evidence] are events (*shi*), and what it relies upon [for making this presentation] is literary language (*wen*)"[75] This formulation of Zhang's seems to me to be an advance over the thought of the famed com-

---

[73] Hayden White has been criticized for dissolving "historiography into fiction." See Arnaldo Momigliano, "Biblical Studies and Classical Studies."

[74] *Time and Narrative* 3: 186.

[75] *WSTY*, p. 144.

mentator, Jin Shengtan (?1610–1661), who declared in his introduction (*dufa*) to the seventy-chapter version of *Shuihuzhuan* (*Outlaws of the Marsh*) that Sima Qian "uses language to put in motion events (*yi wen yun shi*)," whereas the novel "creates events by means of language (*yin wen sheng shi*)."[76] Though Jin's observation is random and undeveloped, as are virtually all such observations in *dufa* commentary, it may be argued that the commentator is trying to distinguish between history and literature on the basis of contrasting a representational view of language with a constitutive or productive one. In the former view, language merely serves to transcribe, and thus to put in motion or convey (*yun*), historical events or experience.

Zhang Xuecheng, on the other hand, seems far more sensitive to the constitutive role of language in the writing of history.[77] It is this sensitivity that leads him to probe the exigencies in writing history when the historian finds it necessary to provide information other than what could be derived from "the transmission through mouths and ears." On these occasions the historian is expected to invent (*chuang*) only that which is "appropriate to the words and events," or to attribute causality (*yin*) only to that which is "appropriate to the aim of the discourse."[78] To put the matter in Western terms, it may be said that Zhang's prescribed goal for the historian is none other than verisimilitude.[79] Elsewhere, Zhang made the observation that although "the language of history (that is, historiography) may have endless variety, . . . to record words and events, however, one must desire to [record] that which is most likely to be the words and events, without any addition or reduction." Furthermore, he made an important distinction between events and words. For the former, the proper method permits only reduction but never addition, "for the addition of one word [about event] is the creation of falsehood." On the other hand, "there is no hard-and-fast rule for the recording of words, but the guidance of the historical author must be his desire to make inference only from the intentionality of the past speaker. If it is in accord with that intentionality, the addition of a thousand words is not too many; otherwise, even one word makes for the creation of falsehood."[80]

Given this view of what is and what is not permissible in history, it is not surprising that Zhang harbors a rather low opinion of what he considers to be fictive. "The ancients," he said, "would not employ language and rhetoric to show off their private opinions, and, therefore, the discourse of history ought

---

[76] "Du Diwu caizishu fa," p. 93.

[77] For a trenchant essay on the dominant role of language in history, see J. Hillis Miller, "Literature and History."

[78] *WSTY*, p. 290.

[79] For further and thoughtful discussion of this topic in relations to Chinese historiography and fiction, see Sheldon Hsiao-peng Lu, *From Historicity to Fictionality*, pp. 74–92; 129–50.

[80] "Yu Chen Guanmin gongpu lun shixue," p. 14.

not be permitted to use untruth to fabricate something else."[81] From this judgment comes the final severance of the literary from the historical. "The flaw of plagiarism in the literati and the merit of deft usage (*yun yong*) in the historian may appear similar, but they are, in fact, irreconcilably different. The plagiarist fears only that people would know of his source; the deft user, that they would be ignorant of it."[82]

The ideas of Zhang Xuecheng discussed here, though enunciated in the eighteenth century, ought not to be regarded merely as a product of the times, for such exalted aims and ideals of historiography, as all students of Chinese civilization recognize, stem from an unbroken tradition from antiquity. The canons of value and the insistence on methodological rectitude have won the just praise of modern non-Chinese historians for their "accuracy, objectivity and devotion to truth."[83] Zhang's prescription for the historian to aim for verisimilitude, to imagine only those words and actions deemed consistent with known historical evidence, by itself bears remarkable semblance to Thucydides' creation of what his characters "have been most likely to express." Despite the ring of nobility in Zhang's utterance, however, what a modern student misses when reading this man universally acclaimed as "a historical genius of the first magnitude" is precisely what one detects so clearly in Thucydides: an awareness of inevitable subjectivity, or what White has labeled "the irreducible and inexpungeable element of interpretation" in his own narrative.[84] To probe the reasons, on the part of the Chinese, for their seeming lack of awareness of this issue of metahistory, I propose to look further at the question of why they wrote as they did, which may provide the most important clues to understanding the principles of traditional historiography.[85] I shall conclude the chapter with a brief consideration of *Hongloumeng* and its reading as a response to the authority of history.

It is general knowledge that a great deal of ancient Chinese historiography existed as annals. The earliest *Book of Documents*, which is by common consent an assortment of pronouncements or papers chronologically arranged (and thus, according to traditional Chinese taxonomy, concerned with the recording of both words and events), exhibits this tendency of pegging separate incidents to specific dates. Most characteristic of all is the *Chunqiu*, putative annals of the State of Lu, and its typical entries read as follows:

---

[81] *WSTY*, p. 89.

[82] "Yu Chen Guanmin gongpu lun shixue," 14.

[83] Earl H. Pritchard, "Traditional Chinese Historiography and Local Histories," p. 198. See also Homer H. Dubs, "The Reliability of Chinese Histories"; and more recently, Yu Yingshi, "The Seating Order at the Hung Men Banquet." The Chinese version of this essay was originally written for a volume of *Festschriften* for the eightieth birthday of Professor Shen Gangbo. See *Shen Gangbo xiansheng bazhi rongqing lunwenji*.

[84] Demiéville, p. 257; White, *Tropics of Discourse*, p. 51.

[85] Lien-sheng Yang, "The Organization of Chinese Official Historiography," p. 46.

In the sixteenth year, in spring, the Marquis of Qi invaded Xu.

The viscount of Chu inveigled the viscount of the Manrong [into his power] and slew him.

In summer, the duke arrived from Jin.

In autumn, in the eighth month, on Jihai, Yi, marquis of Jin, died.[86]

This salient feature of the annal has been succinctly described by Liu Zhiji (661–721) as one that "ties events to the day, and the day to the month; when it speaks of spring, it may contain summer, and when it refers to autumn, it may include winter. Since the year has four seasons, they are presented alternately to name what is recorded" (*Shitong tongshi* 1: 5b). To explain the prominence of the annal, one Western scholar has surmised that "the task of the scribe was probably of a ritual character, and historiography was closely linked with the fortune of the ruling houses. Their success was thought to depend on the ritual in the ancestral temple and on the regular succession of the seasons, to be registered in the calendar."[87]

Although this observation has an accurate insight, I think more can be said about why the Chinese have placed such great emphasis on tying events to the days and months and years. The first reason is manifestly linguistic. Lacking any morphological capacity to differentiate temporality into past, present, and future, Chinese verbs, unlike those of all Indo-European languages, must call upon the assistance of dates to signify the pastness of the past. Other parts of speech or elements of the language (particles, enclitics, adverbs) may help to indicate whether an action is completed or about to be undertaken, but the specificity of chronology is the decisive marker of time in Chinese narrative. That is why Liu Zhiji can declare summarily: "without chronological arrangement, what sort of an annal do you have?" (*Shitong tongshi*, 2: 8b).

The second reason for the intimate bond between chronology and narrative is traceable not merely to the observance of royal ritual but also, and far more importantly, to the basic belief that history of its very nature must be political. This is evident not simply because the historical records are focused upon social and political institutions, upon the exploits and utterances of rulers and ministers, but also because the determination of calendrical time and its proper usage were understood as belonging to the domain of governance. Thus the desired union of historical and astronomical knowledge in Chinese antiquity is located in the high official of Taishi (alternately, Taishigong or Taishiling).

The title of the office, as Joseph Needham has pointed out, may be rendered as "Astrologer or Astronomer-Royal" and as "Historiographer or Chronologer-Royal," the last of which he deems best because "the office was certainly thought

---

[86] "Chaogong, 16th year," modified by Legge, *Chinese Classics*, 5: 663.

[87] P. van der Loon, "The Ancient Chinese Chronicles and the Growth of Historical Ideals," p. 25.

of as combining an earthly archivistic with a heavenly uranographic function."[88] The latter responsibility betokens the advanced state of proto-scientific thought and discovery in Chinese antiquity. For although the Mohists, for example, had no deductive geometry and no Galilean physics (and thus they could not quite come up with the exact conception of motion as change of place functionally dependent on time, which was arrived at by Western physics at the time of the Renaissance), the Chinese had already some sort of luni-solar calendar by the fifteenth century B.C.E.; by the first century they had a calendrical system partly "independent of celestial phenomena,"[89] and the period between 370 B.C.E. and 1732 C.E. saw the production of no fewer than one hundred calendars or sets of astronomical tables that enlisted the service of virtually every known mathematician and astronomer. All this attests to the seriousness wherewith time was taken.

Much of that seriousness can be attributed to the intimate relation between the calendar and state power, and it is in this respect that Chinese astronomy also provides the sharp contrast not only to Greek astronomy but also to Greek historiography.[90] Whereas the recognition of the interdependence of the selection and dating of events did not quite lead to "a fusion of historical and chronological research" in Greek antiquity, it was absolutely necessary for the Chinese, as their documentary and institutional history both testify, to unite calendrical and historical concerns. "In a civilization primarily agrarian the people had to know exactly what to do at particular times, and so it came about the promulgation of the luni-solar calendar (*li*) in China was the numinous cosmic duty of the imperial ruler (the Son of Heaven, Thien Tzu). Acceptance of the calendar was the demonstration of fealty, somewhat analogous to the authority of the ruler's image and superscription on the coinage in other civilizations."[91] Contemporary Western thinkers may be justified in raising the trenchant questions of whether the use of any calendrical system (for example, the single-era count such as the Olympic dating from 7776 B.C.E., the Seleucid from 311 B.C.E., or the Chinese sexagenary periods based on pairing two sets of cyclical characters) for the purpose of constructing a chronology is not already the use of a form of invented encoding, and whether the act of dating itself ought not to be regarded finally as a synthesis of astronomical time with human, social time because it is the conferral of a living present, an "as if" or

---

[88] "Time and Knowledge in China and the West," p. 101. For a detailed discussion of the history of astronomy in China, see *SCC* 3: 178–461.

[89] Needham, "Time and Knowledge," p. 100. For a different judgment on this possibility, see Nathan Sivin, *Cosmos and Computation*.

[90] *SCC* 3: 189.

[91] On the Greeks, see Momigliano, "Time in Ancient Historiography," in *Essays in Ancient and Modern Historiography*, 192. On the Chinese, Needham, "Time and Knowledge," p. 100.

imaginary present, upon a general instant.[92] Such a line of critical reflection, however, was hardly compatible with the weighty concerns of the ancient Chinese to coordinate the dates and seasons with agricultural, ritual, and royal activities.

The powerful bond between history and political governance also, I think, helps to illumine the profoundly didactic character of so much of traditional Chinese historiography. At bottom, the preservation of the memory of the past serves the purpose of instruction, but what history teaches is principally how to explain change, how to account for "the fortune of the ruling houses," the success and failure of significant individuals, the alternating periods of order and confusion that have lasted since the world's beginning (*Mencius*, 3B, 9). Thus "the penetration or comprehension of change" (*tongbian*), a phrase derived from the *Great Commentary* of the *Book of Changes*, has ever been the elevated end of historical knowledge. In the Second Part of this commentary, we have the oft-cited observation, "when one [phase of a cycle of] change had run its course, they [here, a likely reference to the clans of the Yellow Emeperor, of Yao, and of Shun] altered. (Through alteration they achieved continuity.) Through continuity they achieved duration."[93]

Different civilizations, of course, have different ways of interpreting change. Biblical history exalted the will of Yahweh as the final cause for the rejection of Saul and the election of David as king. Homer traced the beginning of the Trojan War to both Paris' foolish infatuation and treacherous divine intervention. Herodotus' account of the Persian Wars stressed a multitude of human motives, perhaps most notably Xerxes' vaulting ambition, whereas Thucydides located in the growth of Athenian power, "which terrified the Lacadaemonians and put them under the necessity of fighting," a triggering incident. For the Chinese, change is accounted for in traditional history primarily in two ways: the moral cause and the natural cause, and these two are not necessarily in opposition to each other.

Whether Confucius did have something to do with that schematization known as praise and blame (*baobian*) is not in dispute here. What is important to note is that writing history in conformity to that kind of an ideal is to take the surprise out of change by placing the events within the fold of an absolute moral order. It may be an overstatement to assert that there are many instances of poetic justice in Chinese historiography, but there is discernible in a text

---

[92] Claude Lévi-Strauss, *The Savage Mind*, pp. 258–60; and see Ricoeur, *Time and Narrative* 3: 181–85 for a brilliant discussion.

[93] *The I Ching or Book of Changes*, pp 331–32. The words denoting nuanced differences in the concept of change in classical Chinese include *bian, hua,* and *yi.* Jacques Gernet's "Sur la notion de changement", focuses on the second of these terms. Another authoritative treatment of *tongbian* may be found in Nathan Sivin, "Change and Continuity in Early Cosmology."

like the *Zuo Commentary* an attempt to weave a moral pattern wherein not only are the good and bad clearly distinguished but they are also "encouraged or censured (*cheng'e er quanshan*)" accordingly (Chenggong, 14th year; Legge, *Chinese Classics* 5: 384). That the incidents recorded are especially germane to the deliberation of statecraft can be seen in the fact that they are not concerned merely with the reward of the virtuous or the punishment of the wicked or tyrannical. The failure to act decisively, to observe proper ritual or propriety, and to heed wise or reasonable counsel can all bring on calamity.[94] This tendency to pass ethical judgments on historical characters by open or implied statements runs through the massive line of standard histories. A modern historian has pointed to the famous or infamous figure of Empress Wu Zetian (r. 690–705) to illustrate the persistence of such didactic intent. "The *Chiu T'ang-shu* roundly condemns the Empress and gives specific reasons for this, but does end with a few examples of her ability and political skill. The *Hsin T'ang-shu* produces an essay on political morality and historical judgment and tries to confirm the meaningfulness of the concept of retribution even though someone evil like Empress Wu was not punished."[95] In either case, the empress' particular location in the moral order has been classified and fixed. "The demand for closure in the historical story is a demand," according to Hayden White, "for moral meaning, a demand that sequences of real events be assessed as to their significance as elements of a moral drama."[96] Focused thus upon the exemplary significance of characters and events, history in China assumes the authority of a kind of realized eschatology, to use Christian terminology, because its judgment is thought to be both impartial and virtually irreversible.[97]

Concurrent with the moral explanation of change is the explanation advanced by what Needham has termed "organic naturalism" in Chinese philosophy, that is, by the attempt to correlate or align the affairs and culture of the human world with the dyadic principles of yin and yang and the posited elemental forces, powers, or "phasal energetics" (*wuxing, wude*) of earth, wood, metal, fire, and water. The School of Zou Yan (Tsou Yen, c. 350–270 B.C.E.), whose biography was prominently written by Sima Qian (*Shiji*, 74), advocated a theory of periods of time in a fixed cycle governed by the Five Phases. Wood, Fire, Metal, and Water are correlated therein with the four seasons and with corresponding colors and directions, while Earth functions as the center and coordinates the changes of the other four phases and their correlates. The

---

[94] See Egan, "Narrative in *Tso Chuan*," pp. 327–32.

[95] Wang Gungwu, "Some Comments on the Later Standard Histories," p. 57.

[96] *The Content of the Form*, p. 21.

[97] Note the succinct words of the 1261 memorial by the Yuan scholar, Wang Ê: "Since antiquity, a state can be destroyed but not its history. In general the history of the preceeding dynasty has been compiled by its successor, because judgment and evaluation can become impartial only with later generations." Cited in Lien-sheng Yang, "The Organization of Chinese Official Historiography," p. 47.

energetics or pulsations of each phase move in a cyclical sequence in which one is overcome by the next in order until the process repeats itself; hence the name of the sequence is mutual conquest (*xiangke*). Later the Han philosopher Dong Zhongshu in his reinterpretation of the *Spring and Autumn* modified the idea of conquest to mutual production or generation of the phases.[98]

Whether these cosmic forces are thought to be essentially in conflict or in harmony, the important point about such theories is that they continue the emphasis of the moral explanation of historical change by the simultaneous naturalization of its immediate cause. Even more than the moral theory, the natural explanation endeavors to endow the flux of history, especially the phenomena of dynastic changes, with the constancy of numerical regulation, for the fundamental function of cyclical concepts, as Nathan Sivin has observed, is "to define order."[99] To Western eyes, "the inconstant moon that monthly changes" may yield an image of fickleness; for the Chinese, instead, the very rhythm of her fullness and wane betokens constancy. Planetary motions and elemental powers thus both provide instructive analogues to human affairs and exert decisive influences upon their interpretation by imposing ultimate limits on the possibilities or directions of historical change. To claim with Mao Zonggang's narrator in *The Three Kingdoms* that an empire, "long divided, must unite; long united, must divide" is to affirm the seamless continuity of the full circle in which, again, there ought to be neither disruption nor surprise. For this reason as well, the success or failure of a human regime in the world can no longer be accounted for merely by political negligence or moral degeneration; cosmic forces must now be placed in view. Paradoxically, however, the stress on the "tide in the affairs of man" does not obviate human obligation and initiative, for "the crucial part of political art was the ruler's ability [and by implication, his ministers' and counselors' as well] to understand the timing of dynastic change and to align himself with the power of the future by introducing measures that bring the state ceremonies and calendar into accord with this power."[100] Once more history functions as the prophetic tutor, because past examples are recorded as a potent guide for present conduct.

Moreover, the cosmological integration of history means that, with sagacity and knowledge, one can detect the secret rhythm and telos of seemingly random temporality. Just as the farmer and astronomer can tell what is about to happen by scanning the heavens and the seasons, so the sage steeped in the learning of

---

[98] For "organic naturalism," see *SCC* 2: 287ff; for Zou Yan, see 2: 232–34. See also Vitaly A. Rubin, "Ancient Chinese Cosmology and Fa-chia Theory," 95–104; John S. Major, "A Note on the Translation of Two Technical Terms in Chinese Science"; Benjamin I. Schwartz, *The World of Thought in Ancient China*, pp. 350–82.

[99] See his "On the Limits of Empirical Knowledge in the Traditional Chinese Sciences."

[100] Rubin, "Ancient Chinese Cosmology," p. 98.

history can decipher the "numerical meaning of the nodal forces, *qishu*," a term derived from the division of the year into twenty-five nodal periods (*jie*, a term in turn derived from the stalk of the bamboo), each with its distinctive character. Interpreting the *qishu* of a person, a household, or a nation is an undertaking entertained not only in historiography but also in novels like *The Three Kingdoms* and the *Investiture of the Gods* (*Fengshen yanyi*), works devoted to dramatize dynastic rise and fall. "The best index to the hegemony of the artificial perspective," as a contemporary theorist has observed, "is the way it denies its own artifiiciality and lays claim to being a 'natural' representation of 'the way things look,' 'the way we see,' or (in a phrase that turns Maimonides on his head) 'the way things really are.'"[101] Thus the power wherewith the cosmic-natural explanation of historical change has validated itself may be seen in the fact that no less a strong-minded person than Qin Shihuang himself, the first emperor of a united China, accepted the Five Phases theory and used it for the legitimation of his rule and the establishment of his institutions. More than a millennium later, the court of the Jin dynasty (1115–1234) was still debating such a view of history, the issues ever gaining new scope and complexity.[102]

That history occupies a position of virtually unrivaled esteem and authority in Chinese culture cannot be doubted. In chapter 5 of the *Shiji*, which is a section bearing the chronicle of the State of Qin, the Grand Historian made the following observation: "In the thirteenth year of Duke Wen [corresponding to 753 B.C.E.] scribes were appointed for the first time so as to record events. Many among the population became civilized." For a modern historian, "this sentence obviously expresses the conviction of a later scribe that the keeping of annals since 753 B.C. had been beneficial, rather than the hope of the first scribe of Ch'in that his activities would have a good effect."[103] This may well be the case, but van der Loon's exemplary exercise of critical acumen misses the point. It does not matter whether that remark of the *Shiji* indicates "the hope of a first scribe" or a latter's conviction, for the assertion of such beneficial effect (whether one agrees or not with van der Loon's rendering of *hua* as reformed) can enjoy no empirical verification. What is important is what that statement reveals about the high estimate of history the Chinese entertained—an already entrenched ideology of history by Sima Qian's time. To possess history is to enjoy the educative and civilizing benefits of that kind of writing which provides a comprehensive ordering of time.

Against the inconsistencies, ambiguities, and chaos of actual life, the clarity afforded by the reductive lens of history in which examples of human evil can

---

[101] W. J. T. Mitchell, *Iconology*, p. 37.
[102] See Hok-lam Chan, *Legitimation in Imperial China*.
[103] Van der Loon, "The Ancient Chinese Chronicles," p. 25.

warn the world and human good can instruct posterity (in Liu Zhiji's words) offers a powerful palliative, if not a real antidote. In a civilization whose basic orientation, by all accounts, is relentlessly focused upon the mundane, human world, not only does history answer the great questions of origin and end— questions which, in other cultures, are classically associated with religion— but also its moral weight and perceived veracity approach scriptural certitude. Its authority is thus the authority of the "Great Code," the Blakean nomenclature for the Bible, which Northrop Frye has used to delineate the "mythological conditioning" of the cultural tradition of the West. It is also this unrivaled importance of historical discourse that lends cogency to a modern scholar's claim: "the world implied in the bulk of classical Chinese fiction is one in which everything 'means' as long as it is related to a historical context. The problem of anachronism in language, costuming, manners and morals, and so forth, though frequently occuring in the narrative of Chinese fiction, is seldom taken seriously by the writer/storyteller and his reader, because more often than not historical data serve mainly as a reminder alerting readers to some *a-temporal* significance of moral mechanism, thereby highlighting a fundamental premise of classical Chinese historiography."[104]

Seen in this light, Sima Qian's statement about the uplifting effect of history, though strictly anachronistic, reveals nonetheless the exalted function assigned to his own project "to narrate past affairs and think about what is to come (*shu wang shi, si lai zhe*)" ("Autobiography" in *Shiji*, 130). This function is, in fact, inalienable from any writing of history, for it is the historian's action alone that makes explicit—indeed assumes—the burden of history. It is what Michel de Certeau has called "the weight of an endlessly present past (an inertia that traditionalists call 'continuity' before declaring it to be 'truth' of history)."[105] Implicit in de Certeau's formulation no less than in Sima Qian's declaration is the recognition that the past as such can have no knowledge of, or use for, future meaning or incidents, or we would have to think that overweening ministers (as Guan Zhong in Confucius's eyes) or murderous subjects acted with intentions of serving as negative examples! It is the insertion of the historian into the process of making history that creates the event from the indeterminacy of the past. The event as occurrence and thus as referent (such as, Li Ling's battle, defeat, and surrender) can no more speak or instruct than signs, omens, and tracks left to themselves. There is thus more than one level of ironic truth when Sima Qian announces in self-ridicule at one point in his famous "Letter in Reply to Ren An": "Your servant's forbearers were not those who had the merit of carving talismans or writing with cinnabar. After all,

---

[104] David Der-wei Wang, "Fictional History/Historical Fiction," pp. 65–66. For further discussion of this theme, see his *Cong Liu Ê dao Wang Zhenhe*, pp. 291–329.

[105] See *The Writing of History*, p. 37.

history and astronomy are quite close (*jin hu*) to what lies between divination and consultation of oracles."[106]

Quite close indeed, for history must be selected, organized, and narrated— all acts of interpretation—with the vested interest (and the presumed moral authority) of the historian to transform through verbal transmission seemingly random occurences into instructive signifiers. Given such a context wherein history must be read as a cognitively and morally privileged discourse, what is the place of fiction and how is it understood? How would fiction's construction and discourse assert a difference of reading? The consideration of this last question brings us directly to the beginning of *Hongloumeng*.

The extraordinary, transgressive disposition of the narrative early in chapter 1 of *Hongloumeng* has elicited from Red Inkstone this observation in the headnotes: "The intentionality expressed in the entire first chapter opening the book has truly broken with the well-worn conventions of novels written here-tofore" (*Pingyu*, p. 10). Although the scholiast does no more to specify *how* his favored text has freed itself from hackneyed tradition than calling the book "worthy to be compared with *Zhuangzi* and *Lisao*," some other literary prece-dents that come readily to mind should help us see the assertive difference of *Hongloumeng*'s beginning.

Among the four monumental works of Ming fiction that preceded the Qing masterpiece, only *The Journey to the West* departs from a steady focus on the human historical order and commences, instead, with a twofold story of creation—first, of the cosmos, and then of the Stone Monkey. To be sure, the narrative makes fleeting reference to various motifs of Chinese cosmogonic lore, to the Three Kings and Five August Ones of mythic history, but there-after, the scene shifts immediately, and the events belonging to a continent of Buddhist cosmology become the sole subject of narration ("This book is solely concerned with the East Purvavideha Continent"; *JW* 1: 66). Indeed, readers will visit with Stone Monkey the highest reaches of Heaven and the lowest depths of Hell for a protracted period of eight chapters before they are permitted to enter the mundane reality of Tang China.

In contrast to the *Journey,* the vision of its three companion novels is firmly trained on the human world. However different they might be in their respec-tive developed forms, *The Three Kingdoms, Outlaws of the Marsh*, and *The Plum in the Golden Vase* all exhibit certain textual features at their beginnings that are consistent with their generic tendency to simulate history. The so-called Hongzhi edition of *Three Kingdoms* compiled by Luo Guanzhong (first printed in 1494) begins in a most matter-of-fact manner:

> Upon the death of Huandi of the Later Han, Lindi succeeded to the throne. He was then twelve years old. At court General-in-chief Dou Wu, Grand Mentor

---

[106] "Biography of Sima Qian," in *Han shu*, p. 62.

Chen Fan, and Minister of Education Hu Guang gave him counsel and assistance. The ninth month of that autumn, the palace eunuchs Cao Jie and Wang Fu arrogated power. Dou Wu and Chen Fan plotted their death, but their plot leaked out and they themselves were killed by Cao Jie and Wang Fu. From then on the palace eunuchs became powerful.[107]

As can be seen from even so brief a citation, the unadorned diction and the simplicity of style are meant to convey the character of a historical narrative. Add to our consideration the printed format and layout, with successive columns of imperial genealogy and of sundry biographies of important ministers, and we can understand why the Preface of the same year by Jiang Daqi declares that this work appears "as if it were history (*shujihu shi*)."[108] When we take up the familiar revised version by Mao Zonggang and his father, we can see that the editors have sought to attenuate the abruptness of starting in medias res typical of Chinese chronicle style by framing the tale with the most venerable law expressive of traditional understanding of history. "The empire, long divided, must unite," proclaims the narrator; "long united, must divide. Thus it has ever been."[109] The narrative then proceeds not only to cite historical examples of such a tendency but also to adduce for the reader "the cause of Han's fall," which underlies the drama of the immediate story. Within the movement of no more than five or six sentences, the Mao version thus conveys to us the unmistakable signal that this story aspires to participate in one cardinal concern idealized by traditional Chinese historiography: to discover and articulate within the recording of the flux of events that principle of permanence in eternal, patterned recurrence.

In both *Outlaws* and *The Plum*, on the other hand, an enlargement of inventiveness and an increase in narrative sophistication are evident. Historical references abound in the beginning of both texts, but they clearly appear as props and pointers leading into the main story. The first lyric (*ci*) that opens the *Outlaws* recalls in both diction and sentiment another lyric (written to the tune of "Immortal at the River") that, taken from the *Ershiwu shi tanci*, is used by Mao Zonggang to preface his *Three Kingdoms*.[110] Even more than the latter poem, the *Outlaws* affirms "former kings and later rulers (*qian wang hou di*)," "their legitimacy or illegitimacy (*zhen, wei*)," to be the stuff of fiction. In this regard, the author of fiction is like the traditional poet who sings of history (*yong shi*); amid laughter and conversation (*xiao tan*) and over wine, both may discuss history with fresh perspective and even invention. History, however, in the guise of the exploits of heroes and princes, remains the entrenched sub-

---

[107] *Sanguozhi tongsu yanyi* 1: 1. In translating titles, I follow Hucker.

[108] Ibid. 1: "Xu," 3b.

[109] Moss Roberts, trans., *The Three Kingdoms*, p. 5.

[110] The first half of the lyric in the *Outlaws* is, in fact, a form of "Immortal at the River (*Linjiang xian*)."

ject of their writings, and the lesson that both history and fiction adduce for their readers also coincide: sic transit gloria mundi.[111]

Thus the lengthy Prologue (*xiezi*) of the *Outlaws* duly rehearses the turmoil of dynastic succession since "the end of Tang." As the narrative moves rapidly through the founding of the Song Dynasty to settle its focus on the reign of Renzong, the aphoristic commonplace of "extreme happiness begetting sorrow" (*le ji sheng bei*) sets the stage, conveniently, for introducing the outbreak of a plague and the imperial quest for its purgation.[112] The fantastic adventures of Marshal Hong Xin, leading straight to the eventual release of the 108 baleful, demonic stars, not only anticipate the subsequent action proper, but they also exploit a device favored by many works of fiction, including *Hongloumeng*. By endowing the outlaws of the marshes with a form of preincarnate existence, the narrative introduces the necesssary mythic background that will work to clarify the ultimate karmic disposition of the mundane plot. More often than not in Chinese fiction, the popular notion of karmic causality (*qianyin houguo*) functions as a form of probability and necessity. Marshal Hong's activities in the Prologue also help to reinforce the story's central irony with its own foreboding twist: it is the imperial envoy seeking a cure for a pestilence that unleashes some violent forces of disorder and destruction.

In the history of the Chinese novel, *The Plum* enjoys the distinction of being the first full-length narrative built on a single, *invented* story. Nevertheless, it still begins not only with an obligatory reference to the Huizong era of the Song but also with a rather stodgy bit of moralizing drawn from recorded history. The prose segment of the first few pages of chapter 1 provides an exposition of the allusion, made in the prefatory lyric to the tune of "Pleasing Eyes" by the thirteenth-century poet Zhuo Tian, to Xiang Yu and Liu Bang, famed contenders for the throne of Han. Expounded in the narrative is the unambiguous lesson that fatal addiction to feminine charms can destroy winner and loser alike in the public realm. Liu and Xiang "were certainly heroes of their day," declares the solemn narrator, "and yet did not escape the fate of suffering their ambitions to be blunted by . . . two women."[113] With such examples from history hoisted high as warning signs, the narrative then proceeds to recount "the passionate story of a lustful woman and her adulterous affairs with a good-for-nothing scalawag" (*Jinpingmei cihua* 1: 3a). Despite the enormous number of literary allusions already built into the first chapter, as David

---

[111] My reading of the lyric in the *Outlaws* obviously differs from that of Deborah Porter, who has written one of the most detailed analyses of this novel's beginning. See her "Setting the Tone."

[112] This most hackneyed formula for cyclic repetition is also rehearsed in the episode of the Stone's temptation to enter the human in chapter 1 of the 1754 text of *Hongloumeng*.

[113] *The Plum in the Golden Vase, or, Chin P'ing Mei*, translated by David Tod Roy, 1: 15.

Roy's annotations have made clear, the implied status of art is also unmistakable: fiction is an elaborate but corroborative repetition of history. If heroes of history could not escape victimization by feminine beauty, so the narrative seems to ask, what chance does a ne'er-do-well like Ximen Qing have?

Unlike these four master texts preceding it, *Hongloumeng* opens with a tantalizing invitation to puzzlement and contemplation.

> Various Honored Readers, what, you may ask, was the origin of this book? When I speak of its root cause, it may border on the absurd, but intimate acquaintance[114] may render it deeply interesting. (*HLM* 1: 1; my translation)

The astounding novelty of commencing a work of fiction in this manner lies first of all in the character it ascribes to its alleged process of production. The text did not come into existence as a form of history; no antecedent events or persons are repeated. What appears on the surface as fault (*huangtang*) will be redeemed by an affective condition or quality (*quwei*) that finds gestation in the difference of repeated contact. The demand exacted by "this book (*ci shu*)" is thus "intimate acquaintance," a metaphor of temporality not of the datable past but of lived experience. If, as Edward Said has argued, "the novel is an institutionalization of the intention to begin," this book's beginning achieves its intention and effect, according to the narrator, only in the replicative act of reading.[115]

The casual, offhanded manner wherewith textual beginning is announced is matched only by the dazzling, complex narration that immediately follows. With its constantly shifting points of view, layered temporal dimensions, and multiple beginnings, the narrative charts a circuitous but captivating course toward the main story through different strands of discourse and levels of illusion.[116] The myth of Nüwa ironically contrasts the public, culture-building nature of a cosmogonic legend with the "uselessness" of a rejected stone and its story. The introduction of the myth of plant and stone, the preincarnate antecedents to the story's human protagonists, sets up the tragic dilemma of the plot—that inanimate objects could be even more involved than humans in desire's entanglement. At another level, the playful, enigmatic debate between a monk, a Daoist, and the Stone provides provocative clues not only to the story's origin but also to its nature and the possible effect of its perusal. Still further removed, at a third level, the parade of human characters who are kinfolk of the Jia clan presumably ushers in the realistic, mundane plane of the

---

[114] I follow the 1754 text here, and read *an* as "knowledge of, acquaintance with, or skilled in." All subsequent versions, as far as I know, have selected the homophone meaning "to examine."

[115] Said, *Beginnings*, p. 100.

[116] See, for example, Lucien Miller's analysis in *Masks of Fiction in "Dream of the Red Chamber,"* especially chapters 2 and 4.

plot, but their names—Jia Yu-cun [false language enduring],[117] Zhen Shi-yin [true events concealed] and Ying-lian [deserving to be pitied]—alert us, if not to the possibility of full-blown allegory, at least to the presence of deliberate rhetorical manipulation of our response.

Through these triple lines of narration and an increasing variety of rhetorical devices as he tells his story, the author is in fact engaging the reader in an unprecedented and continuous discussion on the nature of fiction itself, and simultaneously on the nature of reading. To the question of origin posed at the beginning, the expected answer would have been some source of experience drawn from either national or personal history. Indeed, this anticipation seems so natural and compelling that it may help explain why generations of editors of the novel (including a recent edition dating from 1982) felt obliged to include the paragraph of self-exegesis (discussed above) as part of the narrative's authentic beginning. However that issue may be resolved, the sentence purporting to answer the query about origin, as I have pointed out, is actually no answer at all. Instead of being given the satisfaction of having the rhetorical question answered, the reader is warned at once of deceptive appearance and of hard work. In the structure of the assertion, the tendered question of origin is balanced by the injunction to intimate acquaintance or careful investigation (*xi an*), the absurdity of origin by the reward of intrigue and pleasure.

This revolutionary juxtaposition of the problem of representation and the process of reading—an astonishing measure of the tale's insistent reflexivity—obtains throughout the first five chapters of the work. As we move further through the novel's lengthy course, not only do its characters have occasion to debate the function and merit of all the major literary genres of poetry, drama, fiction, and literary prose (an interesting echo, however distant and unintended, of the *Genji Monogatari*), but the Chinese author also exploits repeatedly a network of polyvalent signification generated by such key terms as *meng* (dream), *huan* (the imagined, the fantasized, illusion, enchantment), *jian* (mirror), and the more colloquial *hulu* (gourd, but metonymically, riddle) to modulate the effects of his creation. By characterizing his story as dream, fantasy, and riddle, the author calls attention to both its fictive nature and an eroticism that intrigues and captivates.

The acknowledgment that the text seeks to exact from its reader is thus not only that fiction betokens a systematic reinforcement of illusion, but also that it focalizes, ironically, both the need and danger of that reinforcement. The need is highlighted because lived experience can appear as transitory and un-

---

[117] Wu Shih-ch'ang's reading of *cun*[1] (village, rural) as *cun*[2] (recorded or preserved, hence enduring) seems preferable to me, since it preserves the strict parallelism, grammatical and tonal, to *zhen shi yin*. See *On the Red Chamber Dream*, p. 65 note 3. On the other hand, it should be pointed out that the phrase *jiayu cunyan* (false language, demotic speech) is explicitly mentioned in the text, in the self-exegetic passage located at the very beginning.

real as dream and fantasy, as the self-exegesis has said of its author's experience, and yet dream or fantasy can be highly revelatory, a potent vehicle of truth, as author, characters, and readers of this particular tale will discover. The profound paradox emerging from Cao Xueqin's story seems to be that the illusion of life, itself a painful avowal of the nonreality and untruth of reality (a view that bears strong overtones of Buddhism), can only be grasped through the illusion of art, which is an affirmation of the truth of insubstantiality (that is, *jia zhong you zhen*), a view that, depending on interpretation, may or may not conflict with the major tenets of Mahayana Buddhism. Echoes and elaborations of this paradox occur often and variously. The titular couplet of the first chapter

> Zhen Shi-yin [true events concealed] through dreams and
>   fantasy comes to know perfect comprehension;
> Jia Yu-cun [false language enduring] in destitution recalls
>   boudoir beauties

again alludes (in its second line) to the mood and language of the self-exegesis in the beginning: "having made an utter failure of my life, I found myself one day, in the midst of my poverty and wretchedness, thinking about the female companions of my youth." In contrast to the "autobiographical" impulse to self-revelation, however, the punning names and structure in the couplet point to the contradictory union of knowledge and concealment, of specious utterance masking realistic depiction. The first line of this couplet with the term *tongling* (tentatively rendered here as perfect comprehension) is difficult to translate because it refers doubly to Bao-yu of the narrative and the sense of numinous intelligence. The line challenges us to consider how a kind of learning or recognition (*shi*) concerning the fictive subject is to be gained from an illusory, dreamlike process. Is the fictive subject Bao-yu a novelistic character, or is it more likely the metaphor for the *textualized* Bao-yu, the stone as inscribed narration that Shi-yin literally handled and examined in one of the opening mythic episodes? Moreover, if reality is hidden or camouflaged, what is the truth that is the delineation of absence, the very opposite of the traditional Chinese understanding of historical truth, conceived literally as the truth of the scribe (*shi³ shi⁴*) or the substance of events (*shi⁴ shi⁴*)?

As we move through the text, questions such as these multiply. Should the reader merely concentrate on learning what, for the Chinese, is the all-too-familiar lesson, old as Zhuangzi's butterfly and the *Laṅkāvatāra Sūtra*, that "human life is but a dream (*rensheng ru meng*)"—a lesson painfully acquired by the book's author, its protagonists, and by many of its characters, driven home by experiences that yield "hot and bitter tears"? How should one regard those "pages full of idle (*huangtang*, literally, absurd or baseless) words" that not only pretend to be lived experience, but also render such pretension irresistibly attractive? If we are to regard life as illusory like fiction, how should we respond to fiction as an engaging illusion? This last question is perhaps *the* principal question posed for the reader in nuanced variations throughout the length of the book.

To perceive more readily the author's inaugural emphasis on a *fictive* beginning, we must note how the reply of the first chapter to the tale's, and the text's, inquiry about its own genesis already stresses the duplicity of the fictive mode of being: it is both baseless (*huangtang*) and entertaining (*you quwei*), at once ridiculous (*da huang*), unverifiable (*wu ji*), undatable (*wu chaodai nianji ke kao*), and yet truthful (*zhen*). The author's representation of his monumental invention thus unwittingly concurs with one prominent notion of Western literary theory that "truth-resembling fiction" works through a form of mediation "that, paradoxically, because of its falseness makes the truth truer."[118] It is, as Bao-yu in chapter 56 speaks of his dream encounter with his fictive double who is a mirror image of himself, "more real than real (*zhen er you zhen*)." To the extent, moreover, that Cao Xueqin seems not merely intent on asserting the "better truth" or different truth of fiction, but also on dramatizing the mendacity of that mediatorial form, *Hongloumeng* insistently calls attention to its own language. What enables "the real to become not-real when the unreal's real" are thus the "idle words" that fill the page, "the flavor" of which no one understands. This notion of the language's susceptibility to misconstrual and misreading—because of its very doubleness of nature in which inhere both "truth" and "fiction"—anticipates with astonishing accuracy the formulation of a modern theorist.

> As it accounts for its own mode of writing, [the text] states at the same time the necessity of making this statement itself in an indirect, figural way that knows it will be misunderstood by being taken literally. Accounting for the "rhetoricity" of its own mode, the text also postulates the necessity of its own misreading. It knows and asserts that it will be misunderstood. It tells the story, the allegory of its misunderstanding: the necessary degradation of melody into harmony, of language into painting, of the language of passion into the language of need, of metaphor into literal meaning. In accordance with its own language, it can only tell this story as a fiction, knowing full well that the fiction will be taken for fact and the fact for fiction.[119]

The "necessary degradation" of misreading intimated by *Hongloumeng* may not involve musical or visual transference of linguistic perogatives, but its language certainly suggests (and this is borne out by the history of its reception) the possibility of literalizing the metaphor of self as autobiography or, as we shall see in Chapter III, of the artifice of reading as a process of religious enlightenment.

---

[118] Said, *Beginnings*, p. 90.
[119] Paul de Man, *Blindness and Insight*, p. 136.

In the domain of Western theory on narrative, furthermore, what distinguishes literary language as a form of mediation lies precisely in the special problem and possibility posed by the presumed mnemonic character of the genre and its relation to temporal representation. "In the chronicle of memory," writes Stephen Crites, "there is the simple temporality of succession of duration, of before and after, but not yet the decisive distinction between past, present, and future, that provides the tension of experience and therefore demands the tenses of language."[120] In such an essentially Augustinian conception of memory and time, our articulated experience—that which expresses a sense of temporal succession and "the power to abstract coherent unities from this succession of of momentary percepts"[121]—would actually authorize those inflected temporal markers developed in all attested Indo-European languages. The sense of sequentiality, which is the constitutive feature of any narrative, historical or fictive, would be impossible to achieve in this view if languages were deprived of their tenses. Not surprisingly, thinkers like Emile Benveniste, Käte Hamburger, Arthur Danto, and Paul Ricoeur have built their theories of narrative squarely on this capacity of language which, "with its system of tenses, contains a ready-made means of modulating temporally all the action verbs throughout the narrative chain."[122]

This crucial feature of Western narratology, built squarely upon the special properties of language, could nonetheless shed some light on the Chinese author's peculiar rhetoric in the characterization of his composition. The most important difference of Chinese as a language in this regard is its want of any structural or morphological demarcation for the action verbs. Without specific citations of year and dynastic reign (*chaodai nianji*), no narrative sentence (in the conventional Western sense) is possible, let alone the kind endorsed by Danto and Ricoeur wherein two events are mentioned, "one that is referred to and one that provides the description in terms of which the first is considered."[123]

The stress on the annal and chronicle as favored modes of writing in much traditional Chinese historiography thus reveals a condition not merely of politics but also of language. Even in the early writings of fiction's formative stage, the names of reign periods are routinely mentioned in the entries of *zhiguai* or *chuanqi* stories because without that concrete marker of time, the incidents of the tale cannot even take on the semblance of occurrence, of having taken place in a certain past or a form of datedness resembling "historical" time. To acknowledge, therefore, history's hegemony and to recognize both the indispensable stylistic feature and the peculiar didactic propensity belonging to

[120] "The Narrative Quality of Experience," p. 301.
[121] Ibid., p. 298.
[122] Ricoeur, *Time and Narrative* 2: 93.
[123] Ibid., 1: 206–7; 2: 69.

traditional Chinese historiography is to understand as well the formal attributes of many of its fictive emulators. This realization in turn helps clarify why so many Chinese readers of literature habitually disdain "using language to discuss literature (*yi wen lun wen*)" and prefer instead "using events to discuss literature (*yi shi lun wen*)." It is in this light, finally, that we may begin to comprehend why Cao Xueqin takes such pains to describe his tale as unverifiable and undatable discourse. His rhetoric does not so much accentuate his story's timelessness or its political innocuousness (as the anxious scholiasts would have us believe) as it does its sharp contrast to a different and rival mode of writing—history itself. All those dissimulations and double entendres, one might argue, constitute part of a strategy of persuasion to dehistoricize his narrative's content and context. For the reader to find the "truth," the "real event," the "substance" of this story, there is nothing beyond the text. Language is all, for only "false language remains (*jia yu cun*)." According to the titular couplet of *Hongloumeng*'s first chapter, however, Jia Yu-cun—the prosopopeia of fictive language—thinks of (*huai*) "boudoir beauties" only because he has fallen on hard times (*fengchen*: literally, wind and dust, a common metaphor for the hardships induced by journeys or wars). Echoing the "autobiographical" disclosure at the book's beginning on the circumstance ("an utter failure of my life," "in the midst of poverty and wretchedness") and motive ("I must not . . . allow those wonderful girls to pass into oblivion without a memorial") of fiction, invention thus springs to life, aptly, from the intervention of desire. But as we shall see in the next chapter, the desire for fiction and the fiction of desire both can be a dangerous thing.

CHAPTER II.

Desire

Was, da ein solcher, Ewiger, war, misstraun wir
immer dem Irdischen noch? Statt am Vorlaüfigen ernst
die Gefühle zu lernen für welche
Neigung, künftig im Raum?
(Rainer Maria Rilke, "An Hölderlin")

ALTHOUGH *The Story of the Stone* seems to have left an unambiguous impression upon its very first reader—the fictive personage named Vanitas—with respect to its principal theme (*da zhi*), subsequent readers down through the last two centuries were far less certain in their construal of what that theme might mean. The problem, of course, is posed by the highly allusive and elusive word, *qing*, used by the narrative to designate the substantive theme of its discourse. Contemporary versions of the work in Western languages, compelled by the need in all translations to choose a single normative reading even when diction or syntax may strongly hint of semantic ambiguity or polysemy, have largely opted for making love as the most appropriate equivalent to *qing*.[1] In this they may have the support not only of the incidents in the story's plot itself but also of numerous groups of readers.[2]

From the scholia penned by Red Inkstone and his associates, however, it is clear as well that readers were quite aware from the outset that *qing*, no different from countless other Chinese morphemes that are "free," can greatly vary its meaning when it is linked with other morphemes to form compounds.[3] By itself, the graph *qing* may connote—depending on usage and context—a variety of meanings ranging from circumstance, content, condition, fact, and matter to feeling, obligation, sentiment, and passion. The usage of *qing* in classical texts is, in fact, preponderantly that of a solitary word. With the steady expansion in textual inscription of the vernacular, the tendency of the morpheme to join others in becoming di- or trisyllabic compounds also increases. Coupled

---

[1] Cf. *SS* 1: 51, Yang 1: 5, and *PR* 1: 12.

[2] For example, the celebrated epithets "qingqing" and "qingbuqing," employed by the Red Inkstone circle of scholiasts to discuss the contrasting attitudes of Dai-yu and Bao-yu toward love. See *Pingyu*, pp. 81 and 827 for an index of these two terms in the collected scholia. See also the comment by one Mad Person of Flower and Moon (*huayue chiren*) in *HLMJ* 1: 54.

[3] For the distinction between "free" and "bound" morphemes and the formation of compounds in Chinese, see Jerry Norman, *Chinese*, pp. 154–56.

with another graph, the resultant meaning of the newly formed nominal, in accordance with the sequence of its morphemic combinations, can fluctuate widely. Whereas, for example, *qingren* denotes lover(s), *renqing* can mean human feelings, human relations, the human condition, or human favor.

That *Hongloumeng* exploits to the utmost both the semantic nuances and cultural overtones of its language—a constitutive vernacular richly interwoven with classical elements—is a marvel acknowledged by all. One factor that adds to both the fascination and vexation incurred in its reading lies, as this study has already noted, in the author's penchant for paronomasic games and riddles. Just as he managed to structure a continuously suggested and suggestive polysemy in numerous proper names, place names, terms, and phrases of his composition, his particular treatment of words homophonic or near-homophonic to *qing* seems to have produced a similar effect. As is well known, the first circle of his historical readership had already read the name of Green-sickness Peak (*qinggengfeng*) as "the root of desire (*qinggen*)" and the "Love-Pure Lane" as the "Favor (*renqing*) Lane" (*Pingyu*, pp. 5, 14). Qin Zhong, Bao-yu's best friend, readily becomes "the seed of desire (*qingzhong*)," while Qin [Bang-]ye is made to signify the "evil karma of desire (*qingye*)" (*Pingyu*, pp. 172, 201). Such readings by Red Inkstone and friends have found resonant echoes in subsequent commentory and criticism. Thus one nineteenth-century annotator fashioned his "Critical Pronouncement" on the differing characters of Zhen Bao-yu and Jia Bao-yu on the basis of their different manifestations of *qing*,[4] and a contemporary critic has analyzed the multiple phenomena of *qing* in the narrative by examining the diverse compounds formed by the morpheme—that is, the romantic love (*aiqing*) of the protagonists, the author's feeling (*ganqing*), and the social mores and human relations (*fengsu renqing*) of the novelistic world.[5] In this kind of analysis, the Chinese readers may have wittingly or unwittingly followed the precedent set by the Ming writer Feng Menglong (1574–1646), whose *Qingshi leilüe* (The Anatomy of Love or, literally, A Topical Outline of the History of Love) was organized taxonomically by twenty-seven classes of *qing*, each of which supposedly exemplified by a number of anecdotes or tales.

The centrality of *qing* in shaping virtually every aspect of *The Story of the Stone*'s structure and meaning cannot be denied, and it is understandable that readers have sought more and more to interpret the novelistic conceptualities in the context of Chinese literary and cultural history. Despite the increase of recent publications in this regard, I believe there is still a need to consider, however briefly, the vast and complex subject of *qing* so as to comprehend better its particular significance, both contextual and textual, for *Hongloumeng*.[6]

---

[4] See "*Duhuaren lunzan*," in *Sanjia* 1: 27, 48.

[5] See Su Hongchang, "Lun Cao Xueqin zai *Hongloumeng* chuangzuozhong di 'dazhi tan qing,'" and Zhou Ruchang, *Hongloumeng yu Zhongguo wenhua*, pp. 193–205.

[6] For recent works on *qing* in *Hongloumeng*, see Haun Saussy, "Reading and Folly in *Dream*

In what follows, I examine the treatment of *qing* as part of the Confucian discourse on desire. The concentration on the most pertinent classical philosophical texts is deliberate, since they exist as the foundational documents for the dominant Confucian culture which the fictive narrative presupposes but against which it also stands in tension. I use the term discourse to characterize Confucian ideas and teachings precisely because they assume a normative, constitutive role in molding China's historical culture, a role inaugurated, nurtured, developed, and perpetuated by successive imperial and local governments since the time of the Han.

The term discourse, moreover, helps to heighten our awareness that whatever cultural conflicts China has experienced in the past, a large portion of those conflicts belongs to the domain of language. Texts of ancient Chinese philosophy, replete with evidence of multilateral references and critiques, justify the title of a modern study of those contentious thinkers as "disputers of the Tao [Dao]," but the disputation is premised on the assumption—most frequently voiced by the Confucians—that whatever the Dao is, it certainly may be regarded as a body of ideas preserved in language and transformative of behavior.[7] In the *Analects*, Dao manifestly has at least three meanings: to speak, to guide, and a way (both literal and metaphorical, personal and diffusive).[8] The disputation is thus a contest for normativeness, for the supremacy of a particular form of language—a school of speech—that aims at practical results. The Dao for the Confucians, as Chad Hansen has formulated it, is the discourse of guidance, and its disputation is, as the Chinese would say later, both product and producer of "wars of the tongue (*shezhan*)" and "wars of the brush (*bi-zhan*)."[9]

Although the following pages will present some close readings of segments of Confucian texts, I hope the exercise will go beyond a rehearsal of notions and arguments familiar to students of classical philosophy. "The manifest discourse," a modern thinker reminds us, "is really no more than the repressive presence of what it does not say, and this 'not-said' is a hollow that undermines from within all that is said."[10] Even without agreeing completely with the totalizing implications of this Foucauldian assertion, I still suspect that what is "not said" in the Confucian discourse may be at least as significant as

---

of the Red Chamber"; Wang Daolun, "Zhongguo chuantong wenhuazhong di qingxue yu *Hong-loumeng*"; and Wai-yee Li, *Enchantment and Disenchantment*, chapters. 4–6.

[7] See, for example, A. C. Graham, *Disputers of the Tao*.

[8] See *Analects*, 16:5 (for "to speak"); 1:5, 2:3, and 12:23 (for "to guide"), and 9:11, 4:15, 5:6 (for "the way").

[9] See Chad Hansen's works: *Language and Logic in Ancient China*, chapter 1; "A Tao of Tao in *Chuang-tzu*"; "Language in the Heart-Mind"; and also his *A Daoist Theory of Chinese Thought*, pp. 68–93 and *passim*. For another discussion of the various meanings of Dao in classical Confucianism, see David L. Hall and Roger T. Ames, *Thinking through Confucius*, pp. 226–37.

[10] Michel Foucault, *The Archaeology of Knowledge and The Discourse on Language*, p. 25.

the declared and enunciated. The last section of this chapter will attempt to show as well how the disputation over desire holds importance not merely for politics and ethics in Chinese cultural history but also for literature and aesthetics. The discourse on desire, I shall argue, serves to focalize in China what may also be seen as the "quarrel" between philosophy and poetry. Accordingly, the related topics taken up in this chapter will be: first, the shifting definition of *qing* in classical texts; second, the dialectics of nature and disposition; third, ritual and the rule of desire, and fourth, pathocentrism and the legitimation of desire.

THE DEFINITION OF "QING"

In A. C. Graham's remarks on "The Meaning of *Ch'ing* [*qing*]," the generalization is advanced that the word in pre-Han literature never means "passions," not even in Xunzi.[11] Citing sources ranging from the *Zuo Commentary* to *Lüshi chunqiu*, Graham seeks to demonstrate that *qing* in the documents of this period frequently takes on the meaning of "essence," in the sense of what is essential to a thing—and by extension, to a human person. In this sense as well, the word is analogous to the Aristotelian concept of essence, but the similarity "relates to naming, not to being."[12] According to Graham's survey of the textual evidence, *qing* and *xing* should be understood as the essential and the natural, two overlapping concepts in antiquity. It follows that early Chinese philosophy did not speak of *qing* in morally pejorative terms, and the compound *qingyu*, in Graham's view, should be rendered as "essential desires."[13] Not until the rise of Neo-Confucianism does Graham find a sharp distinction between *qing*, now understood as passions, and *xing* or nature.

The matter of ontology aside, Graham's brief excursus perforce brings into sharp relief the crucial debate on human nature in classical Chinese philosophy. Although he did not state the matter as such, his contrast of "essential desires" with "passions" clearly implies that, in his view, the early Confucians did not consider *qingyu* in itself necessarily a vice or even a problem. It is only when one submits or yields to such "essential desires" that deleterious consequences may arise. Graham's interpretation, in this regard, has the support of

---

[11] Graham's essay first appeared as a section in "The Background of the Mencian Theory of Human Nature," in the *Tsing Hua Journal of Chinese Studies*. Further discussion of the word *qing* written consistently with a *yan* (language) radical (#149) may be found in A. C. Graham, *Later Mohist Logic, Ethics and Science*, pp. 179–82.

[12] *Studies in Chinese Philosophy and Philosophical Literature*, p. 63.

[13] Ibid. Graham in *Later Mohist Logic* has argued that the same understanding of the term is applicable to the "Qingyu" section (*juan* 2, 3) of the *Lüshi chunqiu*. Hence he translates *yu you qing, qing you jieh* as "among desires there are the essential, for the essential there is measure" (p. 182).

the modern philosopher Tang Junyi. In connection with his discussion of the emphasis on *qing* in *The Record of Rites*, Tang says: "Since the time subsequent to the Han, those who discuss the subject of *qing* mostly construe it as passions (*qingyu*) formed by the union of essential condition *(qing)* with desire (*yu*). They tend to ignore the fact that the natural disposition (*xingqing*) of loving, revering, and honoring one's parents—and the joy, anguish, sorrow, and pleasure relative to such emotions (*xingqing*)—ought really not to be called passions (*qingyu*)."[14] This sort of distinction has also provided Neo-Confucian polemics an alleged ready argument against Buddhism.[15]

Although the word *qing* in classical texts was frequently used in the manner described by Graham and Tang, their observations have not covered all the textual details concerning desire. In particular, one must question whether *qing* and *yu* were always distinguished in the way the two modern scholars have argued, and whether in our consideration of ancient Chinese texts *qingyu* (passion) as a compound could be entirely divorced from *xingqing* (nature or literally, natural disposition). In his book on classical Chinese philosophy, Chad Hansen has defined *qing* as "reality feedback" or "the way reality registers on us. It is the impact of reality on humans that triggers their naming and choosing."[16] Although this systematic and trenchant study achieves the enduring merit of demonstrating how a distinctive view of language underlies and undergirds all schools of ancient Chinese thought, Hansen's consistent emphasis on the external, social ordering of all human reality finally, I think, leaves the Chinese subject virtually bereft of all capacity for subjectivity. Certain remarks of the philosophers, on the other hand, seem to indicate some room for viewing the subject as an agent capable as much of initiating subjective

[14] *Zongguo zhexue yuanlun: yuanxingpian*, p. 89.

[15] For example, see Wang Fuzhi's statement in *Du sishu daquan shuo* 8:10b-11a: "Although rules of propriety are purely detailed expressions of the Principle of Nature, they must be embodied in human desires to be seen. . . . It is only with the Buddhists that principle and desires can be separated. . . . Take fondness for wealth and for sex. Heaven, working unseen, has provided all creatures with it, and with it man puts the great virtue of Heaven and Earth into operation. They all regard wealth and sex as preserved resources. . . . If we do not understand the Principle of Nature from human desires that go with it, then although there may be a principle that can be a basis, nevertheless, it will not have anything to do with the correct activities of our seeing, hearing, speech, and action. They thereupon cut off the universal operation of human life, and wipe it out completely." English translation in Wing-tsit Chan, *Sourcebook in Chinese Philosophy*, p. 700.

[16] Chad Hansen, *A Daoist Theory of Chinese Thought*, pp. 276 and 406. See also pp. 325–27. See also his more recent essay, "*Qing* (Emotions) in Pre-Buddhist Chinese Thought." Developing the same line of argument from his earlier book, Hansen construes the meaning of *qing* as "responses" to "sensory input," "all reality-induced discrimination or distinction-making reactions in *dao* executors" (p. 196). This understanding of the emphatically cognitive aspects of *qing* may have the support of the incipient language philosophy educed by Hansen from classical texts, especially those of Mohism, but it needs to be related to stimuli-response (*ganying*) aesthetics.

action—thinking, deciding, remembering, feeling, and seeking—as of responding to stimuli.

The most succinct statement linking *qing*, *xing*, and *yu* among classical philosophical texts is to be found in the familiar chapter on "Rectifying Names" in the *Xunzi*:

> Now, nature (*xing*) is that which is formed by Heaven; the disposition (*qing*) is the substance (*zhi*stuff, substance) of nature; and desire (*yu*) is the proper response (*ying*) of the disposition. To seek what desire deems attainable is that which the disposition certainly cannot avoid.[17]

Graham's interpretation of this passage (the last sentence is signficantly omitted in his citation) is that the philosopher is distinguishing nature from disposition in the sense of "that by which the living is as it is."[18] That may well be plausible, but what Graham seems not to have noticed in the passage is how the three aspects of the human subject are categorically placed by the ancient thinker on one continuum. In the face of external stimuli, the affective disposition *(qing)*, according to Xunzi, will find it inevitable (*bu ke mian*) to respond in the manner or form of desire (*yu*), causing, as Hansen rightly observes, "a seeking behavior."[19] Even though the Chinese philosopher does not employ such concepts as object of appetite, thought, and movement, the language of Xunzi here strikingly recalls the Aristotelian declaration:

> for that which is the object of appetite is the stimulant of practical thought; and that which is last in the process of thinking is the beginning of the action . . . for the object of appetite starts a movement and as a result of that thought gives rise to movement, the object of appetite being to it a source of stimulation.[20]

Because desire compels such seeking motion, Xunzi's consistent Confucianism posits the necessity for the mind to assert control: "Thus order or disorder rests with what the mind dictates and not with what the disposition desires (*qing zhi suo yu*)." Desire (*yu*), in such a view, seems to be none other than the functional, active manifestation of disposition (*qing*), in turn described as the substantive but latent content of nature (*xing*). Does it not mean, there-

---

[17] *Xunzi jijie*, chapter 22, p. 284. Traditional editions assign "The Rectification of Names" as chapter 22, but Liang Qixiong's *Xunzi jianshi* puts it at 24. Citations hereafter of the *Xunzi* in this chapter will immediately follow the text, with the first number designating the chapter. The annotator Wang Xianqian in *jijie* glosses desire (*yu*) as "that to which the disposition responds (*qing zhi suo ying ye*)," and adds, "that is why humans cannot avoid having desires."

[18] Graham, *Studies in Chinese Philosophy*, p. 65, referring what he calls "the first sense of *hsing*" back to his own definitions on p. 15.

[19] *A Daoist Theory of Chinese Thought*, p. 334. In note 69 on p. 416, Hansen cites both this passage and the parallel one at the beginning of chapter 19 of the *Xunzi*.

[20] Aristotle, "On the Soul" 433^{a}16–20 in *The Complete Works of Aristotle*, 1: 688.

fore, that when aroused (*dong, ying*), the natural disposition (*xingqing* or *qing-xing*) of the human tends to express itself in desire?[21]

Among the numerous passages in the *Xunzi* on *qing* and *yu*, three important, interrelated themes are unmistakably present. First, desire (*yu*), so Xunzi argues, cannot be separated from what I have rendered in the present context as disposition (*qing*). Second, the forms of desire include not merely feelings but also our basic preference and aversion (that is, life and death) and what is commonly called appetite (that is, the delights of the senses) in modern Western languages. Third, the observations about *qingyu* thus touch the heart of Confucian ethics, for how the passions are to be dealt with has ramifications on both the personal and the social-political levels. With unerring pithiness, D. C. Lau has observed: "It is not an exaggeration to say that ancient Chinese thought was man-centered, while the study of man was desire-centered. Thus the notion of desires is at the heart of most of Chinese thought."[22]

Toward the end of chapter 18 of the *Xunzi*, when Song Xing contends for a separation of desire from disposition by arguing that the latter has only a few desires, this is the way Xunzi poses his counter argument:

> "The eye does not desire extreme (*qi*) colors; the ear does not desire extreme sounds; the mouth does not desire extreme flavors; the nose does not desire extreme fragrances; and the body does not desire extreme ease. Can these five extremities be regarded as [the evidence] that the disposition of the human (*ren zhi qing*) does not desire (*yu*)?" [Song Xing] replied, "The disposition of the human indeed desires just so." [Xunzi] said, "If that is the case, then your thesis is certainly not valid. If you consider that the disposition of the human as desirous of these five extremities and still that such desires are few, then it is like arguing that the disposition of the human desires wealth but does not desire goods; or that it loves beauty but does not desire Xi Shi. The people of antiquity did not regard it thus, for they thought of the disposition of the human as desiring much and not desiring little. Therefore, they rewarded by means of wealth and riches, and they punished by means of execution and injury." (*Xunzi jijie*, 18, p. 230)

Notice that not only does Xunzi in this passage forcefully argue for the inseparability of *qing* and *yu*, but he also suggests how desire may proliferate (if someone desires a paradigmatic beauty like Xi Shi, he can also desire Lin Dai-yu and Xue Bao-chai). Such proliferation in turn enlarges the motivation for desire's proper guidance and channeling.[23]

---

[21] Perhaps to steer the reader away from drawing such a conclusion, Mou Zongsan tries to argue that *xing* as the motion of the disposition (*qing zhi dong*) should be understood as *xingneng* or capacity, but that argument is for me unpersuasive. See Mou Zongsan, *Xinti yu xingti* 2: 286.

[22] "The Doctrine of Kuei Sheng in the *Lü-shih ch'un-ch'iu*," p. 59.

[23] Cf. Hansen's discussion of this passage of *Xunzi* on p. 334 of *A Daoist Theory of Chinese Thought*.

Xunzi's ideas are corroborated by passages in the *Lüshi chunqiu*, the only classical text that has a specific chapter titled "Passion (*qingyu*)," in which it is stated:

> In producing humans Heaven has caused them to possess covetousness and desire (*yu*). Desire has its disposition (*qing*), and the disposition its measure. The sages cultivate the measure in order to check the desire, and they, therefore, do not act in transgression of their disposition. Thus the ear's desire for the five tones, the eye's desire for the five colors, and the mouth's desire for the five flavors are the disposition.[24]

As in the observation by Xunzi, *qing* is here depicted once more as desire in its latent condition. The last sentence of this statement is noteworthy, moreover, because the author has substituted disposition (*qing*) for what the earlier Mencius had referred to as nature (*xing*): "The way the mouth is disposed towards tastes, the eye towards colours, the ear towards sounds, the nose towards smells and the four limbs towards ease is human nature (*xing*), yet therein also lies the Decree" (*Mencius*, 7B, 24).[25] The pervasive—dare we say universal— characteristic of *qing* is precisely based on the perception of it as the essential endowment of the human (in the Mencian term, decreed or *ming*) that cuts across social and cultural stratifications; it "unifies the noble and the humble, the foolish and the wise, the worthy and the unworthy" (*Lüshi chunqiu*, 2: 5b). For Mencius and Xunzi as for the *Lüshi chunqiu*, the disposition is the great leveler because all men seem to have the same wants:

> that for food he desires (*yu*) the meat of pastured and grain-fed animals, that for clothings he desires those patterned and embroidered, that for travel he desires a carriage and a horse. Moreover, he desires the wealth of surplus money and accumulated possessions. Even in lean years and stressful periods, he remains ignorant and malcontent. Such is the disposition (*qing*) of man. (*Xunzi jijie*, 4, p. 42)

Because desire (*yu*) is indissolubly bonded to the natural (*xing*) that, as we have just seen, has been eventually glossed as the essential disposition (*qing*)— call it, therefore, the human condition or reality—one cannot, in fact, eliminate or eradicate it. That was the pointed polemic with which Neo-Confucians later would combat what they construed to be one defective doctrine of Buddhism. However, the logical conclusion that one must draw from the philosophical texts discussed hitherto also seems self-evident: that something essentially human—regardless of whether or not the modern scholar wants to call that passion—has to be measured, restrained, and controlled. Only such a somber reading can do justice to this declaration of Xunzi, when he likens a person

---

[24] *Lüshi chunqiu* 2: 5a (*SBBY*).
[25] Translation by D. C. Lau, p. 198.

who "wishes to nurse (*yang*) his desire (*yu*) but unbridles his disposition (*qing*)" to someone who "wishes to nurse his nature (*xing*) but endangers his body (*xing*[2shape, form, body, appearance])" (*Xunzi jijie*, 16, p. 287). "A person like this," says Xunzi, "is no different from an outlaw even though he may be enfeoffed as a lord and called a ruler." The indivisibility of desire and disposition even receives support from the analogy of a linguistic construct: from the names of nature and body (*xing* and *xing*[2]) comes the bond of paronomasic play, a device so frequently exploited by ancient thinkers for the purpose of definition.

In the *Mencius*, the first means of controlling desire seems to focus on an act combining both wilful defiance and deliberate, cultivated choosing. If the sense organs are naturally disposed toward certain things (tastes, colors, sounds, ease), the philosopher says in the above passage (7B, 24), the gentleman will refuse to acknowledge this by not "describing [this tendency] as nature." He subscribes instead to another "Decree (*ming*)" and another conception of nature (*xing*) that exemplify the Confucian way (*dao*) in ordering human relations. If he faces a dilemma of competing attractions (such as fish or bear paw), he will choose one if both cannot be obtained. For Mencius, of course, that well-known observation about his culinary preferences only serves as a pretext for discussing a much weightier issue. "Life is what I want (*yu*); dutifulness (*yi*) is also what I want (*yu*)," he declares in 6A, 10. "If I cannot have both, I would rather take dutifulness than life."[26]

Could all followers of the Confucian way consistently elect this Mencian form of desire: adherence to something a man wants more than life and something that he loathes more than death? Mencius makes a totalizing claim that such an attitude is not limited to the worthies but is common to all. For Xunzi and the *Lüshi chunqiu*, however, the assertion of natural inclination toward principled choice is modulated to the advocacy of prudent calculation or adjudication. Accordingly, Xunzi (*Xunzi jijie*, 4, p. 42) can speak in praise of the action of those who take the long view of things and "moderate what they expend and bridle their desire (*jie yong yu yu*)." The insight of Xunzi and other Chinese philosophers into why humans may delay immediate gratification of their interests is noticeably similar to that of Epicurus: such immediacy, indiscriminately realized, may cut short the ability for maintenance of gratification. Even with knowledge of agriculture, says Xunzi, people dare not consistently use wine and meat for food or silk for raiment—not because they lack desire but because they fear their inability to perpetuate the practice. The desires common to humanity, according to this view, are now superseded by the more sophisticated regard for priorities of ends and means. People thus curb their immediate longings by "harvesting, gathering, hoarding, and storing up goods" so as to prolong the means of satisfaction (ibid.). In the *Lüshi chunqiu*, the

---

[26] Ibid., p. 166.

essentially economic motive adumbrated by Xunzi is further displaced by the psycho-biological motive of exalting and preserving life (*guisheng*). The organs of appetite—the ear, the eye, the nose, and the mouth—must be made sub-servient to life. Therefore, "although the ear desires sounds, the eye desires beautiful forms, the nose desires fragrance, and the mouth desires flavors, a person will stop if such desires become injurious to life. What the four offices [that is, the four organs of appetite] do not desire a person will nevertheless do if it is beneficial to life."[27]

According to D. C. Lau, the author of the *Lüshi chunqiu* has perhaps advanced beyond Xunzi in the recognition that material wealth and goods are not desir-able ends in themselves, as sights and sounds are, but only as means that "make possible the gratification of the desires of the senses."[28] Life is dependent on the senses for its value and thus also on their gratification, but gratification itself must also presuppose life, for "a dead man with no sensations is in-capable of gratification."[29] The circularity of this argument in the text may indeed reveal that the *Lüshi chunqiu* aimed its message ultimately at the "ears of the Emperor," as Lau thinks, for its emphasis on the virtually absolute pri-ority of life represents a significant departure from the views of Confucius (as in *Analects*, 15. 8) and Mencius (as in 6A. 10). Now life, not the Mencian dutifulness, must take precedence as our strongest desire.[30] Whether, however, the postponement of gratification owes its cause to concerns for economics or biology, it should be noted that this "brand of hedonism that reaps the best of both worlds"[31]—that is, enjoying gratification without breaking the bank or cutting short one's natural span of life—is itself based on desire. Momentary acts of self-denial, in fact, enact the desire for temporal extension of desire and its gratification. The subjugation of desire (*yu yu*), therefore, not only entails the adjudication of competitive appetites and the temporalization of gratification; as the Mencian declaration incisively indicates ("dutifulness is also what I want"), virtue is itself a form of desire. The discourse on desire is, therefore, also a discourse of desire.

Seen from such a perspective, Xunzi is logical in pressing home the cultural superiority of "the patterns of life given in the *Odes, Documents, Rituals,* and *Music*" and of the gentleman (*junzi*), for the latter is that person who practices self-cultivation through conscious exertion. He is the princely or exemplary

---

[27] *Lüshi chunqiu* 2: 3a (*SBBY*).

[28] Lau, "The Doctrine of Kuei Sheng," p. 55.

[29] Ibid.

[30] In contrast to the principle of exalting life, the "Yangzhu" chapter in the *Liezi* (dated pre-Qin or Wei-Jin) would emphasize discriminating selection of what desires to satisfy, choosing finally ease and luxury more than long-term health. See *The Book of Lieh-tzu*, translated by A. C. Graham, pp. 135–57, and the discussion by Fung Yu-lan in *History of Chinese Philosophy* 2: 195–204.

[31] Lau, "The Doctrine of Kuei Sheng," 90.

man employing those "patterns of life" to "bring order to [his] disposition (*zhi qing*)" (*Xunzi jijie*, chap. 4, p. 43). Without that order, no civil society is possible, for the desires common to humanity, if pursued fully and individually by each person, can only result in conflict and chaos. For this reason, Xunzi's familiar dictum on the origin of rituals locates it squarely in the necessity to regulate desires so as to avoid the crisis of scarcity.

> How did ritual arise? I say, a human is born with desire (*yu*). If what is desired cannot be found, the attempt to seek it cannot be avoided. Seeking without regard for measure and limit will inevitably end in conflict. Conflict begets chaos, and chaos begets exhaustion. The former kings despised such chaos, and they therefore established ritual principles to limit it so as to make proper provisions for human desires and satisfy what humans seek. They made certain that desire would not exhaust itself because of things, and that things would not deplete themselves because of desire.[32] When both desire and things develop in mutual support, that is the origin of rites. Therefore, rites are a means of proper provision. (*Xunzi jijie*, 19, p. 231)

It might be argued, on the part of those agreeing with Graham's thesis, that what this passage refers to seems to dwell only on the feature of desire (*yu*) and not on the disposition of the human (*qing*). Xunzi, however, makes his meaning unmistakably clear when he advances his equally famous but controversial notion of human nature as evil in chapter 23. Echoing directly his previous discussion of human desires in chapter 4, he declares: "Phenomena such as the eye's fondness for beautiful forms, the ear's fondness for beautiful sounds, the mouth's fondness for delicious flavors, the mind's fondness for profit, or the flesh and bones' fondness for pleasure and ease—these are all produced by man's dispositional nature (*qingxing*). They are instinctive and spontaneous" (ibid., 23, p. 292). Such a natural disposition, nonetheless, is precisely what needs to be disciplined by rites, for anyone who "follows man's nature (*xing*) and obeys man's disposition (*qing*) will inevitably begin with strife and pillage, grow into transgressing limits and violating principles, and end up as a criminal" (ibid., 23, p. 289). Because "ritual principles and regulations were established to bring into order man's disposition and rectifying it," the person who indulges his natural disposition (*xingqing*) is aptly denominated a "petty man" (ibid., 23, p. 290).

The intimate relationship between rites and human nature affirmed by Xunzi, in fact, provides the basis of his argument for considering the latter as essentially evil or vicious. The senses' desire for gratification is as fundamental and spontaneous as one's "desire for satiation when one is hungry, for warmth when one is cold, and for rest when one is fatigued" (ibid., 23, p. 291). When a person acts in a manner that "contradicts man's nature (*xing*) and runs counter

---

[32] My reading of this line follows the exegesis of the Tang commentator Yang Jing.

to his disposition (*qing*)"—as when he dares not eat in an elder's presence, or when the son shows deference to the father—he is acting only on the basis of ritual principles enjoined and learned. Thus filial piety is an acquired virtue, for if one "follows one's dispositional nature (*qingxing*), one would not yield. To practice humility and deference is to run counter to one's dispositional nature." This, concludes Xunzi, makes it apparent that human nature is vicious (ibid.).

So severe and sobering a view of human nature, whether one agrees with it or not, makes Xunzi's philosophy consistent when it exalts rewards and punshiments as "repayment (*bao*)—that which follows in kind" (ibid., 18, p. 219). His emphasis on corporal or mutilating punishment, in fact, correlates its relatioship to ritual or rite (*li*) and throws further light on their mutual implication. At issue here is not whether morality is conventional and artificial, or whether the human person is able to "practice what culture bequeaths."[33] The question provoked by Xunzi's remarks is rather what necessitates in the first place those cultural bequests—in the form of rite, music, and didactic poetry. Even if one were to accept Hansen's view that "reality generates feedback, the *qing*^feelings of the heart and the physical senses," one must still ask why such "feedback" is certain to spawn social strife and scarcity if it remains unchecked.[34] For the ills of scarcity, Xunzi's solution does not aim so much at the redistribution of economic goods, advocated by so many modern social theories both East and West, as it does at a standardized taxonomy of desire itself on the basis of class distinctions.

> To enjoy the honor of the Son of Heaven and the wealth of the world—this is what the human disposition (*renqing*) commonly desires (*tong yu*). But to follow such human desire would result in an intolerable state of affairs because the material goods would not suffice. Therefore the former kings, mindful of this, established rituals and moral principles to make such divisions that there would be ranks among the noble and the base, disparities between the old and the young, and distinctions between the intelligent and the stupid, the capable and the incapable. All of this caused men to do their business in such a way that each would receive his due. Only thereafter would the amount and substance of grain-paid emoluments be made appropriate to their respective stations. This is the Way of group living in harmony and unity. . . . This may be called "ultimate peace." (ibid., 4, p. 44)

Consistent with his Confucian bent, Xunzi looks to posited authoritarian judgment as the best dispenser of equitableness and to hierarchy for the ground of distributive justice.

---

[33] Hansen, *A Daoist Theory of Chinese Thought*, p. 337.
[34] Ibid., pp. 336–37.

For the prior and more vexing issue of rite's implied necessity, Xunzi's reply is not the Kantian notion of radical evil nor the Christian dogma of original sin, but he does locate the problem squarely within what is considered the essential part of the human.[35] The logical implication of his argument in chapter 23 advances beyond the crisis of economic scarcity, for what humanity cannot practice of its own accord are certain ideals society deems essential to its own welfare and survival: the filial deference to a parent or elder, the ministerial loyalty to a ruler. Some form of intervention has to be instituted. It is this understanding of human nature that not only renders Xunzi at odds with tenets of antecedent Confucianism but also imposes far greater urgency on the meticulous justification and establishment of ritual.[36]

Xunzi's understanding, moreover, makes it exceedingly difficult for one to accept Graham's generalization that "in the Neo-Confucinism of the Sung dynasty *ch'ing* 'passions' is contrasted with *hsing* 'nature.' Although the word *ch'ing* is very common in pre-Han literature I should like to risk the generalization that it never means 'passions' even in *Hsün-tzû*, where we find the usage from which the later meaning developed."[37] Graham's remark here, as I hope

---

[35] John Knoblock's observation is unerring: "for Xunzi, the problem of evil was linked to the problem of desire." See his discussion in *Xunzi: A Translation and Study of the Complete Works* 1: 98–100. Heiner Roetz is even more to the point when he says, "the view of man as a deficient being which is unfinished by nature and has to adopt his ability to survive by careful education and organization is surely a main aspect of Xunzi's theory that human nature is evil." For a brief but perceptive discussion of the motif of *natura noverca* and the problem it creates in Xunzi's moral theory, see Roetz's *Confucian Ethics of the Axial Age*, pp. 224–26.

[36] See Benjamin Schwartz, *The World of Thought in Ancient China*, pp. 292–93. To be fair to Xunzi, his ideas seem more incompatible with Mencian doctrines than with those of Confucius. It has often been pointed out that Confucius, though supremely confident in the human capacity for moral achievement, also expresses repeatedly the difficulty of living his surpassing ideal of benevolence (*ren*). See, for example, *Analects*, 14. 1, in which the Master specifically acknowledges the difficulty of not practicing covetousness or desire (*yu*). My interpretation here also differs from Noah Fehl's argument that Xunzi's desires "are not categorically, as in the diagnostic Four Noble Truths, evil in themselves. Nor is it wrong for man to seek what he desires." See his *Rites and Propriety in Literature and Life*, p. 164. The point is not whether the desires are evil or not but Xunzi's contention that certain desires prevent man from seeking the social good above his personal good. In sum, Xunzi's thesis seems to be: selfishness is innate but altruism has to be taught and learned. Hansen's observation is sound when he says that "Xunzi's own argument for the importance of traditional *li*ritual relies on the . . . assumption [that] the natural, uncultivated, and civilized desires are *many*. They are shared with the animals and lead inevitably to disorder and strife. Instead of the Daoist position that conventions multiply desires, he argues that they merely determine what is the proper object of desire. The Confucian traditional rituals, he says, tame and control a myriad of natural desires" ("*Qing* [Emotions] in Pre-Buddhist Chinese Thought," p. 200).

[37] Graham, "Studies in Chinese Philosophy," p. 59. In his latest study of the subject, Hansen faults A. C. Graham for failing to account for how the term *qing* shifted "from referring to something metaphysical and objective (reality, essence, or the facts) to referring to something subjective and psychological (passions)," but nonetheless he avers that "Graham's baseline

my own reading has demonstrated thus far, cannot be supported by the textual details of the *Xunzi*. The noble but misguided rigor of the philologist, by insisting on the single occurences of *qing* in various sentences, quite misses the total semantic field of the word as it is developed in the text, whether the word is used either individually or in combination with other terms. As well, his remark fails to come to grips with the underlying significance of the discourse on desire that prominently threads its way through the history of Chinese philosophy. However limited or distorted the knowledge of Song thinkers might have of their Han and pre-Han forebears, they should be credited in this instance that they knew more about the implications of the term *xingqing* or *qingxing* than Graham would allow. Those implications, in fact, were not lost on Han and Wei-Jin thinkers long before the arrival of the Buddhist critique of human consciousness, emotive life, and its tendency to cling stubbornly to illusions.

THE DIALECTICS OF NATURE AND DISPOSITION

Why did Chinese philosophers recurrently return to the topic of human nature and disposition? Surely, it was not merely to act out their habitual tendency "to think the thoughts of the ancients" and to repeat what their forebears had said. Despite his assertion of the evil of human nature, Xunzi also believes that "it is nature that renders the sage the same as the multitude and not different from the multitude; it is in human activity that the sage differs from and surpasses the multitude" (*Xunzi jijie*, 23, p. 292). The obsessive quest for the realization of sagehood that preoccupies so many of the moral philosophers stretching from antiquity to the present day must thus perforce examine not only the enabling factors but also the disabling impediments. The agreement between Mencius, who holds to the thesis of humanity's incipient goodness, and Xunzi that certain persons among humankind can achieve sagehood has de facto rendered irrelevant their differences on human nature. If for both camps of the Confucians human activity (Xunzi's *wei*) or cultivation matters in the formation of the moral person, the crucial question must then be: what can stifle or pervert such activity?

The answer to this question again returns us to the subject of the disposition

---

insight about *qing* . . . is sound" ("*Qing* [Emotions] in Pre-Buddhist Chinese Thought"). My own survey of the textual materials, however, leads me to question the soundness of this insight and to dispute Hansen's generalization that it is the peculiar emphasis of "the Western Romantic's view that *feelings* are what are definitionally essential to humans" (p. 201). It should be apparent from this chapter's discussion that joy and anger, grief and delight, are considered by many ancient Chinese thinkers as "definitionally essential to humans." If these are not feelings, I for one would like to know what they are?

(*qing*), but this time our discussion must take up as well the emotive overtones enshrined in the word's usage. In my brief exposition of Xunzi thus far, I have concentrated on the verbal and conceptual alliance of *qing* and *yu* in which the latter, under stimulation, is a functional manifestion of the former. Xunzi's remarks, however, make apparent as well that in much of ancient Chinese thought, that process of stimulus and response also defines the emotional contours of the human subject. Depending on context and usage, the notion of feelings or affections shows itself unmistakably, as when Zhuangzi tries to counter the potent sway of emotions by observing both the mystery and the naturalness of their origin.

> Pleasure in things and anger against them, sadness and joy, forethought and regret, change and immobility, idle influences that initiate our gestures—music coming out of emptiness, vapour condensing into mushrooms—alternate before it day and night and no one knows from what soil they spring. Enough! The source from which it has these morning and evening, is it not that from which it was born.[38]

Although Zhuangzi does not specify that those four reactions that open his statement are called emotions,[39] his remark may well have formed the basis for the later formulation by Xunzi when he attempts to define human nature (*xing*) as "what is as it is from birth . . . capable of union with [things] through perception and response to stimulus without effort and spontaneously." As if to concretize such an affective mechanism in the human, Xunzi goes on to say, "the likes and dislikes, the delights and angers, the griefs and pleasures of such a nature are called emotions (*qing*)" (*Xunzi jijie*, 22, p. 274).

These six phenomena, with minor variations in their order of enumeration, are routinely referred to as the six feelings or emotions (*liuqing*) in Han and post-Han documents.[40] However, in chapter 22 of the book, Xunzi also adds passion or desire (*yu*) as a seventh item to his catalog (ibid., p. 277). By the time of the Han compendium of rites, the *Liji* or *Record of Rites*, this list of seven feelings or emotions (*qiqing*) would become the stock formulation for all posterity. "What are called human emotions?" asks the text. "The delights

---

[38] *Chuang-tzu*, translated by A. C. Graham, p. 50.

[39] Elsewhere in chapter 5, Zhuangzi defines *qing* (what Graham renders as "essentials") as "judging 'That's it, that's not.'" One who is "without the essentials" or unfeeling (*wuqing zhe*), he goes on to say, "is a man who does not injure inwardly his person by likes and dislikes, who constantly takes the spontaneous as the cause and thus does not add to life"; *Zhuangzi, juan* 2, 23b (*SBBY*). *Qing*, for Zhuangzi, seems to be the forms of affective discrimination, the ways of saying, feelingly, Yes and No.

[40] See *Zuo Commentary*, "Duke Zhao, 25th Year," in Legge, *The Chinese Classics* 5: 708; "The Biography of Yi Feng" in *Han Shu, juan* 75; "Qingxing pin," in *Bohu tong de lun* [The Comprehensive Discussions in the White Tiger Hall], *juan* 8 (*SBCK*); Lu Ji, "Wenfu," in *Wenxuan, juan* 17.

and pleasures, the griefs and fears, the loves and dislikes, and the desires (*yu*)—these seven [things man] is capable of without having to learn them."[41] This canon delineating man's emotional contour reverberates through the discourse of Tang Confucians and Song-Ming Neo-Confucians.[42]

One interesting feature of this discourse surfaces in how early the emotional disposition (*qing*) assumes a place of opposition to nature (*xing*), for contrary to A. C. Graham's view, such a tendency already manifests itself in Dong Zhongshu (c. 195–115 B.C.E.), traditional putative author of the *Chunqiu fanlu*.[43] "What heaven and earth gives birth to," according to Dong, "is called nature and disposition. Nature and disposition combine to become one, for dormant disposition (*mingqing*) is also nature. If nature is said to be already good, then what could one do with the disposition? Therefore, the sage does not call nature good, for that would inculpate the name." The populace, though endowed with "the stuff of goodness (*shanzhi*)," cannot practice goodness until they are wakened by the cultural intervention of teaching (*jiao*). Echoing the theory of stimulus and response (*ganying*) that undergirds so much of ancient Chinese thought, what guides Dong's reflections here seems also to be the variant dialectic of latency and activation. That dialectic strives to preserve the essential unity of the human subject, for Dong reasons that just as "the eye's closing (*ming*) and its opening (*jue*) thereafter form a comparison of the same level," so human nature asleep or dormant before the waking impact of teaching is still the same nature.[44]

On this same level, however, there are certain elements that should be encouraged to flourish and others that should not. "The fact that a person has nature and disposition is like the fact that heaven has *yin* and *yang*."[45] But in Dong's hierarchical cosmology, those two forces are not equal nor are they equally treated by heaven. This line of thinking thus leads Dong to argue that nature and disposition, though united in one body or self (*shen*), are to be dealt with differently. Again, the analogy to be drawn from "the dual manifestations of *yin* and *yang* in heaven" is that "a person has also the dual natures of covetousness and benevolence."[46] Just as heaven is committed to favor the operation of *yang* and restrain that of the *yin*, so obviously the self must also restrain a certain part of its nature. The grand conclusion Dong elicits from the comparison with the moon is instructive:

---

[41] *Liji xunzuan, juan* 9, 8a.

[42] See Han Yu, "Yuan xing lun," in *Han Changli quanji, juan* 11, 51–6a (*SBBY*); Zhu Xi, *Jinsilu* 2: 1b (*SBBY*); Wang Yangming, *Chuanxilu* 2: 32.

[43] No attempt is made here to treat the question of authorship raised by recent scholarship. For a review of the debate and new proposals, see Gary Arbuckle, "Some Remarks on a New Translation of the *Chunqiu fanlu.*

[44] *Chunqiu fanlu, juan* 10, 4b (*SBBY*).

[45] Ibid.

[46] Ibid., *juan* 10, 3b.

The soul of the moon is frequently repressed by sunlight so that it is made whole or wounded abruptly. If heaven restrains *yin* in this manner, then how could [the self] not diminish its desire (*yu*) and arrest its emotive disposition (*qing*) as a response to heaven? What heaven restrains the self restrains as well. That is why it is said that the self is like heaven. To restrain what heaven restrains is not restraining heaven.[47]

Fung Yu-lan is justified in observing that Dong's "theory of the nature may be said to be a combination of the views of Mencius and Hsün Tzu,"[48] for it apparently presents a view of bifurcated nature (*xing*) that harbors both the stuff of goodness (comparable to the Mencian "seeds or beginnings") and another essential ingredient that requires education and restraint.[49] Elsewhere, Dong is said to have given us even this explicit definition: "Nature (*xing*) is the stuff derived from birth, and disposition *(qing)* is man's desire (*yu*)."[50] This definition, if it is authentically Dong's, not only directly refutes Graham's basic thesis on the meaning of the word *qing* in classical antiquity but also clarifies how Dong can reconcile his own view with Confucian antecedents. To act against man's emotive disposition is, therefore, not an act against nature, for the act itself is part of a natural process, much like sunlight suppressing the light of the moon.

Whether Dong's reasoning by analogy truly persuades is another issue. What his theory clearly announces, echoing the emphasis of Xunzi, is that *qing* must be regarded as an unstable and potentially subversive element of the human, thus setting the stage for legitimating the control of desire.

That discourse will develop with the following emphases. First, the discussions of *qing* will be integrated into the rhetoric of correlative cosmology that became full blown after the Han period. Numerous passages in the *Chunqiu fanlu* assert a comprehensive correlation of man's disposition (often epitomized by the emotive dichotomies of delight and anger, grief and pleasure) with the cosmic regularities of the four seasons, light and darkness, heat and cold, and *yin* and *yang*.[51] From the crucial chapter 43 titled "*Yang*'s Exaltation and *Yin*'s Abasement" comes the unambiguous declaration: "The men might be base born, but they are all *yang*; whereas the women might be nobles, but

---

[47] Ibid.

[48] *History of Chinese Philosophy* 2: 35.

[49] Wang Chong (27-c. 100), who quotes Dong prominently when he discusses man's "proper nature (*benxing*)," struggles mightily to harmonize the opposing views and ends by classifying people into three groups: the good ones described by Mencius, who are "above average"; the bad ones described by Xunzi, who are "below average"; and the "average" ones in whose nature "good and evil are mixed," as described by Yang Xiong. See *Lunheng, juan* 3, 15b (*SBBY*).

[50] Reported in "Biography of Dong Zhongshu," in the *Han Shu, juan* 56.

[51] See chapters 47, 48, 49, 80, and 81.

they are all *yin*."[52] Another sweeping generalization follows in the next chapter: "Categories of evil all belong to the *yin*, whereas categories of goodness all belong to the *yang*."[53] Since all things flourish or decline "following the *yang*," according to our author, "the rectitude of the Three Kings . . . is to be seen in esteeming the *yang* and demeaning the *yin*."[54]

It takes very little imagination to see what consequences may issue from this form of classification, for demeaning (*jian*) is carried out by a deliberate textualized program of active debasement or diminishment of worth. In such a program, metonymic association is all. *Shuowen jiezi*, the first lexicon compiled by Xü Shen in 121, directly echoes Dong's ideas by glossing *qing* as "man's *yin* life-force (*qi*) that has desires (*yu*)."[55] The *Bohutong* offers an expanded definition:

> Nature (*xing*) is the manifestation of *yang*, and disposition (*qing*) is the transfor- mation of *yin*. . . . Therefore the *Goumingjue* says, "Disposition is born of *yin*; it is desire that takes [as its being] the thought of a moment. Nature is born of *yang*; it takes [as its being] reason." The life-force of *yang* is benevolent, but the life- force of *yin* is covetous. Thus disposition has [regard for] profit and desire, whereas nature has [regard for] benevolence.[56]

With this explicit dualism structured in human life, the fate of all phenomena in the cosmos associated with *yin* should also be apparent. Why marriage be- longs to the human way, the *Bohutong* loudly proclaims, stems from the fact that "the importance of disposition and nature [can find] no greater [example] than that of man and woman." Since, however, nature and disposition by now hardly enjoy an egalitarian assessment, their difference are also a trope of the character of social customs and structures. "Why do the rites prescribe that a man takes a wife but a woman leaves her house?" the text asks. "Because *yin* is lowly and not permitted to take the initiative; it goes to *yang* so as to be completed."[57]

This elucidation of ritual principles glaringly reveals the growing tendency to place on the same plane of affinity the categories of *qing, yin,* and the female. Whether in the abstract but graphic symbolism of the *Book of Change* or in the typologies of character and moral virtue found in the burgeoning manuals of family instruction, the metonymic system devised by patriarchy calls for the

---

[52] *Chunqiu fanlu, juan* 11, 4a.

[53] Ibid., 6b.

[54] Ibid., 3b. For a recent critical study of Dong's concept of *yin-yang*, see Wei Zhengtong, *Dong Zhongshu*, pp. 76–83.

[55] *Shuowen jiezi zhu* 10b, 24a (*SBBY*). Annotation by Duan Yucai.

[56] *Bohu tongde lun, juan* 8 (*SBCK*).

[57] Ibid., *juan* 10.

regulation and subordination of these categories.[58] "*Yang*'s exaltation and *yin*'s abasement" elides easily into "Heaven's exaltation and Earth's abasement." In chapter 5 of the famous *Nüjie* (Commandments for Women) by Ban Zhao (c. 45–116), there can be no more totalizing definition of a male spouse than what the learned woman proffers: "Husband is Heaven. Just as Heaven should not be disobeyed, so a husband should never be forsaken."[59] For the chapter entitled "Lowliness and Weakness, the First" which opens the treatise, a Ming annotator writes: "Heaven's exalted and Earth's lowly, *yang* is sturdy and *yin* is weak—these are the orthodox moral principles for woman. If she is unwilling to be lowly and desires to exalt herself, unyielding to weakness and desires to strengthen herself, then she transgresses these moral principles and is no longer orthodox. Though she had other abilities, how could she be held in esteem?"[60]

In his study of the early history of Chinese philosophy, Tang Junyi rightly tells us that Han Confucians tended to "exalt nature but demean disposition (*zun xing er jian qing*)" without, however, offering us a clue for such proclivity.[61] Our charting of the discourse on desire, for this very reason, has attempted to find the explanation in their heightening awareness of the state of *qing* and its intimate connection to human desires and emotions. That connection, particularly as it has been adumbrated by the likes of Xunzi and Dong Zhongshu, would pose a vexing question for the important ideal of sagehood, a question that, at least on the ethical dimension, touches the problem of evil. In the Chinese context, however, the classic formula for theodicy in Westen culture will have to be modified thus: sicut sapiens bonus, unde malum—if the sage is good, whence comes evil? If the sage shares with all men the one natural disposition (*xingqing*) or dispositional nature (*qingxing*), however this binome is ordered, how shall we account for the *qing* part of the equation?

In its attempt to address this issue, the second emphasis of the discourse on desire will seek, in Tang Junyi's words, to "exalt nature but demean disposition" either by distancing the sage from the potent sway of *qing* or by fashioning a comprehensive system of control. It is thus no accident that the writer He Yan

---

[58] For this tendency in the *Book of Change*, see Richard W. Guisso, "Thunder over the Lake," pp. 51–4; for typologies of character and moral virtue, see Ban Zhao, *Nüjie* (Commandments for Woman), chapters 2 and 3. The pejorative interpretation of *yin* and its classified associations extends, for example, down to the Qing thinker Wang Fuzhi (1619–1693). See his *Zhouyi neizhuan, juan* 3, where he says: "The operative virtue of *yin*, in terms of humans, will become petty men, women, and barbarians. In terms of mind, it will become greed and desire." Perhaps the only part of the cultural ideology that truly seems to treat *yin* and *yang* as what Andrew Plaks calls "complementary bipolarity" is to be found in early medical texts. See the *Neijing suwen, juan* 2, chapters 5–7; *juan 24*, chapter 79.

[59] Ban, *Nüjie*, p. 17.

[60] Ibid., p. 4.

[61] *Zhongguo zhexue yuanlun* (*Yuanxingpian*), p. 80.

(d. 249) argued that the sage "lacks either joy or anger, grief or pleasure." On the other hand, Wang Bi (226–249), the influential annotator of classical philosophical texts, affirmed that the sage "is like all men since he possesses the five emotions (*qing*). . . . The sage's disposition is thereby such that he can respond to things without being tied to them."[62] Wang's contention prepares the way for those repeated discussions on the part of the Song Neo-Confucians of how the sage can feel and act like a human subject without at the same time succumbing to the transgressive potency of emotion and desire. Cheng Hao (1032–1085), for example, sought to displace the origin and character of affective stirrings from mind to things by arguing that "the joy and anger of the sage are not tied to the mind but tied to things."[63] If the seven emotions can "flare up and become increasingly wanton (*dang*) to such extent that one's nature is pierced," it will be the task of "the enlightened person to control his disposition (*qing*) and make it fit the Mean."[64]

At the font of Confucian tradition in antiquity, did not the Master himself already indicate an achievement of serene self-possession when he declared that at forty he had no doubts or delusions (*huo*)? Did not Mencius, his most ardent disciple, assert some two hundred years later (with rhetoric perhaps too pointed to be entirely accidental) that at forty he, too, had acquired an unmoved mind-and-heart (e.g. *Mencius*, 2A, 2ff.)? If emotions and desires are acknowledged dangers, the sage—be it his nature (*xing*) or his mind-and-heart (*xin*)—must be shielded in subsequent Confucian discourse from the taint of weakness. In Platonic and Aristotelian terms, the sage cannot be an akratic individual subject to moral failings because of intellectual or affective errors. The enterprise of "rectifying the mind and nourishing one's nature" for Cheng Hao thus aims at rendering one's entire response with such perfect appropriateness to the stimulus that the sage's "constancy" may be understood as how "his feelings accord with all things without himself having those feelings (*wu qing*)."[65] Perhaps reminiscent of Zhuangzi and also influenced by the Buddhist critique of desire, Cheng seems to want to argue, with occasionally tortuous rhetoric, for a form of sagely detachment that not only isolates and preserves the mental equanimity—and thus, the moral integrity as well—of the person, but also makes the agent of stimulus responsible for the character of the response.

Cheng's argument, in a real sense, was anticipated by the Tang Confucian Li Ao (774–836). In his celebrated "Letters for the Restoration of Nature

---

[62] These two views are reported by Pei Songzhi (372–451) in his annotation of *juan* 28 of the *Sanguozhi*; see 3: 795.

[63] Zhu Xi, *Jinsilu, juan* 2, 3b (*SBBY*).

[64] Ibid., 1b.

[65] Ibid., 2b.

(*Fuxingshu*)," Li has bluntly stated at the outset, "that which makes a man a sage is nature; that which deludes (*huo*) his nature is his disposition (*qing*). Joy and anger, grief and fear, love, hate, and desire—these seven are all doings of disposition. When disposition obscures nature, it becomes concealed."[66] Paving much of the way for later Neo-Confucian attacks on the passions, Li's assessment of *qing* is virtually wholly negative. Though it is admittedly "born of nature" and is defined as "nature in action or motion (*xing zhi dong*),"[67] it is also denominated as "the deviant (*xie*) of nature"[68] and "the disorderly (*wang*)."[69] The restoration of nature from the delusive grip of *qing* thus involves for Li on the one hand the resistance to "thinking and deliberation" so as to make the mind quiescent and unmoved or inactive,[70] and on the other "the measuring (*jie*)" of one's response to stimuli by "acting or moving in accord with ritual (*dong er zhong li*)."[71]

This last formulation, along with Cheng Hao's injunction to make *qing* "fit the Mean," directly recalls the familiar opening chapter of *The Doctrine of the Mean*, where the thesis is developed by the commonplace device of paronomastic play of *zhong*[1] (the mean, the middle, the center) and its verbal form, *zhong*[4] (to hit upon). "[The condition] prior to the arousal of joy and anger, grief and delight," the text says, "may be called the center or mean. When they are aroused and they all hit upon the measure (*jie*), this may be called harmony."[72] For Li Ao, ritual is clearly the concrete manifestation of the measure.

---

[66] *Li Wengong ji shiba juan, juan* 2, 5a (*SBCK*).

[67] Ibid., 5b. Li's statement here may be an echo of Xunzi's in chapter 22 of his treatise, when he defines the emotions as "the likes and dislikes, the joy and anger, the grief and delight of nature. When the emotions are such that the mind makes a choice," Xunzi goes on to say, "this is called deliberation. When the mind deliberates and puts that into action, this is called the artificial." See *Xunzi jijie*, p. 274.

[68] *Li Wengong ji*, 8b, 11b.

[69] See ibid., 8a: "Without thinking and deliberation, *qing* will not arise; when *qing* does not arise, this is thinking in rectitude (*zheng si*). Thinking in rectitude means no deliberation and no thinking"; and 8b: "*Qing* is the deviant of nature. When one knows its deviancy, one knows also that it originally is nothing. The mind thereby is still and inactive, and deviant thinking will become extinguished by itself. If only nature shines brightly, how could the deviant arise. When *qing* is used to terminate *qing*, this is indeed Great *Qing*." Li's rhetoric here seems an obvious blend of classical Daoist vocabulary and that of Zen Buddhism.

[71] Ibid., 6b. The implied character of such motion again anticipates the Neo-Confucian emphasis that the sage "arrives at things (*ge wu*)" with such transparent mental discrimination that "he [in himself] does not respond to things" (ibid., 9a). At one point (11a), Li cites chapter 5 of the *Shu Jing* (Book of Documents) to argue that "when Yao and Shun elevated the sixteen ministers, this was not [an indication of] their joy. When they banished Gong Gong, exiled Huan Dou, and imprisoned Gun—in sum, when they chased away these three barbarians, this was not [an indication of] anger."

[72] *Sishu duben*, p. 22.

RITUAL AND THE RULE OF DESIRE

To speak of ritual perforce returns us to Xunzi, whose extensive discussion of desire is dialectically contextualized by his even more comprehensive disquisition on ritual and rite. Moreover, however multifaceted and complex the significance of ritual may be in his thought, one central theme in his philosophy centers on the regulatory role of ritual in regards to *qing*.[73] The meaning of that term in Xunzi's text, as we have seen, ranges from the essential or dispositional part of human nature to emotive states (joy and anger, grief and delight) and desires (likes and dislikes) that include what in modern languages is referred to as needs or appetites (sex, food, wealth, life). This wide scope of *qing* in Xunzi's understanding in turn reveals the felt necessity for constructing elaborate instruments of control that are designed, in the philosopher's words, "to nurse (*yang*) *qing*" (chap. 19), to "rule or put in order *qing*" (chap. 4), or to "secure *qing* in ritual" (chap. 2).[74] This kind of recurrent emphasis, one may argue, bespeaks the thinker's profound awareness of *qing*'s menacing potency. At one point, he goes as far as saying that "he who considers happiness to consist in the advocacy of *qing* will surely perish" (*Xunzi jijie*, 19, p. 233).

Because *qing* threatens the health of both the personal and the social body, an effective countermeasure is called for. The Daoists and later the Buddhists have their own curative proposals, but for Xunzi the Confucian, there seems no better antidote to this volatile power than one central ideal of his own tradition: namely, ritual (*li*) that can function as a marker or sign (*biao*). As he puts the matter, "those who travel through water mark (*biao*) the deep places. If the marker is unclear, [those who follow] would fall in. Those who govern the people mark the way, and if the marker is unclear, disorder follows. Rites (*li*) are markers. If rites are denied, the world becomes blind" (ibid., 17, p. 212).

The literal force of the analogy with wading through deep water makes

---

[73] See, for example, Fehl, *Rites and Propriety*, pp. 151–212 for discussions of ritual's relationship to learning, law, and life in *Xunzi*.

[74] The usual translation of the word *yang*[3] as nourish or nurture is not wholly satisfactory, because the verb in classical texts contains a range of meanings that no single English word can account for. The *Zhou Li, juan* 5, 2b (*SBBY*) speaks of using "the five flavors, the five grains, and the five kinds of medication to *yang*[3] one's illness," and the sentence can hardly have the sense of feeding or nourishing (in the sense of providing sustenance for) the malady. The modern phrase of *yang*[3] *bing* thus points to the meaning of proper treatment by giving the ailment its due. On the other hand, the all too familiar but cryptic remark of Mencius in *Mencius*, 2A, 11 ("I am good at *yang*[3]ing my floodlike *qi*") may well have the meaning of nourishing by protecting the object of care from excessive exploitation or dissipation. Hence the idiom, nourishing one's spirit (*yang*[3] *shen*), refers in modern, secular usage to the conservation of energy. Shades of both lines of meaning (treating properly and preventing wastage) may obtain in Xunzi's phrase *yang*[3] *qing*, and my translation attempts to make that clear.

apparent the parlous consequence of the negligence of rites. The acts of omission (leaving unclear markers or no markers at all) and commission (a wilful disregard of the marker because one insists on one's own way) may both spell disaster. What Xunzi and Li Ao in other passages call "the measure (*jie*) of *qing*" is in this sense similar in meaning to the sign or marker (*biao*), for both terms serve a prescriptive and a prohibitive function. Consistent with the distinctive topos of classical Chinese philosophy, which construes Dao as a way and a guiding discourse, the prescriptive aspect of the sign delimits the normative locale of the ritual action and specifies its proper content. The prohibitive aspect, on the other hand, cautions against the transgression of its boundary.

It is this understanding that in Xunzi renders ritual a channel for desire,[75] and the capacity is perhaps best illustrated by the philosopher's discussion of funeral rites. The discussion is premised first on the assumption, fundamental to all Chinese philosophy, that the affective stirrings of the human and human desires are ineradicable traits of nature. The problem, as the Confucians saw the matter is thus not with the elimination of emotions and desires but rather with their regulation. The second premise of the discussion is an equally distinctive assumption that the human subject is only constituted by the social bodies of family and state.[76] Kinship and political structures, therefore, will define the normative location of subjectivity, its expression and operation to be guided and conditioned by rites that are invented to serve those structures.[77]

What can cause greater grief to humans than the loss of kin, and what greater loss can one suffer than the loss of one's parents? To put the question in this manner is already to contrast the Chinese understanding of the duty of mourning with a Western formulation such as Plato's remark (in *Republic* 387 e) that the loss of one's friend or comrade (*hetairos*) afflicts no less keen an impact than the loss of brother or son. Plato's thought, in fact, finds proper example in the final books of the *Iliad*, in which Achilles' rage and grief for the death of Patroklos provide a poignant counterpoint to Priam's suffering for Hector's demise. To the Chinese, on the other hand, this equation of friends with kin

---

[75] See Hansen, *A Daoist Theory of Chinese Thought*, p. 312.

[76] This is, of course, a familiar theme of scholarship on classical Confucianism. For a convenient recent study, see Ambrose Y. C. King, "The Individual and Group in Confucianism."

[77] In this sense, Chinese rituals aptly illustrate the thesis of Jonathan Z. Smith, who argues cogently in *To Take Place* that ritual is fundamentally a category of the locative; it concerns place and placement. The zones of operation of classical Chinese ritual are hierarchical—itself another locative notion—and ubiquitous: from the inner chamber to the public hall, from the living quarters to the gravesite, from the studio to the ancestral shrine, and from the house and courtyard to the state. For the specific Confucian defense of why the ruler (*jun*) must supercede in importance all kin, including one's parents, see *Xunzi jijie*, chapter 19 (pp. 248–49). Citing the ode "Jiongzhuo" (Mao 251), as his authority, the philosopher reaffirms the Mencian dictum that the prince is the parent of the people (*Mencius*, 1A, 4, 5; 1B, 7, 6).

must appear problematic, for the ordering of human relations must grant kin their due priority in their claim on our emotions. The expression of grief on such occasion as the death of parents, for the Confucians especially, is not only natural but morally obligatory. "All those born between heaven and earth—those with blood and breath—must have intelligence. And those with intelligence," so reasons Xunzi in the lengthy chapter 19 of his treatise, "must love their own kind. . . . Among those with blood and breath none is more intelligent than man. Therefore a man will love his parents endlessly even until he dies. . . . If all of a sudden one's revered parents perish but he who attends their burial is neither grieving nor reverent, then he is no better than a beast" (*Xunzi jijie*, 19, pp. 247, 241).

The philosopher, moreover, makes a distinctive contribution to ritual theory by not merely enjoining the duty of showing grief and reverence but also by specifying the conditions wherewith such display may be both facilitated and regulated. Funeral rites are plays in which the prescribed actions assist the surviving kin in acting out their emotions. According to Xunzi, "it is customary for funeral rites in the event of death to adorn [the dead], to move [the dead] by taking it to a distance, and to make [the dead] permanent by rendering its condition ordinary."

Why must the dead be treated in this manner? The reply of Xunzi's keen insight is that the duty of grieving for the departed, even for a loved one like a parent, can itself be grievous or onerous. "It is the way of the dead that if it is not adorned, it will be despised; what is despised cannot elicit grief. When the dead one is nearby, it will become a familiar object. What is familiar will become loathsome, and the loathsome begets forgetfulness. Forgetfulness will produce irreverence" (ibid., p. 241). The props and measures of funerary rites—dressing a corpse, for example, or placing food in the mouth and combing the hair—are thus meant to benefit the living as much as the dead.

Reducing, supposedly, the repulsiveness of the dead provides a means of minimizing—perhaps even purging—the otherness of death, and is thus a means of control and domestication. In the tales of the anomalous (*zhiguai*) that flourished in the post-Han period, I have noted in another study that the language of the genre often emphasizes, by means of formulaic parallelism, the disparity between the worlds of life and death, of humans and spirits.[78] From the Confucian point of view, ritual is precisely the instrument devised to bridge the vast gulf separating the living and the dead. Confucius had taught that "sacrifice as though (*ru*) present should mean sacrifice to the spirits as though they were present" (*Analects*, 3. 12). Consistent with his emphasis on the requirement of inward rectitude for moral action, Confucius' remark might have been directed pointedly at the attitude of the ritual performer. His injunction, interestingly enough, receives direct expansion by Xunzi: "All things are offered as though

---

[78] See my "'Rest, Rest Perturbed Spirit!,'" pp. 413–15.

the spirits would taste them; . . . the host lifts the sacrificial goblet as though the spirits would drink it" (*Xunzi jijie*, 19, pp. 250–51). Such a formulation, however, turns ritual into a full-fledged aesthetic, since it is constructed on the perceived, hypothetical likeness (*ru*) of action and setting. Moral psychology has given way to dramatics. Food is placed in the dead one's mouth as though the person were living (ibid., p. 243), and the grave and grave mound formally imitate (*xiang*) a house, while coffin and hearse covers imitate draperies of doors or rooms (ibid., p. 245). Ritual's suppositional character, in Xunzi's climactic summation, is a form of staging that seeks to bestow presence on absence: "How full of grief, how full of reverence! To serve the dead as though alive, to serve the departed as though present. What concerns the seemingly shapeless and shadowless thereby attains, nonetheless, a signifying pattern (*wen*)" (ibid., p. 251). Ritual, in sum, is potent drama.

Despite this aesthetic's elaborate character, however, the activity itself embodies no intrinsic, transcendent imperative. The socio-political interests of the living human, supremely personified by the sage and by the superior man, must take unquestioned priority, for, in the last analysis, honoring the dead is another means of confirming the rectitude of the living by registering his refusal to contemn one who has lost consciousness (ibid., p. 238). Xunzi's philosophy has been noted for its exaltation of "heaven" and of "ritual," but the anthropocentric tenor of those concepts is also apparent in the constant emphasis that human conscious activity (*wei*) must join and complete the productive forces of the cosmos to order the world. Thus opines the philosopher: "Heaven can beget things but it cannot distinguish them; Earth can carry people but cannot govern them. The myriad creatures, the living people, and the like in the world must await the sages before they can reach their proper places" (ibid.).[79] Funeral rites are "eschatological" acts in the sense that they are unrepeatable, but their orientation is entirely this-worldly because they provide the last occasions when a superior man can show respect to the ruler or a son to his parents (ibid., p. 239). These "rituals [that] adorn the dead by means of the living, [that] send off the dead by grandly imitating the living" (ibid., p. 243) are therefore only aborted fictions. The dead one's mouth is planted with raw rice and closed with dried shell while the ears are stuffed with wads of silk floss, much as the corpse on the way to burial is accompanied by a horseless carriage, untuned lutes and zithers, and unsounding pipes and reeds. These imitations, says Xunzi, make clear (*ming*) the fact that for the dead, a different path has been taken and the artifacts are of no real use (ibid., pp. 244–45). If the aesthetics of funeral rituals is ordered by the supposed similarity between life and death, the rituals themselves thus finally become allegories of realistic difference.

---

[79] The text of this quotation is revealing, although this paragraph is generally considered a misplaced one (see Watson, *Hsün Tzu*, p. 102).

To the extent, therefore, that the principle of fiction in ritual is firmly held in check by "the reality principle," so to speak, and that aesthetics must be subordinate to politics, we may also discern how ritual for Xunzi must serve to order and countermand its genetic impulse, the ground of its being. Make-believe has its limits because desires and emotions—and the expression thereof—must also have their limits. Herein again the dialectical relations between ritual and *qing* and between aesthetics and *qing* become evident.

Sacrificial rites, declares Xunzi, arise from "the feelings of recollection and longing (*aimu zhi qing*)" (ibid., pp. 249–50), but this specific association only serves to accentuate how desires and feelings are the basis of all rites because *qing* is pervasively characteristic of the human. If the superior man is always careful to treat birth and death, the auspicious and the inauspicious events of life (ibid., pp. 238, 240) through ritual, the feelings of grief and joy (*you yu*) also epitomize, in Xunzi's view, human emotionality because they are the persistent antipodes (*duan*) of human life (ibid., p. 243). The manifestation of these two feelings as man's response to life's vicissitudes thus runs the gamut of expressivity, for it encompasses the signs of both nature and culture, the natural and the artificial. Just as a smiling or sorrowful look betokens the emergence (*fa*) of joy or grief in the countenance, and songs and laughter, weeping and lamentation betoken joy or grief in the voice, so even the use of diverse foodstuffs, garments, and lodgings may indicate the varying subjective states of the person (ibid., pp. 242–43).

It should be apparent at once that this understanding of ritual's semiology ("changes in feeling and countenance should be sufficient to distinguish between the auspicious and the inauspicious") is entirely concordant with the aesthetics of what modern scholars have labeled the expressive theory of literature in the Chinese tradition.[80] Briefly stated, that theory maintains that literary writings, like other natural signs (such as bodily gestures) or cultural ones (such as musical tones), are sufficient and real indices of a person's inward disposition, be it in the form of aspiration or intent (*zhi, yi*) or feelings. Though it is one among several views of literature in the tradition, its preeminence and influence, particularly amid the dominant Confuian culture, are not to be minimized.

As early as *The Book of Documents*, there is the notion—accepted virtually throughout the full length of Chinese literary history—that certain signs (in this case, poetry and musical notes) are able to express the intent/aspiration (*zhi*) of the heart-and-mind (*xin*).[81] A variant view, possibly stemming from Lu Ji (261–303), substitutes the affective disposition (*qing*) as the ground for expressivity, and thus a controversy developed early with respect to whether intent/aspiration and disposition are similar or different things.[82] However that

---

[80] See James J. Y. Liu, *Chinese Theories of Literature*, pp. 53–87.

[81] "Yaodian," in *Shangshu jishi*, p. 28; cf. Legge, *The Chinese Classics* 3: 28.

[82] On this question, see the informative essay by Bi Wanchen, "Yanzhi yuanqing manyi."

question is resolved, the crucial agreement between the two views is evident in the direct conduit linking subjectivity and its external appearance. As Liu Xie (c. 465–522) later declared in chapter 27 of his magisterial *Wenxin diaolong*: "When *qing* is moved, words will endow it with form; when principle (*li*[2 principle]) arises, signifying pattern (*wen*) will render it visible. In this way runs the course from the latent to the manifest, and thus the external may be talismanic of the internal."[83]

Situated in its particular moment of transition from the classical to the imperial age, Xunzi's discourse on ritual, music, and desire not only echoes antecedent notions but also looks prospectively toward such Han writings or compilations as the "Record of Music (*Yueji*)" in the *Record of Rites*, the "Treatise on Music (*Yueshu*)" in the *Historical Records*, and the "Great Preface" to the *Poetry Classic*. The affinity of the philosopher's ideas with this group of texts is well known.[84] However, Xunzi's accord with the general psychology of stimulus and affective stirring that yields expressivity is not as germane to our discussion as his tenacious advocacy of normative regulation of that stirring and expressivity.

According to the familiar assertion of the "Great Preface,"

> Poetry is where the intent/aspiration (*zhi*[3]) goes (*zhi*[1]). What is held in the mind is intent/aspiration; what emerges in words is poetry. The disposition (*qing*) inwardly moved will take shape in words. The inadequacy of words provides the reason for sighing about them. The inadequacy of sighs provides the reason for singing about them. The inadequacy of singing causes unconsciously the hands to dance them and the feet to tap them. The disposition emerges in sounds; when sounds attain a signifying pattern we call these tones.[85]

This passage, which has elicited so much commentary, nonetheless still has the capacity to invite more. First, we must note the placement of intent and

---

See also the discussion by Owen in *Readings in Chinese Literary Thought*, pp. 130–31. Both Bi and Owen seem to argue that intent/aspiration and affective disposition are different. Owen thinks (p. 131) that "Lu Chi [in the line 'the poem (*shih*) follows from the affections (*ch'ing*) and is sensuously intricate' found in his *Wenfu*] 'broadens' the originary definition of *shih* to account more perfectly for poetry's true range." Perhaps. But in the context of the discourse on desire, Lu's definition may be more of a unifying than a broadening focus, for if the discussion of poetry's or music's origin is placed within the discussion of ritual's origin, the centrality of *qing* is immediately apparent. Indeed, the rhetorical structure of the Great Preface provides the most intimate juxtaposition of *zhi* and *qing*.

[83] *Wenxin diaolong zhu, juan* 6, 8a.

[84] On the line of descent from Xunzi to the ideals of ritual extolled in the *Record of Rites* and the didactic potency of poetry in the Mao Prefaces, see Bernhard Karlgren, "The Early History of the *Chou Li* and *Tso Chuan* Texts"; Tang Junyi, *Zhongguo zhexue yuanlun* (*Yuanxingpian*), pp. 79–89; Knoblock, *Xunzi*, 1: 36–44; Haun Saussy, *The Problem of a Chinese Aesthetic*, pp. 100–5, and note 73 on p. 224.

[85] Ruan Yuan, *Shisanjing zhushu*, 1, 5a.

disposition in relation to mind. Although the preface does not clarify further the exact positioning of these three human features, their aggregate significance here in the text apparently concerns the interior "spaces" of subjectivity, and in that sense, it contributes toward a theory of art founded on "a more broadly conceived psychology."[86] Second, the escalating scale of seemingly spontaneous reaction surprisingly consigns language to the least effective level of expressivity. For a preface purported to extol the importance of a poetic anthology, a collection of verbal artifacts, the scale magnifies instead other kinds of signs: nonlinguistic, physical gestures can attain shape or form ($xing^2$) that qualifies as signifying pattern (*wen*). Its intimation of tonal and rhythmic activities makes apparent the emphasis in Chinese antiquity of poetry, song, and dance as, in fact, analogous modes of speech stemming from a common source.[87] It also helps explain why in the texts of early Confucianism the concern for ritual control of auditory symbols has found perhaps even more frequent statement than concern for control of linguistic ones. Third, the passage posits the irresistible drive for outlet once the emotive disposition is aroused.[88] If one expressive means does not satisfy, the enlistment of other means unconsciously or unknowingly (*buzhi*) takes place; it becomes, as it were, instinctual and automatic.

Read in isolation, this passage on affective motion that brooks no suppression or compromise would seem strangely at odds with Confucian ritualism, because for someone like Xunzi the fact that joy and grief define the antipodal states of the human condition does not mean therefore that these and other forms of *qing* are to enjoy untrammeled manifestation. The affective reactions may have a natural origin, but nature is always in need of human superintendence. "If one can cut or stretch them [the affections], broaden or narrow them, increase or reduce them, classify or exhaust them, let them flourish or adorn them so that their beginnings and ends are all properly aligned and sufficient to be a standard for all times, then this is ritual indeed" (*Xunzi jijie*, 19, p. 243). The pithy series of verbs in Xunzi's remark not only spells out concretely the interventionist character of ritual action, but also clarifies the relations of *qing* to either ritual or aesthetics. The remark gives substance to the kind of summary statement in the *Record of Rites*: "When the sages establish rules, they would always make heaven and earth as the origin, . . . ritual and righteousness as the utensils, and human *qing* as the fields [for cultivation]."[89]

---

[86] Owen, *Readings in Chinese Literary Thought*, p. 41.

[87] For a statement of this emphasis, see Yu Kuang-chung, "Shi yu yinyue [Poetry and music]," *Zhongguo shibao* (China Times), December 5, 1993, p. 39.

[88] See Stephen Owen's interesting reading of the passage, in which he resorts to a theory of *qi* to elucidate the gradations of intensity in the affective stirring. See *Readings in Chinese Literary Thought*, p. 42.

[89] *Liji xunzuan, juan* 9, 10a.

The agrarian metaphor, although wholly consistent with the Confucian emphasis on nature's subservience to culture, also sheds light retroactively on Xunzi's definition of ritual's character and ideal.

> All rites begin in simplicity, are brought to completion in signifying patterns (*wen*), and terminate in delight and pleasure. When rites are performed in the ultimate, most adequate manner, the affects (*qing*) and signifying patterns are exhaustively [present]. On the next level, the affects and patterns prevail by turns. On the lowest level, everything reverts to the affects so as to return to the Great Oneness. (ibid., p. 236)

The Great Oneness (*dayi*), glossed by a commentator as "substantive purity the return to which is also ritual" (ibid., p. 236)," might have been a rhetorical sop for those in sympathy with early Daoist philosophers, but its humble location in Xunzi's taxonomy is revealing. In both Xunzi and the *Record of Rites*, as in other Confucian texts generally, the raw condition of *qing* can never be accorded preeminence or normative stature. The requisite avoidance of its excessive manifestion thus not merely encourages the rules and instruments of regulation, but also motivates the philsopher's repeated call for the "middle state (*zhongliu*)" as the ideal ritual economy (ibid., pp. 238, 242).

Xunzi's prescription, moreover, may help us realize as never before that signifying pattern (*wen*), which presides as the foundational concept for literature in the total sweep of Chinese civilization, is no neutral term for abstract design or innocuous marking, as lexicon and etymology would have us believe.[90] In the discourse on desire, signifying pattern is already imbued with the ideology of curbing desire. It is only in this light that we can understand the logic of the aphorism found in the "Great Preface" to the *Classic of Poetry*: "Therefore, the altered Airs emerge from the affective disposition (*qing*), but they do not go beyond ritual and righteousness. That they should emerge from the affective disposition stems from the nature of the people, but that they should not go beyond ritual and righteousness is the beneficent legacy of the former kings."[91] There is thus no contradiction, after all, between the Preface and Confucian orthodoxy, for the waving hands and dancing feet, though semblances of spontaneous, unruly gestures, must be swiftly directed toward principled movement.

Indeed, the one continuous thread of argument running through what might be called the Confucian view of the arts is this contradictory desire for sponta-

---

[90] See Liu, *Chinese Theories of Literature*, pp. 7–9 for a brief but succinct discussion. See also Stephen Owen, *Traditional Chinese Poetry and Poetics*, pp. 18–27; Owen, *Readings in Chinese Literary Thought*, pp. 183–298 (on *Wenxin diaolong*); Peter Bol, *"This Culture of Ours,"* pp. 84–107. Bol is especially informative in detailing the cultural centrality of writing for medieval Chinese civilization and the effectiveness of official dynastic histories in upholding and transmitting the ideology of *wen*.

[91] Ruan, *Shisanjing zhushu*, 1: 14a.

neity and calculation, freedom and control. "Music is pleasure," declares Xunzi in a visual tautology (the graph for music and pleasure being the same), "what the human disposition cannot avoid. . . . Therefore, a human cannot not feel pleasure, and pleasure cannot not assume a form (*xing*²). When forms are not directed by the Dao, disorder is inevitable. Because the former kings hated disorder, they set up the sounds of the hymns and odes to guide it [that is, the human disposition or *renqing*]" (*Xunzi jijie*, 20, p. 252). In this agon between two kinds of necessity, the inevitability of affective movement must yield to the perceived requisite of its discipline.

The imposition of form (*xing*², *wen*) in such a view cannot be merely a matter of expressing or miming the affective experience, for aesthetics must serve the superintending ideals of a prior guiding discourse, the Dao itself.[92] That discourse will hierarchize not only politics and aesthetics but also ethics and psychology. If it is in the nature of the common people (*min zhi xing*) to let affections blossom into poetic songs, as the "Great Preface" alleges, that predilection in turn must submit to what "the former kings" like or dislike. In the Confucian discourse, order and disorder, similar to what Mencius has said of righteousness, can finally be seen as the inventions of desire which are, however, heralded as the "beneficent legacy" of kings, sages, and gentlemen. That class or social status breeds ethical difference is thus an assumption no more foreign to the Confucian outlook than it is to the classical Athenian one.[93] "It is said, music is pleasure. The gentleman (*junzi*) is pleased to carry out the Dao, but the little man is pleased to carry out his desires (*yu*). Using the Dao to regulate the desires, we shall have pleasure without disorder. Using desires to forget the Dao, then we shall be deluded and unhappy. Thus music is the Dao that guides pleasure" (ibid., 20, p. 254). The Confucian argument has thus come full circle as well: aesthetic expression, the unavoidable creation of human affectivity, must also preside as the discourse that guides that affectivity. In such a discourse on desire, there is neither innocent nor neutral speech or, for that matter, dance or song.

PATHOCENTRISM AND THE LEGITIMATION OF DESIRE

The circularity of the Confucian argument about the nature and function of the artistic media also imposes on them their special burden. Because "forms that do not attain [the status] of guiding discourse (*dao*) cannot but end in chaos," Xunzi's theory of music asserts that the very means of expressivity must become

---

[92] For an articulation of such a view in Western terms, see Susanne K. Langer, *Philosophy in a New Key*, and *Feeling and Form*.

[93] On this point about Greek morality, see Moses I. Finley, *Ancient Slavery and Modern Ideology*.

at the same time the instrument of regulation. No feature of music is exempted from this all-encompassing didactic and prescriptive purpose. The odes and hymns fashioned by former kings are meant to cause "the tones to be joyful without being wanton; the pattern to be manifest but not worrisome; their directness or indirectness, complexity or simplicity, sparsity or abundance should be sufficient to activate the mind of goodness in humans and to prohibit the devious and excessive energies from approaching" (*Xunzi jijie*, 20, p. 252).

This sweeping moralism, as we have seen, directly and profoundly bears upon poetics as well. If literature can realistically and accurately mirror human nature, what should be the scope and content of such reflection? If part of that nature is construed to be problematic and susceptible to disorderly or illegitimate manifestation, how should one exercise the media of its expression? Questions such as these, in fact, underlie the persistent conundrum of whether poetry articulates the mental or affective intent (*shi yan zhi, yan qing*), and the correlative concern for restraining excessive sounds (*yin* or *liu sheng*) or diction (*yin ci*). They reveal, moreover, that within the Confucian discourse, all outward manifestations of the inward disposition must be held liable to censorious scrutiny, because every expressive medium—speech, sound, language, gesture, complexion—can be a tale-telling sign that signals either waywardness or rectitude. It therefore requires scrupulous monitoring, regimentation, and interpretation. The historicist's argument that Confucius's praise for the "Osprey Ode" refers only to its sound but not its content (hence that semantic censure only began with Han scholasticism) may be a correct interpretation that nonetheless misses the point. For to declare any sequence of tones—that is, a musical composition—"delightful but not wanton or licentious (*le er bu yin*)" is already a value-laden interpretation.

The venerable slogan *shi yan zhi* (poetry expresses intent/aspiration) impresses its importance in the literary tradition by the way it affects both poetic practice and theory, for it spawns far-reaching ramifications for such hermeneutical issues as authorial intent, poetic or linguistic effect, the nature of representation, poetry's pragmatic context, poetic reference, and the theory of reading. Not merely a Confucian notion, the assumed significance of the saying surfaces even in a Daoist document like the *Zhuangzi*.[94] Wherever the slogan is heard among the ancient texts, one of the first questions that naturally comes to mind must be: whose *zhi* is being expressed by the poetry? In certain passages often cited from the *Zuo Commentary* ("Duke Xiang 16"; "27"; "Duke Zhao 16") to illustrate the practice of reciting poems from the *Poetry Classic* for diplomatic transactions, there is a discernible tendency to subordinate whatever authorial intention is in the poetic specimen so deployed to the intent of the recitalist.

---

[94] For example: "The *Poetry Classic* states (*dao*) the intention or aspiration (*zhi*); the *Book of Documents* states events; the *Ritual Classic* states conduct." See *Zhuangzi*, chapter 33.

The incident reported in Duke Xiang 16, for example, indicates that a quotation deemed inappropriate or unfit (*bu lei*) can incite anger and the threatening verdict of a disaffected or divergent aim (*yi zhi*). Poetry, so deployed, is already a political commodity, and it is its consumers, not its original creator(s), that are held most responsible for its putative meaning. On the other hand, another story of the *Zuo Commentary* ("Duke Zhao 12") tells of an ode ("Qizhao") composed (*zuo*) by the minister Moufu in his attempt to prevent King Mu from making extensive tours of his realm. Although it is not clear whether Moufu happens to be the ode's creator or merely its user, the story accentuates one cherished conviction of Chinese poetics: namely, the remonstrative power of poetry. As in the famous tale of the "Seven-Step Poem" by which the Emperor Wen of Wei (Cao Pei, r. 220–226) was moved to spare his brother by the latter's original allegorical quatrain on the bean and beanstalk, King Mu is said to be momentarily devastated by the ode.[95] Ultimately, however, he—unlike Emperor Wen—is unable to fulfil the Confucain ideal of "self-conquest (*zike*)" and curb his excessive *Wanderlust*.

It is no accident that a saying of Confucius is prominently featured to sum up the moral of the tale recounted in the passage from "Duke Zhao 12" ("to subdue the self and return to ritual is benevolence"), for the Confucian tradition has indeed forcefully shaped the development of the concept of *shi yan zhi*. The slogan appositely articulates that tradition's concern for characterology. Confucius's injunction in *Analects*, 1.11—"Observe what a man has in mind to do when his father is living, and then observe what he does when his father is dead"—belongs to the hermeneutics of action, of which speech and language both figure unambiguously as crucial texts. If a person's activities can be scrutinized or read (*guan*) for moral assessment, so, too, can his verbal and linguistic expressions that must serve as signs of his intent or aspiration. The long episode reported in *Analects*, 11.26, wherein Confucius directly examines several of his disciples by luring them with an imaginary offer of political office into "stating their *zhi*" (here equivalent to how each of them would govern), not only demonstrates the enormous consequence of speech but also the characteristic Confucian emphasis that a man's moral stature is ineluctably tied to his political disposition. The response of a condescending snicker from the Master, itself a sign that elicits questioning and interpretation, both elucidates and judges a disciple's impropriety in the episode.

Zilu, who invited his mentor's scorn, is said to have spoken immodest or unyielding words, but the Chinese clause itself, *qi yan bu rang*, can refer to either content or deportment. Add the clause to the narrated description of Zilu's act of speaking (immediately or hastily, *shuai'er*), and we may certainly draw the conclusion that he transgressed in both speech and manner. Both the way he jumped to answer his mentor's inquiry without deferring to his fellow

---

[95] See *A New Account of the Tales of the World*, translated by Richard B. Mather, p. 126.

students and the scope of his claim (to instill in three years a sense of courage and direction in the citizens of a large, troubled state) offended the quintessential Confucian sentiment loudly affirmed by the Master—"It is by rites that a state is made."

Confucius' reaction to Zilu, in turn, helps clarify the problem that is the focus of our discussion at this point: namely, the relationship between *zhi* and *qing*. The little tale begins to show us again that in the Confucian tradition, there appears to be the recognition that moral aspiration and political ambition cannot but be the products of desire, itself defined, as we have seen, as a stubborn but malleable part of nature (*xing*). When that nature is aroused, according to such a view, its manifestation can assume the guise of the affective, the moral, or the political. Thus a passage on the origin of ritual in "Duke Zhao 25" of the *Zuo Commentary* provides a revealing gloss of the key terms: "There were love and hatred, pleasure and anger, grief and joy, produced by the six vital energetics (*qi*). Therefore, [the sage kings] scrutinize the relations and put in order the categories [of ritual] so as to regulate the six impulses (*zhi³*) (Legge, *The Chinese Classics* 5: 704, 708; text modified).

The six impulses, as we have seen, are referred to in other ancient documents as the six emotions (*liu qing*), and it is thus not surprising that the Tang commentator Kong Yingda (574–648) concludes in his annotation of the passage: "What remains in the self (*ji*) is the disposition (*qing*); when the disposition stirs (*dong*), it is intent or aspiration (*zhi³*). Disposition and aspiration are one."[96] Xunzi would readily agree with the first part of Kong's definition, but in Xun's view of the matter, the result of an aroused disposition, we recall, would more often than not end in desire (*yu*). It is, therefore, again no surprise that the early Han annotator Zhao Qi would gloss *Mencius* 5A:4 with the definition: "*Zhi³* is what the poet records as the things he desires (*shiren zhi suo yu zhi shi*)."[97] But switching the use of *zhi³* to that of a verb, Zhao's gloss decisively links intent with desire itself (*yu*). We may hence conclude that the Confucian discourse on desire continuously recognizes the propensity of the affective to slide into the oretic, and what is moral aspiration (*zhi³*) in one case (the desire to govern or serve a state, the passionate love for one's spouse) may degenerate into unbridled ambition or unfilial infatuation.[98]

Seen in this light, the familiar observation of someone's "bosom cradling great aspiration/intention (*xiong huai da zhi*)" becomes a morally parlous de-

---

[96] "Chunqiu Zuozhuan zhushu" in Ruan, *Shisanjing zhushu, juan* 46, 4b.

[97] *Mengzi zhengyi*, compiled by Wang Yunwu, p. 101.

[98] The word "oretic" derives from the Greek word *orego*, meaning to reach or stretch out. The noun form, *orexis*, was used by Aristotle to indicate forms of desire, affective movements that are "object-directed, active inner reaching-out." See the discussion in Martha C. Nussbaum, *The Fragility of Goodness*, pp. 273–89. For further discussion of the complex relations between *zhi* and *qing*, see Zhu Ziqing, "Shi yan zhi bian," 1: 183–234; Guo Shaoyu, *Zhaoyu shi gudian wenxue lunji*, 1: 23–26; and Steven van Zoeren, *Poetry and Personality*, chapter 3.

scription, for the subject entertaining such a state of affairs, in the Confucian view, may harbor either legitimate or self-aggrandizing sentiments. Moreover, all the signs of such a subject's disposition—a gesture, a word, a poem authored or quoted—may betray revealing disclosures. As if to leave no doubt whatever, one saying attributed in the *Record of Rites* to Confucius provides a characteristic assertion that also illumines the topic at hand. When questioned by the student, Zixia, on what are the "five ultimate reaches (*wuzhi*^{5}),"

> Confucius replies, "Where the intent (*zhi*^{3}) reaches (*zhi*^{5}), poetry also reaches. Where poetry reaches, rite also reaches. Where rite reaches, pleasure also reaches. Where pleasure reaches, grief also reaches. When pleasure and grief mutually beget each other, it is the cause for rectitude. . . . The intentional energetics (*zhiqi*) fill up heaven and earth, and these are called the five ultimate reaches."[99]

Confucius's statement here apparently belongs to the tradition, exemplified by the passage from "Duke Zhao 25" of the *Zuo Commentary* I cited earlier, that maintains the virtual synonymity of *zhi*^{3} and *qing*. The statement epitomizes the relationship not only by its immediate appeal to the paronomastic play on the phoneme, *zhi*, but also by its picking up, intertextually, the absent graphs of that phoneme. The passage powerfully and unmistakably recalls such foundational dicta as "poetry is where the intent goes (*zhi*^{1})," poetry "arises from the affective disposition but stops at (*zhi*^{2}) rites and righteousness" (both from the "Great Preface"), and a passage like that from "Duke Zhao 12": "Moufu composed the Qizhao poem to still (*zhi*^{2}—literally, to stop) the king's mind." In its emphasis on poetry's affective origin and both its need and capacity for moral and political regimentation, the complex of verbal play and echo confirms a modern scholar's conclusion that the heart of the Confucian pedagogical project is "to mobilize the emotional nature in their service [that is, to carry out moral judgments] in a spontaneous and unconflicted way. The central problematic was not the question of how to *determine* the good (for the norms were already known, or at least knowable through study) but how to *be* good."[100]

Transferred to the specific field of literature, the questions posed by Chinese literary history are whether such mobilization can indeed result in "spontaneous and unconflicted" exercises of moral judgments, and whether a literary composition arising from the movement of the affective disposition can always stop within the bounds of propriety. Translated further into the realm of reading and reception, the question next surfaces in the guise of how one must treat a text whose content perceptibly violates established Confucian norms. If literature is one lawful means of expressing desire, how legitimate is a work that is unreservedly devoted to that expression? And finally, if one's speech, language, and writing are inevitably true indexes of one's disposition, is there room for a

---

[99] In the chapter, "Confucius at Leisure (Kongzi xianju)"; see *Liji xunzhuan, juan* 29, 1a.
[100] Van Zoeren, *Poetry and Personality*, p. 54.

concept of fiction as imagined reality, as outright fabrication? Studied in the context of Chinese literary history, these questions help in turn to bring to the fore the issues of allegoresis or the deliberate displacement of meaning in literary creation and interpretation, the increasingly gendered conceptualization of both the affections and certain literary genres, and the problematic relations posited for fiction and the creator of fictive representation. As we can readily see, all these issues can be directly pertinent to a reading of *Hongloumeng*.

In his impressive account of the history of hermeneutics relative to the *Poetry Classic*, Steven van Zoeren has credited the Song poet Ouyang Xiu (1007–1072) for re-interpreting certain poems of that anthology—from didactic allegories to passionate love songs. Ouyang thus joins a wider movement of the eleventh century wherein, supposedly, "discussions of the Odes began to mention an idea that had been energetically and effectively denied for a thousand years: the possibility that certain of the Odes expressed sentiments and attitudes which were not only not canonically correct and normative but actually inimical to the foundations of the Confucian vision of society and morality."[101] Given Ouyang's penchant in authoring some rather daring poems himself, his affirmation of erotic presence in that foundational text of Chinese culture is perhaps not surprising.[102] What is of interest to our reflection here, however, is whether Ouyang or other interpreters of the odes of the time can truly be said to represent a new understanding of the nature of these poems, and whether the millenium-long tradition of denial is in fact based on the specific recognition of erotic presence in the classical anthology.

Consider the poem (Mao 73) on the "Great Chariot (*daju*)" in the "Royal Domain (Wang Feng)" section, which reads as follows:

> My great carriage rumbles and tumbles,
> My felt robe (green) like the young sedge.
> How could I not long for you!
> But I fear you will not dare.
>
> My great carriage creaks and groans,
> My felt robe (red) like the millet.
> How could I not long for you!
> But I fear you won't run off.
>
> In life we dwell in different rooms;
> In death we share the same pit.
> You dare say I am faithless!
> I am like the bright sun.

[101] Ibid., p. 169.
[102] See, for example, various lyrics in *QSC* 1: 150–55.

Although the diction and syntax of this poem are not particularly difficult, the reading of specific words, as in the case of so many other Chinese poems, will determine the overall meaning assigned to the work. One locus of contention lies in the last word of the second stanza, *ben*, which I have rendered, for the sake of the present discussion, in as in general what would be indicated by the English "run off." How the word is understood, however, divides the interpretations historically.

If we begin with the "Lesser Preface," its summation of what the poem is all about goes like this: "The 'Great Chariot' is a critique (*ci*[4]) directed against the Grand Masters of the Zhou. When rites and righteousness are in fragments, men and women elope (*yinben*) at will, and that is why the past is narrated in order to criticize the present."[103] This passage makes apparent at once the commentator's identification of the verb as an abridged form of the term for elopement,[104] used for the acts of men and women meeting not in accordance with ritual prescriptions and thus termed licentious, wanton, or excessive (that is, *yin*).[105] The practice allegedly is recorded in the *Zhou Li* (Rituals of the Zhou). In the section on the "Ministry of Education (*diguan*; literally, officers of the Earth)," under the entry of the "Marriage Monitor (*meishi*),"[106] it is written that "during the second month of the spring period, the [monitor] would order men and women to meet. At that time, those who elope (*ben*) would not be prohibited."[107]

Some textual scholars have argued that such a description of the marriage monitor might well have been a late addition of the Han to an earlier text. Whatever the problem in dating this passage, the provisional allowance of elopement "in obedience to the seasons," as the textual commentator says, or elopement as simply a transgressive social practice was clearly presupposed in many Song discussants of the *Poetry Classic*, including Ouyang Xiu and Zhu Xi.[108] We can see, therefore, that neither the ancient reader(s) represented in the "Lesser Preface" nor the medieval Song critics had any difficulty in recognizng the erotic in the odes, especially if "Great Chariot" was indeed a text that voiced a woman's challenge to her lover to elope with her. The problem of reading posed by the text is thus not strictly a matter of perception or recog-

---

[103] Ruan, *Shisanjing zhushu, juan* 4, 16a.

[104] Such a reading is also accepted by Bernhard Karlgren, as can readily be seen in his translation. See *The Book of Odes*, p. 49.

[105] I thus disagree with van Zoeren's translation of the word as "debauched" (see *Poetry and Personality*, p. 169), for in the discussions of the commentators, beginning with the "Lesser Preface" and proceeding to such Song critics as Ouyang Xiu and Zhu Xi and beyond, *yinshi* or licentious poetry/poems is clearly related to the practice of *yinben*, literally licentious flight or elopement. "Debauched" may not be inaccurate, but it is a clumsy adjective in this context.

[106] In the translation of titles, I follow Hucker.

[107] *Zhouli Zheng zhu, juan* 14, 6b (*SBBY*).

[108] See, for example, Ouyang Xiu, *Shi benyi, juan* 1, 7b–8a (*SBCK*); Zhu Xi, *Shi jizhuan, juan* 4, 29a–b (*SBCK*).

nition of the literal sense of the text. It is, rather, the construal of what that sense or meaning is supposed to serve. The venerable pairing of intent (yi^3) and meaning (yi^4) turns on, in fact, the fine line of such a distinction.[109]

In this regard, it is instructive to note how the "Lesser Preface" proceeds to deal with the purport and meaning of the text. Once the erotic is duly acknowledged, its purpose in terms of its literal presence is immediately displaced—"the past is narrated in order to criticize the present." Whatever reality the past is meant to embody, and however offensive that reality thus recorded and textualized may be, it now serves an acceptable mission. As Haun Saussy has perceptively written of Confucian poetics and musicology, "the musical theory of poetry ends in expression; the theory that supplants it ends in exemplarity. . . . Music mimics local conditions, but musicology is pan-Chinese."[110] In line with this observation, we may say that the poem is expressive of specific circumstance and affect, but the poetics that hopes to justify both poem and poet will elevate the individual to the universal, the incidental to the paradigmatic.

I say the poet as well, because in its treatment of the expressive arts, the Confucian discourse does not want any aspect thereof to be left to chance; the source, the medium, and the effect must all be examined and regulated. The posited influence of King Wen in the production of the odes, the alleged power of regional and temporal mores to alter (bian) poetic content and styles, and the transhistorical application of literary meaning all constitute the basic tenets of Han hermeneutics of poetry as evident in the "Great Preface" and "Lesser Preface." Those documents themselves represent the culmination of a long process of development, parts of which hark back to Confucius. The operative assumptions fundamental to such a hermeneutics are certainly not changed, let alone abandoned, in the Song, as we can readily see in a remark from Zhu Xi's own Preface to his Shi jizhuan (Collected Commentaries of the Odes):

I have heard that all the odes named Airs had by and large emerged from the songs and ditties composed in back alleys—what men and women chanted and sung to each other to declare their affects (qing). Only those sections, "Odes of Zhou and the South" and "Odes of Shao and the South," had been changed by King Wen's personal influence to [statements] of virtue, through which people may rectify their natural dispostion (xingqing). Hence what they express in words are pleasing but not transgressive in being licentious, sad but not to the extent of being injurious.[111] For this reason only these two sections constitute the proper canon of the "Airs of States." From the "Airs of Pei" downward, the various states differed in being well or chaotically governed, and their people in their being worthy or not. Thus what they expressed in response to stimuli also

---

[109] For a helpful discussion of these two words, see van Zoeren, *Poetry and Personality*, pp. 162–66. I have not, however, adopted his translation of yi^4 as significance.

[110] *The Problem of a Chinese Aesthetic*, p. 108.

[111] A slightly expanded quotation of *Analects* 3. 20.

possessed the asymmetry of rectitude and perversion, of right and wrong. The so-called Airs of former kings, on account of this, underwent a change.[112]

This statement by the venerated Song thinker and teacher, a reply to a rhetorical question on the reason for the difference of forms obtaining in the main sections of the *Poetry Classic*, makes apparent the various strands of complementary emphasis converging to align literary history and genre theory with the topoi of "moral history."[113] The central thrust of this summation once more relies on the ascribed character of the odes, depicted as a kind of ethical and political barometrics that constantly calibrates the expression of that all-important human element, *qing*.

A poetics of such concern, moreover, is not confined merely to critics of premodern times. A contemporary reading of the "Great Chariot" by Chen Zizhan also may betray the attempt to purify the acts and the emotions.[114] Whereas in the "Lesser Preface" the erotic is merely the instrument of political satire or critique, the modern reading purges it completely by changing the alleged historical referent. Chen takes his cue from the fact that the ode's last stanza is quoted verbatim in a story about one Lady Xi found in the *Lienüzhuan* (Biographies of Women). Taken captive by the conquering King of Chu and forced into his harem, the lady comforted her defeated husband (now a door-man in the king's palace) with the pledge of undying fidelity and a recitation of the ode's last stanza, cited in the tale as her own spontaneous composition. Thereafter, both she and her husband committed suicide that same day. Commended by the Chu King for her chastity and righteousness, the two were accorded burial rituals befitting feudal lords.[115] In Chen's differently historicized reading of the ode, therefore, the poem, far from being a passionate invitation to elopement, becomes an equally ardent declaration of spousal loyalty that would win high Confucian praise.

Chen's interpretation takes for granted the literal accuracy of the tale thus recorded, for his reading depends crucially on the truth of Lady Xi's association with those ringing words of the last stanza. For Chen and the textual authorities he cites, in fact, that last stanza might well have been the generative unit for the entire ode in antiquity, its nobility of rhetoric justifying its ultimate inclusion in the "Royal Domain" section of the anthology. It never dawned on Chen that the reverse could equally be true, that a portion of the ode was appropriated by the Han compilers of the biographies to authenticate the exemplarity of Lady Xi's behavior.[116] Indeed, no one reading the biographies should fail to notice

---

[112] *Zhu wengong wenji, juan* 76, 13b-14a (*SBCK*). For a translation of the complete Preface, see Richard John Lynn, "Chu Hsi as Literary Theorist and Critic."

[113] An apt phrase from Owen, *Readings in Chinese Literary Thought*, p. 47.

[114] In *Shi Jing zhijie*, 1: 225–26.

[115] For the story, see *Lienüzhuan, juan* 4, 4b (*SBBY*); an English translation may be found in Albert Richard O'Hara, *The Position of Woman in Early China*, pp. 112–13.

[116] The various documents and commentators of the ode cited by Chen had as their principal

that the organizational principle of grouping these stories of women lies in the taxonomy of virtues (Lady Xi's entry being included in the section on "Chastity and Obedience"), or that the various biographies routinely cite—often out of context, as is characteristic of Confucian discourse—the *Poetry Classic* as a proof text for assessing character and event.

In its exclusive emphasis on the last stanza, Chen's interpretation wreaks havoc on the ode's preceding two, as can be seen from his own vernacular translation. Instead of reading *zi* as the word for you in the final lines (i.e., "I fear you don't dare," "I fear you won't run off"), Chen makes the word a title and *zi* thus becomes, for him at least, an ellipsis of Chu Zi or the Prince of Chu. Although such a move may be defended on a strict philological basis, it turns poetic sense into nonsense, for Chen's translation makes the woman say in the stanzaic punch lines: "Could I not think of you!/But fearing the Chu Prince I dare not! . . . Could I not think of you!/But fearing the Chu Prince I'll not flee!" Understandable sentiments for a woman in Lady Xi's situation, but hardly conducive to the heroic commitment declaimed in the last stanza or the ensuing act of self-immolation.

Lest there be any doubt that still lingered about how the expressive signs were to be safeguarded, the Confucian discourse sought to stabilize the very character of the affects themselves as they are manifest in verbal artifacts. To do this, the motive to create itself had to be secured, as can be seen from the following two remarks. I quote first from the *Jinglun* (Discussions of Classics) by the Southern Song minister Li Liwu:[117]

> In my youth I read the "Ballad of Drooping Corn" by the Viscount of Ji and became so sad that tears flowed.[118] A little older I read the "Crafty Youth"[119] from

---

concern only the lady's historical identity. Their protracted discussion thus dealt with such questions as who Lady Xi was and whether she had another name. No one worried about the issue of the rhetorical use of the odes in the tales.

[117] Cited in Chen Zizhan, *Shi Jing zhijie*, 1: 264. Li, who refused further civil service after the Song's demise, was a friend of the loyalists Wen Tianxiang and Xie Fang. For a brief account of his life and work, see Huang Zongxi, comp., *Song-Yuan xuean, juan* 28.

[118] The story of this ballad (another name of which is "A Dirge for the Yin [*Shangyin cao*]") is to be found in the *Shiji*, where it is recorded that Viscount Ji, on his way to the Zhou court, was deeply saddened by the ruins of the old Shang capital, now overgrown with corn and millet. The sight made him want to weep, but fearing that tears might "render him too much like a woman," he composed the ballad instead to mourn the site. Part of the ballad goes: "The corn is flourishing,/The grains are luxuriant./O, that crafty youth!/He is not good to me." People understood that by "crafty youth" he was referring to King Zhou (the last ruler of the Shang). The remnant of Shang all wept when they heard it.

[119] This is the ode, "Jiaotong (Mao 86)," which reads:

> O, that crafty youth!
> He does not talk to me!
> It's because of you
> That I'm unable to feed.

the "Airs of Wei" and my licentious mind (*yinxin*) began to grow. When I went out and beheld some women who were my neighbors, they all seemed to be inviting me with their eyes and beckoning with their hearts. Feeling guilty led me to self-examination. Now these two lines—"O, that crafty youth!/He is not good to me"—I read them at one place and they produced feelings of loyalty (*zhongxin*); at another place, and they produced feelings of licentiousness (*yinxin*). Could these poetic lines have two meanings? It must be the fault of the poem's interpreter who, however, should be more careful. For it has ever been the case that whenever there is friction between ruler and subjects, between friend and friend, [the poet] will entrust the matter to words to satirize it. There are many "Airs of State" that employ this style. Interpreted with recklessness, they become contaminated and lost to licentiousness. The ancient doctrine that classics have no deviousness, I suppose, cannot be at all like this.

Whether Li had ever made this remark is not at issue here, nor is the question of whether the poem "Crafty Youth" is indeed a so-called licentious poem (*yinshi*)—a topic of raging debate among scholars down through the dynastic periods.[120] Of greater pertinence and interest, rather, are Li's reported reactions to the two poems and how he proposed to reconcile them. The first problem we must notice in Li's remarks is his hasty identification of the two poems as having the same lines. No doubt the construction and diction are virtually identical, but within the compact economy of ancient Chinese poetry, the difference of a single word can indeed make a difference. In the "Ballad of Drooping Corn," the line in question is: "O, that crafty youth!/He is not good to me (*bu yu wo hao*)." The line's meaning is ambiguous because good (*hao*) is a rather general description. Detached from any contextual illumination, the subject of unkindness may be a lover, a superior, a friend, or a relative. How we are to give content to the word "good," however, depends on who we think the "crafty youth" is. More knowledge is, therefore, needed, but once it is supplied (in this case by the Grand Historian), one may thereby accept both the people of Yin's understanding that "crafty youth" is a veiled reference to King Zhou and Li Liwu's sympathetic response to such a plaint about royal neglect and negligence.

By contrast, the two stanzas bearing the title of the same two words preserved in the anthology detail not only the concrete instances of the subject's un-

---

O, that crafty youth!
He does not eat with me!
It's because of you
That I can't rest at all.

[120] I have not been able to discover whether the *Jinglun* still exists. Li's remark was cited by the Qing scholar Shi Runzhang in his lectures on poetry. The lecture notes, in turn, were compiled by Mao Qiling and edited as the book, *Bailuzhou zhike shuoshi*. See Chen, *Shi Jing zhijie* 1: 263.

friendliness (refusal to converse, to eat together) but also the poetic speaker's resultant grief (inability to eat, loss of sleep). The specificity of action and condition in these lines betoken a far greater degree of intimacy—whether actual or longed for—between speaker and subject. The intimacy makes apparent that the "crafty youth," however the identity of this person is to be construed, is very much an object of the speaker's desire, manifestly with erotic overtones. Such a perception, in turn, explains the equally sympathetic response of reader Li Liwu, the "naturalness" of his transferring the identity of the ode's addressee to himself and reading the women of the neighborhood into the sign system of the text.

When Confucian nurture and culture intervene to alert Li to the present danger of his own desire, his movement of resistance does not attempt a different construal of textual meaning by taking into careful account the difference between the two texts, as I have just tried to elucidate. Rather, his is an effort—one that ought to be familiar to all readers of the Han prefaces to the odes—to displace the text's literal meaning by announcing for the ode a different sort of intention: "whenever there is friction between ruler and subject, between friend and friend, [the poet] will entrust the matter to words to satirize it." For Li as well as for the entire tradition of premodern Chinese poetics, one may argue, it does not take a disjunction of ontological realms or dualistic metaphysics to bring forth the allegorical. The deliberate manipulation of the creative will is all that is required to exploit the essentially algebraic nature of linguistic signs and produce the ironic or the satiric, both modes of discourse that use one thing to say something else.

What is of supreme importance for us to notice at this point is that this intent to manipulate, the impulse to allegoresis, is always an asserted intent, a claim that the sequence of signs one sees (or even hears) does not mean what it seems to mean. For example, the statement "Monkey is a heroic character" can be literal, ironic, or allegorical, but by itself it cannot suggest that its reader/audience should take it as anything but literal. To move beyond that semantic level of understanding, it requires further contextualization in the form of a direct statement ("By that I mean . . ."), or an elaborate scheme of rhetorical clues and directives (by writing a hundred-chapter novel to try to illustrate what I mean), or an interpretive assertion by someone else as reader-author ("what Anthony Yu means by this statement . . .").[121] In distinguishing between

---

[121] I thus agree with E. D. Hirsch's attempt to clarify his position advanced in his widely discussed book, *Validity in Interpretation*, in which he argued for authorial intention as the normative determinant of meaning in the act of interpretation. Much of the controversy spawned by the book centers on the questions of whether authorial intention means the original author and how we determine that intention. In a current essay, Hirsch seems to have come to the conclusion that author should be regarded as a logical and functional rather than an empirical category in this debate on hermeneutics. See E. D. Hirsch, Jr., "Transhistorical Intentions and the Persistence of Allegory."

different levels of semantics, one further point of emphasis is in order: the discernment of the allegorical, the satiric, and the ironic—in sum, the non-literal—must depend on the posited existence of the literal. No linguistic construct can be said to be *intrinsically* ironic or satiric. It is only the presupposition of the literal meaning that the old adage—this does not mean what it says—makes sense at all. Thus puns, paronomasias, irony (often, the exact opposite of literal meaning), and allegory work as an assertion of difference in which the literal must enjoy tacit recognition.[122]

This brief excursion into semantics should now enable us to see more clearly the significance of Li Liwu's claim about poems like "Crafty Youth." First, the typing of this ode as satire (*feng*) simply echoes the precedent set by the "Lesser Preface": "it criticizes *(ci)* negligence: inability to seek service from a worthy person because powerful subjects are usurping [the ruler's] command."[123] Second, this claim about the modal change of the poetic discourse, from literal to satirical or admonitory, acknowledges the reality of the literal—in this case, the presence of excessive, if not downright illicit, desire. The claim thus may represent an attempt, in ancient Han no less than in the Song, to deflect poetic meaning from the morally dangerous embodiment of the oretic. For such a claim to attain its maximum weight, however, the Chinese interpreters realize that they must ground its authority finally on an assertion of direct knowledge of poetic intention, as is evident not only from the critical remarks I have cited, but also from another source in late imperial China. In his treatise on "Fuxue (Women's Learning)," the Qing Confucian Zhang Xuecheng declares unambiguously: "the ancients, when thinking of the ruler or yearning for their friends, frequently entrust such feelings to the depiction of ardent sentiments between men and women, much like how poets satirize (*feng*) or admonish (*ci*) perversity and licentiousness (*xieyin*)."[124]

Zhang Xuecheng's contention, of course, can find antecedent substantiation not merely in Han exegesis of the *Poetry Classic* but also in the rhetoric of the poet in *The Songs of the South* (especially in such sections as "Encountering Sorrow" and "Nine Pieces") and the writer of many Han rhapsodies. These

---

[122] This is true even of a statement in which the linguistic signs seem to be signifying two things at once. Jacques Derrida uses the statement, "I see giants," as an example. As a description of the object of vision, the statement, according to him, may be only metaphoric; but as an expression of fear, the statement can be labeled "literal." See *Of Grammatology*, pp. 275–76. Derrida's understanding, however, is premised on the supposed impossibility of "giants" in our common construal of the world as such. But if a young boy of five catches sight of five players on a professional basketball team and exclaims, "I see giants," that statement may well be meaningful as a literal one, and the emotions signified by the linguistic signs need not be confined to fear; they can range from astonishment to admiration.

[123] Ruan, *Shisanjing zhushu, juan* 4, 11a; 1: 173.

[124] *Wenshi tongyi, juan* 5, 29a (SBBY). For a recent study of the entire treatise, see Susan Mann, "'Fuxue' (Women's Learning)."

texts indeed reveal the direct and explicit tendency of the court poet to assume the voice and role of the female and "to represent the ruler-subject relationship in gendered terms (e.g., the emperor as the absent lover, the poet-minister as the abandoned woman)." That act of appropriation betokens both the poet's aspired aim to teach and his self-serving desire to ingratiate, for as Wai-yee Li astutely analyzes the matter, "feminine self-adornment" as elaborated in Han *fu* often "unfolds through the interplay of seduction and instruction."[125]

This imposed transference of voice and role can become a standard practice in Chinese literary history precisely because it can serve so well the Confucian goal of camouflaging and containing desire. If Li Liwu's poet can entrust political and social friction to a certain kind of words (*tuoyan*) for representation, Zhang Xuecheng's observation asks for an even more thoroughgoing program in the prevenient transferrence of subjectivity (*tuoqing*). Allegoresis is an ethical, and thus also a political, necessity because, as van Zoeren contends, "the traditional promise of the Odes had been to provide a kind of model—a *zhi* 'aim' in the medieval hermeneutic, an *yi* 'intention' in the Song version—around which the personality of the reader was to form itself."[126] That personality, it goes without saying, must have another worthy personality as its object of emulation. The question of whether a morally troubling spectacle can nonetheless yield legitimate visions of learning and pleasure (such as we find in Aristotle's theory of tragedy) or whether an ethically flawed sensibility can nonetheless produce an enduring and ennobling fiction (such as we find animating Wayne Booth's *The Company We Keep: An Ethics of Fiction*) can command scant sympathy in this sort of poetics.

Because Confucian poetics has little basis to sanction the representation of what it considers illicit desire, an inevitable paradox ensues: tragedy in real life and history may abound, but tragedy in art brooks meager toleration. Even the merest hint of possible excess must be checked by interpretation. The first poem of the *Poetry Classic*, familiar to every schoolboy (and some educated girls) in premodern China, is ostensibly a poem celebrating a young man's romantic passion. Because, however, its opening line mentions in passing ospreys, a bird whose alleged behavior might prove an edifying model, the Han commentator leaps to its elaboration.

> Ospreys are passionate but observe separation [of the sexes]. . . . The consort delights in her lord's virtue, always seeking to fulfill his wishes, and yet does not lead him to become infatuated with her beauty. She is careful, constant, retiring, and pure, just as are the ospreys with their separation of the sexes. As a consequence, [the consort] is able to change [*feng-hua*] the world. *When husband and wife keep apart, fathers and sons are close; when fathers and sons are close, the*

[125] Li, *Enchantment and Disenchantment*, p. 19.
[126] *Poetry and Personality*, p. 247.

relation of ruler and subject is one of respect; when the relation of ruler and subject is respectful, all is proper at court, and when all is proper at court, the royal influence [wang-hua] is complete.[127]

The political obligation of displacing one kind of desire by another, established by Confucian exegesis more than two millennia ago, retains remarkable constancy. The ardent sentiments of men and women (*nannü yinqing*), according to Zhang Xuecheng's prescription in the Qing, can expect legitimation only in the guise of normative patriarchal desire.

The foregoing discussion should make it apparent that in the Confucian discourse on desire—structured in literature (poetry), poetics (commentary, philosophy), ethics, politics, and history—there is an interlocking network of meaning governing its understanding of subjectivity, of the nature and operative modalities of the affective disposition called *qing*. When we examine the word's appearance from antiquity to later periods, the valorization of the affective as the essential not only colors and problematizes its usage, particularly in literary contexts, but it also decisively influences the Chinese notions of language and representation.[128]

The expressive theory of the arts to which we have alluded in previous sections avers that the essential as aroused subjectivity (e.g. *qing dong yu zhong*) would give rise to the activities of poetry, song, and dance, in such a way that "the more profound the feeling (*qing shen*), the more manifest would be the pattern (*er wen ming*)."[129] Even the disposition or "state of mind" of the sage, his *qing*, will become manifest in words.[130] In the stimulus-reponse conception of how humans and things interact, the aroused mind-and-heart (*xin dong, dongxin*) is thus frequently the equivalent to the aroused disposition (*qing dong, dongqing*). If things could "sway the natural disposition (*yaodang xing-qing*)," as Zhong Rong (469–518) asserts in the "Preface" to his *Shipin*,[131] speech and writing as the "sound (*sheng*)" and "picture (*hua*)" of the mind are "that by which both the superior man and the petty man [indicate] an aroused disposition."[132] This grand motif of the complex association uniting human subjectivity, stimuli, behavior (inclusive of speech, gesture, and all other sign systems of song and dance), language, and form will reverberate in documents dating from the pre-Han to the Tang.

Emerging from this development comes another conviction foundational to Chinese literary aesthetics, that the affective and emotive can be effectively

---

[127] *Maoshi zhengjian, juan* 1, 2b. I quote the fine translation by Haun Saussy in *The Problem of a Chinese Aesthetic*, p. 97; emphasis mine.

[128] An exhaustive survey of this topic is to be found in Siu-kit Wong's "*Ch'ing* in Chinese Literary Criticism." Wong's thoroughness is not quite matched by analytic precision.

[129] The clause occurs at least twice in book 19 of the *Liji*.

[130] From book 2 of the *Xici zhuan*. See *Zhouyi jinzhu jinyi*, p. 416.

[131] *Shipin, juan* 1, 1a (SBBY).

[132] Yang Xiong (53–18 B.C.E.), *Fayan, juan* 5, 3b (SBBY).

transmitted in language. Verbal art can reach the exalted height of what, in later periods, is called "the composition of sentiment (*qingwen*)" because language is believed to have the capacity for transparent conveyance of feelings and emotions. One early and unambiguous affirmation of such a belief is found in Ban Gu (32–92), celebrated historian and rhapsody writer:

> To the extent that poetry becomes a branch of learning, it concerns nothing but the nature and dispositions (*xingqing*). The qualities of the five viscera are not mutually injurious; the six affects alternate in flourishing and decay. One observes nature (*xing*) by means of what has been experienced; one observes disposition (*qing*) by means of metrics (*lü*).[133]

If Ban Gu's statement seems to anticipate T. S. Eliot's dictum that prosody is a product of heightened emotions, it is hardly surprising.[134] The Chinese emphasis, though it does not focus entirely on formal properties of poetry, does accentuate with Eliot the linguistic capacity for the communication of feelings and even ideas about feelings. Poetry is thus an activity that "intones and sings of the dispositional nature (*yinyong qingxing*)," as many authors during the Wei-Jin Six Dynasties period routinely assert, but the meaning of this venerable formula from the "Great Preface" would undergo steady transformation.[135]

The original context of that formulation makes the familiar justification of allegory on the ground of political necessity: "The historians of the states understood the traits of success and failure. Because they mourned the abolition of proper human relations and lamented the severity of governance by punishments, they intoned and sang of their dispositional natures in order to criticize those above."[136] In this view of Han Confucianism, the alleged practice of the *Poetry Classic* could find no better corroboration than the utterances by the frustrated poet in *The Songs of the South*:

> Grieving, I make my plaint,
> to express my feelings (*shuqing*).

---

[133] Ban Gu, "Biography of Yi Feng," in *Han Shu, juan* 75. The language of this passage may well be related to the microcosmic side of the correlative cosmology flourishing in the Han, in which the five viscera are thought to be generative of different emotive and moral qualities. See the chapter on "Disposition and Nature" in the *Bohu tongde lun, juan* 8.

[134] Poetry, according to Eliot, is an effective medium to communicate emotions, thus making it also an effective means to arrive at the general or the universal. "The human soul in intense emotion strives to express itself in verse. . . . if we want to get at the permanent and universal we tend to express ourselves in verse." See T. S. Eliot in *Selected Essays*, p. 46. He declares further in *On Poetry and Poets*, p. 87, that "the peculiar range of sensibility can be expressed by dramatic poetry, at its moments of greatest intensity. At such moments, we touch the border of those feelings which only music can express."

[135] Zhong Rong, "Preface" to *Shipin, juan* 1: 1a (*SBBY*); Pei Ziye, "Diaoconglun," in *Quanliangwen, juan* 53, 16a (*SGLCW*); Xiao Gang, "Yu Xiaodongwang shu," in *Quanliangwen, juan* 11, 3b (*SGLCW*).

[136] *Maoshi zhengjian, juan* 1: 1b (*SBBY*).

I set out in verse my secret feelings (*weiqing*),
    to offer and send to the Fair One.
With whom could I enjoy the fragrance thus left behind?
Long I faced the wind, giving vent to my feelings.[137]

For countless Chinese readers of Qu Yuan down through history, lyricism provides the apposite and privileged outlet for thwarted political desires.[138]

Zhong Rong's articulation of the formulation, on the other hand, makes a different but audacious claim about language. Poetry not only facilitates untrammeled transmission of the affects and desires, but, as Lu Ji alleges, "follows (i.e., in accordance with) *qing* [of a given particular subject or occasion] and becomes sensuously refined and elegant (*shi yuan qing er qimi*)."[139] Just as Confucius himself and the "Great Preface" tradition of exegesis had declared that musical tones could be imbued with certain moral qualities because of *qing* in its double guise as feelings and desires, so now language could itself directly attain affective characteristics as a result of its potent impact. *Qimi*, if Xiao Huarong's annotation is accepted, refers to the "luminous transparency of language (*yuyan di xianming*) and the refinement of description."[140] A genre such as threnody (*lei*) defines itself by the very emotive quality of its diction, according to Lu Ji in the *Wenfu*, but Liu Xie makes the relations between word and sentiment more comprehensive. "Just as paintings give forms to colors, literary phraseology exhausts the disposition (*qing*). Whereas differing colors produce dogs and horses of different shapes, the variegated disposition (*qing-jiao*) varies the styles from gracefulness to vulgarity."[141] Such an assertion would help to establish in subsequent literary history a taxonomy of both poetry and prose that is based on stylized subjectivity. Since the moods and emotive qualities are felt to be enshrined in language, large segments of a major genre such as the Song lyric (*ci*), for example, have been divided according to an

---

[137] The citations are from the "Xi Song (Grieving I Make My Plaint)," the "Chou Si (Outpouring of Thoughts)," and the "Yuan You (Far-Off Journey)" chapters of the anthology.

[138] See the discussion in Xiao Huarong, "'Yinyong qingxing'—Zhong Rong shige pingpan di lilun jichu." Xiao's essay, however, seeks to differentiate between the position of *shi yan zhi*, which he allies with the Confucian emphasis of political and moral didactics, and the position of *shi yan qing*, which he sees, at least in the usages of Lu Ji and Zhong Rong, as a beginning of literary aestheticism.

[139] Lu Ji, *Wenfu, juan* 17, 7a (SBBY). This famous idiom of Lu should be understood in the light of similar linguistic constructions found in his other writings. In the "Rhapsody on Thinking about Retirement [*Sigui fu*]," Lu has the line, "Grief follows *qing* and seduces itself." In the "Rhapsody on Lament of Transience [*Tanshi fu*]," he declares, "Sorrow follows *qing* and comes to reside." See *Lu Shiheng ji, juan* 3, 3a. Both lines indicate a conception of *qing* as the essential disposition of a human subject, a thing, or an event that, in turn, occasions specific affective response (such as grief, sorrow, joy, and so on).

[140] Xiao, "Yinyong qinqxing," p. 167.

[141] *Wenxin diaolong, juan* 6, 30: 24a.

index of either "delicate restraint (*wanyue*)" or "heroic abandon (*haofang*)."[142] From the point of view of traditional Chinese poetics, therefore, literary language is nothing if not pathocentric, in the sense that the orientation of thought is toward an order of meaning that presumes the unproblematic presence of subjectivity, the immediate and accurate representation of the inner by the outer.[143] The concept of *qing* as emotion, desire, and cognition is conceived as a self-existing foundation.

As developed by the literati of the Wei-Jin Six Dynasties period, this pathocentricism acquires the significantly new characteristic of being both projective and imagined. It is not accidental that persons like Lu Ji, Zhong Rong, and Liu Xie all advance repeated claims on the writer's unrivaled capability of transcending space and time. In his discussion of "thinking by means of spirit (*shensi*)" (chap. 26 of *Wenxin diaolong*), Liu Xie emphasizes not merely the writer's mental ability to think across ages and geography but also his capacity to depict the imagined or the inanimate "feelingly." The operation of such "divinatory thought"—another possible translation of *shensi*—both liberates the writer from the bondage of rules or laborious effort and inserts the human into the represented objects, in such a way that "ascending mountains, one's dispositon (*qing*) will fill the mountains, and viewing the seas, one's intent (*yi³*) will overflow the seas."[144] This projective subjectivity that at once

---

[142] For brief discussions of these concepts of lyric criticism, see Pauline Yu, "Introduction" to her *Voices of the Song Lyric in China*, and Shuen-fu Lin, "The Formation of a Distinctive Generic Identity for *Tz'u*." Although these two labels enjoy established relations with the genre of lyric, prose can also be characterized as "heroic," "warm and refined," and so forth.

[143] My rehearsal of this pathocentricism obviously relates to what certain modern Chinese scholars have termed "the lyrical tradition (*shuqing chuantong*)" in Chinese literary history. In his brief pioneering essay, "*Zhongguo di shuqing chuantong*" (collected in *Chen Shixiang wencun*, pp. 31–37), Chen Shixiang made the perceptive (though undocumented) observation that "from the point of view of its totality, it is no exaggeration to say that China's literary orthodoxy is one of lyricism (*shuqing di daotong*)" (p. 34). In "Lyric Vision in Chinese Narrative," Kao Yu-kung [Gao Yougong] has developed the notion of expressive lyricism into a conceptual category for the criticism of fictive narratives. The final section of his two-part essay, "Wenxue yanjiu di meixue wenti," also makes the familiar linkage between lyricism and the "expression of intent (*yanzhi*)" (p. 44–45).

The merit of Chen and Kao's views notwithstanding, there are problems—both linguistic and philosophical—with the use of the word "lyric" as the customary translation of *shuqing*. Relative to etymology, lyric (Gk. *lyra*, a lyre) would appear to have more to do with musical and auditory features than with emotive expressivity as such. Lyric in the Classical view of the West simply means any non-narrative and non-dramatic verse and not by definition a privileged vehicle for the emotions. In their formulation of the Chinese lyrical tradition, on the other hand, these theorists refuse to acknowledge the conjunction of *qing, zhi,* and desire (see Gao, "Wenxue yanjiu," p. 45). Such a denial obscures the pathocentric emphasis in the Chinese view of language and literature and thus also the correlative stress on regulation in both ethics and politics. For a more recent and realistic discussion, see Lü Zhenghui, *Shuqing chuantong yu zhengzhi xianshi*.

[144] *Wenxin diaolong zhu,* juan 6, 26: 1a.

animates the circumambient world and emotionalizes it through language antic-ipates the much discussed topic of "affective scene or setting (*qingjing*)" in later poetics.[145]

Consistent with his steadfast adherence to Confucian precepts, of course, Liu Xie throughout his lengthy treatise privileges what he thinks are real emo-tions of real persons. His preference for "literary compositions created for the sake of the emotions (*wei qing zuo wen*)" over "the emotions created for the sake of literary compositions (*wei wen zuo qing*)" is based on his belief that actual resentment produced the "Airs" and "Elegantiae" sections of the *Poetry Classic*. The philosophers, on the other hand, indulge in the rhetorical manip-ulation of their audience's disposition for the sake of personal gain, and their styles, according to Liu, thus tend to be "prolix and diffuse."[146]

Liu's conclusion that literary compositions "created for the sake of emo-tions would be measured and truthful"[147] can be contrasted with the view of Zhong Rong, who injects a stronger note of the imaginative into his poetics by virtue of his realization that an aroused disposition (*qing*) could be detected in certain *typical* situations.

> A felicitous gathering depends on poetry to inculcate intimacy, and separation relies on poetry for mourning. In such instances as when a Chu subject [i.e., Qu Yuan] departs from the state and a Han consort [i.e., Wang Zhaojun] takes leave of the palace; or when the bones are strewn in the desolate wilds and the souls chase after flying reeds; or when one bears arms at the frontier and his bellicosity dominates the border; or when the chilled wayfarer feels his garment's thinness and the widow her tears's exhaustion; or in those instances when a scholar unties his girdle-pendant to leave the court never to return, and a maiden receives imperial favor with uplifted brows, ready to topple the state with a second glance—in all these [situations] in which the mind-and-heart has been moved and swayed, what could unfold their meaning if not the recitation of poetry, and what could give rein to the disposition (*qing*) if not a lengthy song? Hence it is said, "poetry can promote group living and give voice to complaints."[148]

Notice that for Zhong Rong, the "truth" of literary composition is not neces-sarily premised on real emotions conveyed by actual human subjects, though no doubt he would regard Qu Yuan and Wang Zhaojun as true figures of history. Rather, the examples he cites point to circumstances—both recorded and imag-ined—that should create an air of typicality, a condition certain to produce the truthfulness of feeling. According to Xiao Huarong, the first sentence of Zhong

---

[145] For a fine study of Liu Xie on this point, see Zhang Shuxiang, *Shuqing chuantong di shensi yu tansuo*, pp. 63–84. For *qingjing*, see Cai Yingjun, *Bixing wuse yu qingjing jiaorong*.

[146] Ibid., *juan* 7, 31: 1b.

[147] Ibid.

[148] "Preface" to *Shipin*, 5b–6a. The terminal quotation comes from *Analects* 17. 9.

Rong in this section cited, in fact, denominates two basic kinds of feeling—pleasure (*huanqing*) and grief (*yuanqing*)—that can serve to categorize the subsequent representations of aroused subjectivity. Thus the meeting with friends and a maiden's reception of imperial favor both indicate pleasant occasions, while the rest of the examples all enumerate a lamentable condition.[149] As such, Zhong's list echoes and exemplifies the ancient classification of *qing* as joy, anger, grief, and pleaure. A closer scrutiny of Zhong's statement, however, should reveal that virtually all the examples of subjective arousal are also occasioned by desire, inasmuch as the upright scholar's resolute self-exile bespeaks his dissatisfaction with ruler and court, and a girl's exuberant facial expressions betoken her delight in the favor bestowed.

As typologies of desire, Zhong Rong's examples conventionalize the affects through standardization, a process in which the precedents of both historical and literary constructs become paradigmatic models. Zhong's remark, we should note, does not specify with any clarity who are the persons whose minds have been so moved and swayed that they would burst forth in poetry or song. If the question is put to him, Zhong Rong may well reply that he has in mind both the historical Qu Yuan and any literate person similarly situated. Thus he who would learn about political loyalty or a sense of integrity must liken himself and his own disposition to Qu Yuan, much as he who would understand desolation or loneliness should remember the poor wayfarer or the tearful widow. Literature can indeed fulfill the exalted ideal of sociality predicated by Confucius of the *Poetry Classic*, since even stock images and characters can transport us beyond the isolation of a private, independent subjectivity. They can do this precisely because the virtue of the imagination in literature is believed to lie not so much in the invention of the new and the particular as in the recollection of the typical. In this way the tradition of literature, as constituted by the Confucian discourse, functions once more as moral paideia (the material and process of education), for it serves both to guide the manifestation of *qing* and delimit its possibilities. To the extent that Qu Yuan is canonized in the tradition through interpretation and exegesis, one may emulate his solitary rectitude but one ought not to aspire to be wilder or more unrestrained than "the mad poet of Chu." Hence Liu Xie can conclude that "poetry is regulation—that which regulates the dispositional nature (*qingxing*) in humans. The single meaning of the entire three hundred poems in the *Poetry Classic* may be summarized as 'no deviant thought.' To teach that poetry is regulation tallies with [Confucius'] observation."[150]

Liu Xie's all too orthodox definition of poetry, following Confucian glosses, may conveniently return us to the initial topic of discussion of this chapter—the philological disputation on the word *qing*. A. C. Graham, we recall, has

---

[149] Xiao, *Yinyong qingxing*, p. 172.
[150] *Wenxin diaolong zhu, juan* 2, 6: 1a.

argued that the word in classical antiquity means something like "essence" or "the essential," never "passion" in the pejorative sense. His conclusion, as it stands, is not incorrect, for *qing* is, indeed, the essential not merely in the human but in the myriad objects of the whole universe. Such an understanding also accounts for the stubborn Confucian insistence that, in principle, it should never be denied or suppressed, let alone subjected to eradication. As can be seen in the discussions of other ancient writers, however, the semantic field of *qing* has a reach and range far beyond Graham's limited philological excursions; not unlike the vast literature on emotions in the West, the Chinese thinkers from pre-Han to the pre-Tang periods have already included in their conceptualization of the term elements of what we today would denominate as affect, desire, and cognition.[151] Arguably, in fact, the distinctive contribution of ancient Chinese thinkers to the topic is their widespread contention that desire undergirds as much our affective stirrings as it does our moral or political strivings.

As we have seen in our readings of Xunzi and related thinkers, there is the repeated argument that we humans have the same feelings (the seven *qing*) of pleasure or grief only because we have the same likes and dislikes, the same responses to food and sex as our basic appetitive needs. This insight into the crucial link of desire with affect, it must be pointed out, is often lost on modern Chinese scholars, who never tire in their attempt to distinguish between what the vernacular refers to as the general affective ties binding all humans (*ganqing*) and the specially potent "boy-girl sentiments (*ernü shiqing*)." Such a distinction often bears the explicit assumption that the former constitutes the proper provenance of literature, whereas writings cut from the cloth of erotic love would be labeled too "confining and inviting of criticism."[152]

---

[151] For a convenient discussion of such an understanding of the emotions, see Justin Oakley, *Morality and the Emotions*. Though somewhat dated, the most informative survey of pertinent literatures on the subject in the West is still *Feeling and Emotion*, by H. M. Gardiner, Ruth Clark Metcalf, and John G. Beebe-Center.

[152] So, Xiao, *Yinyong qingxing*, p. 167. See also, for example, Zhou Ruchang, *Hongloumeng yu Zhongguo wenhua*, p. 219, citing a portion of Feng Menglong's "Preface" to his *Qingshi*. Reading Zhou's brief exegesis of Feng's remark, I find it astonishing that so erudite a person as he could miss so completely Feng's irony and the latter's pointed use of the venerable *qing-zhi* construction to highlight the Ming novelist's own unorthodox aspirations and attachments. Whereas Feng's remark thus articulates his strongest affirmation of the priority and pervasiveness of *qing* in human life, including the realm of erotic love (though that specific sentence is omitted in Zhou's citation), Zhou's comment resolutely insists that *qing* in Feng's conception has "nothing to do with the passion between young men and women." The discomfort with erotic attachments that leads the Chinese characteristically to allegorical displacement can be ubiquitously felt. Opening the "Preface" to a collection of his miscellaneous essays, the contemporary poet Zhang Cuo (Zhang Zhen'ao) announces: "When you finish reading this book, you should realize that the so-called private feelings of boys and girls (*ernü siqing*) are actually the great affairs of family and state (*jiaguo dashi*)." (See Zhang Cuo, *Ernü siqing*, p. 1). If even

Against such a strand of modern moralism, the bluntness of an ancient text like the *Record of Rites*—"Eat, drink, man, and woman: herein are found the great desires of the human. Death, destruction, poverty, and suffering: herein are found the great dislikes of the human"[153]—not only reveals and refreshes, but it can even inspire magnificent filmmaking in late twentieth century. Because the great desires indeed constitute "the essential" of the human condition, the paradox emerging from this Confucian discourse on human nature maintains that "the essential" cannot be granted unbridled manifestation. The actualization, the development, and the fulfilment of what is deemed the most fundamental and enduring in the human individual, the self—these obsessively recurrent themes of Western consciousness that pervade its literatures ranging from ancient epic and tragedy to the modern *Bildungsroman*—thus can expect little unqualified endorsement in traditional Chinese culture. For obvious reason as well, the canons of Confucian aesthetics repeatedly emphasize that the media of artistic representation must also function as their instruments of discipline.

Does this mean that Confucian misgivings about the wayward propensities of both poet and poetry have been able to curb the tide of affective stirrings and stifle thereby both creativity and expressivity? To find a firmly negative answer to this question, one has but to glance at a recent chronicle of banned books down through China's long history.[154] The lengthy list of such proscribed volumes is revealing: the persistence of writing stems directly from the persistence of the affects and thus of desire itself, and that stubborn combination is what induces perpetual conflict with an ethos determined to question desire's legitimacy. The opposition between desire's affirmation and its regimentation is thus also a longstanding one in traditional Chinese culture.

Although one may not agree completely with a modern historian's thesis that "the end of the Han dynasty witnessed the rise of individualism," since the meaning of individualism may significantly differ between that of the Han and that of the modern world, there can be no dispute that the Wei-Jin period was the first epoch of Chinese history in which many of the established Confucian tenets with respect to the social, political, and moral orders were radically

---

a poet like Zhang feels obliged to maintain that personal, erotic subjectivity must find its most meaningful expression only in the consciousness of the collective, as "affairs of family and state," then a critic of Chinese literature may find it difficult to fault Fredric Jameson's now famous verdict: "Third-world texts, even those which are seemingly private and invested with a properly libidinal dynamic—necessarily project a political dimension in the form of national allegory: *the story of the private individual destiny is always an allegory of the embattled situation of the public third-world culture and society.*" See "Third-World Literature in the Era of Multinational Capitalism," 69.

[153] *Liji xunzhuan, juan* 9, 8b.

[154] See *Zhongguo jinshu daguan*, edited by An Pingqiu and Zhang Peiheng. This interesting book on proscribed writings is admirably thorough in enumerating titles indicted in the imperial era but, of course, it has nothing to say about the period of Chinese history after 1911.

challenged.[155] Not only were the foundational relationships governing ruler and subject, parent and son, and husband and wife repeatedly questioned, but this revolt against normative moralism carried with it the audacious affirmation of nature and the untrammeled expression of affect and desire.[156] It is a familiar tale that Ruan Ji (210–263) achieves fame or notoriety for "destroying public morals" by indulging his passions and giving free rein to his nature. Criticized for going to see his sister-in-law in her parents' home and bidding her leave, thus violating the prohibition against contacts between such kin, Ruan replies, "Were the rites established for people like me?"[157] Assaulting the Confucian curriculum that seeks to curb desire with ritualism, Xi Kang (224–263) declares:

> The basic aim of the Six Classics lies in restraint and guidance, but human nature delights in following one's desires. Restraint and guidance go against one's wishes, but following one's desires is how we attain the natural (*ziran*, self-so). This being the case, the attainment of the natural does not stem from the restrictive Six Classics, and the foundation of perfecting one's nature does not rely on rites and laws that offend our *qing*.[158]

In a similar vein and even more pointedly, Xiang Xiu (c. 222–c. 300), to whom some have attributed the authorship of the *Commentary of Zhuangzi*, answers Xi with the following observation:

> Where there is life there is *qing*. If one follows *qing*, then one becomes natural. If one cuts it off and leaves it out entirely, then one is no different from the lifeless. Now could such a person be as worthy as someone alive? Furthermore, to indulge in such desires as the love of glory and the dislike of humiliation, the love of leisure and the dislike of exertion all arise from the natural. . . . What the living takes as pleasure is to be in touch with what one favors and loves—Heavenly principles and human relations, the gentle beauty that delights the mind, the glorious wealth that pleases one's aspiration. To enjoy the tasty delicacies is to express our five emotions; to indulge in songs and sensuality is to vent our natural vitality. This is the self-so [condition] of Heavenly principles—what is suitable for humans and what the Three Kings would not alter.[159]

Statements such as these lead Yü Ying-shih to argue that Wei-Jin sentiment and thought, despite twists and detours, constitute a direct line of influence

---

[155] Ying-shih Yü, "Individualism and the Neo-Taoist Movement in Wei-Chin China," p. 122; Thomas C. Heller et al., eds., *Reconstructing Individualism, Autonomy, Individuality and the Self in Western Thought*.

[156] Yü, "Individualism," pp. 122–25.

[157] From Gan Bao, *Jinji*, cited in *A New Account of Tales of the World*, translated b Richard B. Mather, pp. 372, 374.

[158] Xi Kang, "Nan Zhang Liaoshu ziran haoxue lun," in *Quan sanguo wen, juan* 50, 6b–7a (*SGLCW*).

[159] "Nan Xi Shuye yangsheng lun," in *Quanjinwen juan* 72: 6a–7a (*SGLCW*).

that reaches across the centuries to the author of *Hongloumeng*, for in his view the "anti-traditionalism" pervasive in the master narrative finds its mainspring precisely in the irreconcilable opposition of *qing* and ritualism.[160] Although the literary representation of that opposition, as both the primary materials and recent scholarship reveal, presents too lengthy and complex a history to be accounted for in the present study, the high points of its contour may be noted.

Despite a poetics of didactic moralism and remonstration that continuously analogizes desires between the sexes with relations between ruler and subject, the poetic tradition itself has never ceased to produce bodies of works that ill fit an allegorical hermeneutic. And, despite such convenient devices as coopting the feminine voice and equating an exiled subject with the abandoned woman exploited by the like of Cao Zhi (192–232) and countless other male poets, folk and literary specimens—perhaps authored by both sexes—abound in the *Yuefu shiji* (Collected Poems of the Music Bureau) and other preserved "ancient style poems (*guti shi*)" that seem to articulate the joys and sorrows of marital commitment. "Within a family system regulated by clan rules and customs," observes a contemporary critic, "deep spousal affection itself exercises a decentering (*lixin*) effect on despotic parental will."[161] The validity of this modern insight, however, has been anticipated by Ming iconoclasts like Li Zhi and Lü Kun—who would argue for a re-positioning of marriage as the primary of the Five Relations—and perhaps unwittingly affirmed by many poets.[162] The famous lyric to the tune of "Phoenix at the Hairpin's Tip (*Chaitoufeng*)" by Lu You (1125–1210), allegedly composed in anguish after he met again his wife whom he had been forced by his mother to divorce, might not have been sufficient protest to reverse maternal edict. But along with the wife's reply in the same tune, the poem has been justly canonized as a tribute to genuine affection born of marriage.[163]

Nursed in the experience of dream and fantasy and propagated by literary representation, such affection strives to perpetuate itself and thereby aspires to transcend the vicissitudes imposed by inhospitable space and time. Herein lies the seed of the utmost daring in a later drama, *The Peony Pavilion*, where "desire at its limit (*qing zhi zhi*)" would seek through invention to abolish even the boundaries of life and death.[164] For an imagination less given to a reach of such magnitude, the shorter and simpler form of the poetic elegy

---

[160] "Cao Xueqin di fan chuantong sixiang," *HLMYJJK* 5 (1980): 165.

[161] Kang Zhengguo, *Fengsao yu yanqing*, p. 132. For a brief discussion of the exiled subject as forsaken woman in comparative literature, see Lawrence Lipking, *Abandoned Women and Poetic Tradition*, pp. 127–34.

[162] For Li Zhi, see his *Fen Shu*, p. 90; for Lü Kun, see Joanna F. Handlin, "Lü K'un's New Audience," p. 34.

[163] For Lu's lyric, see *QSC* 3, 1585; for the reply by the wife, Tang Wan, see 3: 1602.

[164] For the text of the author's "Preface" to *The Peony Pavilion*, see Xü Shuofang, ed., *Tang Xianzu ji* 2: 1,093.

becomes a time-tested but no less potent vehicle for conveying remembrance, grief, and yearning. In this sense, the lyric to the tune of "River Town" by Su Shi (1037–1101) for Lady Wang accomplishes considerably more than the transformation of derivative diction and conventional topoi through "the substitution of deceased wife for deserted courtesan."[165] Similar to the group of elegies penned by the Tang poet Yuan Zhen (779–831), Su's poem arguably memorializes marital sentiment (*qing*) that stubbornly defies the reductive politics of interpretation structured in the Confucian discourse.[166]

Courtesans, abandoned or not, nonetheless augment significantly the field of literary representation that explores and celebrates the desires between the sexes. The increase of the number of "official courtesans (*guanji*)" in the Tang may also have multiplied, ironically, the number of literate women.[167] Literary activities of both those flourishing in court or aristocratic households and those living on the fringe of social respectability as palace consorts, song girls, courtesans, or Buddhist and Daoist nuns do not merely add to the records of history; they also complicate the whole question of the legitimation of desire in literature.[168]

On the one hand, both their own writings (which frequently give voice to distinctive women's concerns and grievances[169]) and their persons provide a potent impetus for male desire: the beautiful, talented woman who inhabits the sordid quarters of aristocratic or commercial entertainment can also in poetic self-representation appear to be the devoted lover. In depiction a quintessential symbol of purity and pollution in one body, a projected goddess and whore, her persona thus provides a damning contrast to the faithless (*wu qing, bo-xing*) and fickle poet-official (cf. Yu Xuanji's famous couplet: "Easier to acquire a priceless treasure/Than to land a man possessive of *qing*") and anticipates later male idealizing belief that it is woman, in or out of the home, who most peculiarly incarnates *qing*.[170] On the other hand, relations with such women

---

[165] Ronald C. Egan, *Word, Image, and Deed in the Life of "Shu Shi*," p. 317. For the text of Su's poem, see *QSC* 1: 300.

[166] For Witter Bynner's translation of three of the best-known, repeatedly anthologized elegies of Yuan Zhen, see *The Jade Mountain*, pp. 215–16; for the Chinese text, see *QTS* 4: 4,509.

[167] See the publications by Wang Shunu, Kishibi Shigeo, Ishida Mikinosuke, and Chen Dong-yuan.

[168] For examples see Hu Wenkai, *Lidai funü zhuzuo kao*, pp. 17–39. New translations of representative women poets of the Tang and other periods may be found in *An Anthology of Chinese Women Poets*, edited by K'ang-i Sun Chang and Haun Saussy.

[169] See examples cited by Chen Dongyuan, *Zhongguo funü shenghuo shi*, pp. 98–101. For a brief discussion of the three Tang women poets Li Jilan, Yu Xuanji, and Xue Tao, see Maureen Robertson, "Voicing the Feminine," pp. 74–79.

[170] On this point, the ideas of the Ming writer Lü Kun are representative. See Joanna F. Handlin, "Lü K'un's New Audience," pp. 13–38; also, *Action in Late Ming Thought*, pp. 149–60. For further important studies of women's poetry in late imperial China and the pervasive celebration of romantic love, see Paul S. Ropp, "Love, Literacy, and Laments"; K'ang-i Sun

not only continuously fuel the male tendency both to inscribe the frankest erotic within the lyric forms (e.g., Ouyang Xiu), or to colonize the feminine voice and experience, thereby authenticating its own moral existence and assuaging its political anxiety.[171] Ironically, the very expansion of this latter genre of writing undertaken in the guise of exploring "boudoir grievance (*guiyuan*)" and "boudoir condition/sentiment (*guiqing*)" may also have served to refine male poetic technique and sensibility in such a way that would not have been imaginable without the "sexual reversal."[172]

It is no accident that Yuan Zhen, author of some moving poetic tributes to his deceased wife Wei Cong, also composed a large body of glamorous/erotic verse (*yanshi*) possibly based on his affairs with his lovers. These two kinds of verse, as one modern scholar points out, provide in fact the typologies for the collection of Yuan's poems that the poet himself compiled.[173] That a poet so devoted to the celebration of heterosexual desire (*nannü qing*), licit or illicit, also happens to be the author of the tale *Yingying zhuan* should hardly occasion surprise, for the enduring appeal of that story (however one may assess finally the fate and self-understanding of its heroine) finds its most compelling testimony in its repeated reembodiments in dramatic form and in the kind of key motivational and rhetorical role it assumes in a later narrative such as *Hongloumeng*. In the context of our present discussion, however, the greater significance belongs to the fact that this work, like so many other preserved texts of the Tang tale (*chuanqi*), has immensely escalated the literary representation that exalts pathocentrism.

We have been concentrating our discussion on poetry and poetics, but the Tang tales, along with the developed dramas of the Yuan-Ming periods, radically increase the variety and the quantity of literary genres devoted to this theme, and thus directly affect later developments in the full-length works of prose fiction. If even centuries of moralistic exegesis cannot stifle a young girl's immediate, erotic response to one archaic poem in the *Poetry Classic*, as Tang Xianzu would comically stage for us, what sort of discursive symbolics

---

Chang, *The Late Ming Poet Ch'en Tzu-lung*, chapters 2 and 3, and her "Ming-Qing Women Poets and The Notions of 'Talent' and 'Morality.'"

[171] See Robertson, "Voicing the Feminine," p. 69: "In such poetry [i.e., that written by male Chinese poets], the dramatized speaking voice is marked as a form of feminine voice, but the source of this speech and the actual subject position is easily disclosed by the poems themselves. They indicate the eye of the voyeur in their presentation of passive, narcissistic women, romanticized suffering, and displays and inventories of boudoir furnishings and clothing. . . . They feature a non-referential, iconic image and projected voice, an empty signifier, into which the male author/reader may project his desire." Not all the male poets in China's lengthy tradition write in this mode. For significant exceptions in the later period of imperial history, see Paul Ropp, "A Confucian View of Women in the Ch'ing Period."

[172] Lipking, *Abandoned Women and Poetic Tradition*, p. 132.

[173] Chen Yinque, *Yuan Bai shijian zhenggao*, p. 81.

is needed to cope with hundreds, even thousands, of texts that are more accessible economically and linguistically? What will be the effect and fate of reading imposed by such narratives as *The Story of Jiaohong* (*Jiaohongji*) and *A Sequel to The Journey to the West* (*Xiyoubu*) and such dramas as *The Western Wing* and *The Peony Pavilion,* not to mention even more scandalous works as *The Plum in the Golden Vase* (*Jinpingmei*) or *The Carnal Prayer Mat* (*Rouputuan*)?[174]

The reception history of many literary works of the Ming-Qing period can thus appear as one long crisis of the containment of desire, indeed, but that development, as I have just intimated, has its antecedents. If the content of *The Anatomy of Love* (*Qingshi leilüe*) by Feng Menglong (1574–1646) shows its compiler "focusing on the point at which the heroic and romantic meet," as Patrick Hanan has observed, that kind of meeting surely could find notation and exploration as early as such medieval tales as "Han Ping and his Wife (*Han Ping qi*)" and "The Maid Who Sold Mercuric Powder (*Maifener*)" of the Wei-Jin period, and "Li Wa," "Bu Feiyan," and "Miss Ren (*Renshi zhuan*)" of the Tang.[175] Although many such compositions may well betray the belief that "female sexuality is fraught with inherent dangers" requiring suppression or regulation,[176] there are just as many others that portray women of such gallantry, generosity, and fidelity that they must be hailed as mimetic models. Thus Miss Ren, a woman conceived as the monstrous Other (*nüyao*), validates at the story's end the narrator's conclusion that "the disposition of a strange creature (*yiwu zhi qing*) can find its human embodiment (*you ren ye*)," and that her proper appreciation requires fathoming her dispositional nature (*qingxing*) and not merely delighting in her beauty.

To advocate understanding the female on her own terms is already to challenge the foundational hierarchy long established, much as to privilege *qing*, especially the affects between the sexes, as both the educative and regulative force in life potentially subverts the norms of orthodoxy. What Feng Menglong declares in the long pentasyllabic *gāthā* of his "Preface" to the *Anatomy* through his proposed "religion of the affects (*qingjiao*)" is nothing short of a trans-

---

[174] For an informative study of the novel *Jiaohongji* and late Ming cultural predilections, see Richard G. Wang, "The Cult of *Qing*"; for what may have been a shared fund of motifs between *Xiyoubu* and *Hongloumeng*, see Chow Tse-chung, "*Hongloumeng* yu *Xiyoubu*." For the influence of *Jinpingmei* on *Hongloumeng*, see Mary Elizabeth Scott, "Azure from Indigo."

[175] English translations of the first, third, fourth, and fifth stories may be found in *Traditional Chinese Stories*, edited by Y. W. Ma and Joseph S. M. Lau. The second tale, originally anthologized in Liu Yiqing's *Youminglu*, is preserved in Li Fang, comp., *Taiping guangji, juan* 274, 3: 2157.

[176] This is the conclusion of William H. Nienhauser, Jr. after studying three groups of texts, including the *Li Wa zhuan*. See his "Female Sexuality and the Double Standard in Tang Narratives." For further study of the transgressive nature of sexual love in Tang stories, see Feng Minghui, "Tang chuanqi zhong aiqing gushi zhi pouxi."

valuation of Confucian values: "With *qing* the unrelated become kin (*shu zhe qin*);/Without *qing* even kin become aliens (*qin zhe shu*)." Astonishing is the phenomenon now increasingly evident in the Ming wherein poetry, drama, prose fiction, philosophical treatise, anecdotal jotting, and epistolary writing all seemingly join to respond to Feng's call couched in Buddist diction: "I wish to gather all feeling/sentient persons (*you qing ren*)/To proclaim together this Dharma (*yiqi laiyan fa*)." To dilate or expound the Dharma (*yan fa*) of *qing* may indicate much more than a cultic indulgence in fetish and fad. Just as Feng's own compendium provides a capacious taxonomy of the various appearances, phenomena, or forms (Skt. *lakṣaṇa, nimitta*, Chin., *zongzong xiang*) of *qing*, so the sheer prolixity and scope of other writings in the Ming-Qing period distill the manifold manifestations of pathocentrism, now further complicated by the potent impact of Buddhism.[177] At a late stage of this movement will appear a narrative which, with its self-proclaimed intention of "speaking principally about *qing*," may have realized more than any other text the legitimation of this "religion's" law and truth.

---

[177] For the text of Feng's "Preface," see the front page of *Qingshi leilüe* (Qing edition).

CHAPTER III.

Stone

Though cold like you, unmov'd and silent grown,
I have not yet forgot myself to stone.
(Alexander Pope, *Eloïsa to Abelard*)

THE STONE OF FICTION

The previous chapter sought to indicate, by means of the constructed and partial genealogy of the Confucian discourse on desire, how this discourse may assist in contextualizing our study of *qing* in *Hongloumeng*, because the intent and subject of the narrative are declared specifically to be pathocentric (*da zhi tan qing*). We should note at once, however, that desire is introduced in the narrative by an awareness of imperfection (a cosmos that requires repair, a stone that has been rejected) and of lack—of need, dissatisfaction, and longing suffered by Stone as the mythic protagonist. From this perspective, it may be contended that from the very beginning, one principal problem that the novel addresses has to do not merely with the legitimacy of desire but also with its understanding. The mythic stone's origin, his dialogue with the mysterious clerics, his eventual and eventful sojourn to the world of Red Dust, and his final transformation into a scripted and carved stone all revolve around the questions of how desire is generated and experienced, and how it is to be represented and comprehended.

To explore those questions in relation to the larger narrative, we need to begin with the myth of Stone that frames the mundane story, bringing our discussion back to the end of Chapter I, where I have noted some of *Hongloumeng*'s rhetorical devices to dehistoricize its own content and context. For the text, in other words, the time signified concerning the tale's genesis stems from ambiguous antiquity. The tale of Nüwa's rejected stone and its preincarnate peregrinations, which endows the narrative with its "original" name and which ostensibly forms part of the narrator's attempt to spell out origin in detail (*ci shu cong he er lai*), repeatedly emphasizes surface absurdities masking authentic explanations. The assertion that the narrative lacks proper identification by dynastic reign and year explicitly serves to dissociate its function from the historiographic one of reinscribing the narrative time within the time of the universe—that is, within a specific chronological construct based in turn on a scale of time aligned with the "history" of the cosmos.[1] The location of the

---

[1] See Paul Ricoeur, *Time and Narrative* 3: 104–26 for a detailed rehearsal of this historio-

tale's origin within mythic temporality nonetheless purports to explain change, because undatable and unverifiable events are summoned to dispel the reader's perplexity (*shi yuezhe liaoran buhuo*) by revealing narrative logic, the motivation of the stone's entrance into the world of Red Dust. What seems at first glance to be no more than a conventional bit of plot construction, based on the popular notion of karmic reciprocity, actually plays a double, cardinal role of plot advancement and the establishment of textual identity. The principal motif of rock, stone, and jade, in sum, is used by the narrative to accentuate its own mode of existence, its fictiveness. This chapter purports to argue that the narrative is as much a story about a piece of stone (Stone as one protagonist) as it is about what that story is (Stone as script, as linguistic representation and fictive writing) and how it is to be received (the effect of reading Stone). Such an argument follows quite literally what the text itself suggests: that the experience of one novelistic protagonist—his need of and quest for enlightenment, for disentanglement from the net of desire (*qing*)—can also trope the process of genesis and reception of fiction. As well, it will be my contention that both the story of the Stone—told in such profound, human terms—and the reflexive drama of its telling and reading achieve their impact only if we reckon seriously with certain major themes in Chinese philosophy and religions.

Those themes and their nuanced import require us to begin by determining how Nüwa's story has been used in the tale's early pages. Scattered among ancient documents, the sources indicate that there are at least two major motifs embedded in the various and sometimes conflicting accounts of this famous goddess.[2] On the one hand, Nüwa and her frequently mentioned companion Fuxi seem to belong to part of creation mythology, although the pre-existence of the universe, as Derk Bodde has observed, denies them the status of true creators.[3] If her very name evokes the mystery of beginning, it is only the

---

graphic undertaking; and also Michel de Certeau, *The Writing of History*, pp. 88–99.

[2] Studies of the Nüwa-Fuxi story are numerous. I have found the following discussions informative: Wen Yiduo, "Fuxi kao" and "Gaotang shennü chuanshuo zhi fenshi"; Marcel Granet, *Danses et légendes de la Chine ancienne*, pp. 485–503; Mori Mikisaburō, *Shina kodai shinwa*, pp. 15–22; Izuishi Yoshihiko, *Shina Shinwa densetsu no kenkyū*, pp. 37–70, 325–43; Derk Bodde, "Myths of Ancient China," pp. 62–65; Yuan Ke, *Zhongguo gudai shenhua*, pp. 40–46; Wang Xiaolian, *Shenhua yu xiaoshuo*, pp. 13–57; K. C. Chang, "Zhongguo chuangshi shenhua zhi fenxi yu gushi yanjiu," and "A Classification of Shang and Chou Myths"; Yue Hengjun, "Zhongguo yuanshi bianxing shenhua shitan," pp. 159–72; Mao Dun, *Shenhua yanjiu*, pp. 63–93; Andrew H. Plaks, *Archetype and Allegory in the "Dream of the Red Chamber"*, pp. 27–42; Liu Chenghuai, *Zhongguo shanggu shenhua*, pp. 545–87; Martin J. Powers, *Art and Political Expression in Early China*, pp. 113–23, 263–69; Wu Hung, *The Wu Liang Shrine*, pp. 111–18, 156–57, and 245–47; and Jing Wang, *The Story of Stone*, pp. 42–62. This last title represents the most through examination of most of the sources on the motif of Nüwa and the symbolism of stone in Chinese lore known to me.

[3] The creation mythology derives notably from the *Fengsutong* as preserved in *TPYL* 1: 365 (*juan* 78, 5a); Bodde, "Myths of Ancient China," p. 65. I follow both Bodde's translation and interpretation here.

mystery of an unresolved etiology which invites the sort of questioning found in the "Tianwen" chapter of *The Songs of the South*: "Nüwa had a body. Who formed and fashioned it?" The infinite regressiveness of this query erodes her significance as any symbol of absolute beginning.

A different account, like that of *Huainanzi* 6: 7a (*SBBY*),[4] on the other hand, emphasizes the work of Nüwa as restorer and organizer of culture, because her recorded labors (fusing stones to repair the sky, cutting off turtle feet to prop it up, collecting reed ashes to check wild waters) redeem the wreckage caused by the arch rebel Gonggong. Whatever its separate origin, the story of Gonggong is intimately linked with the primal catastrophe of the Flood, because his ramming Buzhou Mountain, which capsized the support of heaven, might have also triggered the deluge.[5] His defeat and banishment thus readily symbolize the victory of Order over Chaos, and Nüwa's work of repairing the sky by refining or smelting five-colored stones may also be regarded as a crucial contribution to the establishment of Order.[6]

In his pioneering study of certain kinds of symbolism in *Hongloumeng*, Andrew Plaks has sought to join these two motifs discernable in the Nüwa myth—world parenthood through conjugal union with Fuxi and suppression of the forces of disorder—to fashion part of the archetypical underpinning of his reading. Thus the paradoxical separateness and unity of the primal couple, "originally two unrelated deities" but brought together in Han mythology and iconographically depicted, would be seen in Plaks's view as emblematic of "the Chinese cultural preference for the simultaneous presence of comple-

---

[4] Details echoed or varied in 1: 1a–b; Wang Chong, *Lunheng* 15: 15a-b (*SBBY*); *Liezi* 5: 3b (*SBBY*).

[5] William G. Boltz in "Kung Kung and the Flood," pp. 147–48, argues on structural and lexical grounds that Gonggong is a "personification of the Flood itself." Although his observations are not unpersuasive, his specific contention that the word *liu* as used in both the *Book of Documents* and *Mencius* ("Tengwen gong" section) means "to flow" seems highly questionable. *Liu* in this context simply refers to the longer banishment that formed part of the five punishments of antiquity: caning with bamboo (*chi*), caning with wood (*zhang*), shorter banishment (*tu*), and death. To *liu* Gonggong is to banish him for a long time, perhaps permanently, to the Land of Stygian Gloom (*youzhou*). It has little to do with the rebel's nature being "amenable to 'flowing' or being 'drained away'," as Boltz tries to establish in his exegesis, unless the ancient texts are punning.

[6] Granet, *Danses et légendes*, pp. 236–73; Boltz, "Kung Kung," pp. 145–48. See Plaks in *Archetype and Allegory*, p. 39: "The repair of the dome of Heaven now emerges as the reestablishment of the harmony of the universe after a temporary loss of equilibrium (what Lévi-Strauss might call the restoration of continuity out of discontinuity). Similarly, the fusion of five-colored stones for this purpose must reflect the harmonious ordering of the five elements necessary for maintaining this equilibrium, much like the corresponding orderly sequence of the eight trigrams ascribed to Fu-hsi." For further discussion of the connection of Fuxi and *Yijing* materials, notably the "Great Commentary" section, in Han art, see Wu Hung, *The Wu Liang Shrine*, pp. 160 ff.

mentary forms," a preference he finds pervasive in his delineation of narrative meaning and structure.[7]

Whatever merit this interpretation may have in illuminating the larger aspects of narrative design, it does not bring into sufficient relief the adumbration of beginning and motivation of the immediate story. As the text of the novel indicates, the tale of Nüwa is invoked solely as an agent of negativity in initiating the plot: of the thirty-six thousand, five hundred and one pieces she had melted to repair the sky, one was rejected, for lack of innate capacity or talent, as unworthy of selection (*du ziji wu cai, bu de ru xuan*). However it is to be explained and defined, the one element decisive of the stone's fortunes first concerns *cai*, a word variously written in ancient and modern script and perhaps best understood in this context as talent or native endowment.[8] It is this lack that propels the stone from the mythic to the mundane level of existence. As Martin Huang incisively comments on the passage:

> Dismay over the lack of opportunities to use one's talent is clear here. The number 36,501 is worth careful analysis: Nüwa uses only 36,500 blocks, the number of the days in a century (in the traditional Chinese calendar) and leaves one block unused (which is apparently superfluous). The symbolic implication of someone that is unwanted is obvious. Furthermore, in referring to the number of days of a calendar year, the author (or the narrator) calls attention to the powerful traditional idea of timing (*shi*) or "not being born in a right age" (*sheng bu feng shi*), [an idea which] played an important role in a literatus's rationalization of his political misfortune.[9]

Whether such "rationalization" indeed belongs to the novelistic author may always invite speculation, but there can be little denial that the Stone of the

---

[7] Hung, *The Wu Liang Shrine*, p. 117. Plaks, *Archetype and Allegory*, p. 40.

[8] The text of 1756 uses the word *cai* with the wood (*mu*) radical on the left side, and this graph is also used in several of the Red Inkstone manuscripts. The printed version of 1791/1792, however, changes the word to *cai* without the wood radical. Zhou Ruchang in *Hongloumeng xinzheng* 1: 15, takes this as decisive evidence for the redactor Gao E's political vulgarism. Zhou argues that *cai* with the wood radical means innate capacity or serviceability, a respectable diction of antiquity, whereas *cai* without the wood radical refers to the specific quality or qualification that renders a person fit for civil service through the examination system, a late word redolent of the career worm mentality. In view of the fact that these two words were considered interchangeable as early as the *Shuowen,* the first lexicon, and that *cai* without the wood radical was used exactly in the first sense throughout such ancient texts as the *Poetry Classic*, the *Analects*, the *Mencius*, and the *Kongzi jiayu*, Zhou's raging critique seems puzzling and baseless. Moreover, the full-length *Qianlong* manuscript also employs the *cai* without the wood radical. The two homophones appearing variedly in the Red Inkstone manuscripts and the first full-length versions (hand-copied or printed) thus might indicate no more than an editor's, a copyist's, or a typesetter's routine substitution and not a purposive subversion.

[9] *Literati and Self-Re/Presentation*, p. 86.

narrative's opening is afflicted at once with a keen, Miltonic sense of "an age too late," as the testimonial hymn (*gāthā*) on the inscribed Stone readily testifies.

> Found unfit to repair the azure sky
> Long years a foolish mortal man was I.
> My life in both worlds on this stone is writ:
> Pray who will copy out and publish it.
>
> (*SS* 1: 49; *HLM* 1: 4)

Straightforward as the meaning of this poem may appear to be, its language is not without problems. Most readers take the first line to be a declarative sentence, but the word *ke* (can, permit) renders the syntax ambiguous. If read as a rhetorical question (Could I, without talents, repair the azure sky?), the line would heighten the mournful, querying tone of the entire poem, stressing not merely the disqualification by divine verdict but also the poetic speaker's self-doubt and self-questioning. Was his banishment justified? Was he truly so unfit to take up the grandiose task of cosmic restitution?[10] The poem's second line, too, continues the ambivalent tone with the word *wang* (to waste, to wrong). If, on the one hand, it is taken in the sense of vain or futile, the word would substantiate the common reading that the life of the banished Stone on earth is as useless as its previous incarnation. Rejected for lack of native endowment to help in the mighty task of rebuilding the dome of the sky, the Stone even in the world of Red Dust remains incapable of altering its destiny. If, on the other hand, *wang* is construed as the sufferance of wrong or injustice, the line would strengthen the implicit voice of protest heard in the preceding line.

However such ambiguities are to be resolved with regard to the meaning of the events of "both worlds," the poetic speaker's desired resolution to have his experience, now already recorded and inscribed, transmitted (*qichuan*). The English "publish" of the cited translation lacks the allusiveness of the French *un merveilleux récit* (Li 1: 10), for *qichuan* echoes at once the idiom *wenshi chuanqi* (literally, to appear in the world and transmit the marvelous) struc-

---

[10] Zhou Ruchang in *Hongloumeng xin zheng*, 1: 33–37 follows the common view of interpreting *butian* (repairing the sky) as a symbol of cultural reformation through political office, which he takes to be the proper aspiration of Jia Bao-yu (!) and, of course, his creator, Cao Xueqin. However, Zhou also mentions (1: 38) several Qing authors, notably You Tong (1618–1704), who have titled their song or poetry collections *Butianshi* (The Sky-Repairing Stone), and argues that *butian* may thus be viewed as a metaphor for the use of literature as a private means of protest and idealization when the person is frustrated in his political aspirations. See also Cheng Peng, "Cao Xueqin 'butian' sixiang zai tantao." Although Zhou's comment in this context is particularly suggestive, it should be pointed out that some of the songs he cites (2: 811–37) from the dramas of You Tong are about the failure of a talented scholar to pass the examination (such as, the poem to the tune of "Jun tian yue") or the unrecognized beauty of Wang Zhaojun (such as, the poem to the tune of "Diao pipa"), themes certainly present in the novel but used for radically different purposes.

tured in the narrative (*HLM* 1: 4) and clearly intends to make a specific literary point. *Chuanqi* or the transmission of the marvelous, of course, designates first the short prose tale composed in the classical language dating from the Tang, and second the "southern style" dramas popular in the Ming-Qing periods. The salient characteristics of the prose tale include a stylized opening sentence providing names, dates, and places, the frequent use of an initial and terminal frame bracketing the main plot, the insertion of lyric poetry in the narrative, and explicit didacticism. As for the plays, the construction often involves multiple scenes (thirty to forty) for dramatic narration and the use of an artifact (hairpin, lute, fan) as an emblematic metaphor.

Hongloumeng, as we can readily see, incorporates and exploits all these characteristics for its own purpose. Some longstanding devices are radically altered or parodied, as when the opening of the narrative, instead of indicating pertinent names, dates, and locales, teases and baffles us with layered beginnings and amphibolous geography. When the allegorical figure Zhen Shi-yin is introduced in chapter 1, for example, the names of his native district and address have all prompted commentators to seek to decipher their hidden meanings through homophonic extensions. Thus *hulu miao* (literally, Bottle-Gourd Temple) has been read as "marvelous riddles" (*HLMJ* 1: 185), and *shili jie* (literally, Ten-Mile Street) has been construed as "Worldly Way" or "Truthful Way" (*Sanjia* 1: 6).[11] On the other hand, the prominence given to Bao-chai's gold locket and Bao-yu's jade in the narrative certainly renders them emblematic metaphors, although the work's complexities make it apparent that no single symbol (dream, mirror, gold-and-jade affinity, wood-and-stone affinity) can fully encompass the narrative's plenitude of meaning. Most importantly, this fleeting reference to two traditional genres enlists literary history to reinforce the fictive nature of the tale. At the same time, however, the question raised by this explicit appeal to *chuanqi* again hints of mischief and irony: what sort of fictive marvel is to be transmitted by this tale when it owes its beginning to failure and rejection, and when it can describe its own origin as baseless, absurd, and unverifiable?

Part of the answer, of course, comes in the form of how the rejected stone is to be ushered into the mundane human world, where the story proper will find its peculiar development. As we have it in the full-length narrative, the transmigration has to do first with the sudden appearance of a monk and a Daoist on the scene. Catching sight of the stone's lustrous translucency in the shrunken form of a fan-pendant (for, having undergone Nüwa's refinement, it possesses both sentience and magic powers of transformation [*lingxing yi tong*]), the "Buddhist mahasattva Impervioso and the Daoist illuminate Mysterioso" de-

---

[11] David Hawkes's translation as "Worldly Way" apparently follows the reading of the Red Inkstone Scholiast (see *Pingyu*, p. 14).

cided to take it to "a nation of enlightened prosperity, a clan of genteel aristoc-
racy, a place of sensual opulence, and a home of genial riches, there to live and
enjoy a career (*HLM* 1: 3; my translation)."[12] Although these words, structured
in the classic literary style of symmetrical parallelism, are meant to move their
auditor to acquiescence, the initiative to seek an incarnate existence for the
stone remains with the clerics. Stone might have been lamenting its fate of
rejection, but despite its so-called attainment of numinous capacity of both
sentience and beautiful form, it could do nothing to alter its condition until the
arrival of the clerics.

In the earlier version of this episode preserved only in the 1754 text, however,
the author seems to have dwelled much more on Stone's own initiative. Its
"worldy mind (*fan xin*)" bestirred by an overheard conversation on the "glory
and riches of the Red Dust world," Stone begs to be taken there, only to be met
by this rebuff from the clerics:

> Although there are certain pleasures in the world of Red Dust, they cannot last
> forever. Moreover, the eight words presenting the truth of "flaw in every perfection,
> suffering for the virtuous" are indivisibly joined. In a little while you will reach
> the extremity of pleasure that begets sorrow, the passing of humans and the alter-
> ation of things. In the end all will be a dream, all phenomena will return to
> emptiness. It would have been better for you not to go there. (1754, 4–5; see
> *HLM* 1: 3, my translation)

Such stern warning, however, does nothing to abate the stone's desire for a
taste of worldly pleasures, and the clerics relent with the observation: "this,
too, indicates the fated change of 'extreme repose giving rise to movement, of
nothing begetting something.'"

The textual history of *Hongloumeng* does not make clear why this particular account of the stone's initial encounter with the agents of its change, so to
speak, has been drastically shortened in the 1760 manuscript and, apparently,
in all subsequent versions.[13] Despite some trenchant remarks by Red Inkstone
(who described the assertion, "at the end all will be a dream," as "the overall

---

[12] The last phrase of this quotation, "there to live and enjoy a career (*anshen leye*)" is actually found in the 1754 version of the story, preserved (interestingly enough) in the hand-copied
Qianlong version but not in the 1791/1792 120-chapter printed version. The last instead has
the word "for a little trip" to end the sentence. The 1982 edition has made an unusual decision
of collating the 1754 text with the longer version, unusual because the 1754 text is the only
version, as far as I know, which has a much longer episode (an added 492 characters) on the
first encounter of the Stone with the monk and the Daoist.

[13] Hu Jingzhi, in "Wangru hongchen ruoxu nian," thinks that the 1760 version is closest to
the author's "original intention," but this argument presents no substantive evidence. Moreover, Hu seems to have completely misread the text when he asserts (p. 148) that the Goddess
Disenchantment does not appear in the 1754 text. The truth is that the Goddess is prominently
mentioned on p. 6b.

subject of this book"), the extensive dialogues between the stone and the clerics might have been excised for reason of narrative tonality. The caution uttered by the clerics might have struck the author himself as too banal and too overtly didactic. Moreover, the declaration of the stone that it "ardently desires the glory and prosperity of the human world" not only might have rendered its character somewhat inconsistent with the incarnate protagonist's disdain for wealth and power (if Jia Bao-yu was meant indeed to be the human Stone), but the verbal exchange could also inadvertently distract from the other part of the myth soon to be introduced in the narrative—namely, the stone's karmic relations with a plant and how that affects their transmigratory process.

On the other hand, the decision of the contemporary 1982 edition to insert this passage of the 1754 text into the 120-chapter 1792 text may represent an editorial recognition not so much of a superior textual reading (based on temporal priority) as of a different focus on the problem of motive. By emphsizing the blazing arousal of the stone's worldly mind (*fanxin yi chi*), the 1754 manuscript highlights *desire* (*qing, yu*) as an element fundamental to the understanding of the stone's actions and their consequences, thus validating, at least partially, the later observation by Wang Guowei (1877–1927) that the puns on jade and desire (both *yu*) resound throughout the work as a leitmotif.[14] By refusing to heed the clerics' solemn warning, the stone's assertive behavior renders it responsible for its own fate. It might have been rejected by Nüwa for obscure reasons, but it chooses of its own accord to enter the world of Red Dust. Its action in the 1754 version thus lights up the ironic contrast between its refined condition and implied numinous intelligence (*lingxing yi tong*) and its mocking denomination by self and others as a "stupid thing (*chun wu*)," a contrast that throughout the novel's lengthy course will serve to define the character and development of its male protagonist in relation to the perplexing problems of ignorance and perception, renunciation and desire. It is not surprising that the terminal section of the full-length narrative has sought to depict Bao-yu's journey toward enlightenment with, among other experiences, his parlous hold on the piece of jade that has accompanied his entrance into this world. If the name of his beloved Dai-yu (literally, Black Jade) can be punned as "carrying desire (*dai yu*)," the repeated episodes of his birthstone's mysterious loss, recovery, and final loss can also be allegorized as his attempts "to give back his jade/desire (*huan yu/yu*)" (see chapters 94, 106–7).

However the textual problem is to be resolved, it should be clear that even at this early stage the narrative has already brought into view the karmic process of Stone's incarnation no less than the *form* of such a process. As the narrative unfolds, the Stone will next appear to its reader not simply as he is, an actor in a story; rather, he comes through the form of double mediation—that is, as

<hr />

[14] "*Hongloumeng* pinglun," in *Haining Wang Jing'an xiansheng yishu* 4: 1,604–9.

narrative, as a script or a text to be read. The "speaking Stone (*shi neng yan*)," a figure derived from a passage in the *Zuo Commentary* that has served as the font of numerous later allusions, thus must live out its desire as a scripted or textualized stone. In response to the stone's highly ironic appeal (*HLM* 1: 2) to the cleric's "sky-repairing and world-succoring talents (*butian jishi zhi cai*)," the transformed shape (*huan xing*) with which the monk (*HLM* 1: 3) will contrive by "a mighty exercise of Buddhist power (*da shi fo fa*)" to make the stone truly intelligent (*ling*) and marvelously noble (*qigui*) involves not merely incarnation and its implied accrual of worldly experience, but also fictionalization (true-events-concealed, false language enduring) and inscriptionalization (the clerics carving the text of the stone's fiction on the stone). The account of the stone's life in both worlds (*shen qian shen hou shi*) is told in its entirety initially only as a summarized, hence completed, process of reading and reception by a dramatized figure in the narrative named Vanitas or Kongkong Daoren, its details then to be filled out at great length in retrospect.[15] This, I think, is the implication of Cao Xueqin's highly original narrative technique, that his *Story of the Stone* must always exist for its reader in an act of proleptic reading, for no actual reader can antedate or supercede Vanitas. Another part of this implication is that the working out of the stone's aroused subjectivity must materialize— quite literally—in the writing of desire, a pathocentric fiction that focuses on the many lives of desire.

One principal source of that desire will be introduced when the reader next meets the stone as another mythic figure: the "Divine Luminescent Stone-in-Waiting in the court of Sunset Glow" (*SS* 1: 52; *HLM* 1: 8). The episode is structured as the narrative's second beginning: whereas the presentation of

---

[15] The story of the "Speaking Stone," found in the 8th year of Duke Zhao in the *Zuo Commentary*, mentions the explanation of this prodigy by the music master Kuang to a querying marquis of Jin: "A stone cannot speak, but perhaps it is possessed by a spirit. . . . And yet I have heard that when things are done out of season, and discontent and complaints are stirring among the people, then speechless things do speak. Now palaces are built, lofty and extravagant, the strength of the people is tasked to exhaustion, and both discontent and complaints are rife. . . . Isn't it fitting that a stone should speak?" (Legge, 5: 622, modified). Citing Ming Yi, a late mid-Qing reader of the novel who made an explicit reference to this story (*HLMJ* 1: 12), Liu Mengxi in *Hongloumeng xinlun* (p. 181) thinks that the narrative's first name of *Story of the Stone* and the source story of "A Speaking Stone" both "reflect the basis of Cao Xueqin's hatred for, and resistance to, the feudal ruling class of a waning dynasty." Echoing Liu's thesis, Marion Eggert's *Rede vom Traum*, p. 150, asserts also that the source story brings to speech a political grievance. In this context a 'Story of Stone' will function plainly as a challenge of power ([eine] politische Misstände. . . . In diesem Kontext wirkt ein 'Bericht eines Steins' geradezu als Herausforderung der Macht)." Although I agree in part with this line of interpretation, I cannot accept Liu's observation (p. 191) that the book *Hongloumeng* uses "the account of romantic love (*tan qing*) to conceal the realistic description of political conflicts." The problem of *qing* is itself a major problem of Chinese politics and thought which the text addresses. It is not an integument of some other important issue.

Nüwa's rejected block supposedly introduces the "origin" of the story of the stone as a tale, a literary composition, this part of the narrative traces for the reader the preincarnate ancestry, so to speak, of the male and female protagonists in the mundane plot and clarifies the preconditions of their fated relationship. The stone in the shape of a fan-pendant was said to have been carried by the monk to the court of the goddess Disenchantment, the regnant deity over the Land of Illusion. As if to underscore once more the surreal nature of its rehearsal, the narrative again has a monk and a Daoist disclose the story of the stone's experience to a framing character named Zhen Shi-yin (true-events-concealed) in a dream.

What Zhen was told is too familiar to require summary. One point, however, bears closer scrutiny: namely, the stone's action at the court and its consequence.

> By the Rock of Rebirth, he found the beautiful Crimson Pearl Flower, for which he conceived such a fancy that he took to watering her every day with sweet dew, thereby conferring on her the gift of life.
>
> Crimson Pearl's substance was composed of the purest cosmic essences, so she was already half-divine; and now, thanks to the vitalizing effect of the sweet dew, she was able to shed her vegetable shape and assume the form of a girl.
>
> This fairy girl wandered about outside the Realm of Separation, eating the Secret Passion Fruit when she was hungry and drinking from the Pool of Sadness when she was thirsty. The consciousness that she owed the stone something for his kindness in watering her began to prey on her mind and ended by becoming an obsession. (*SS* 1: 53; *HLM* 1: 8)

As a response to the stone's action, the plant eventually vowed to reciprocate with "the tears shed during the whole of a mortal lifetime" if they were reborn in the human world.

In the light of its antecedent condition, this particular stage of the stone's transformation is striking. The rejected instrument of one deity previously, it was "filled with shame and resentment and passed its days in sorrow and lamentation" (*SS* 1: 47; *HLM* 1: 2). Whatever might have been the reason that rendered it unfit for repairing the firmament, however, this did not handicap or restrain it from performing an act of vigilant kindness (from the point of view of the act's recipient) as well as of overt sexual overtones (from the point of view of a contemporary reader) when it had been placed in the Land of Illusion.[16] The issue of its "usefulness," whether it possesses sufficient "natural endowment (*cai*)," in this light, must now be reconsidered: its irrigation of the plant may well be understood as a different act of restoration or nourishment (*bu*), for it literally confers upon its object human form and feelings.

---

[16] See Louise P. Edwards, *Men and Women in Qing China*, p. 59.

The "magical" effect of the stone's action on the plant, in other words, constitutes another reflexive gesture by which the text calls attention to its own nature and language, for the opening sequences in the narrative should enable us to see by now the repeated and brilliant use of the rhetorical device of prosopopoeia. The personification of inanimate things, to be discussed in the following section, will summon into view one of the most perduring idioms of conventional Chinese wisdom enshrined in thought and literature, because the notion of plants and stones without affects (*mu shi wu qing, cao mu wu qing*) in contrast to the assumed "fact" that "humans are not plants and wood (*ren fei cao mu*)" arguably provides a symbolic leitmotif crucial for the full-length narrative's overall emplotment. That plot development will incorporate into itself, as we shall also see, the sustained contest between opposing strands of symbolic discourse (the gold-and-jade affinity vs. wood-and-stone affinity; the Confucian myth of jade and stone vs. the Buddhist myth of stone; the Daoist and Buddhist ideas about dream and the text's appropriation and reinterpretation of these ideas).

The action of the stone and the marvelous transformation wrought in a supposedly insensate object thus have enormous ramifications. Although the stone in the beginning seems to have been denied access to Nüwa's legendary fertility, its behavior toward the plant may betoken another kind of creativity.[17] Obviously attracted to the plant, its attentive care in turn provides for "her" the enabling power of transfiguration, much as the monk's action brings about the stone's desired and wondrous transformation. The stone's fecund potency may thus be regarded as part of its original stirring of desire, the process described by the clerics previously as "the fated change of 'extreme repose giving rise to movement, of nothing begetting something (*wu zhong sheng you*).'" The last clause, of course, is a direct inversion of the famed declaration by Laozi (chap. 40) that "something is begotten of nothing (*you sheng yu wu*)." Whereas that philosopher's statement in context seems to assert some kind of cosmogonic process, the clerics' verdict on Stone's longing to enter the human world refers sardonically to the foolish potency of desire. Now an entrenched idiom of the modern vernacular, the expression *wu zhong sheng you* signifies a kind of absurd or baseless reasoning, fixing itself as a metaphor in perpetual denigration of fiction. In terms of the novel, however, desire is double-edged: it impels the stone to seek remedy for a supposed lack in its own existence, but for this experience to generate the plot of an entire work of fiction also presupposes a prior need of a writer to create something out of nothing.[18] Seen in this light, the function of Nüwa's supposed "fecundity" is doubly displaced. Instead of being one of the progenitors of humans, as her mythic role purportedly suggests,

---

[17] Wang Jing, *The Story of the Stone*, p. 219.

[18] My nominalized translations of *you* and *wu* follow the discussions of A. C. Graham. See his "'Being' in Western Philosophy," and his *Disputers of the Tao*, pp. 410–14.

her work in the narrative becomes the genesis of fictive origins. And, instead of joining her in the fertile enterprise of cosmic restitution, the rejected stone engages in a different kind of productive labor. Both of their actions, in turn, also mirror the "life-giving" and "form-endowing" activities of the artist, activities that are actually illusory and thus must dwell, appositely, in the Land of Illusion.

Once aroused by the stone's attention, on the other hand, the plant is moved to "obsessive" desire for reciprocity, and it is this fierce character of their mutual involvement that marks their relations as fated, as a debt that inexorably demands repayment. The representation of desire indeed understands its operation as the economics of exchange, but the novelistic text takes pains to suggest as well that such an activity may always take on the character of delirium or madness (*chi qing*). Against the political and moral constraints distinctive of Chinese culture, the novel affirms that the mutuality demanded by this kind of desire can permit no origin or object other than the solitary individual self. It may be disseminated—and thus shared—through the contagion of representation found in art, music, and language (as we shall see in Chapter IV), but *qing* in its most intense manifestation between the sexes brooks no substitution or collectivization. This notion of *qing* as desire, feelings, sentiments, sentiency, and love is thus answerable to the discursive presentation I have tried to sketch in the previous chapter. As well, it explains why the intense esteem in which both Stone and Plant hold each other must hurtle them along the karmic path of transmigration. Thrown into incarnation, they must settle their "case (*gongan*)" in the human world by working through a life governed by memory and emotion, illusion and enlightenment.

THE GATE OF EMPTINESS

Enlightenment, this word that looks forward at once to the protagonist's experience at the end of the narrative and his dramatic resolve possibly to embrace the Buddhist faith (or, at least, a life of renunciation away from home), refers to a concept the signficance of which, throughout China's historical culture, has been nurtured by Buddhism. In the narrative itself, the concept has been alluded to in all the classical terms used by both Daoism and Buddhism to translate or expound the notion of intuitive apprehension of (and thus entrance into) what is considered ultimately real: *wu* (to apprehend, to realize, to be aware of, to grasp intuitively), *jue* (to waken, to realize, to feel), and *xing* (to wake up, to gain consciousness of). These concepts that point to an altered perception and a knowledge that liberates and transforms in turn bring into view their implied, dialectical opposites: *mi* (to delude, deceive, confuse, mislead; Skt., *māyā, moha*), *huan* (illusion, hallucination, conjurer's trick; Skt., *māyopama*), and *ye* (karmic causality). Such concepts enjoy intimate relations with Buddhism, but the conceptual genealogy of *qing*, a part of which we have sought to sketch in the previous chapter, also cannot be complete without considering the term's meaning and its Buddhist accretions. Accordingly, this and the next sections of this chapter will examine the Buddhist complication of desire by looking at Bao-yu's lengthy journey to the Gate of Emptiness, illumined by the two cardinal images of dream and mirror structured in the narrative. The chapter's final section will argue that Buddhist conceptualities, however unsystematically rehearsed in the course of the tale, not merely facilitate the construction of its plot and characters but also modulate and enhance the narrative's reflexive adumbration of its own fictionality.

Although the beginning of *Hongloumeng* has succeeded in impressing many readers with a dazzling display of technical virtuosity, the opening five chapters deftly constructing a triple frame (mythic, realistic, narrativistic) wherein to introduce the setting and characters of the tale and to lay much of the groundwork for subsequent development of its immense plot, the ending of the full-length novel, in my judgment, betokens a no less extraordinary accomplishment. Whereas Buddhist clerics of both sexes—the monk and the nun—were by no means strangers to the world of Chinese fiction since the early Tang, and whereas certain figures like the mad, scabby monk Ji Gong and Bodhidharma, the legendary founder of Zen Buddhism, were much celebrated in both literature and art, a full-length novel that locates the driving impulse of its story squarely upon the protagonist's desire for liberation from his sufferings and upon his final resolve possibly to become a monk has little precedent. The momentous significance of young Bao-yu's act cannot be fully fathomed without our perception of how carefully and variously it has been foretold and prepared for by the devices of the so-called camouflaged-predictive brush (*fu bi*) of the author, of the kind of alarm and misgiving it has caused whenever there is but the merest hint of the prospect, and of the pain and terror it induces in family members when in the end he turns a contemplated threat into an accomplished act.

Why, then, one may ask, would the young hero's decision to take, as it were, "holy orders" from the Buddhist sangha incite such commotion and dread? The answer is not difficult to find, for the assumption of that particular form of religious vocation represents at bottom Buddhism's most severe conflict with the social and ethical ideals of Chinese culture. To be committed to the life of *pravarājya* (*chujia*, literally, leaving one's family), is to renounce those ties to the family that the Chinese, in the spirit and letter of Confucian orthodoxy, most deeply cherish and the importance of which they most assiduously seek to inculcate. The person of such a religious profession would be regarded as someone unfilial and therefore disloyal (in both the familial and political sense), someone who is, in the words of Han Yu's famous memorial against receiving Buddha's relics, "ignorant of the obligations between ruler and subject, of the sentiments between father and son."

In their efforts to remove this stumbling block from the path of faith, Buddhists have tried to dissuade the Chinese from their stubborn clinging to their cultural emphasis and turn toward a supposedly better ideal. They have, for example, debated the merits of remaining at home (*zaijia*) and of leaving home (*chujia*) in a text like the *Wenshushiliwen jing*, or they have argued with the Huayan master Zongmi (in his commentary on the *Yulanpen jing*) that "Sakyamuni left the household life to become a monk in order to repay the love and affection of his parents."[19] The Buddhist must be deemed superior to the Confucian in his practice of filial piety, goes the argument, for the former's submission to the Law and performance of rituals may bring about the ultimate salvation of parents and ancestors. This line of reasoning, in fact, informs Wang Guowei's assessment of Bao-yu's departure from his family at the end.

> Realizing the errors of his father and ancestors, he [Bao-yu] therefore could not bring himself to repeat them and thereby redouble their guilt. How could this be called unfilial? Thus Bao-yu's idea that "when one son leaves the family, seven generations of ancestors would find deliverance" may well be construed as a true insight, if the problem of so-called filial piety is looked at one way and not another [that is, from a conventional point of view]. His thought is no mere self-justification.[20]

What success this kind of Buddhist apologetics, exemplified by Wang's argument, achieved among the Chinese audience varied with the circumstance. One thorny problem that no amount of theological sophistry can entirely surmount concerns not merely the care of parents or elderly loved ones but also the supreme responsibility of a male to provide an heir. The obligation to ensure biological perpetuity of the familial line is jeopardized, indeed obviated, once the life of celibacy has been taken up. It is in the light of the all-too-familiar Mencian maxim, "there are three ways of being a bad son; the most serious is to have no heir," that we can comprehend why the term *chujia* sounds such an ominous and hateful note within the Jia mansion of *Hongloumeng,* a novel that is supremely concerned with, among other things, the waxing and waning of familial fortunes.[21] When a person faces insuperable frustration and suffering, or a household irreversible disaster, the "Gate of Emptiness" promises a soothing place of refuge precisely because its entrance supposedly requires the severance of all ties, all relations or affinities. From a certain point of view, however, this kind of peaceful shelter is suitable only for maids and servants,

---

[19] For the *Wenshushiliwen jing*, see *T.* 468, 15: 505; for Zongmi's commentary, see *T.* 1792, 39: 505–12; for Sakyamuni, see Kenneth Ch'en, *The Chinese Transformation of Buddhism,* p. 31. For another study of the relationship between Buddhism and the family in traditional Chinese society, see Stephen F. Teiser's perceptive chapter in his *Ghost Festival in Medieval China,* pp. 196–213.

[20] "*Hongloumeng* pinglun," 4: 1,620.

[21] *Mencius,* translated by D. C. Lau, 4A: 26, p. 127.

derelict soldiers or disgraced officials—the kind of people, in short, who are for one reason or another already adrift from the mooring of kinship.[22] For someone like Xi-chun, the cousin of Bao-yu, however, the very fact of her having been born into an aristocratic family made it "inconvenient" for her to think of becoming a nun (chap. 87; *HLM* 3: 1,255). When she shaves her hair later and insists on entering a nunnery, the words of her aunt Lady Wang in giving grudging consent are to the point: "it would look very bad for a girl from a family such as ours to enter a nunnery. That really is unthinkable" (*SS* 5: 318; *HLM* 3: 1,605). If it is "unthinkable" for a young woman of noble birth to take such drastic action, how much more inconceivable it would be for a person like Bao-yu, who is in the novel the sole heir of the family because his elder brother had died young. Nonetheless, the prospect of his becoming a monk runs through the story like a long continuous thread.

It begins at the very beginning, for we are told in the first intriguing pages detailing the story's origin that one of its evolving titles happens to be *The Tale of Brother Amor* or *Qingsenglu* (*SS 1:* 51; *HLM 1:* 6). At this point we have no knowledge, of course, of Brother Amor's identity, for the title indicates only that the story concerns a clerical figure. It is noteworthy, however, that his very name betokens an oxymoronic predicament, an ironic clash of nature and vocation, that solicits both attention and further explanation. In the first few chapters following, part of that explanation will be given, to the reader as well as to the unknowing novelistic characters, in the form of warnings against amorous entanglement and against impending disasters. While the first type of warning may give the initial impression that the story confronting us is essentially a didactic, cautionary tale, an impression that the intricate art of the narrative will eventually alter and rectify, the second type of warning renders *Hongloumeng* unique in its unhesitant announcement from the beginning of tragic developments and ending.

This note on human sorrow and suffering, on scuttled dreams and shattered loves, and on the finality of death and destruction of the family, is sounded again and again in the first episodes. When the young Bao-yu tours in his dream the Land of Illusion in chapter 5, he is granted by the goddess Disenchantment a sort of preview—twice in fact—of the fate of the twelve girls with whom he would be most involved in his youth and adolescence. As he reads and hears uncomprehendingly the oracular verses that seem to foretell

---

[22] This is precisely the line of reasoning that an old prioress uses in chapter 77 to persuade Lady Wang to give permission to allow three young maids to become nuns: "these three young people have no parents and are far from the place where they were born. Having had a taste of luxury during their years here with you, yet being born to a lowly fate and trained in a profession that at best is vanity, they cannot but tremble when they think what the future may hold for them. I believe that is why, out of the midst of this sea of suffering, they have turned toward the light and resolved to abjure the world and its vanities and prepare themselves for the life to come" (*SS* 3: 552; *HLM* 2: 1113).

the wretched destiny of these Twelve Beauties of Jinling and of himself, the lines of the last song proclaim:

> The disillusioned to their convents fly,
> The still deluded miserably die.
>
> (*SS* 1: 144; *HLM* 1: 89)

Athough the subject of this particular song seems to encompass generic types (the office jack, the rich man, the kind, the cruel, and so on) rather than specific individuals (as do the previous songs of the suite), the expansive character of the language prohibits the exclusion of the protagonist from its prophetic predication. However much the story of Bao-yu may resist facile summary, one central ingredient certainly has to do with his process of growth, change, and the attainment of some form of insight or enlightenment. At the moment when he hears the songs, he might be moved by their melodic melancholy *(HLM 1:* 85), but the telescopic content of the future baffles and mystifies him. "Silly boy! You still don't understand, do you?" is the apt verdict of the goddess (*SS* 1: 145; *HLM* 1: 89), and it takes a long time before the boy arrives at the realization not only that love is an illusion in "the immortal precincts," but also that "the love of your dust-stained, mortal world must be doubly an illusion" (*SS* 1: 146; *HLM* 1: 90). Only when he has tasted the intoxication of romance, the ambivalence of age, the bitterness of betrayal, and the ineradicable pain of mortal separation can he lay claim to the perspicacity of Buddhist vision (the song's *kanpodi* [literally, to see through it]).

One critic has noted that of all the many male characters in the text, only Bao-yu practices the exclamatory habit of chanting Buddha's name.[23] Although the Prospect Garden's rather sheltered environment defines the immediate world of the young man and his female cousins, there is ceaseless traffic between the larger household of the Jia Mansion and a series of religious houses that include monasteries, nunneries, Taoist and Buddhist temples.[24] Since Bao-yu's infancy, a certain Mother Ma (chap. 25), possibly a Buddhist deaconess, "had been arranged . . . to ensure him the protection of her powers" *(SS 1:* 495), and his frequent companions included the attractive but pretentious nun Adamantina. The bustle of his daily life certainly does not preclude visits to religious houses or even participating in the ritual of burning incense and worshiping the images. These activities by themselves need not be decisive in inducing in Bao-yu, as it were, "an awakening to faith," for they could be thought of as part of the common routines of late imperial Chinese society. As we have it in the narrative, his first thought of becoming a monk, even if it was meant as a jest at the moment of its utterance, is traceable directly to the relationship between himself and his cousin Dai-yu, to the disturbing alternation of intense pleasure and

---

[23] Zhang Bilai, *Manshuo Honglou*, p. 455.
[24] For a detailed list, see Sa Mengwu, *Hongloumeng yu Zhongguo jiu jiating*, pp. 111–12.

pain, of gratification and frustration, of rapport and misunderstanding that persistently accompany their blossoming experience of love. This occurs during one of the episodes (chap. 30) in which the two lovers end up bickering because they are caught in the dilemma of being both desirous and wary of disclosing their true feelings to each other.

Dai-yu had been meaning to ignore him, but what he had just been saying about other people "coming between" them seemed to prove that he must in *some* way feel closer to her than the rest, and she was unable to maintain her silence.

"You don't have to treat me like a child," she blurted out tearfully. "From now on I shall make no further claims on you. You can behave exactly as if I had gone away."

"Gone away?" said Bao-yu laughingly. "Where would you go to?"

"Back home."

"I'd follow you."

"As if I were dead then."

"If you died," he said, "I should become a monk."

Dai-yu's face darkened immediately:

"What an utterly idiotic thing to say! Suppose your sisters were to die? Just how many times can one person become a monk? I think I had better see what the others think about that remark."

Bao-yu had realized at once that she would be offended; but the words were already out of his mouth before he could stop them. He turned very red and hung his head in silence. It was a good thing that no one else was in the room at the moment to see him. Dai-yu glared at him for some seconds—evidently too enraged to speak, for she made a sound somewhere between a snort and a sigh, but said nothing—then, seeing him almost purple in the face with suppressed emotion, she clenched her teeth, pointed her finger at him, and with an indignant "Hmmm!," stabbed the air quite savagely a few inches away from his forehead:

"You—!"

But whatever it was she had been going to call him never got said. She merely gave a sigh and began wiping her eyes again with her handkerchief.

Bao-yu had been in a highly emotional state when he came to see Dai-yu and it had further upset him to have inadvertently offended her so soon after his arrival. This angry gesture and the unsuccessful struggle, ending in sighs and tears, to say what she wanted to say now affected him so deeply that he, too, began to weep. In need of a handkerchief but finding that he had come out without one, he wiped his eyes on his sleeve.

Although Dai-yu was crying, the spectacle of Bao-yu using the sleeve of his brand-new lilac-coloured summer gown as a handkerchief had not escaped her, and while continuing to wipe her own eyes with one hand, she leaned over and reached with the other for the square of silk that was draped over the head-rest at the end of the bed. She lifted it off and threw it at him—all without uttering a word. . . . Bao-yu picked up the handkerchief she had thrown him and hurriedly wiped his eyes with it. When he had dried them, he drew up close to her again and took one of her hands in his own, smiling at her gently.

"I don't know why you go on crying," he said. "I feel as if all my insides were shattered. Come! Let's go and see Grandmother together."

Dai-yu flung off his hand.

"Take your hands off me! We're not children any more. You really can't go on mauling me about like this all the time. Don't you understand *anything*?" (*SS* 2: 94–96; *HLM 1:* 420–21)

I quote this episode at length because the charming scene of a young lovers' squabble may also be seen as a little prophetic drama, revelatory of the complexity of emotions underlying the words and gestures of the teenagers and hinting at the possibly tragic devolution of their fate. For Lin Dai-yu, the narrative has progressively made it clear that the journey through pubescence toward young adulthood is one fraught with increasing anxiety over her marital prospects. That she finds herself drawn more and more to her cousin Bao-yu only exacerbates her worry over her plight as an orphan lodging in a borrowed residence, her declining health that a physician would later attribute to consumption, and the possibility of rivalry for Bao-yu's affections among their kin in the Jia mansion.[25] Thus her injunction for him not to go on "mauling" her in the present incident indicates neither simply a directive of anger nor an inclination to observe the Confucian proscription against physical contact between grown members of the opposite sexes. It betrays, rather, her sharp awareness of the peculiar ramifications of their being "no longer children." This awareness, I believe, helps explain the provocative tone of her exchange with Bao-yu and the severity of her reaction to his unthinking but not wholly unpurposeful pledge to become a monk if she should die. Even prior to this episode, Dai-yu's mounting anxiety had already led her to devise different ways of ascertaining the intentions and feelings (all rendered by the word *xin,* translated as both mind and heart) of Bao-yu, though the efforts result more often in bitter quarrels than in harmonious communion, earning, in fact, from the doting Grandmother Jia in the previous chapter the remark:

'Tis Fate brings foes and lo'es tegither, . . .

(*SS* 2: 91; HLM 1: 417)

Although this saying with its ironic suggestion of predestined union and discord is a familiar Chinese maxim, used primarily for describing a married couple, the narrator pointedly remarks that the novelistic cousins heard it for the first time only at this point, "and its impact . . . was like that of a Zen perception: something to be meditated on with bowed head and savoured with a gush of tears."

---

[25] For further elaboration of these points, see Chapter 5 below.

It is in this immediate context that Dai-yu further tries to plumb Bao-yu's mind by taunting him with the possibility of her departure or death. "I won't dare try to be near Master Number Two ever again. Master Number Two can behave exactly as if I had gone away." These literal words of hers and their sarcastic tone barely mask the agitated query of an insecure lover: what would you do if I were absent?

Bao-yu's reply surprises both her and himself. He had arrived at Dai-yu's room intent not only on seeking a reconciliation with her but perhaps, if the opportunity beckoned, also on disclosing what was on his mind—his true feelings for her (Hawkes' "highly emotional state" does not capture the full flavor of the term *xinshi*, literally, the affairs of the heart-and-mind). In his dealings with this special cousin of his, however, he is depicted in these chapters of the novel as particularly prone to a kind of "Freudian slip" of the tongue, of blurting out some of the deepest secrets of his heart that he cannot articulate calmly and coherently (see chapter 32 for another such incident). The narrator in the present episode asserts that he "had realized at once that she would be offended," but why she was offended is never actually mentioned. Dai-yu's chiding once more reveals the discrepancy between her words and her unspoken thought.

Dai-yu's rhetorical question to Bao-yu—whether he would become a monk if his sisters were to die—camouflages her recognition that his description of his own future can well be construed as the serious pledge of a lover, far more serious in implications than when sometime earlier (chap. 26) Bao-yu teases her and her maid with two lines from the drama of romantic love, *The Story of the Western Wing*:

> If with your amorous mistress I should wed,
> 'Tis you, sweet maid, must make our bridal bed.
>
> (*SS 1:* 517; HLM 1: 367)

Whereas the dramatic comparison merely hints at marriage, which Bao-yu advances more in mockery than in earnest (hence Dai-yu's complaint of becoming "a source of entertainment for the *menfolk* now, it seems"), to enter the priesthood is itself a far more drastic act. Sisters and other kinfolk may die, but the grief they cause is not as likely to induce a resolve to submit to the Buddhist Law as does the romantic passion that leads to the proverbial insistence of not marrying any person other than that one particular beloved (*fei qing mo qu, fei jun mo jia*). Her reference to his other siblings thus ironically implies a query that seeks to dissociate herself from their status: am I someone who means more to you than your sisters? If just before his visit she had been thinking about his words and how they suggested that "he must in *some* way feel closer to her than the rest," Bao-yu's abrupt announcement must appear to her now to be a troubling confirmation of such felt intimacy.

It is troubling in two ways. On the one hand, it offends as any open declaration of love would offend in traditional Chinese society, and no reader can believe that Dai-yu quite meant what she said when she declared that she had better see "what the others think about that remark." Her impulsive outburst, in fact, provides a poignant contrast to *his* self-serving realization "that no one else was in the room at the moment to see him" making such a statement. This is, of course, her agonizing dilemma: she needs above all Bao-yu's assurance, which, however, is forbidden by social constraint. Teenagers in imperial China can hardly be expected to say, with Juliet, "If thou doest love, pronounce it faithfully," for this pronouncement directly affronts the parental prerogative in determining the "great enterprise of lifelong settlement (*zhongshen dashi*)." Even if he were to offer it in an offhand manner, as he apparently does at the moment, propriety dictates that she regard it as trivial or frivolous. That is precisely how she behaves in a different setting—lighthearted and indifferent—for when Bao-yu parodies himself soon thereafter and publicly repeats his pledge to become a monk if his maid Aroma dies, Dai-yu mocks him with two upheld fingers, and Aroma's scornful rejoinder is for him to be more serious (chap. 31).

In the privacy of Dai-yu's chamber, on the other hand, the shocking implications of Bao-yu's promise cannot have escaped her notice, for given the grave misgivings she has about her own future, her careless intimation of death can suddenly loom as an ominous forecast (*chenyu*). This is the other side of her dilemma, for she could hardly wish for her own end to be the ultimate test of her lover's sincerity or fidelity. Moreover, she cannot be oblivious to the meaning of priestly vocation, because that act for Bao-yu would be a denial of all the familial responsibilities expected of him as sole heir and future master. "Master Number Two (*erye*)" carries particular resonance here because Master Number One has long since died. The life of celibacy, since it is a life without posterity, is veritably a life in death. For good reason, therefore, Dai-yu's instinctive reaction to his promise is the stinging retort: "I think *you* must really want to die!" which unfortunately has been deleted in the English translation. Her reference to his sisters and how many times he can become a monk may thus imply another silent query: if you can't do it even for your sisters because you really don't know what it entails, how could you say such a thing to me if you don't mean it? How could you insult me with so casual an offer of so serious a pledge? Even at the height of her turmoil, however, she cannot very well proceed to demand a satisfactory answer, to discover whether he truly means it. Her rage, vividly portrayed, accordingly stems as much from a complex mixture of bewilderment and embarrassment as it does from desperate hope and heightened fear.

However turbulent their encounter might have been, this episode also reveals something extraordinary of the nature of love that flourishes between the two cousins and eventually consumes them. Within the traditional culture of imperial China, where parents are invested with the absolute authority of all marital arrangements, premarital affection between the sexes seldom exists precisely because the parties have so little opportunity to meet, let alone to enjoy any form of acquaintance and courtship. The novel's two most prominent literary antecedents (also prominently alluded to in the novel) that may be considered exceptions to this custom nonetheless resort to depicting the unmarried lovers either as engaging in furtive intercourse that ends eventually in disaster (the stories and plays associated with *Western Wing*), or as establishing contact through the mysterious medium of premonitory dreams (*The Peony Pavilion*). Cao Xueqin is unique in so constructing a tale that his hero and heroine are permitted prolonged and intimate association in a hospitable setting. The unbreakable bond that unites the two assumes a natural course of development, proceeding from intuitive childhood attraction, through shared periods of camaraderie, banter, communion, and growth, to poignant moments of heated dispute and passionate disclosure.

That their relation is erected upon a genial friendship which deepens into a quest for mutual understanding belies the opinion of some critics that the experience of the two teens does not move much beyond infatuation and romantic longing. Lin Dai-yu might appear to some readers as a particularly neurotic and even egotistic girl, obsessed with her own problems. Nonetheless, it is moving to observe that time and time again, Bao-yu is the one who signals for her the deliverance from excessive self-preoccupation. She may have been racked by grief and anger in the episode of chapter 30, but Bao-yu remains the cherished and attended other; her care for him even extends to worry over his soiling a new summer gown. At the close of this episode, the two young persons are allowed to come to a sort of temporary truce again, but the perplexities crowding their minds are never quite resolved.

In the larger context of the novel, such resolutions are not found until much later. If the last forty chapters of the narrative are adjudged authentic—at least in spirit, if not in every letter—to Cao Xueqin's original vision, as I believe they essentially are, the question of whether Bao-yu has to live out his pledge will find the most dramatic answer.

The seeds for such a development are abundantly sown in the first two-thirds of the narrative. Though they may be too numerous for detailed examination in this chapter, those worthy of citation may include the incidents of Bao-yu's peculiar identification of a line of the play *Zhishen at the Monastery Gate*—"Naked and friendless, I roam without care or concern" (chap. 22)—as his own destiny, and of his subsequent attempt to compete with Dai-yu and Bao-chai in Zen perception by writing *gāthās*. This segment of the story terminates with Bao-yu giving up the pursuit of Zen for the moment, but once more it serves to focus powerfully on the paradox of his existence: his delight in unbridled commerce with the female companions of his household and his latent desire to transcend the disappointment, frustration, and all other kinds of emotional tumult such relations invevitably entail.

By the time we reach the last third of the narrative, our protagonist, perhaps no more than seventeen years of age (the narrative ends when he is nineteen), has lived through what for many might well be considered a lifetime of experience. He has known the first ecstasy of sexual pleasure (chap. 5), the elation of sudden communion and the deepening of trust (chaps. 32 and 33), the agony of paternal wrath and discipline (chap. 33), the exuberance of familial festivities (chap. 53), and the anguish of mortal loss (chaps. 77–78). Having traversed the polar extremities of emotion, Bao-yu has yet to find the liberating insight into the contradiction of his existence, marked, as it were, by the contrary desire for human community with all its attendant obligations and burdens and the longing for escape and freedom. An episode in chapter 21 presents a revealing glimpse of his youthful attempt to unravel this riddle.

> After dinner Bao-yu came back flushed and slightly tipsy, having taken a few cups of wine with his meal. Normally this would have been the occasion for an evening of hilarity with Aroma and the rest, but today he would have to sit by his lamp alone in cheerless desolation. The prospect was a depressing one. Yet if he were to go running after her, it would seem too much like a capitulation, and her nagging would thenceforth become insufferable. On the other hand, to frighten her into some sort of compliance by asserting his mastery over her would be heartless. There was nothing else for it: he would just have to grin and bear it.
>
> "Just pretend they are all dead," he said to himself. "After all, I myself will have to go one of these days." The thought was strangely comforting. He was able to stop worrying. He even began to feel quite cheerful. Having instructed Number Four to trim up the lamp and brew him a pot of tea, he settled down to a volume of *Zhuangzi*. Presently he came to the following passage in the chapter called "Rifling Trunks":
>
>> Away then with saints and wise men, and the big thieves will cease from despoiling. Discard your jades, destroy your pearls, and the little thieves will cease from pilfering. Burn your tallies, smash your seals, and the common people will revert to their natural integrity. Break all the bushels and snap all the steelyards, and they will have no further grounds for dispute. Obliterate those sacred laws by which the world is governed, and you will find yourself at last able to reason with them. . . .
>
> The words wonderfully suited his present mood. He read no further. Impulsively picking up a writing-brush, and with the inspiration lent him by his tipsiness, he added the following lines in the margin:
>
>> Away then with Musk and Aroma, and the female tongue will cease from nagging. Discard Bao-chai's heavenly beauty, destroy Dai-yu's divine intelligence, utterly abolish all tender feelings, and the female heart will cease from envy. If the female tongue ceases from nagging there will be no further fear of quarrels and estrangements; if Bao-chai's heavenly beauty is discarded there will be no further grounds for tender admiration; and if

Dai-yu's divine intelligence is destroyed there will be no further cause for romantic imaginings. These Bao-chais, Dai-yus, Aromas and Musks spread their nets and dig their pits, and all the world are bewitched and ensnared by them. (*SS* 1: 420–21, text modified; *HLM* 1: 291–93)

To deliver himself from such nettlesome bewitchment, Bao-yu would follow the gleeful nihilism of Daoist philosophy and strike at the root of his troubles. With one stroke of the brush and in stylistic flair answerable to Master Zhuang, he would kill off all those beautiful companions and that would end his discomfort. The problem with this attempted solution, of course, is that it is only a pretense, a fictive creation, and that the boy in his intoxicated insouciance has failed to come to grips even with the meaning of the condition his brush has invented. Could he truly suffer the destruction of Dai-yu's intelligence, the abolishment of all tender feelings?

The answer to this question is what lends to the last part of the narrative its immense pathos, for Bao-yu throughout his ordeal of mysterious illness, his unwitting wedding of a substitute bride, and his inconsolable grief for the departed Dai-yu reveals that he is no more capable of giving her up than she is able, even in the last hours of her life, to banish him from her thoughts. Months after her death, when he visits her residence in the Prospect Garden, now "a scene of utter desolation" (chap. 108) both because of declining familial fortune and the steady departure of its residents, a servant's accidental reference to a weeping ghost drives him to the tearful outcry: "Oh, Cousin Lin! Cousin Lin! How could I have wounded you so! Please don't reproach me! Don't feel bitter towards me! It was my father and mother who made the choice. In my heart I was always true to you!" (*SS* 5: 170; *HLM* 3 1,497).

The plain directness of the plea and protest presents the sharpest contrast to the elaborate elegy Bao-yu prepared for Skybright, a maid who earlier had obviously enjoyed his affection. In the speculation of many readers, the tender scene of the mortally ill Skybright having a last interview with her young master, who held her in his arms and who received from her a fragment of her nail as a dying memento (chap. 77), seems to be deliberately "prefiguring" what might also have taken place later at the death of Dai-yu. I believe, however, that the difference in language tells a different story. That the boy and the maid are drawn to each other cannot be doubted, but the ornate, effusive style of the literary exercise after Skybright's passing renders it only a fitting vehicle for part of a carefully but playfully designed rite to "show proper respect" (*SS* 3: 575; *HLM* 2: 1,129). Significantly, the narrator calls attention to the elegy's wildness and exuberance, and it is justly criticized by Dai-yu for its "shopworn" phrases (chap. 79). Even the second lyric he writes later in memory of Skybright (chap. 89) expresses no more than lingering sorrow brought about by the cape she had once knitted for him. In contrast to all this, the pain of Dai-yu's memory, for Bao-yu, defies and defeats poetic language.

Indeed, the closing chapters of the narrative seem to dwell on the many bouts of tears in which Bao-yu indulges, though admittedly not all of these occasions are triggered by his grief over Dai-yu. Nonetheless, his implacable sorrow both causes concern for his health (chap. 109) and elicits this assessment from the maid Cuckoo (chap. 113):

> It seems plain that the family conspired together and tricked him into the wedding at a time when he was too ill to understand. Then afterwards, when he knew what he had done, he suffered one of his attacks and that's why he hasn't been able to stop weeping and moping ever since. He's obviously not the heartless, wicked person I took him for. Why, today his devotion was so touching, I felt really sorry for him. What a dreadful pity it is that our Miss Lin never had the fortune to be his bride! Such unions are clearly determined by fate. Until fate reveals itself, men continue to indulge in blind passion and fond imaginings; then, when the die is cast and the truth is known, the fools may remain impervious, but the ones who care deeply, the men of true sentiment, can only weep bitterly at the futility of their romantic attachments, at the tragedy of their earthly plight. *She* is dead and knows nothing; but *he* still lives, and there is no end to his suffering and torment. Better by far the destiny of plant or stone, bereft of knowledge and consciousness, but blessed at least with purity and peace of mind! (*SS* 5: 255; *HLM* 3: 1,559)

What leads Cuckoo to alter her opinion of Bao-yu is precisely the tenacity of his memory. She is right in discerning that he cannot, in the words of the Chinese text, forget his feeling of love (*wang qing*), and his endless torment may indeed bespeak his fidelity and his being a hapless victim of familial intrigue. But she is wrong in thinking that "the destiny of plant or stone, bereft of knowledge and consciousness," is superior, for in terms of the mythic— indeed, often Buddhist—suppositions undergirding the novel, this is precisely the destiny of plant and stone!

As we have already learned from the novel's beginning, the decisions of the stone and plant to enter the mortal world of Red Dust were adjudged an infatuous involvement with the mundane (*si fan*), a foolish act certain to bring catastrophe. In the actuality of their earthly existence, however, their initial encounter nonetheless continues their preincarnate drama of fated entanglement, for at the first sight of each other they both express the feeling—out loud or in silence—that they seem to have seen each other before (chap. 3). This is, of course, the narrative enactment of their karmic origin and destiny, and the shock of recognition is but a confirmation of their common memory in this human stage of their rebirth.

It is at this point as well that the Indian legacy of the Buddhist vision becomes apparent, for as Wendy Doniger has pointed out, "the key to the persistence of memory, and hence the persistence of rebirth, lies in the persistence of emotion. . . . Emotion is what drives karma forward; it is what causes us to be reborn."[26] Understandably, therefore, Buddhist salvation, which seeks to terminate the karmic motion of *samsara,* aims at breaking this vicious cycle of memory and emotion.

From the point of view of the novel, emotion is in truth "what drives karma forward," but susceptibility to this fatal weakness is not confined to humans. Whereas numerous works of Chinese literature have made use of the Buddhist notion of rebirth or the transmigration of souls in such a way that characters appearing as reincarnations of figures (divine, human, and sometimes even animal) of a different time must work out the karmic consequences of their previous fate, only *Hongloumeng* has the originality to echo and parody this tradition by introducing in its opening myth certain inanimate objects that are also highly sentimental. The proverbial wisdom of the Chinese scattered among ancient writings of various genres has long posited that such objects as plants, trees, and stones would define the condition of nonsentiency, and thus of apatheia. Witness these testimonies: from the *Xunzi* ("Fire and water possess vital breath but have no life. Plants and trees possess life, but lack awareness");[27] from Sima Qian ("I am [not unfeeling] like wood and stone [*shen fei mu shi*], though I keep company with prison guards");[28] from Xi Kang on the destructive potency of emotions ("Delight and anger would disarrange one's proper vital breath; thought and worry would dissolve one's essential spirit; grief and pleasure would upset one's equanimity. . . . Thus a body easily given to exhaustion is attacked without and within. Since a body is not wood and stone, could it endure [such onslaught]?");[29] and from a line of Bao Zhao's poem ("The mind's not wood and stone (*xin fei mu shi*), how could it not feel?").[30]

The celestial agents in *Hongloumeng* may warn us repeatedly against the delirium induced by irrational passion (*chi qing*), but the same story shows us that even a stone or a plant is not without emotion (*wu qing*) or memory. This notion of the affective presence in inanimate things, once an important and controversial issue in Buddhist dogmatics, may have made its appearance in as early a document as the *Literary Mind and the Carving of Dragons* (*Wenxin diaolong*). In a passage devoted to the familiar injunction that language must faithfully express intentionality, Liu Xie remarks,

> peach and plum trees do not speak, but paths are formed beneath them because they have fruits [to offer to people]. For even an orchid will have no fragrance if a man plants it, for he lacks the proper affects (*wu qing*) within. Now if trivial

---

[26] Wendy Doniger O'Flaherty, *Dreams, Illusions, and Other Realities,* pp. 225 and 227.

[27] *Xunzi jijie* 9. 16a; John Knoblock, trans., *Xunzi* 1: 103.

[28] Sima Qian, "Letter in Reply to Ren An," in *Wenxuan, juan 41.*

[29] Xi Kang, "Essay on the Nurturing of Life (Yang sheng lun)," in *Wenxuan, juan 53.*

[30] Bao Zhao, Poem 4 in the series of poems titled "Yi Xinglunan," *Gushixuan 2, juan 2,* 10b (*SBBY*).

things like plants and woods must bear fruits that are in accord with their affective disposition (*yi qing dai shi*), how much more should this be the case with literary writing?[31]

The use of *qing* makes the passage difficult to translate because it is one of those that fully exploits that word's double sense of essential disposition and the affects. The familiar defense of writing as talismanic of inward reality turns on the genderized assumption (perhaps first expressed in Book Ten of the *Huainanzi*) that a woman inherently has greater capacity for *qing* than a man, which explains why his orchid plant would not produce the desired fragrance. On the other hand, the analogy between the vegetative condition and the human one which leads Liu to make his a fortiori argument obtains only if one shares his premise that even grasses and plants enjoy a disposition that feels (*cao mu you qing*).

Does this suggest that Buddhist thinking has already made its first inroads into the thought of Liu Xie who, despite the persistent ring of Confucian discourse in his monumental ars poetica, did become a monk during his final years? However we may answer this interesting question, the important point to note here is that Liu's observation is directly germane to our reflection on the myth of plant and stone so central to *Hongloumeng*. For from the perspective of Buddhism, sentiency is virtually synonymous with sentiment, and this interpretation may well be Cao Xueqin's subtlest reading of the Buddhist term *you qing*.[32] If plants and stones, too, are capable of feelings, what chance does a sentient being have for enlightenment? Bao-yu's comment in chapter 77 has, in this light, the function of an ironic gloss on the action of the entire narrative:

Not only plants and trees, but all things that live and grow have feelings. And like us, they are most responsive to those who most appreciate them. There are plenty of examples from history: the juniper tree in front of the temple of Confucius, the milfoil that grows beside his tomb, the cypress in front of Zhuge Liang's shrine, the pine tree that grows in front of Yue Fei's grave: all those paragons of the vegetable world, mightily endowed with vital essence and able to withstand the ravages of the centuries, have withered and dried up in times of disorder, only to flourish once more when times were prosperous. In the course of a thousand or more years all of them have died and come to life again several times over. If those are not portents, what are they? On a somewhat less exalted level there are the peonies beside Yang Gui-fei's Aloeswood Pavilion, the rhododendrons of the

---

[31] "Qingcai," in *Wenxin diaolong zhu, juan* 7, 1b.

[32] This observation does not imply that Cao Xueqin was the first Chinese author to have made extensive use of the theme of *qing* (feeling, desire) to fashion a story. In the history of Chinese prose fiction, the most important antecedent might well have been *Xiyoubu*, attributed to Dong Yue (1620–1686). See the discussion by Frederick P. Brandauer, *Tung Yüeh*, pp. 88–93; and Robert E. Hegel, *The Novel in Seventeenth-Century China*, pp. 148–66.

Duanchenglou and the evergreen grass on Lady Bright's grave. Surely you can't deny that all these are instances of sympathy between plants and humans? (*SS* 3: 540–41; *HLM* 2: 1,105)

Although Bao-yu's reasoning apparently stems more from Chinese lore than from Buddhist doctrine, his attribution of feelings to trees and plants cannot but strike a resonant chord in those readers familiar with this religion's history, evoking for them in faint but distinctive overtones the once hotly debated issue in both China and Japan of whether trees and plants may attain enlightenment or Buddhahood.[33] This is not to suggest, however, that doctrine is ever blatantly or crudely adumbrated in the narrative. Whereas the cardinal concern of erudite priests was to settle the question of whether Buddha's infinite compassion extends to inanimate and inorganic matter in such a way that even it could proclaim the Law, Cao Xueqin's purpose was unwavering in making the abstract and abstruse the vital ingredients of aesthetics. The excellence of *Hongloumeng* is thus to be found in its masterful translation of the mythic and religious into the realistic, so that this particular instance of sympathy between a plant and a stone is told in the most unforgettable human terms. The wood and stone of the novel are no mere parasitic portents of historical legends; they come to life in the illusion of art. Lacerated by guilt and grief over his beloved's death, Bao-yu can find no solace in anything or anyone. "Do you people think that I am an unfeeling person (*wuqing di ren*)?" is the question that continues to haunt him (chap. 104). His relationship with Bao-chai, his wedded wife, seems to be marked more by contrived and constrained affection than by spontaneous self-giving. The distance of his spirit despite physical union virtually enacts the scene sketched out in one of the oracular songs of Chapter 5 (see *SS* 1: 140; *HLM* 1: 84–85). Because his mind cannot banish "that fairy wood forlorn" that has left the world, the end the "every good" that still holds in the end "some imperfection" for Bao-yu includes the promise of offspring (for Bao-chai is pregnant) and of office (for he has finally passed the provincial examination). Uncomforted, the young man flies into the Gate of Emptiness.

Is *Hongloumeng* a grand parable of Buddhist quest and enlightenment? In view of the experience of its male protagonist and many of the other characters, three of the four titles supposedly given to their story (*Tale of Brother Amor, A*

---

[33] The classic text on the subject is the *Jingangbi* (Diamond Stick) by Zhanran (711–782) of the Tiantai School (*T.*, no. 1,932 in 46: 781–86). See William R. La Fleur's two-part study of "Saigyo and the Buddhist Value of Nature." In the *Mengzhan yizhi*, the Ming scholar and specialist on dreams, Chen Shiyuan (fl. 1537–1579), has a chapter on vegetative symbolism in dreams and the categorical correspondence (*leiying*) between plants and human physiology. Chen's concluding remark in the chapter is: "though it is said that plants are without feelings, we nevertheless see that there are signs for divination by dreams." I use the *Congshu jicheng* edition of the *Mengzhan yizhi*, edited by Wang Yunwu, p. 68. On the possibility of even "nonsentient beings expounding the Dharma (*wuqing shuo fa*)," see *The Record of Tung-shan*.

Bejeweled Mirror of Romance, and *Dream of the Red Chamber),* and the vast and vibrant network of echoes and allusions to Buddhist themes and rhetoric, it is virtually impossible not to consider seriously an affirmative answer to such a question. Not only do the final five chapters provide us with what is arguably a lengthy and vivid account of Bao-yu's last leg in his journey toward disillusionment, but in his final debate with his wife Bao-chai, he refers specifically to the Buddhist notion of four delusions *(kleśas)* in reference to the ego (greed, anger, folly, and desire) to counter her desperate admonition to cultivate the virtues of the Confucian sage (chap. 118), "a heart full of loyalty and filial devotion." For Bao-yu, however, all that occupies his attentive meditation is "how to rise above all this, how to escape the net of this mortal life? 'This floating life, with its meetings and partings'—I can see now why in all the ages since it was first uttered the true meaning of this expression has never been fully grasped" (*SS* 5: 329; *HLM* 3: 1,613).

When at last he thinks he has grasped its true meaning, he uses the occasion of his leaving home for the provincial examination as the most appropriate— and certainly the most ironic—moment for making his permanent departure. The total rupture of communication between him and his family, the complete cross purposes of their words and actions, cannot be more powerfully dramatized (chap. 119). After kneeling in tears to thank his mother and bowing deeply to his wife, Bao-yu leaves with raised head and laughter, crying, "I'm going! I'm going! No more of this foolery! It's all over!" If the reader has journeyed with the young hero to this point of the narrative, it is almost unnecessary for him to be prompted by the final envoi to reflect on life being a dream (chap. 120), to see that the "silly boy" has at last arrived at some form of understanding concerning the illusion of life. So to regard his action is also to acknowledge the centrality of the dream metaphor that both depicts his earthly existence and defines the nature of his story.

THE DREAM AND THE MIRROR

We recall Bao-yu's preview of the destiny of his female companions, which in turn reveals significantly his fate and that of his family. At one point, in fact, the goddess reports that the spirits of the Duke of Ning-guo and his brother, the Duke of Rong-guo, had revealed to her that their family fortunes would suffer a fated eclipse "because its stock of good fortune has run out, and nothing can be done to replenish it (*SS* 1: 137; *HLM* 1: 82). To the youth, however, who has hitherto never experienced anything other than familial success, parental dotage, and soon thereafter imperial favor, the prospect of

> Fall'n the great house once so secure in wealth,
> Each scattered member shifting for himself;

> And half a life-time's anxious schemes
> Proved no more than the stuff of dreams. . . .
>
> (*SS* 1: 145; *HLM* 1: 88)

simply defies understanding. Such knowledge as the goddess Disenchantment seeks to impart to him requires far greater experience, and the implied delay in turn imposes the necessary constraint on narrative time. It is in regard to this that the multiple, receding frames of the narrative bring to the fore one of their most dazzling ironies inherent in the plot construction: the lesson that a dream purports to teach concerning the dreamlike impermanence of life and fortune cannot be quickly learned, for when the young initiate wakes from that immediate dream, the waking reality he encounters is for many years itself a dream, the "golden days" (literally in Chinese, the dream of the red towered buildings) celebrated by the songs he heard in his sleep. Not until he has tasted the sweetest and bitterest of experiences does he come to the true awakening and realize that, "contrary to our hopes and projections, all the phenomena and relationships we experience in our daily lives are bound to disappear with time."[34] The epic peregrination of the narrative thus not only raises for the reader the questions—common to both Indian thought and Daoist philosophy—of what is and is not a dream, of who is the dreamer and who the dreamt, but it also asserts the paradox that only time can proffer to us a sense of the brevity and insubstantiality of our world. In this way *Hongloumeng* participates in certain elemental traits of dream literature from China and elsewhere.[35]

To speak of life as a dream is, indeed, not an insight peculiarly original with the Buddhists. Those familiar with classical Chinese Daoism are quick to recall the famous butterfly dream of Zhuangzi and its verdict on the difficulty of differentiating between waking and oneiric reality. Even more to this point are his observations elsewhere:

> How do I know that to take pleasure in life is not a delusion? How do I know that we who hate death are not exiles since childhood who have forgotten the way

[34] William R. LaFleur, *The Karma of Words*, p. 5.

[35] See in the works of Shimizu Eikichi, Uchiyama Tomoya, Uchida Michio, David R. Knechtges, and Liu Wenying listed in the bibliography. The last is the contemporary Chinese scholar who has probably done the most research on Chinese dream—lore and theories. For a stimulating discussion of the use of dream in Chinese literature, see Andrew Jones, "The Poetics of Uncertainty in Early Chinese Literature." Recent Western scholarship that attempts to relate the Chinese dream topos to various disciplines include the studies by Roberto K. Ong, Michael Lackner, and Carolyn T. Brown. In this last volume, the essays by Michel Strickman ("Dreamwork of Psycho-Sinologists") and Roberto K. Ong ("Image and Meaning") are especially illuminating for our present study. One major analysis of a portion of *Hongloumeng* that utilizes a good deal of the literature cited here is to be found in Shuen-fu Lin, "Chia Pao-yü's First Visit to the Land of Illusion." Finally, the most systematic treatment of Chinese dream literature in relation to literary embodiment is Marion Eggert's *Rede vom Traum*.

home? . . . Who banquets in a dream at dawn wails and weeps, who wails and weeps in a dream at dawn goes out to hunt. While we dream we do not know that we are dreaming, and in the middle of a dream interpret a dream within it; not until we wake do we know that we are dreaming. Only at the ultimate awakening shall we know that this is the ultimate dream. Yet fools think they are awake, so confident that they know what they are, princes, herdsmen, incorrigible! You and Confucius are both dreams, and I who call you am also a dream.[36]

In addition to these remarks, one can also cite the famous third chapter of *Liezi*, where among its several anecdotes is the hilarious story of "a woodcutter of Zheng," who, when he failed to remember where had hidden a hunted deer, decided that he had to be dreaming. He told this to a passerby, who succeeded in retrieving the deer for himself. When he credited the woodcutter with a true dream, his own wife disputed the conclusion and said that his success meant that it was he who had a true dream. Eventually the woodcutter brought the passerby before the chief justice to contest his right to the deer. When the chief justice's counsel for the two to divide the deer was rejected, the prime minister who was consulted brought in the opinion: "It is beyond me to distinguish dreaming and not dreaming. If you want to distinguish dreaming from waking, you will have to call in the Yellow Emperor or Confucius. Now that we have lost the Yellow Emperor and Confucius, who is to distinguish them? For the present we may as well trust the decision of the Chief Justice."[37]

Although both philosophers emphasize the difficulty of distinguishing between dream and reality, there is little suggestion from the Daoist sages that "meditation can penetrate illusion."[38] We can either learn to live with the knowledge that life is a dream until death, the "great awakening," or we can be practical and do the next best thing. The Daoist feeling is perhaps best summed up in the last song of the Tang story, "Scholar Zhang":

> Why speak of being in a dream
> When life is all but a dream?[39]

In contrast to the note of casual merriment of the philosophical Daoists, however, the treatment of dreams in a number of other works of prose fiction registers a more somber, if not a wholly pessimistic, outlook. In such Tang tales as "The World inside a Pillow" (*Zhenzhongji*), "The Magistrate of the Southern Branch" (*Nanke taishou zhuan*), and "Cherry and the Blue Robe Maiden" (*Yingtao qingyi*), the experience of dream is frequently used as a

---

[36] *Chuang-tzu*, translated by A. C. Graham, pp. 59–60.

[37] *The Book of Lieh-tzu*, by A. C. Graham, p. 70.

[38] Ibid., p. 59.

[39] Originally collected in *Zuanyiji*, compiled by Li Mei (fl. 827), it can now be found in the *Taiping guangji* 282.

cautionary device. Supposedly without undergoing the actual vicissitudes in real life, the dreamer through his dream is made aware "of the ways of favor and disgrace, the vagaries of distress and prosperity, the patterns of accomplishment and failure, the emotions of life and death."[40] A dream thus assumes exactly the function of fiction.[41] It teaches by means of vicarious knowledge, but the particular lesson its polymorphic situations convey invariably dwells on the emptiness of worldly attainment and the brevity of human happiness— shorter, as it is observed in one story, than the time required to steam millet.

Does such emphasis reflect the Buddhist teaching on illusion? The plausibility of this question is certainly heightened by the rhetoric of *Hongloumeng*. Having fallen ill in chapter 25, Bao-yu is given this prognostication by a monk appearing from nowhere:

> From drunken dreaming one day you'll recover:
> Then, when all debts are paid, the play will soon be over.
>
> (*SS* 1: 505; *HLM* 1: 357)

The condign conjunction of dream with stage, of waking with debt retirement, accords well with Buddhism, for not only does the monk's observation point to the illusion of existence and its theatrical brevity, but it also highlights the more important issues of knowledge, the status of mind and of ego, the possibility of rectifying the mortal tendency of erroneous perceptions, and the proper deliverance from our stubborn attachments. A *gāthā* from *The Diamond* or *Vajracchedikā-prajñāpāramitā Sūtra (Jingangjing)* admonishes us:

> All things phenomenal
> Are like dreams, *māyā*, bubbles;

---

[40] The words are from "The World inside a Pillow," translated by William H. Nienhauser, Jr., in *Traditional Chinese Stories*, edited by Y. W. Ma and Joseph S. M. Lau, p. 438. In one of the few scholarly essays that explicitly examine the theme of dream in relation to the novel, Zhou Ruchang thinks that dream in the novelistic context has less to do with Zhuangzi than with its literary antecedents in Tang *chuanqi* tales and Ming dramas. See his "*Hongloumeng* jie," in *Hongloumeng xinzheng* 2: 822–31. His brief remarks completely ignore the possibility of philosophical and religous ideas underpinning Chinese dream theory.

[41] This point was similarly noted by Xie Zhaozhe (1567–1624), who declared in his *Wu Zazu*, p. 447: "A play is similar to a dream, because the feelings they produce—the joys and sorrows related to union and separation—are not real feelings, and because the situations they create—exaltation or debasement, wealth or poverty—are not real situations. The brevity of human life, which passes in the twinkling of an eye, is also thus. Nonetheless, the foolish will rejoice when he experiences a dream of good fortune and worry over a dream of ill omen. Similarly, he would change his countenance sadly when witnessing a drama of suffering, or laugh in glee when encountering a drama of prosperity. In sum, he has not yet been liberated from the view point of real life. Nowadays men of letters are fond of using historiographical materials to point out the falsehood of popular dramas. This is exactly like expounding a dream in front of foolish people." See also Uchida Michio, "Tōdai shōsetsu ni okeru yume to genesetsu," p. 12.

Like dew and lightning flashes.
Thus one should regard them.[42]

"There are some Brahmans and Sramanas," declares also the *Laṅkāvatāra Sūtra,* "who recognising that the external world which is of Mind itself is seen as such owing to the discrimination and false intellection practiced since beginningless time, know that the world has no self-nature and has never been born; it is like a cloud, a ring produced by a firebrand, and castle of the Gandharvas, a vision, a mirage, the moon as reflected in the ocean, and a dream."[43] The majority of the human race, devoid of such luminous perception, are only attracted to, in the words of the Chinese, castles in the air or flowers in the mirror and moon in the water (*kongzhong louge, jinghua shuiyue*).

Salvation for the deluded must therefore take the form of the removal of illusion *(māyā* or *huan),* to disabuse the mind of such mistaken calculations and discriminations *(vikalpa),* and to purge from it all sorts of undesirable attachments (*abhiniveśa*). The goal to be realized is, of course, Nirvana, which is the symbol of a state of emptiness (*śunyatā* or *kong*). Such a state is not so much given as it is actualized by the self by means of supreme wisdom (*prajñā, āryajñāna*). Moreover, to attain such enlightenment, at least according to the *Laṅkāvatāra* tradition, "there must be a revulsion (*parāvṛtti*) at the deepest sea of consciousness known as the Alayavijñāna, . . . a kind of mental receptacle where all the memory of one's past deeds and psychic activities is deposited and preserved in a form of energy."[44] Given this understanding, it is not surprising that one modern reader steeped in the Zen tradition (directly descended from the *Laṅkāvatāra*) has thought of Bao-yu's terminal rebellion against his family as a drama of this "revulsion," and tries to argue that the entire novel is but an allegory of the process whereby Bao-yu as novice or yogin (*xingzhe*) seeks liberation from this storehouse consciousness.[45]

Whether one judges a reading of this sort to be ingenious or farfetched may depend finally on one's basic sympathy. What I want to emphasize here, however, is that the affirmation of the Buddhist view of reality is but one side of *Hongloumeng.* To perceive only that affirmation is to miss a more profound aspect of Cao Xueqin's art, namely, how the author has succeeded in turning the concept of world and life as dream into a subtle but powerful theory of fiction that he uses constantly to confound his reader's sense of reality.

The suggestion is there again from the beginning, as we have seen in the first section of this chapter, when the author indulges in some of the most elaborate moves in the history of Chinese literature to explain how his story

---

[42] *T.* 235, 8: 752. The translator was Kumārajīva.
[43] *The Laṅkāvatāra Sūtra, A Mahayāna Text,* translated by D. T. Suzuki, pp. 37–38.
[44] D. T. Suzuki, *Studies in the Laṅkāvatāra Sūtra,* p. 128.
[45] Xiaoxiang [Liu Guosiang], *Hongloumeng yu chan.*

has been brought into existence. The quatrain in the narrative's chapter 1 that speaks of "all men [calling] the author fool" actually refers to him as *chi* (foolish, delirious). Given the prominence of the dream metaphor in the entire work, it is virtually impossible for the Chinese reader not to bring to mind the well-known phrase, "disclosing a dream to a foolish person (*chi ren shuo meng*)." By itself, the phrase can easily be taken to mean the opposite, as it has been indeed so regarded in many instances: that a foolish person is telling of his dream, although the source of the phrase indicates otherwise.[46] In an anecdote, a certain monk was touring Southeast China when

> he was asked, "What is your name (*ru he xing*)?" He replied, "What is my name (*da yue he xing*)." He was asked again, "What country did you come from (*he guo ren*)?" and he replied, "What country I did come from (*da yue heguo ren*)." Li Yong of the Tang was making an inscription, and he did not understand such language. He therefore wrote in the monk's biography: the master's name is What (*he*) and he came from a country named What. This is exactly what is called disclosing a dream to a foolish person (*dui chiren shuo meng*). Since Li Yong regarded the dream to be true, he was truly the most foolish.

The irony of misperception and misreading in this story of slapstick repartee is not lost, of course, on our Qing author, for his poem at once stresses the disparity between the readers' assessment of him and their lack of understanding. Who are the fools, the *chiren*? Are they the protagonists ("silly boy" for Bao-yu, "silly Frownie" for Dai-yu) who persisted in their deluded clinging to amorous feelings; or the readers, who read with varying lack of comprehension; or the author, who took such pains to write such a story? The ambiguous meaning of the phrase reverberating throughout the book seems to mock the efforts of both author and reader.

Why should the author be called a fool, one still might ask. A brief answer may lie in the fact that he, too, engages in a kind of hide-and-seek game with his readers, in the verbal trickery employed by the monk of the anecdote. This is apparent not merely from the ostensibly deprecatory description he confers on his own writing ("pages full of idle words")—though as we shall see in the next chapter, idle words or *huangtang yan* might well be the most audacious and politically dangerous caption he could confer on his own creation—but also from the very first sentence in what is sometimes considered a sort of Prologue to the novel proper:

> In the opening first chapter of this book, the author himself has declared that having undergone a dreamlike and illusory experience, he deliberately had the true events concealed and instead composed this book, *The Story of the Stone.* That is why he speaks of True Events Concealed (Zhen Shi-yin), who by means

---

[46] See *Lengzhai yehua*, 41a.

of a dream makes acquaintance with Perfect Comprension. (*HLM* 1: 1, my translation)

Although most scholars of the novel concentrate on this statement's autobiographical intimation, the repetition of the words dream and illusion *(meng, huan)* should also intrigue, because they focus not merely upon the quality of the author's alleged experience but also on the instrumentality of his art. He will use illusion to discourse on illusion. What Victor Mair has said of the etymological meaning of Dunhuang transformation texts provides us with an illuminating background for seeing the novel's opening perspective:

> "Transformation" here implies the coming or bringing into being (i.e. into illusory reality, Skt. *māyā*) of a scene or deity. The creative agent who causes the transformational manifestation may be a Buddha, a Bodhisattva, or a saint. . . . Highly skilled storytellers and actors . . . were also thought to be able to replicate transformational acts of creation. The ultimate religious purpose of such transformations was the release of all sentient beings from the vicious cycle of death and rebirth (*saṃsāra*). By hearing and viewing these transformations and reflecting upon them, the individual could become enlightened.[47]

Whether the ultimate aim of telling the story of *Hongloumeng* entertains such exalted religious purpose is open to debate. But Cao Xueqin certainly understands this purpose when he ushers his Bao-yu at the very beginning into the Illusory Realm of the Supreme Void (*taixu huanjing*), for the medium of warning and enlightenment is poetry, song or, if you will, literary fiction.

Not only is Bao-yu's journey in chapter 5 a dream within a dream, a fiction within a fiction, but the very way that the episode has been related (complete with a wet dream, which is *the* evidence repeatedly cited in Buddhist writings for the realistic function of dream) prolongs the running debate in which Cao seeks to engage his readers: the nature of truth and falsehood, reality and unreality (*zhen, jia*). Shuen-fu Lin's meticulous analysis of this episode in the narrative has argued that the lesson the goddess Disenchantment seeks to impart to the uncomprehending youth concerns the paradoxical nature of erotic love. Passion can bring enormous pleasure and satisfaction, so the argument goes, but "because love and passion are illusory and may lead a person to unspeakable lust, they are not things one should be obsessed with. . . . The catch is that unless one has tasted the sweet experience of love and passion, he or she cannot realize their illusory nature."[48]

---

[47] Victor H. Mair, *Tun-huang Popular Narratives*, pp. 2–3. For further discussion of the importance of illusion in Chinese arts, see Fu Tianzheng, "Fojiao dui Zhongguo huanshu di yingxiang chutan," in *Fojiao yu Zhongguo wenhua*, pp. 237–50. On *māyā* artistic and creative power with connotation of magic, illusion, and deceit, see O'Flaherty, *Dreams, Illusions and Other Realities*, pp. 114–22.

[48] Lin, "Chia Pao-yü's First Visit," p. 105.

Although this interpretation may square with part of the narrative's surface meaning, it misses the ironic play of linguistic and conceptual doubleness that its rhetoric consistently exploits. Taken at face value, the message of Disenchantment, with its sly suggestion of moralistic strictures against sensuality and desire, may sound indeed as a didactic, cautionary lecture. But the lesson that the goddess purports to teach ends Bao-yu's dream with the young boy's sexual initiation. He dreams of having intercourse with the goddess's sister, who, however, is also named Ke-qing, the boy's niece-in-law. When Bao-yu wakes up from this erotic dream (presumably late in the afternoon), the evidence of his so-called nocturnal emission quickly seduces him and his attending maid Aroma to continue the dream, so to speak, by engaging in "real" sexual play.

That Bao-yu's erotic dream is followed by another sexual experience, this time with a live partner, emplots the textual implication that a dream is both product and agent of desire. In modern language, a dream has the elements of both day dream and nocturnal dream; it is both a real or true experience and a wish. In the language of psychoanalysis, it has both latent content and manifest content. To recognize the doubleness of the oneiric phenomenon means that one can no more regard a dream as merely a metaphor of impermanence and insubstantiality than Disenchantment can call love and passion illusory. If calling life a dream is designed to wean us from the objects of our misplaced attachment, the discovery is doubly vexing when we realize that not only do we resist such enjoined severance or decathexis, but that we are actually attracted to the very instrument of warning, the dream itself. The illusion of reality, exposed for what it is, nonetheless continues to delude because it continues to enchant. Desire (Bao-yu excited by the person and bedroom of Qin Shi), which brings on dreaming as wish-fulfilment (Bao-yu's wet dream), can through oneiric representation further beget desire. The testimony of both psychoanalysis and literature—East and West—seems to be that we not only persist in dreaming, but our love of the dream, our obsession, ensures its persistence.

The acknowledgement of our enjoyment of this self-perpetuating circuit of dream and desire brings us to one additional consideration: namely, the problem of the difference between reality and the oneiric illusion of reality. To speak again in Freudian terms, the pleasure principle in this instance is directly germane to the reality principle. It is no coincidence that both Indian philosophy (inclusive of historic Buddhism) and Western psychoanalysis have addressed this issue by reference to the physiology of sex, for it is here that the puzzling ontological doubleness of dream makes its most apparent manifestation. The following questions thus arise: if we dismiss a dream or its experience as unreal, how are we to explain the discernible physical symptoms and effect of a sexual dream? If we acknowledge the dream's "reality," then what precise sense of the real are we to assign to its experience and content?

"The evidence of semen after an orgasmic dream is ambiguous," writes Wendy Doniger, "because it is proof not only of the latent content (the emotion of sexual passion) but also of the manifest content (the experience of a *real* orgasm, as real as those *really* wet feet). The dream adventure of making love to a woman in the other world is thus a record of the dream that most vividly straddles the line between reality and illusion."[49] It straddles the line because both latent and manifest content can be experienced, perceived, recounted, "read," and shared without a material or physical referent of that content. A dream about sexual union instantiates behavior of unambiguous solipsism masked as action of mutuality. It is thus a form of presence in absence, the classic sign of a sign. If a literary dream such as that depicted in chapter 5 of *Hongloumeng* can both mediate and create pleasure and passion for its fictive character who experiences that dream, literary fiction—of which this literary dream in chapter 5 is but a diminutive analogue—can have the same effect because its very nature, like a dream, also "vividly straddles the line between reality and illusion." What Cao Xueqin forces his readers to acknowledge in chapter 5 of his narrative is not necessarily the truth of Dischantment's lecture about romantic love but what the entire episode of Bao-yu's dream tour elaborately enacts: the power and persistence of representation. Appropriately, therefore, the couplet hung over the entrance to the Land of Illusion visited by Bao-yu greets us with this lesson:

> Truth becomes fiction when the fiction's true;
> Real becomes not real when the unreal's real.

Reinforcing the metaphor of dream in the narrative is the pervasive use of the mirror image, which in itself is probably the most enduring metaphor-simile in all Buddhism for revealing assumptions and attitudes. According to Alex Wayman, there are three strands of thought tied to this image:

First, the early Buddhist use of the mirror as a metaphor of the mind, which becomes dirtied as a mirror collects dust, eventually led to the highly evolved philosophical position of Asanga and his school called the Yogacara, and then in Buddhist tantric ritual to the washing of the mirror while a deity was reflected therein. Second, the rise of the Prajñaparamita literature as interpreted by the teacher Nagarjuna avoids the metaphorical mirror and employs the mirror simile for such illustrative purposes as the theory of *dharmas* (natures, features), and the meaning here is succinctly shown in the brief tantric ritual, initiation of the mirror. Third, the ancient use of a mirror for predictive purposes . . . develops . . . eventually into remarkable forms of mirror divination.[50]

---

[49] O'Flaherty, *Dreams, Illusions and Other Realities*, p. 46.

[50] Alex Wayman, "The Mirror as a Pan-Buddhist Metaphor-Simile," p. 252. See also his "The Mirror-like Knowledge in Mahayana Buddhist Literature"; the magisterial seminal essay of Paul Demiéville, "Le miroir spirituel"; and John R. McRae, *The Northern School and the Formation of Early Ch'an Buddhism*, pp. 144–47. For an illuminating study of the mirror as a source for the threefold knowledge of self, other, and spirituality in Chinese literary and cultural history, see Florence Hu-Sterk, "Miroir connaissance dans la poésie des Tang."

Echoes of all three strands of the mirror theme may be detected in the novel. The first instance is found in the highly satiric episode of the dissolute Jia Rui, whose lechery lands him in fatal illness. As he tries desperately to find a cure by swallowing every kind of medication, a mysterious Daoist suddenly appears to hand him a mirror inscribed with the words, Bejeweled Mirror of Romance (*fengyue baojian*) on its back. When he looks into the instrument, he sees the woman of his desires (Phoenix) beckoning him to enter. After they make love inside the mirror, he finds himself back on his bed, where in horror he discovers that the mirror, turning itself round of its own accord, has presented him with the image of a grinning skull. He dies in a pool of his own sweat and ejaculated semen (chap. 12).

The identification of the Land of Disenchantment as the mirror's origin and the duplication of one of the novel's titles as the mirror's name make it apparent that the episode continues not only the cautionary note struck in chapter 5 but also the play of fiction within fiction. The sudden appearance of the skull image to supplant that of a beautiful woman repeats, in fact, a familiar emphasis in Buddhism, particularly in Zen, which was already alluded to earlier in two lines of verse: "Who yesterday her lord's bones laid in clay,/On silken bridal-bed shall lie today" (*SS* 1: 64; *HLM* 1: 18). The point in the Jia Rui story is, of course, more than the transitory nature of physical beauty; it is also the swiftness of retribution for unbridled passion. The instrument of Jia's death may suggest the image of the defiled mind and the judgment laid down in the *Mahāyāna-Sūtrālamkara*: "As in a broken water-pot the reflection of the moon cannot be seen, in the same way to those that are evil the Buddha does not manifest himself."[51] What is most noteworthy is the question of reality and nonreality (*zhen, jia*) posed by this episode masquerading as a tale of superstition. A mirror image, insubstantial as a dream, can nonetheless dispense shattering, lethal self-knowledge. To destroy by burning, however, this mirror "held up" to Jia Rui's corrupt nature, as Jia Dai-ru, the schoolmaster, and Jia Rui's grandfather, wanted to do, is no more enlightened action than the beatings and burnings reported by Xue Bao-chai (chap. 42) when her family tried to prevent her and other members from reading works of proscribed fiction.[52] As the flames flare up to consume the mirror, according to the masterful account in chapter 12,

> a voice was heard in the air saying, "Who told him [Jia Rui] to look in the front? It is you all who are to blame, for confusing the unreal with the real (*yi jia wei zhen*)! Why then should you burn my mirror?"
>
> Suddenly the mirror was seen to rise up and fly out of the room, and when

---

[51] Cited by Wayman in "The Mirror," p. 256.

[52] For further analysis of Bao-chai's conversation with Dai-yu in chapter 42, see Chapter 4 below.

Dai-ru went outside to look, there was the lame Taoist shouting, "Give me back my *Bejeweled Mirror of Romance!*" He snatched it as it flew towards him and disappeared before Dai-ru's very eyes. (*SS* 1: 253, text modified; *HLM* 1: 172)

To those in the immediate novelistic situation who have witnessed Jia Rui's gruesome, comic end, the mirror has become some frightful weapon of a "fiendish Daoist," which, "if not destroyed, would continue to cause great harm among the people of the world" (*HLM* 1: 172). But what Jia Rui sees in the mirror when he "confuses the unreal for the real" is, in the apt phrases of Umberto Eco, "the *symptom* of a presence, . . . the shadow of a semiotic phenomenon."[53] In other words, the mirror image is the fiction of a sign. But this is apparently too profound for someone like Jia Dai-ru, the aged scholar in charge of the Jia family school who is bitingly named, literally, Surrogate or Moronic Confucian. Bent on protecting the world's insouciant mirror viewers and readers of fictive images that nonetheless can produce such dire sexual response as the fatal loss of semen, he would destroy all such wicked reflective instruments. He quite forgets, as readers of *Hongloumeng* may also be led to forget quite frequently, that Jia Rui, the lecherous schoolboy in his charge, is literally but a False Omen.[54]

For Bao-yu's development throughout the narrative, the mirror provides the crucial symbol of mind and knowledge. In the episode where he competes with Dai-yu in writing *gāthās* (chap. 22), Bao-chai follows their competition with the most familiar story of the paradigmatic contest between two Zen masters. To establish his credentials, the head monk Shenxiu at the time of the Fifth Patriarch wrote a quatrain that stresses the need to polish the mirror (as symbol of mind) constantly lest it be sullied by dust. The boy Huineng, who according to legend later became the Sixth Patriarch, countered with his own verse:

> No real Bo-tree the body is,
> The mind no mirror bright.
> Since of the pair none's really there,
> On what could dust alight?
>
> (*SS* 1: 443; *HLM* 1: 209)[55]

The poems by the two masters have always been regarded by the Buddhist tradition as the decisive differentiation between the doctrines of gradual and sudden enlightenment.[56] In the novelistic context, however, their story only

---

[53] *Semiotics and the Philosophy of Language*, chapter 7, "Mirrors," p. 209.

[54] My reading here is stimulated by Eggert's excellent discussion of the episode. See *Rede vom Traum*, pp. 242–43.

[55] The source of this story may be found in *The Platform Scripture*, translated by Wing-tsit Chan; see also McRae, *The Northern School*, pp. 1–4, and 235–40.

[56] Demiéville, "Le miroir spirituel," pp. 132–35.

serves to illustrate Bao-chai's mockery of Bao-yu that he is hardly ready to practice Zen meditation, let alone attain enlightenment.

The most remarkable incident occurs in chapter 56, and this is an episode in which the images of both dream and mirror are seamlessly merged. Earlier, the narrative had already played on the convenient coincidence that there could be persons in this wide world with not only the exact same names but also identical personalities, and had revealed that Bao-yu had a double whose name was Zhen (true) Bao-yu, as opposed to his surname of Jia (false). On being reminded of this double in the present chapter, Jia Bao-yu falls into a troubled sleep in which he dreams of visiting a garden exactly resembling his own Prospect Garden, complete with similar appointments and familiar-looking maids. At length he encounters his Doppelgänger, a boy who is his mirror image.

> "I came *here* looking for Bao-yu. Are you Bao-yu then?" Bao-yu could not help blurting out.
>
> The youth leaped down from the bed and seized Bao-yu by the hands:
>
> "So you are Bao-yu, and this isn't a dream after all?"
>
> "Of course it isn't a dream," said Bao-yu. "It couldn't be more real!"
>
> Just then someone arrived with a summons;
>
> "The Master wants to see Bao-yu."
>
> For a moment the two Bao-yus were stunned; and then one Bao-yu hurried off and the other Bao-yu was left calling after him:
>
> "Come back, Bao-yu! Come back, Bao-yu!"
>
> Aroma heard him calling his own name in his sleep and shook him awake.
>
> "Where's Bao-yu?" she asked him jokingly.
>
> Though awake, Bao-yu had not yet regained consciousness of his surroundings. He pointed to the doorway:
>
> "He's only just left. He can't have got very far."
>
> "You're still dreaming," Aroma said, amused. "Rub your eyes and have another look. That's the mirror. You're looking at your own reflection in the mirror."
>
> Bao-yu leaned forward and looked. The doorway he had pointed to was his dressing-mirror. He joined Aroma in laughing at himself. (*SS* 3: 86–87; *HLM* 2: 795–96)

The marvelous drama in this little episode not only permits a revealing glimpse into Bao-yu's psyche and its characteristically adolescent search for true identity, but the dizzying, topsy-turvy dialogue, punning repeatedly on the names of the two Bao-yus, alights again and again on the problem of what is real and not real. For the moment, Jia Bao-yu who is presumably the real Bao-yu (though false in terms of being sunken in the dream of life) has yet to find his true self, his true identity. Much later, in chapter 115, when he once more encounters his mirror double, Zhen Bao-yu, the narrative hero there will discover that there is the sharpest division of mind despite identity of appearance.

The conflict, as we shall see in the last section of our chapter here, materializes between two competing discourses about stone and jade that will hasten the protagonist's process of awakening. Repetition *is* difference, and with a technique worthy of the modern Borges or Philip Roth, the Chinese author proceeds to present the dazzling transfer or exchange of attributes between the Zhen and the Jia Bao-yu, so that their words and mutual discovery of the other become virtually a living embodiment of the truth inherent in a dream, a mirror image, or a fiction: that there is the real in the false, and the false in the real *(jia zhong you zhen; zhen zhong you jia)*. The Buddhist ontology of the world has now become in a sense the transformed analogue to the ontology of narrative art.

With all this in mind, we can begin to see how the author would have us hear his "secret message" or, literally, savor the "flavor" of his work. He would have us ponder why "idle words" penned in "hot, bitter tears" could become so irresistibly attractive. What kind of knowledge does fiction communicate? Is it to be dismissed as untruth, as the ephemeral stuff of dream or mirage, or is mirror knowledge (*ādarśa-jñāna*) the purest kind of knowledge, as the Buddhists say, because it is untouched by the soil of phenomena or discursive thought?[57] Once more we are compelled to ask: if life is illusory like a dream or fiction, what are we to do with so engaging an illusion as fiction? This last question brings into relief both the paradoxical function of Buddhism in the novel and the cunning of Cao Xueqin's art.

The trajectory of the plot, since it follows Bao-yu's quest for deliverance from his sufferings, may tempt the reader to think that the novel supplies but a mimetic enactment of the Buddhist vision. If the analysis in the present study thus far is not far off the mark, however, then I believe that the "flavor" or "secret message" of the work lies in the differentiation between the Buddhist "reading" of the world and our reading of literary fiction. Buddhism may regard the world as dreamlike and unreal much as a person might regard fiction as something false and unreal *(jia)*, but there is one crucial difference. Whereas Buddhism draws from its "reading" the conclusion that detachment is the ultimate wisdom, the experience of reading fiction, at least according to our author, is nothing if not the deepest engagement. In *Hongloumeng,* therefore, the medium subverts the message, the discourse its language. It is interesting to observe that Cao has left, at the very beginning, what might be construed as a description of the "effect" of reading his novel for us to ponder.

> For a long time Vanitas stood lost in thought, pondering this speech. He then subjected the *Story of the Stone* to a careful second reading. He could see that its main theme was love; that it consisted quite simply of a true record of real events; and that it was entirely free from any tendency to deprave and corrupt. He there-

[57] Wayman, "The Mirror-like Knowledge," 353–57.

fore copied it all out from beginning to end and took it back with him to look for a publisher.

As a consequence of all this, Vanitas, starting off in the Void (which is Truth) came to the contemplation of Form (which is Illusion); and from Form engendered Passion; and by communicating Passion, entered again into Form; and from Form awoke to the Void (which is Truth). He therefore changed his name from Vanitas to Brother Amor, or the Passionate Monk, (because he had approached Truth by way of Passion), and changed the title of the book from *The Story of the Stone* to *The Tale of Brother Amor*. (*SS* 1: 51; *HLM* 1: 6)

Approaching "Truth" by way of "Passion" and "Form (which is Illusion)" may be the most difficult route for many Chinese readers to comprehend, accustomed as they are to mistaking every sign of concealment for a signifier of the actual or the historical. Small wonder that the author who had written himself into his own fiction could loudly mock Vanitas, who serves as the projected reader, similarly situated, of his work: "You in your insistence on ferreting out facts are like the man who dropped his sword in the water and thought to find it again by making a mark on the side of his boat; you are like a man playing a zither with the tuning-pegs glued fast" (*SS* 5: 375; *HLM* 3:1647–48). To resist "ferreting out facts" is to participate properly in the "game" and "diversion" of the text which, in the tongue-in-cheek pronouncement of the narrative, "author, copyist, and reader" alike seem not to understand.

For a scholarly explanation of the magic of art, the writer as conjurer, I can do no better than to cite again the words of O'Flaherty: "the artist, midway between the yogin and the ordinary person, receives the dream passively but learns to control it actively, to transform it into a material object that all of us can see and touch. Instead of merely telling his dream, he shows his dream, drawing us inside his own experience in a way that nonartists can usually do only when they are in love. In this way, the mere illusion of the shared dream becomes a true form of maya, the artistic creation of another reality."[58]

The Buddhist explanation puts the matter in slightly more abstract terms. "The best thing (to say) is that illusory matter (*rūpa*), inasmuch as it lacks any inherent substance of its own, cannot be differentiated from emptiness; and that genuine emptiness, being all perfect, penetrates to what lies beyond existence. By viewing matter as empty we achieve Great Wisdom, so that we do not abide in (the cycle of) life and death. By viewing emptiness as matter we achieve Great Pity, so that we do not abide in *Nirvāṇa*. Only by creating no dualism between matter and emptiness, and no differentiation between pity and wisdom, do we reach Truth."[59]

---

[58] O'Flaherty, *Dreams, Illusions and Other Realities*, p. 289.

[59] From the *Hua-yen huan-yuan kuan*, cited in Fung Yu-lan, *A History of Chinese Philosophy*, translated by Derk Bodde, 2: 342–43.

The novel's view of the "emptiness" of literary art is perhaps best epitomized in the final quatrain.

> When grief for fiction's idle words
> More real than human life appears,
> Reflect that life itself's a dream
> And do not mock the reader's tears.

(SS 5: 376; HLM 3: 1,648)

Not to mock the reader's tears (literally, do not laugh at how silly the mortals could be—*xiu xiao shiren chi*) is to avow both the potency and illusion of fiction, and that is great pity and wisdom, indeed!

THE FICTION OF STONE

If *Hongloumeng* seems to assert that the Buddhist reading of life is both like and unlike a person's reading of fiction, this thesis may also find exemplification in the very experience of the novelistic protagonist. The story of Stone, in other words, not only will find its proper development and closure, but the very resolution of the story elucidates and clarifies its own nature as story, script, and effective fiction. The education of Bao-yu, a protracted process that has led many readers to consider the narrative as a Chinese specimen of Bildungsroman, provides also the education of the reader, but the two levels of education radically differ. The way the text goes about this self-imposed and reflexive task, within the immediate context of the novel's opening and closing episodes, centers on the choice of a rather simple colloquial expression to indicate and complicate the process of enlightenment, to suggest something much more profound and far-reaching as the narrative advances the plot.

Hearing the clerics' promise that they would carve some words on it and take it to a world of glory and prosperity, the stone begs for a clear indication of what words and the whereabouts of the place, but this is the answer he receives: "Do not ask. You will know soon enough when the time comes" (*SS* 1: 48; *HLM* 1: 3). The vernacular "know" (*mingbai*) has the meaning of both knowledge and understanding, and in many passages of the novel the word retains its uncomplicated, common sense. In other passages, however, the phrase implies something much more than the presence or absence of the right kind of information, for it refers, rather, to the proper grasp of the meaning of an event or situation in either its retrospective or prospective aspect.

In his dream tour of the Land of Illusion in chapter 5, for example, Bao-yu is portrayed as not being able to "make much sense (*bu shen mingbai*)" of certain verse and pictures shown to him by the goddess Disenchantment. Because these objects constitute, in fact, a kind of tableau prophetic of the fates of the female companions in his life, Bao-yu finds them "mystifying (*shi he yisi*)" and "fails to make sense (*bu shen mingbai*)" of what he sees (*SS* 1: 133; *HLM* 1: 77–78).[60] To be sure, he can feel the "melancholy" generated by a couplet that intimates human responsibility for needless emotional entanglements (*SS* 1: 132; *HLM* 1: 76), but he himself readily admits his bafflement over the meaning of "passion that outlasts all time" and "love's debts" (*SS* 1: 131; *HLM* 1: 75). The didactic intent of such object lessons for him, according to the goddess Disenchantment's announcement, cannot be more explicit. The spirits of the Duke of Ning-guo and his brother, the Duke of Rong-guo, had revealed to her that their family fortunes would suffer a fated eclipse "because its stock of good fortune has run out, and nothing can be done to replenish it" (*SS* 1: 137; *HLM* 1: 82). Thus commissioned by the dukes to forewarn their offspring, the goddess chooses as the peculiar means of caution "a full exposure to the illusions of feasting, drinking, music, and dancing," in hopes that it "may succeed in bringing about an awakening in [Bao-yu] some time in the future."

Not only does the method chosen for Bao-yu's education echo the purpose for the Stone's incarnate experience assigned by the clerics in chapter 1, but both instances of explanation are also deeply reflective of Buddhist understanding of phenomenal existence. "When the roots are deep and firmly embedded, and the erroneous notion of self not yet destroyed," declares the ancient master Huiyuan (334–416), "then one makes the passions one's garden, sounds and colors one's promenade."[61] That is exactly the kind of life prophesied for both the Stone and Bao-yu, but a "full exposure," of course, will require at least several turbulent years of his young life, since the span of the 120-chapter narrative will take Bao-yu from his early teens to a time probably just before his twentieth birthday. Although in the course of the dream tour in chapter 5 Bao-yu's curiosity is occasionally aroused to such extent that he indeed is determined to "make an effort to understand these things" (*SS* 1: 131; *HLM* 1: 75), it is also apparent that the brief confine of his dream allows little possibility of comprehending the full meaning of his vision and experience. "Silly boy! You still don't understand, do you?" is the apt verdict of the goddess (*SS* 1: 145; *HLM* 1: 89), and it will take a long time before the boy arrives at the realization not only that love is an illusion in "the immortal precincts," but also that "the love of your dust-stained, mortal world must be doubly an illusion" (*SS* 1: 146; *HLM* 1: 90). When at last his story draws to its proper termination, Bao-yu in the narrative will be the one whose actions and words increasingly become a source of perplexity to those around him, even as he himself gains greater understanding of his situation (for example, chapters 116–17).

---

[60] It should be pointed out that the phrase *bu shen mingbai* (literally, did not quite understand) is not found in the family of hand-copied manuscripts, and it may have been a later editorial insertion in the full-length versions. The phrase *bujie* (did not understand or comprehend), however, was used repeatedly in all versions from the beginning.

[61] Huiyuan, "Shamen bujing wangzhe lun." I use the English translation by Leon Hurvitz, in "Render unto Caesar in Early Chinese Buddhism," p. 98.

Such a development may readily be seen in the episode on Bao-yu's second tour of the Land of Illusion, which is induced by a remark of Musk, the maid, when his lost piece of jade is returned to him by another mysterious monk. Ostensibly cheered by this reunion with his birthstone, Bao-yu nevertheless lapses into a deathlike faint when Musk makes the unthinking observation: "What a treasure that stone of yours is! Just seeing it has made you better! Thank goodness you never managed to smash it to pieces!" (SS 5: 283; HLM 3: 1,580). That these words can cause such a sudden, violent upsurge of emotions in Bao-yu is undoubtedly attributable to the unintended but unerring uncovering of his dilemma. Had he managed to smash his yu (jade/desire) from the beginning, when he first met Dai-yu (see the highly dramatic scene in chapter 3), he might have altered significantly the course of his life. On the level of the narrative's realistic plot, the smashed stone might have vastly reduced the chance of his family's exploitation of the myth of gold-and-jade affinity that eventually clinched the choice of Bao-chai as his mate (see chapters 8, 28, 29, 84, 96). Furthermore, it would therefore have prevented its mysterious loss which, in turn, brought on his strange illness that resulted in his unwitting marriage to a substitute bride. On another level of the narrative's allegorical rhetoric, on the other hand, Bao-yu's success in smashing or losing his jade might signal, in fact, his success in severing himself from his oretic entanglements.

As it turns out in the novel, however, neither alternative proves a possibility for him up to this point: he cannot have Dai-yu, the object of his desire, nor can he forget her even long after her death. His dilemma thus necessitates a second visit to the Land of Illusion so that certain crucial moments of his life, this time witnessed with greater retrospective clarity, can work to provide him with the needed illumination. His journey to the mythic realm provides, therefore, a structural emphasis on thematic recapitulation in the narrative, "a return," as he himself acknowledges, "to the scene of [his] childhood dream" (SS 5: 286; HLM 3: 1,582). His serial encounters with certain figures resembling deceased female companions—Faithful, You San-jie, Skybright, and Dai-yu— serve primarily to underscore the lesson that a Buddhist monk seeks to drum into his consciousness: "predestined attachments of the human heart are all of them mere illusion, they are obstacles blocking our spiritual path" (SS 5: 293; HLM 3: 1,587).

When he awakes from his comalike condition, which has sent his loved ones into fits and weeping, his mother, Lady Wang is moved to remark:

> When Bao-yu was ill before, another monk came, I remember, and told us that Bao-yu had a precious object of his own at home that could cure him. He was referring to the jade. He too must have known all about its magical properties. It is extraordinary that Bao-yu came into the world with the Stone in his mouth! Have you ever heard of such a thing happening, in the whole of history? Who knows what will become of the Stone in the end? And who knows what will

become of *him*! It seems to be an inseparable part of his life, in sickness and health, at his birth and . . . (*SS* 5: 295; *HLM* 3: 1,588)

These words of the mother, in dwelling upon the stone's mysterious appearance and alleged "magical properties," point up only her continuous bewilderment over the events that had befallen her son. For her and so many other members of the large Jia household, the stone remains an opaque, enigmatic object whose inexplicable movements of appearance and disappearance seem to defy rational comprehension.

By contrast, Bao-yu's wordless reaction at this time indicates plainly that he has experienced another crucial breakthrough in his perception. Whereas Lady Wang could not bring herself to mention her son's death or the deathlike coma he just experienced, and broke off her sentence with weeping, "Bao-yu felt in his own mind that he now knew the answer to her questions only too well (*xinli queye mingbai*). Thinking back, he understood more clearly the significance of his visit to the 'other world.'" From this moment on until the time Bao-yu finally leaves home—ostensibly to take his civil service examination but thereafter also to enter the Buddhist sangha—the narrative use of the term *mingbai* increases in both frequency and irony as it seeks to depict the growth of his understanding in contrast to the uncomprehending alarm and apprehension afflicting his loved ones. When Bao-yu meets at the door another monk resembling the one who served as his guide in his dream, "the truth began to grow clearer in his mind (*xinli zao youxi mingbai liao*)" (*SS* 5: 301; *HLM* 3: 1,592), as a result of which he eventually decides to hand back the jade to the cleric. In reponse to Aroma's frantic pleadings to desist, since she fears that the jade's departure would again induce his illness, Bao-yu pointedly replies: "Now that I know my true purpose (*you liao xin*, literally, possess my mind), what do I need the jade for?" (*SS* 5: 302; *HLM* 3: 1,593).

Later, when his cousin Xi-chun resolves to cut her hair and become a nun against all protests, Bao-yu's singular approbation of her action provokes his mother to say: "I'm afraid I completely fail to understand (*wo suoxing bu mingbai liao*) what's going on in your mind" (*SS* 5: 319; *HLM* 3: 1,606). In those highly charged episodes just prior to Bao-yu's departure from his household, Lady Wang is not the only person who fails to understand his mind. Even his wife Bao-chai, with whom he has recently consummated their marriage (chap. 109) and for whom this new-found intimacy has yielded occasional insight into his thoughts and behavior, nonetheless still finds his words and actions baffling most of the time. Unable to comprehend his growing gravitation toward the ideal of complete detachment and world renunciation, Bao-chai makes one last desperate attempt to "remonstrate the idiotic person," as the titular couplet of chapter 118 declares, to wean him away from books that emphasize "quitting the world and rising above the mortal plane" (*SS* 5: 329; *HLM* 3: 1,612) by urging her spouse to study diligently for the civil service examination. Their pointed debate on whether he should uphold the Confucian values of "a heart full of loyalty and filial devotion" or merely subscribe to a "world-fleeing, society-denying (*chushi liqun*)" philosophy ends ostensibly with his concession, much to her surprise and delight. Such Daoist and Buddhist classics as the *Zhuangzi* and *The Compendium of the Five Lamps* he orders his maid to store away, with the explanation: "Now I understand. . . . None of those books is worth anything. It would be best to burn the lot and be rid of them once and for all!" (*SS* 5: 332; *HLM* 3: 1,615).

In the immediate context of the story, Bao-yu's profession of understanding (*mingbai*) ironically accentuates the sharpest disparity of knowledge between him and his wife, and thus also the complete rupture of their communication. She may interpret his behavior as an acceptance of her remonstration, but he is now ready to sever his familial ties once and for all. That is why, I suspect, he can reply to her pleadings with the cryptic remark: "Doing well in the examination is not that difficult. And what you say about *never achieving anything else* and making *some return for Heaven's favour and our ancestors' virtue* is very much to the point" (*SS* 5: 330; *HLM* 3: 1,614). Her point, however, is not the same as his: he will make some return for Heaven's favor and his ancestors' virtue by going to the examination and passing it, but that occasion will also mark his exit from his family. That resolve will render superfluous even those books he loves to read.

Bao-yu's decision to embrace "the Gate of Emptiness" and take up a life without the family is indeed of momentous significance because the act itself, as we have pointed out, may betoken the sharpest conflict between Buddhist practice and the ideals—social and ethical—of traditional Chinese culture. As the sole male heir of the family, Bao-yu is saddled with the special burden of ensuring for his family's biological perpetuity. If his unborn child whom Bao-chai is carrying turns out to be a girl and he has already become a monk and taken up the life of celibacy, the line of that particular Jia house will be terminated. In this light, part of the tragic finality that the narrative denouement so powerfully conveys lies in the fact that such misfortunes as unjust conviction, confiscation of property, and even imprisonment can all be reversed by a so-called "enlightened monarch" (chap. 119). The destruction of the source for male issue, however, is a catastrophe no amount of imperial favor can undo. The Bao-yu who has vanished (if he is going into the monastery, as his words have darkly hinted prior to his departure for the examination) is as good as a dead Bao-yu. Hence the pathos of the futile search authorized by a royal edict. Far from political pandering to possible readership from the court, as critics skeptical of the last forty chapters' authenticity have sometimes charged, the author/redactor here has in fact heaped irony upon irony in his treatment of the Jia household and its future prospects.

Again, we have mentioned how apologists for Buddhism have sought to reconcile their faith with Chinese culture by urging that the believers' submission to the Law and practice of rituals may bring about the ultimate salvation of parents and ancestors. With respect to Wang Guowei's interpretation of Bao-yu's motive cited earlier, just how much of the young man's decision to leave home is governed by the motive of repaying his parents (in the sense of accruing religious merit for them) is very much subject to debate. His words of leavetaking just prior to his departure for the examination—"I could never repay you adequately for all you have done for me, Mother. But if I can do this one thing successfully, if I can do my very best and pass this examination, then perhaps I can bring you a little pleasure. Then my worldly duty will be accomplished and I will at least have made some small return for all the trouble I have caused you" (*SS* 5: 336; *HLM* 3: 1,620)—clearly emphasize only his momentary accommodation of her wishes for him to succeed in a worldly career. In view of the fact that scholastic success eventuates in his permanent departure from the home, at a time when his wife is pregnant with his child (though the reader will be forever ignorant of its sex, and thus will also be ignorant of whether the Jia family will have an heir), one may justly wonder what sort of "pleasure" would be brought to Lady Wang, and whether such "repayment" is as insubstantial and unrewarding as his final, wordless bow to his father (chap. 120).

If it is unclear how his assumption of a religious vocation can benefit his family members, his motivation concerning his own prospect is perhaps more apparent: to rid himself from a painful and guilty memory primarily incurred by Dai-yu's death, he must sever all oretic entanglements. Whether he actually succeeds in his quest for personal release after he becomes a monk is again open to speculation. Nonetheless, his flight from the family may certainly be construed as the most concrete expression of his "enlightenment"—the attainment of knowledge and perception (*mingbai*) that contrasts with his youthful condition of nonperception at the narrative's beginning, a state of ignorance or unenlightenment (*wuming*, Skt., *avidyā*) which Buddhist doctrines explicitly take to be "the source of the net of delusion.[62] Bao-yu's development at the end of the narrative thus fulfills the promise made to the preincarnate Stone by the clerics at the novel's beginning: "You will know (*mingbai*) soon enough when the time comes."

The mythic Stone's attainment of knowledge provides at the same time the final clarification for the reader, thus fulfilling also the promise of dispelling the reader's perplexity by the exposition of origin (*zhuming laili*—*HLM* 1: 1), for the very "history" of its story "in both worlds (*shen qian shen hou shi*)"— as the preincarnate rock, then the Divine Luminescent Stone-in-Waiting, and finally the incarnate Bao-yu—constitutes the fiction of the narrative under perusal. The story of the Stone is also the inscription "writ" on the Stone. In tracing for us the lengthy but circular process of how the Stone became jade

---

[62] Huiyuan, "Mingbaoying lun," p. 76.

and returned to Stone's "primitive form" again (see *SS* 1: 3; *HLM* 1: 48–49; *SS* 5: 369–76; *HLM* 3: 1,643–48), fiction and narrative coincide.

Even the inscription itself, however, possesses the double quality of revelation and concealment. After it had been refined by Nüwa, the stone supposedly attained a certain numinous power (*tongling*) signaled by its translucent luster. Capable of growing big or small at will, it first caught the attention of the monk and Daoist, in fact, as a small piece of fan-pendantlike jade. Then it was shown to Zhen Shi-yin again by the clerics to help him understand (*mingbai*) the "heavenly mysteries" embodied in the story about the Stone Page and Crimson Plant they have been telling. Dubbed the "absurd creature" by the clerics, the small piece of jade nonetheless now bears the incised name of "Precious Jade of Numinous Knowledge" (*tongling baoyu*), the examination of which brought Shi-yin to the frontier of the Land of Illusion. Finally, the jade made its mundane appearance (Chap. 8) as Bao-yu's birthstone held in the boy's mouth when he was born. In the episode in which Bao-yu is asked to show it to his cousin Bao-chai, the narrator directly intrudes into the narrative to remind his reader again of the fictive origin of both stone and jade by citing a regulated verse of some later "jesting poet":

> Nü-wa's stone-smelting is a tale unfounded;
> On such weak fancies our Great Fable's grounded. . . .
>
> (*SS* 1:189; *HLM* 1: 123)

Immediately thereafter, however, the narrator goes on to remark:

> That foolish Stone had also recorded its transformed image bearing the seal script carved on it by the scabby monk. Below we have made a sketch of the script; but its true size is exceedingly small, for only thus could it be held in the mouth of an infant still in the womb. If we draw the characters in their true size, they will be so tiny that the reader's eyes will be severely taxed. That's not pleasant. For this reason we have preserved their form but have enlarged them slightly according to scale, so that they may be read even in lamplight or if the reader's tipsy. We offer this explanation to protect us from the cavil: how big is an infant's mouth that it can hold such a clumsy object? (*HLM* 1: 124, my translation)[63]

These words have in turn elicited a remarkable headnote from the Red Inkstone scholiast:

> All of a sudden he [the author] writes these few sentences, causing the imaginary (*huan*) to become real (*zhen*) and the real to become imaginary. [Interweaving] the real and the false (*zhenzhen jiajia*), he delights in the play of brush and ink. He may be described as the most cunning indeed! As a person, one should be honest; as a writer, one should be cunning. (*Pingyu*, p. 184)

[63] The passage is not included in Hawkes' translation, but it is well attested in virtually all versions since 1754. See Li 1: 194; Yang 1: 120; Itō 1: 112.

What impresses the scholiast in this instance is, of course, the author's self-conscious mockery of his own creation. Immediately after a poem that continues to harp on the fictive origin and nature of his tale, the narrator provides a fastidious apology for one particular aspect: the jade inscriptions have been deliberately enlarged, but such deception is supposedly required to protect the writer from the charge of unrealistic mimesis. As if the reader who has been invited hitherto to accept a far more incredible invention now requires this sort of blatant reminder to maintain a proper perspective on narrative probability and verisimilitude, the double irony of feigning acknowledgment of misrepresentation to gloss fiction—itself already a form of representation that leaves the real or the truthful (*zhen*) for the imaginary/illusory (*huan*) and the false (*jia*)—displays such verve and craft of rhetoric that it justly wins the scholiast's praise.

The commentator's generous words, perceptive as they are, touch on only one dimension of authorial guile. They miss a deeper level of textual cunning. For as we have it in Chap. 8, the narrative seems to indicate that "the words which the scabbyheaded monk had incised on the stone when he found it lying in its diminished shape under Greensickness Peak" (*SS* 1: 189; *HLM* 1: 124) are composed of only the few seal-script characters that enjoin its proprietor to vigilant ownership ("mislay me not, forget me not") by reason of its magical power to ward off evil. Readers who have traversed earlier episodes, however, cannot so readily forget the report of what the monk actually said to the stone on that first occasion of meeting: "Ha, I see you have magical properties! But nothing to recommend you. I shall have to cut a few words on you so that anyone seeing you will know at once that you are something special" (*SS* 1: 48; *HLM* 1: 3). Those "few words" that the monk eventually carves on the stone will turn out to be, in the course of the whole narrative, not merely the talismanic signs but, in fact, the entire "history" of its life in both worlds, *The Story of the Stone* itself.

Within the mundane plot of the narrative, the brief markings of the jade appear indeed as omen of its alleged supernatural power. Both word and object in this mode may be said to foreshadow those episodes in the narrative in which the jade's mysterious disappearance and reappearance will crucially affect the immediate welfare and ultimate destiny of its owner (chaps. 25, 94–95, 115–17). Since the phrase *tongling* implies both numinous intelligence and efficacy, the jade birthstone is symbolic of both Bao-yu's capacity for understanding or the lack thereof and, at the same time, the coveted charm custodial of his well-being. As such, the jade may seem to be that "something special" that the monk declared he would make of the rejected stone in the opening episode.

But this piece of jade thus inscribed, we must remember, is also a mask, the "transformed" appearance of another slab of stone bearing another kind of inscription: namely, the story of the "obdurate stone" (*wanshi*). Used throughout the narrative, the adjective *wan* applied to the stone has the meanings of ignorant, inane, stubborn, and playful.[64] In this slightly pejorative though never malicious description, the term resonates with other appelations assigned to the incarnate Bao-yu by the narrator and other narrative characters: stupid (*chun, yu*), moronic (*dai*), silly (*chi*), idiotic (*sha*), and mad (*feng*). These teasing but unflattering epithets, deliberately counterpointed to other references of Bao-yu's natural talents (*tianfen*) and sharp wit, thus alert us to what a critic has called "the double-voiced orientation" of the narrative.[65] The obdurate Stone is also verily the intelligent/efficacious Jade, and its story of how one becomes the other when their juxtaposed existences are finally merged is also one that substantiates the injunction of Bao-yu's ancestors to the goddess Disenchantment, that "the pleasures of the flesh" into which the boy was to be inducted must discharge the educative responsibility of shocking "the mad obdurateness out of him (*jingqi chiwan*)" (*HLM* 1: 82).

Nowhere perhaps is such a dramatic summation of "the double-voiced orientation" more apparent than when Jia Bao-yu speaks to his double, Zhen Bao-yu, toward the end. Irked by what he considers to be worldly platitudes and insincere laudation of their common name mouthed by his mirror image, Jia Bao-yu says: "Your praise is alas undeserved. I am but a dull and foolish creature, a mere lump of senseless stone [*wanshi*]! How can I compare with a person of such quality and nobility as yourself? It is I who am unworthy of the name [that is, Bao-yu or Precious Jade] that we both bear" (*SS* 5: 274; *HLM* 3: 1,573). Occuring, as it does, almost immediately before Bao-yu's final resolve to leave his family (ostensibly for the civil service examination but ultimately for the Buddhist priesthood), this encounter of the two look-alikes represents the most poignant experience of Bao-yu's reckoning with himself and all that he regards as unworthy defilements of mind and spirit.

As a response to his guest's conventional compliment, Bao-yu's words also simulate ritual modesty, the required etiquette of self-deprecation. The central point in this verbal jousting, ostensibly over the question of who is more worthy to bear their shared name of Precious Jade, actually concerns a much deeper issue of the meaning of that name. As such, the debate touches on the most crucial ramifications of the protagonist's self-understanding, for his name and all its symbolic and literary associations either created or activated in the total narrative are what finally defines his sense of identity.

As it is used in the novel, the name Jia Bao-yu most certainly recalls a famous passage in *Analects* 9. 13, where

> Tze-kung said, "If you had a piece of beautiful jade (*yu*) here, would you put it
> away safely in a box or would you try to sell it for a good price (*jia*)?" The Master

---

[64] See Lucien Miller, "Masks of Fiction in 'Dream of the Red Chamber,'" pp. 36–37, note 76, and p. 82 notes 252–53.

[65] See the fine analysis by Wang Jing, *The Story of Stone*, pp. 193–98.

said, "Of course I would sell it. Of course I would sell it. All I am waiting for is the right offer (*jia*)."[66]

The novel's specific allusion to this classic is made apparent as early as chap. 1, where the first line of a couplet composed by the framing character Jia Yu-cun reads: "The jade (*yu*) in the casket awaits a good price (*shan jia*)" (*HLM* 1: 13, my translation). In the paronomasic rhetoric of the narrative, Jia Bao-yu literally can mean False or Pricey Precious Jade.

The passage in the *Analects*, we must note, has been interpreted at least since the time of the Song dynasty as a favored disciple's ingenious query on whether Confucius wishes to serve in government and the Master's unambiguous reply that his willingness is dependent on a favorable condition.[67] So understood, it stands in traditional Chinese culture as a supreme example of legitimate vocational aspiration. Sanctioned by the words of Confucius, the educated man has both moral duty and right to serve, to aim his life at officialdom.

Unfortunately, public office is the state of affairs to which the Jia Bao-yu of the narrative shows complete aversion. Throughout the story, it is the self-indulgence of this young boy, his preference for poetry and games with his female companions over preparation for the examinations of the first degree, that cause continuous friction between him and his anxious father. By the last third of the narrative, Bao-yu is said to have made better efforts at his studies, but his disdain for officialdom remains constant and undiminished.

Bao-yu's attitude is what endows the episode in chapter 115 with its ultimate significance. Ignorant of his host's disposition, Zhen Bao-yu's reply to the former's gesture of affected politesse continues to play upon what may be termed the Confucian myth on jade.

> "When I was young," mused Zhen Bao-yu aloud for his new friend's benefit, "I was blind to my own limitations and entertained ideas far above station. But then my family fell on hard times, and we have all spent the past few years in greatly reduced circumstances. . . . You, on the other hand, have lived in the lap of luxury all your life, you have lacked for nothing, and you have, I am sure, been able to achieve great distinction in your literary compositions and in the study of public affairs, a distinction that has caused your honourable father to hold you in high esteem, and to view you with great pride and affection. I say again, you are worthy of the fine name that we both bear." (*SS* 5: 274; *HLM* 3: 1573)

The first sentence of this speech should read in literal translation: "When I was young, I thought I could have been carved and ground." The actions so described (*zhuo, mo*) refer once more to a passage in *Analects* 1: 15:

---

[66] Confucius, *The Analects*, translated by D. C. Lau, p. 81.
[67] See *Lunyu jizhu buzheng shusu* 5: 26a–b.

Tze-kung said, "'Poor without being obsequious, wealthy without being arrogant.' What do you think of his saying?"

The Master said, "That will do, but better still 'Poor yet delighting in the Way, wealthy yet observant of the rites.'"

Tzu-kung said, "The *Odes* say,

> Like bone cut, like horn polished,
> Like jade carved, like stone ground

Is not what you have said a case in point?"[68]

As the passage makes clear, the quotation from the *Poetry Classic* is used by the disciple to liken Confucius' refinement of his own moral formulation to the actions deployed in the poem: the cutting, polishing, carving, and grinding are efforts of cultivation (*xiu*) that turn objects of elemental crudity into prized artifacts.[69] A comparison that wins the teacher's immediate approbation, it has been regarded by most commentators down through the ages as a succinct conceit for the arduous but rewarding process of educative and ethical discipline.

The resonance of Confucian diction and sentiment is certainly not lost on Jia Bao-yu, but its overall impact amounts to "the telltale rhetoric of the career worm" (*SS* 5: 274; *HLM* 3: 1,573). So completely repulsed is Bao-yu by his interlocutor's speech and character that their meeting ends with the former's quick return to his room of his wife, Bao-chai, in "profound depression" (*SS* 5: 277; *HLM* 3: 1,576). The coveted meeting with his own alter ego unalterably confirms his distaste for a worldly career, so he reports his disgruntlement to his mate, and the subsequent debate with Bao-chai on another Confucian theme—the expected duties of a filial son—only strengthens and hastens his resolve to quit the family altogether.

---

[68] Lau, trans., *The Analects*, p. 7.

[69] See *Lunyu jizhu* 1: 59a–63a. The gloss on this passage made by either Xunzi or some of his disciples is also revealing. See Book 27, "The Great Compendium," in Knoblock, *Xunzi*, 3: 227–28:

Learning and culture are to men what polishing and grinding are to jade. An Ode says:

> Like bone cut, like horn polished,
> like jade carved, like stone ground.

This refers to studying and questioning.

The *bi* disc made from the Bian He and the stone from Jingli, having been polished by men, became treasures to the whole world. Zigong and Jilu, who were originally men from a frontier district, clothed themselves in culture and learning and wrapped themselves in ritual and duty so that they became distinguished scholars of the world.

As Guo Shaoyu points out (*Zhaoyu shi* 1: 155–56), the school of Xunzi's understanding of culture reflects deep influence of the Confucian discourse. Needless to say, this sort of culture and learning (*wenxue*) is a hateful garment to Jia Bao-yu.

Read in such a context, Bao-yu's reference to himself as the obdurate stone (*wanshi*) now takes on a signficance that far transcends the dictates of polite repartee. Not only does the term recall the original form of his previous existence and the vicissitudes that it has undergone "in both worlds" up to this point, but it also undoubtedly evokes for many Chinese readers the well-known idiom stemming from Buddhist lore: "the obdurate stones nod their heads (*wan-shi dian tou*)." As it is reported in the Qing collectanea *Tongsubian*,

> Zhu Daosheng [c. 360–434], a monk of the Jin period [265–420], once gathered on Mount Huqiu some stones to be his disciples. He expounded to them the *Nirvāṇa Sūtra*, and all the stones were moved to nod their heads. Nowadays this expression of "obdurate stones nod their heads" is used to indicate how great is the power of spiritual illumination.[70]

The Buddhist sutra, we must recall, has been intimately identified with this famous cleric because he seeks to wed its interpretation to the fundamental Mahayana tenet "that all sentient beings poseess the Buddha-nature in them, and that all are capable of attaining Buddhahood." When the sutra's first Chinese translator, Faxian, indicated in certain passages that the *icchantikas* (demons) were devoid of such capability because they were creatures "whose primary interest was the gratification of their desires," Zhu Daosheng thought it had to be an error of translation.[71] He vigorously contended that the totality of Mahayanist doctrine could not support such a point of exclusion, and for him, even *icchantikas* were endowed with Buddha nature. The stones nodding their heads in the tale hence illustrate both the boundless scope and sudden nature of enlightenment, Zhu Daosheng's cherished interpretation of Mahayanist soteriology.

Given the web of meanings surrounding the anecdote, we can now see how profoundly and appositely evocative that term "obdurate stone" is meant to be when it is used in the narrative to denominate the protagonist. As the pre-incarnate Stone rejected from a heaven-building task, it became entangled within a specific network of karmic relations while on its way to human incarnation. As the Stone-in-Waiting befriending a Crimson Plant by watering it, its action elicited from its object of attention a similar motion of gratitude to repay its kindness with the tears of a lifetime. This initial stirring and reach of desire, to be vastly expanded and played out as a magnificent tale of reciprocal love in the world of Red Dust, also give the lie to the common Chinese adage that "wood and stone have no feelings or consciousness" (*mu shi wu qing*). Indeed, the incarnate young Bao-yu is diagnosed by the goddess Disenchantment as "the most lustful person . . . ever known in the whole world," which

---

[70] *Tongsubian*, compiled by Zhai Hao, *juan* 2, "Dili," p. 37.

[71] Kenneth Ch'en, *Buddhism in China*, p. 115. See also Whalen Lai, "Tao-sheng's Theory of Sudden Enlightment Re-Examined."

means in the sense of her further explanation that not merely is he susceptible to feminine charm but also that his young being has been filled by nature with "blind, defenceless love" (*SS* 1: 145–46; *HLM* 1: 90). Most appropriately, as the Red Inkstone scholia repeatedly declare (*Pingyu*, pp. 199, 354, 367, 405, 455, 477, 551), Bao-yu as a character is someone who can "make the unfeeling feel (*qing buqing*)."[72]

If Bao-yu is thus seen against his intricate and protracted involvement in the life of desire, those following his development may well be compelled to ask: could there be enlightenment at long last for this uncomprehending Stone that is also very much a special species of *icchantika*? When *wanshi* is first applied to Stone near the beginning of the narrative, the reader is given little clue as to why such usage of the Buddhist nomenclature has peculiar relevance. When Bao-yu finally refers to himself as *wanshi* toward the end of his sojourn in his human household, however, the irony cannot be more poignant and profound. The conversation between Zhen and Jia Bao-yu in actuality makes explicit drama of the confrontation between two myths of stones: the Confucian and the Buddhist. The encounter with this young man who is his mirror image, his self as other, brings to a climax the male protagonist's prolonged search for the knowledge of who he is and what he is to do with his life. Significantly the narrative tells us that he hopes to find in Zhen Bao-yu a *zhiji* (translated as alter ego by Minford, but having the literal meaning of one who knows the self), a term that in previous times he reserves almost exclusively for his beloved Lin Dai-yu. At this stage of experience, it seems that a decision must be rendered as to which myth of stones shall have a more authentic claim on the existence of Bao-yu.

In the words of Zhen Bao-yu, his "other" self, Jia Bao-yu is lauded as someone who has won paternal esteem and affection by virtue of literary accomplishments and excellence in the study of public affairs. He presents, in fact, a vision of certain social and familial roles in conformity to Confucian orthodoxy that are totally at odds with the "real" Jia Bao-yu's character of the narrative and untrue to his experience. If "repairing the sky" is to be understood as the traditional metaphor for distinctive service through public office, this stone has long since been found unfit for such undertaking. The stone's failures in his efforts to prepare for public life in the human world are, in short, fated, but this rejected stone is also destined to transmit another kind of wonder (*chuanqi*), to bear another form of testimony. Jia Bao-yu's self-reference so expressive of his self-identity—a sense of which has been progressively discovered and con-

---

[72] This well-known epithet of the scholiasts is notoriously difficult to translate because the first *qing* in the phrase is a verb, but the sense, unlike most translations known to me, does not refer to the subject (in this case Jia Bao-yu) who feels something, but that he has the capacity to evoke or elicit feeling from an unfeeling other.

firmed through the last third of the narrative—thus also signals a resounding repudiation of a worldly vocation, both the obligations and economics of Confucian culture. He is the stubborn, stupid Stone that, even in this world, resists Confucian refinement. If Zhen Bao-yu and his Ruist aspirations represent his "mirror image," his "second or divided self," then this Doppelgänger will have to be rejected like so many similar figures in modernist literature.[73] Jia Bao-yu's rhetoric contriving modesty ("I am a dull and foolish creature") serves but to camouflage a mind almost fully awakened to his true condition and the beckoning promise of Buddhist deliverance. This "lump of senseless stone" is about to nod its head.[74]

To perceive the plenitude of meaning in Jia Bao-yu's self-designation, a plenitude of intertextual allusiveness, is also to recognize the importance and high regard of fiction upheld in the narrative. If the rejected Stone must undergo a certain fullness of experience before it comes to understand its purpose and worth, the script detailing that experience carved on its back (starting with the account of Nüwa smelting stones and going through the entire "Great Fable," as the poem of chap. 8 says) is what endows it with genuine appeal (*shizai di haochu*) and transforms it into "something special" (*qi wu*). Its true talismanic power, akin to magic, is its literary erotics, for it is indeed that account that

---

[73] For a stimulating account of this form of fictive doubles in modern literary representations, see Sau-ling Cynthia Wong, *Reading Asian American Literature*, pp. 77–117.

[74] Another impressive literary antecedent to the name *wanshi* in this narrative must be that found in the erotic novel, *The Carnal Prayer Mat (Rou putuan)* by the late Ming writer Li Yu (1611–1680). The libertine hero of this familiar tale, prior to embarking on a life of unfettered sensual indulgence, was amply warned by the Buddhist monk, Lone Peak, about possible perils facing him. At the story's end, when he faced Lone Peak once more and in repentance sought to take the Buddhist vow, the hero "selected his own name in religion: Stubborn Stone [*wanshi*]. It signified regret over his slowness to repent, which showed the stubbornness of a stone, and also gratitude for Lone Peak's skillful preaching, which had persuaded a stubborn stone that hadn't nodded its head in three years to start nodding again." See Li Yu, *The Carnal Prayer Mat*, translated by Patrick Hanan, p. 304 (Chap. 20). As this passage readily reveals, Li Yu seems conversant with the story of Zhu Daosheng, the Buddhist preacher in the story of "The Obdurate Stone Nodding Its Head," for his novel's hero is unquestionably a kind of sensual demon, an *icchantika*. Jia Bao-yu, of course, is no overt profligate, nor is *Hongloumeng* an erotic novel in the same genre as Li's work, but the use of the stubborn/obdurate stone motif in both novels shows such remarkable parallels that a direct influence seems likely.

A second, little noticed but no less significant antecedent to the stone may be found in another seventeenth-century work of prose fiction, the *Fengshen yanyi* or *Investiture of the Gods* attributed to Xu Zhonglin. Detailing the epic struggle between the righteous forces of the conquering Zhou King and the human and superhuman warriors defending King Zhou, the last tyrant of the Shang, the novel contains a brief episode (in chap. 13) wherein one Lady Rocky Bluff (Shiji Niangniang) was captured and killed by the Immortal of the Great Monad (Taiyi Zhenren). The motif relevant to *Hongloumeng* is that the lady is identified as a piece of obdurate stone (*wan shi*) who through cultivation has succeeded in becoming a spirit by gathering the numinous ethers (*ling qi*) of heaven and earth. See *Fengshen yanyi* 1: 120–26.

catches the attention of Vanitas, a character structured in the opening and closing sections of the narrative as a sort of reflector for the author-as-reader, and causes his realization that this is "a stone of some consequence" (*SS* 1: 49).[75]

The text carved on stone, a practice reserved for those documents deemed worthy of the greatest duration, has long been the chosen medium for transmitting and preserving historical and Buddhist writings. Though employed in earlier times, it was in the Han period that flat steles (known as *bei*) were regularly inscribed "to commemorate historical occasions, to preserve the memory of individuals and to standardise sacred texts in correct and permanent form."[76]

Our *Story of the Stone*, when compared to such an illustrious and venerable line of inscribed rocks, again reveals its paradoxical character. Lacking "the authentication of a dynasty and date" (*SS* 1: 49; *HLM* 1: 4) or any rehearsal of "statemanship" or "social message of any kind" (*SS* 1: 49; *HLM* 1: 4), as Vanitas tells the stone, the text nevertheless purports to relate the "history" of a significant individual. No sacred text or "moral examples of moral grandeur among its characters" (*SS* 1:49; *HLM* 1: 4), it still recounts "the life of a man" in both worlds before he finally seeks refuge in the Gate of Emptiness. Small wonder that Vanitas, having encountered in the mythic realm the Stone which had returned from its incarnate journey to assume its original form, and having read the entirety of its story, would voice his fear that "the people in the world would not want to read it" (*HLM* 1: 4) even if it were copied and published.

The stone's reply to Vanitas' critique amounts to a tongue-in-cheek apology for redefining the genre of prose fiction that is at the same time a parody and a rewriting of the old *dufa* (how to read) commentary of fiction. Against the charge of no "artificial period setting," Stone argues that its way of telling its "*Story of the Stone* exactly as it occured" actually improves the text. It shuns "stale old convention" and it endows the story with a "freshness" that the "old romances" do not have (*SS* 1: 49; *HLM* 1: 5). Its content does not, as did "historical romances," pile up "scandalous anecdotes" about politicians or "scabrous attacks on the reputations of long-dead gentlewomen." It does not exploit obscenities like the "erotic novel" nor thrive on formulaic constructions of plot and language.

The subject on which the stone "spent half a lifetime studying with [its] own eyes and ears" consists of a "number of females," characters who, according to Vanitas after his first reading, are "conspicuous . . . only for their passion or folly or for some trifling talent or insignificant virtue" (*SS* 1: 49: *HLM* 1: 4). This explanation for such an unusual choice of subject matter once

---

[75] The clause, "knowing that he is a stone of some consequence," is not found in the early manuscripts.

[76] "Paper and Printing," by Tsien Tsuen-hsuin, p. 28, in *SCC* 5/1. For further idealized accounts of stone inscriptions, see Liu Xie, *Wenxin diaolong*, chapter 11, "Ming Zhen (Inscription and Exhortation)."

more stresses technique over content. There is no claim that these women are "better people" than those who populate other books. Rather, the stone highlights the possibility that its text can elicit "the contemplation of their actions and motives" (*SS* 1: 50; *HLM* 1: 5). So casual and passing a remark, in fact, directs us to an extravagant prerogative of the fiction writer that is also passed on, through his creation, to the reader: namely, the prerogative of knowing other minds and feelings. It is a privilege that, in Western understanding, turns the writer into someone godlike and, in the Chinese tradition, makes the person an arch rival of the historian. The exercise of this privilege, so imply the words of Stone as author, is what endows its tale with the ring of sincerity and authenticity: "All that my story narrates, the meetings and partings, the joys and sorrows, the ups and downs of fortune, are recorded exactly as they happened. I have not dared to add the tiniest bit of touching-up, for fear of losing the true picture" (*SS* 1: 50; *HLM* 1: 5). The trope *chuanzuo*, though it has the literal meaning of boring and chiseling (which may explain Hawkes' choice of "touching-up" as a translation), actually carries the metaphoric significance of forcing one's way through—a train of thought or an argument. Thus *chuanzuo fuhui* means to offer farfetched or dubious explanation by the use of superficial details or non sequitur arguments to gain a sense of literary coherence and cogency, and these are the pitfalls that the stone's tale claims to have eschewed.[77] The "truth" (*zhen*) of its tale is not based merely upon the record of observable and experienced events ("exactly as they had happened"), but founded much more on probing and weighing the causes of actions and motives (*yuanwei*), a truth less dependent on mimetic fidelity than on the rationale and probability internal to the text.

How is the reader supposed to react to such a text? A clue to answering this question, I believe, can be found in the narrative's description of Vanitas' reaction. As a consequence of reading the tale for a second time, pondering it, copying it, and taking it with him to look for a publisher, "Vanitas, starting off in the Void (which is Truth) came to the contemplation of Form (which is Illusion); and from Form engendered Passion; and by communicating Passion, entered again into Form; and from Form awoke to the Void (which is Truth)" (*SS* 1: 51; *HLM* 1: 6). This sentence of such sinuous length and complexity, formed as it is by the appropriation of classical terminologies from the tradition of *Prajñapāramitā* (perfection of wisdom) descending from Nagarjuna's philosophy but influential in virtually all subsequent major divisions of Chinese Buddhism including Chan, ostensibly depicts the effect of reading in religious terms.[78] The rhetoric directly recalls Feng Menglong's remark in his Preface to

---

[77] Chapter 43 of *Wenxin diaolong*, bears the title of *fuhui*, translated by Stephen Owen as fluency and coherence. See his *Readings in Chinese Literary Thought*, pp. 267–72.

[78] For discussions of the tradition, see Bodde, trans., *A History of Chinese Philosophy* 2: 237–92; and Kenneth Ch'en, *Buddhism in China*, pp. 57–120.

an edition of Tang Xianzu's play, "The Dream of Handan (*Handanmeng*)": "whereas 'The Purple Hairpin (*Zichai*)' and 'The Peony Pavilion (*Mudanting*)' rely on love (*qing*), and 'The Southern Branch (*Nanke*)' on illusion (*huan*), only this [play] gains entrance into the Dao by means of love and awakens one to the real (*wu zhen*) through the instrumentality of illusion."[79] As the result of encountering one kind of reality, Vanitas acquires a certain knowledge that alters his perception and understanding of that reality.

According to the Buddhist paradigm evoked by the language, the "void" or emptiness (*kong*, Skt., *śūnyatā*) is indeed posited as the real nature of the world, but it does not thereby negate the "reality" of phenomena. "In the dialectic apprehension of Nagarjuna," as one modern scholar has observed, "voidness is both the true understanding of existence and the expression of the true nature of existence which is without an ultimate ground."[80] Voidness is therefore not an ontological absolute in the sense that it enjoys no independent meaning or validity apart from its dialectical relationship to the phenomenal world, to forms or *se* (*rūpa*). The *prajñā* (intuitive wisdom or nondual knowledge) stemming from "thorough comprehension of the empty, unreal, or relative nature of all phenomena" must be gained, in the succinct summary by Kenneth Ch'en,

> only by going through a relative or worldly level of truth. Here we have the double level of truth of the Madhyamika. The relative level consists of man's reasoning and its products. It causes man to see the universe and its manifold phenomena, and to consider them as real. He cannot dispose of this relative truth by his arguments, just as a person in a dream cannot deny his dream by any argument. Only when he wakens can he prove the falsity of the objects in the dream. In this relative level one sees the distinctions between subject and object, truth and error, *samsara* and nirvana. . . . [However], acceptance of the doctrine of *śūnyatā*, or the unreality of all phenomena, does not mean that we have to devaluate all human experience. Before attaining the final absolute truth, beings still have to move in the world of phenomenal appearances, where the laws of karma and empirical understanding are applicable.[81]

If this understanding of emptiness and phenomenon (or form) indeed underlies the language used to render the experience of Vanitas, then we may conclude as well that the highly abstract paradigm expressive of his progres-

---

[79] Mao Xiaotong, comp., *Tang Xianzu yanjiu zhiliao huibian* 2: 1,305.

[80] Frederick J. Streng, *Emptiness*, pp. 156–57. For a more recent discussion of this all-important concept of *śūnyatā*, see C. W. Huntington, Jr., with Geshé Namgyal Wangchen, *The Emptiness of Emptiness*, pp. 55–59.

[81] Ch'en, *Buddhism in China*, pp. 85–86. See also his discussion of Tiantai Buddhism, which follows Nagarjuna's emphasis on developing the threefold truth of void, transitoriness, and mean (p. 311). On the possibility of explicit textual echoes of Tiantai Buddhism in the novel, see David Hawkes, "*The Story of the Stone*."

sion from one state to another is in fact a deliberate but ironic parallel to the experience of Stone as protagonist. For the latter, too, may be said to have started in an original Void and proceeded through "the contemplation of Form (which is Illusion)," the engenderment of Passion, the reentrance into Form by Passion's communication, to the final awakening to the Void again. In more specifically human terms, much as the young Bao-yu has been led to a grudging acknowledgment of life's impermanence and emptiness through the most intense entanglements in the world, so the reader must work through a contemplation of Form (itself equivalent to Illusion) and the Passion it engenders and communicates to reach some kind of truth, which is also the Void.

If life has shown Bao-yu, the incarnate Stone, the emptiness of his existence, what is the knowledge of the Void that reading his story provides? Is it a knowledge of some truths external to the text? Is the story to be received as a parable of Buddhist teachings, an autobiography of authorial vicissitudes, a chronicle of familial fortunes, a document of social customs, or an allegory of royal and palatial intrigues? For an illuminating answer, we must again refer to that part of the text quoted at the end of this chapter's second section: it is the very end of this lengthy novel where Vanitas, having copied the story of the stone, is told by Jia Yu-cun (false language enduring) to find Cao Xueqin for its proper transmission. When Vanitas presses for an explantion for Cao's willingness to assume the authorial role ("How is it that you know Jia Yu-cun that you are willing to transmit it?"), the latter's reply also rebukes the habitual error, characteristic of so much of traditional Chinese literary culture, of seeking external authority to validate art.

> These may be rustic words, but they contain no careless errors or nonsensical passages. It would be a pleasure to share this with a few like-minded friends. . . .
> No need for some self-important being to commend it or publish it. You in your insistence on ferreting out facts are like the man who dropped his sword in the water and thought to find it again by making a mark on the side of his boat; you are like a man playing a zither with the tuning-pegs glued fast. (*SS* 5: 375; *HLM* 3: 1,647–48)

The liberating knowledge to be gained by Vanitas, the Void into which he must awaken, is just that: the emptiness of fiction. Just as the real world is considered empty and unreal in the Buddhist vision, so the invented world of story is "baseless" (*huangtang*), "absurd" (*da huang*), "unverifiable" (*wuji*), and "undatable" (*wu chaodai nianji*). Both the inhabitants (Jia Bao-yu, Lin Dai-yu, Jia Zheng, Xue Ying-lian, and so on) and geography (Worldly Way, Carnal Lane, Bottle-Gourd Temple) of that world owe their existence to the play of language. Thus Vanitas must be told at the end by Jia Yu-cun, who had fallen asleep (during the lengthy duration of fictive time) "in the little hermitage at Wake Ness Ferry [*Juemi du*] by Rushford Hythe [*Jiliu jin*]," that he (false language enduring) had already "seen all this [the story of Stone] first hand"

(*SS* 5: 373, 375; *HLM* 3: 1,646–47).[82] Fiction is thus the dream product of "false language," much as plot is actually a progeny of rhetoric, for the tragic relations of Bao-yu to his two beloved cousins unfold as a process literalizing, with ironic commentary, the adage *jinyu liangyuan* (the goodly affinity of gold and jade). The facts of such a world can no more be pinned down in relation to historical and empirical reality than marking a boat to anchor a sword dropped in water. The referent of the sign simply slips away in a shifting sea of signifiers and signifieds.

In view of such intimated parallel between Buddhist tenet and literary theory, does it mean that Cao Xueqin has played the ultimate Buddhist trick on the reader? In inventing such a grand and irresistible illusion of art to break down the illusion of human life and world, is he not resorting to the most subtle exercise of the Buddhist doctrine of skillful means (*upāya*)? Does not art, in this final analysis, finally serve the cause of faith? Although one is tempted to answer yes to all three questions, I believe there is one crucial difference. For the Buddhist at least, "the awareness of 'emptiness' . . . is the cognition of daily life without the attachment to it."[83] For Bao-yu of the narrative, a life of detachment must be carried out, in fact, by leaving the family, by cutting all ties to his human community. On the other hand, the effect of reading for Vanitas is anything but detachment. Having gone through *The Story of the Stone*, "he changed his name from Vanitas to Brother Amor, or the Passionate Monk (because he had approached Truth by way of Passion), and changed the title of the book from *The Story of the Stone* to *The Tale of Brother Amor*" (*SS* 1: 51; *HLM* 1: 6). So captivated is he, in other words, with the illusion conjured up by the text that henceforth its reality will completely supplant his identity.

This narrated transformation of Vanitas would, for me, call into question Andrew Plaks' fundamental thesis concerning the novel, that "within the breadth of vision that characterizes the work as a whole, even truth and falsity, reality and illusion must be treated as complementary possibilities rather than dialectical antitheses." Those complementary possibilities so dear to Plaks' conceptualization of Chinese cosmology indeed pervade the fictive universe, but the cosmology thus affirmed cannot be the same as the felt aesthetics. If, as Plaks avers, "the apparent opposition of being and non-being [in the novel] emerges

---

[82] So the fine comment by Eggert, *Rede vom Traum*, p. 246: "On the level of allegory, however, Jia Yucun is none other than a homonym for 'false language enduring' (the word play that will be used a little later), and thus in the end another expression for the novel itself as the fictive end-product of life's experience. If now the person Jia Yucun is a sleeper, what else can be inside him (that is, as novel) other than a dream? [Jia Yucun ist jedoch auf der allegorischen Ebene nichts anderes als ein Homonym für 'fiktive Worte bleiben übrig' (das Wortspiel wird wenige Zeilen später verwendet), letzlich also ein anderer Ausdruck für den Roman selbst als das fiktive Endprodukt einer Lebens-erfahrung. Wenn nun aber Jia Yucun (die Person) ein Schläfer ist, was kann sein (des Romans) inhalt anderes sein als ein Traum?]"

[83] Streng, *Emptiness*, p. 160.

as an example of the sort of interpenetration of reality and illusion for which the dream is the nearest analogue in human experience," the novel itself is a "dream" that neither expires nor dissolves into any confluence of complementary opposites (*ke you ke wu*).[84] It is, in sum, an "analogue" that eventually subverts a metaphysics of illusion, as the author has so cunningly developed his idea throughout the tale: the cosmos may be regarded as illusory and dream-like, but the world of fiction, its "reality" and appeal far more resistant to such dismissal, remain paradoxically a more potent and permanent illusion.[85] That is why, in the final analysis, Vanitas the fictionalized reader, and not Bao-yu, is Brother Amor.

Such a distinction, in fact, crucially differentiates between two different kinds of understanding or enlightenment (*mingbai*) the treatment of which is thoroughly interwoven in the text. For the stone of the narrative, the comprehension of its origin—from whence it came (*laili*)—entails the vital, incarnate experience of living through the consequences of desire. Hence the trajectory of the plot with respect to Stone as protagonist is fundamentally circular. For to the extent that it echoes the tenets of both philosophical Daoism and Mahayana Buddhism, it renders the stone's experience as a process in both illusory or inventive transformation (*huanhua*) and material transformation (*wuhua*), in which the stone exists in successive stages as Stone Page, jade amulet, and a human being. The process, however, is in actuality a journey of recursive motion, for its final destination is the stone back in its original or substantive form (*yuanxing*). The stone's final condition, I would argue, amalgamates the Daoist concept of "returning to one's roots (*gui gen*)" mentioned in *Daodejing* 16, glossed by the commentator Wang Bi as "each returning to its origin (*ge fan qi suo shi ye*)," with the Buddhist notion of "returning to one's origin (*fan ben huan yuan*)."[86]

When after the passing of aeons the stone encounters Vanitas, the dramatized reader, it has attained once more its original condition of "stillness," for it knows itself as stone and rests content in that knowledge. The highly suggestive line in chapter 16 of the *Daodejing*—"returning to one's roots is known as stillness (*gui gen yue jing*)"—thus exerts its intertextual potency as part of the

---

[84] Plaks, *Archetype and Allegory*, pp. 222–23.

[85] In his more recent publication, *The Four Masterworks of Ming Fiction*, p. 180, Plaks offers a somewhat altered view of the matter. Discussing Zhang Zhupo's comments on the *Jinpingmei*, Plaks writes: "these abstract dialectics of reality and emptiness may sound like a bit of sophistry, but they have a special significance here for the art of the novel, which in a sense consists in turning the empty illusion of fiction into an affecting, and to that extent 'real,' human experience." In view of what the entire sweep of Chinese civilization has to say about the affect (*qing*) and its reality—not to mention, centrality—in human life, "that extent" is considerable.

[86] For a noncyclical interpretation of *gui gen*, see D. C. Lau, "The Treatment of Opposites in Lao Tzu."

initial stirring of desire that thrusts the stone into the world. For according to the clerics' verdict in the 1754 version of the novel, "this, too indicates the fated change of 'extreme repose or stillness giving rise to movement (*jing ji sheng dong*).'"

The knowledge that is gained by Stone through lived experience, however, is at the same time scripted as narrative, to be transmitted to the world and published. Small wonder that Jia Bao-yu, the incarnate text, story, and stone, at the end receives from the emperor the hilarious epithet, "Magister Verbi Profundi" (*SS* 5: 366; *HLM* 3: 1,641). *Profundi* is the word John Minford selected to translate the graph *miao*, an adjective meaning wonderful, marvelous, and ingenious, which has been used countless times by the first scholiasts themselves to praise their beloved author's writing. For Bao-yu to be named Wenmiao Zhenjun (literally, The Realized Immortal of Writing Marvelous) is hardly another shameless pandering to imperial favor on the part of Gao E or the redactor, as modern Redologists would have it, but rather a none-too-subtle apotheosis self-conferred on the fictive script.

For Vanitas, the reader, the understanding of the stone's origin (*laili*) when he reads its story depends also on the proper recognition of its true form, which is nothing other than fiction itself. The effect of reading in this instance, however, is hardly "stillness"; it produces, by contrast, a circuit of interminable desire fed by interminable involvement with created Form. "He who wakes from the sleep of spiritual ignorance is as one awakening from a dream," according to the Mādhyamika classic, *The Entry into the Middle Way*, but the effect of dreaming and the encounter with dreamlike representation, as I have already argued, may exert an even more tenacious hold on the supposedly enlightened person. Thus "even though he has awakened, a foolish person may remember the objects apprehended during his dream and become attached to them."[87] Some foolishness indeed, for Brother Amor as affected reader must henceforth exist in a state of endless contradiction implied by the oxymoronic predicament structured in his name: knowing something as illusory, unreal, and dreamlike as fiction, he nonetheless must live by the need of constant attachment to it. He lives the siege of contraries—perception and delusion, knowledge and obsession. The talismanic inscription on the stone of fiction ("mislay me not, forget me not"), which is also the fiction of Stone, thus realizes its efficacy in its erotics, the power for perpetual engagement.

---

[87] The quotations are taken from Huntington's translation of the *Madhyamakāvatāra* in his *The Emptiness of Emptiness*, pp. 163, 162.

CHAPTER IV

Literature

Llenósele la fantasí de todo acquello que leía en
los libros, . . .
(Miguel de Cervantes, *Don Quijote de la Mancha*)

MARRIAGE, LEARNING, EXAMINATION

When Chu Hsien-fu married Mr. Lu's daughter, even before he realized how
accomplished she was, he was almost bowled over by her beauty. She was not
one of the usual run of accomplished young ladies, however; for her father, having
no son, had brought her up as if she were a boy. When she was five or six he had
engaged a tutor to teach her the *Four Books* and the *Five Classics*, so that by the
time she was twelve she could expound the classics and read essays, having
thoroughly mastered the works of Wang Shou-hsi. She had also learned to write
the Octopartite essays with their divisions into eight paragraphs: "broaching the
theme," "advancing the theme," "embarking on the subject," "the first strand,"
"the central strand," and so forth. Her tutor was paid as highly as if he were
teaching a boy, and he supervised her studies just as strictly. She was an intelligent
girl with a good memory. By this time she had read all the works of Wang Shou-
hsi, Tang Shun-chih, Chu Ching-chun, Hsueh Ying-chi and other famous essayists
as well as the examination compositions from the chief provincial examinations,
and could recite over three thousand essays. Her own compositions were logical,
concise, and elegant; and her father often declared with a sigh that, had she been
a boy, she would have sailed through all the examinations.

Whenever the compiler had leisure, he would tell his daughter: "If you write
Octopartite essays well, then whatever literary form you use—and this applies
even to lyrics or descriptive poems—you will have bite and concision in your
language. If, however, you cannot write Octopartite essays well, then your expressions have as much authority as those by wild foxes, perverse demons, and
heretics."

Miss Lu took her father's instructions to heart. Her dressing-table and embroi-
dery-stand were stacked with essays, and every day she annotated and punctuated
a few. As for the poems, odes, elegies and songs that were sent her, she did not
even glance at them, giving the various anthologies of poetry in the house to her
maids to read, and occasionally asking them to compose a few verses for fun.

Now Miss Lu and Master Chu appeared an ideal couple, perfectly matched as
regards family status, appearance, and accomplishments. She took it for granted

that her husband had completed his studies and would soon pass the metropolitan and palace examinations; yet, even after they had been married for nearly two weeks, he still paid not the slightest attention to the essays which filled her room.

"Of course, he must know all these by heart," she thought. "And he is newly married; he wants to enjoy himself and thinks this is no time for study."

A few days later her husband, returning from a feast, took from his sleeve a volume of poems to declaim by the lamp, and invited his wife to sit beside him and read with him. Too shy at the time to remonstrate, she forced herself to look at the poems for an hour until it was time to sleep. The next day, however, she could bear it no longer; and, knowing that her husband was in the front library, she took a piece of red paper and wrote down an essay subject: "When a man cultivates himself, his family will be well governed."

Then she called Tsai-ping and said to her: "Take this to the young master and say that my father requests him to write an essay for our edification."

Chu Hsien-fu laughed when he received this message.

"This is hardly in my line," he said. "Besides, not having been a month yet in your honourable house, I would prefer to write something more cultured. I really have not the patience to engage in such vulgar activities."

He thought this would impress his brilliant young wife, not realizing that this was just the sort of talk she disliked most.

That evening, when the nurse went in to see her young mistress, she found her frowning, sighing and in tears.

"Why, miss!" exclaimed the nurse. "You have just had the luck to marry a good husband: whatever is the matter with you?"

The girl told her what had happened that day.

"I thought he had already completed his studies and would soon pass the metropolitan examinations," she concluded. "Who could have imagined this? My whole life is ruined!"

The nurse reasoned with her for a little, until Chu Hsien-fu came in, to be treated rather coldly by his wife. Knowing what had caused this aloofness, he felt a twinge of shame; but neither of them liked to say anything. After this, they were not on the best of terms and she was very unhappy. But if she raised the question of the examinations, her husband would not reply; and if she insisted, he criticized her as worldly. So she became more and more depressed, until a frown never left her face. (*Rulin Waishi*, chapter 11)[1]

Except for the names of the characters thus portrayed, the above passage might well have been a scene straight out of *Hongloumeng*. Although Xue Bao-chai in the latter novel may not be depicted explicitly as sharing Miss Lu's mastery of the canonical materials and rhetorical method requisite for success in the examination system, Xue's knowledge of Confucian classics,

---

[1] English translation taken from Wu Ching-tzu, *The Scholars*, pp. 141–43; translation slightly modified.

her unquestioning subscription to their enshrined values, and her zeal in practicing them are consistently portrayed in the full-length narrative. Similar to the young man in *The Scholars*, Jia Bao-yu's "inveterate contempt for worldly success" (*SS* 5:298; *HLM* 3: 1,590) has received constant emphasis as the cause of parental irritation and familial strife. After their marriage in the latter part of the book, Bao-chai certainly does not miss any opportunity to try, as does the young lady in *The Scholars*, to "talk sense" into her ostensibly willful and irresponsible spouse. When Jia Zheng commands Bao-yu (chap. 115) to write some sample examination essays for the father to review, Bao-chai is said to be "rather pleased" to learn of this (*SS* 5: 268; *HLM* 3: 1,569). When Bao-yu reacts to the news of Tan-chun's imminent marriage with one of his characteristic weeping spells (chap. 100), his wife's mild rebuke is redolent of Neo-Confucian sentiment: "The goal of all people reading books is the understanding of Principle (*ming li*). How is it that the more you study, the more muddle-headed you've become?" (*HLM* 3: 1,409, my translation)

As it is apparent to the attentive reader of the last twelve chapters of the full-length narrative, Bao-chai's marriage to Bao-yu marks another stage of her ordeal in being tested and refined as an "[object] of paternalistic molding" after the precepts of Confucian orthodoxy.[2] She faces struggles much more opprobrious than Miss Lu's of *The Scholars*, for the latter has to contend with only a spouse given to "bohemian" predilections.[3] On the other hand, Bao-chai must not only deal with the ongoing legal difficulties of a roguish brother and a rather dim-witted and ineffectual mother; her marriage also lands her in the care of a husband half-crazed by grief for her chief romantic rival, his psychological instability further undermining his scant capacity for serious preparation for the examinations. It is not surprising, therefore, that the narrator in chapter 98 refers to her actions in her attempt to bring Bao-yu to his senses as that of constantly "probing him judiciously, like an acupuncturist with a needle" (*SS* 4: 374; *HLM* 3: 1,382). The medical metaphor *zhenbian* (literally, stabbing with a stone needle) in the immediate context undoubtedly refers to her abrupt disclosure to him of Dai-yu's death, in hopes "that by severing his attachment once and for all she would enable his sanity and health to be restored" (*SS* 4: 375; *HLM* 3: 1,382). But such "shock treatment" clearly does not exhaust the meaning of her "needling" him, for the narrative portrays her "repeatedly admonishing him with words of rectitude (*meiyi zhengyan quanjie*)" (*HLM* 3: 1,382).

This process of admonition receives more narrative treatment, first in the episode of the two Bao-yus meeting and her advice to her Jia Bao-yu to take a worldly career more seriously (chap. 115), and second, in the far more elaborate episode of chapter 118, when she counters her husband's all too obvious

---

[2] Charlotte Furth, "The Patriarch's Legacy," p. 202.
[3] The adjective is used ibid., p. 204.

Buddhist interpretation of Mencius's "heart-and-mind of a newborn infant" with her own Confucian argument. There is, assuredly, no direct reference on her part to his love of poetry and drama as a stumbling block to his success in vocational aspiration, but one particular sentence of hers during the debate is particularly revealing of the kind of cultural conflict surfacing in the narrative. "Since we are husband and wife," she says at one point, "I should be able to look to you for lifelong support, the kind that is not merely based on the private interests of passion" (*SS* 5: 329, slightly modified; *HLM* 5: 1,613).

The obvious platitudes of Confucian orthodoxy that inform her remark none-theless take on significance precisely because they indicate how that ortho-doxy seeks to regulate marital relations. Though affirmed to be one of the "great relationships" of humanity (*ren zhi da lun*), marriage is, in the tradi-tional Chinese view, inherently unstable. From the perspective of entrenched patrilineality, it is the only familial relationship that is established by the introduction of a person alien to the immediate kinship structure of the husband's household. According to Susan Mann, "we can point to the Chinese family system as an institution whose critical stress point centered on women. Like women in all male-centered family systems, Chinese women posed an implicit danger to the long-term stability of the family structure. They were the liminal or marginal members who were constantly violating family boundaries: entering and exiting as brides, they produced not only the sons of future generations, but also the bonds of conjugal solidarity that threatened to tear brothers apart."[4]

---

[4] "Widows in the Kingship, Class, and Community Structures of Qing Dynasty China," p. 44. Mann also refers to Maurice Freedman for a description of the "ambivalent role of women as mothers and wives" in his *The Study of Chinese Society*, p. 272. Patricia Ebrey dates the beginning of the modern system of patrilineal surnames to the Qin dynasty in "Women, Marriage, and the Family in Chinese History," p. 201. Her conclusion may find corroboration in *The Book of Rites* or *Liji*, completed in its present form probably in the first century B.C.E., which declares: "In taking a wife, one does not marry someone with the same surname (*tong xing*)" (*Liji xunzuan* 1: 12a). I am indebted to Wai-yee Li, however, for pointing out that such a custom was already recorded in the *Zuo Commentary*. See James Legge, trans., *The Chinese Classics* 5, "Duke Xi," 23. 6, "Duke Xiang," 23. 9, and "Duke Zhao," 1. 12, and also the *Guoyu*, "Jinyu," 4. Critical studies on women's history in China have increased enormously since Lin Yutang's article, "Feminist Thought in Ancient China," and Chen Dongyuan's pioneering *Zhongguo funü sheng-huoshi*. For the discussion here, I have consulted Erwin Rousell, "Die Frau in Gesellschaft und Mythos der Chinesen"; Albert R. O'Hara, *The Position of Woman in Early China*; Liu Hengjing, *Funü wenti wenji*; Yuasa Yukihiko, "Shindai ni okeru fujin kaihōmoron"; Elizabeth Grisar, *La femme en Chine*; Machii Yōko, "Shindai no josei seikatsu: Shōsetsu wo chusin to shite"; Margery Wolf and Roxane Witke, eds., *Women in Chinese Society*; Yamakawa Urara, *Chūgoku josei shi*; Liu Ziqing, *Zhongguo lidai xianneng funü pingzhuan*; Siegfried Englert, *Materialien zur Stellung der Frau und zur Sexualität im vormodernen und modernen China*; Lionello Laniciotti, ed., *La donna nella Cina imperiale e nella Cina repubblicana*; Paul S. Ropp, "The Seeds of Change"; Mark Elvin, "Female Virtue and the State in China"; "Women in Qing Period China—A Sym-posium," *JAS* 46 (February 1987); Rubie S. Watson and Patricia Buckley Ebrey, *Marriage and Inequality in Chinese Society*; and Susan Mann, "The Education of Daughters in the Mid-Ch'ing Period."

Indeed, from the point of view of the husband's home, it is not just the brothers but all other relations of that home who are potentially threatened. The new bride thus personifies all the dangerous subversiveness of a mole or spy implanted by the enemy. Although a married couple's surface affability may help to promote the ideal of harmony within the household, any sign of excessive affection may be viewed with alarm, because the Chinese know only too well what potency belongs to sexual passion. In the scriptural traditions of the Jewish and Christian West, the notion of marriage as the union of life with life to create a new life cycle is based on required rupture: "therefore a man *leaves his father and his mother and cleaves to his wife, and they become one flesh*" (Genesis 2: 24).[5] By contrast, not only does much of the accepted living arrangement and psychological disposition of married couples in premodern China contradict the condition implied by this scriptural assertion but the claims of young couples also can never be allowed to supercede those owed to parents and kinfolk, for that would upset the so-called Three Bonds and Five Relationships (*san gang wu lun*), advocated and propounded for the purpose of minimizing social conflict through the imposition of a rigid code of hierarchy.[6] That is why the numerous "Household Instructions" (*jiaxun*), written down through the centuries as so much exegetical extension of those bonds and relations, vehemently restrict the time or condition in which a married couple can be together, and they even proscribe such activities as the couple taking meals by themselves or engaging in pillow talk.[7] What such strictures seek to prevent is precisely what Bao-chai speaks of—the private gains or interests engendered by passion (*qingyu zhi si*).

C. T. Hsia's translation of this Chinese phrase as "our selfish feelings and

---

[5] Citation from the Revised Standard Version, emphasis mine.

[6] On this point the observation by Richard W. Guisso is right on target. Referring to the *Five Classics* (*wu jing*) of China's antiquity, he says: "the *Classics* have little to say of women as persons, but deal almost entirely in idealized life-cycles of daughter, wife and mother. They have in common an insistence, not that woman is the servant of man, nor that her function in life is less important than his, but that there is a natural and immutable difference between male and female. They suggest that since this difference is part of the cosmic order, it must be maintained to preserve and continue that order. In other words, woman's place in the classical canon was not determined by the fiat of any supernatural force or deity, but rather by the Confucian certainty that order and harmony were supreme values and that only in hierarchy were they preserved." See his "Thunder over the Lake," p. 48. Since order in such a conception is virtually synonymous with hierarchy, as Guisso is quick to recognize, Chinese cosmology is not one that places emphasis on the equality of its constituent elements. "Each sex had a distinct and complementary function and woman's place was neither dishonourable nor necessarily inferior to man's except in so far as earth was inferior to heaven or moon inferior to sun. . . . In other words, the *Five Classics* did not initiate female subordination but justified it. They did so largely by speculating on the nature of woman, and by demonstrating her natural inferiority" (pp. 50–51).

[7] Furth, "The Patriarch's Legacy," p. 196.

desires," represents a plausible alternate reading that nonetheless accentuates the disturbing meaning of the word *si*.[8] One central problem posed by the relations of the sexes, further exacerbated by marriage, is this matter of the private and privacy (*si*). Because the domain of the family belongs to the patriarch, nothing in principle can be hidden from the parents or move beyond their concern and control. Communal order is imposed through ritual, precisely because ritual, as process and action of hierarchy, is defined as "that which determines nearness and distance in kinship, decides on the causes of suspicion and dubiety, distinguishes between the points of agreement and difference, and clarifies right and wrong."[9] The private is tainted in this perspective since personal tastes, interests, and preferences all may run counter to the prescriptions of ritual (*li*). Both morally and semantically, therefore, whatever smacks of the personal or private self may slide easily into the realm of selfishness; hence the tautology of *zi si*, or literally, one's own privateness.

"While his parents are still alive, . . . [a son] will have no personal [*si*] wealth" (*Liji xunzuan* 1: 6b). A male youth is counseled not to "listen with the head inclined on one side" so that, as one scholiast says, "he will not be suspected of receiving someone's private [thoughts or words]" (ibid., 1: 11a). "Male and female should not sit together in the same room; they may not share the same clothing rack, or the same towel or comb, nor may they touch each other's hands when giving or receiving" (ibid., 1: 11b). "These four prohibitions," comments the Yuan scholiast Chen Hao (1261–1341), "will distance the persons from the suspicion of private intimacy (*si xie zhi xian*)."[10]

For a daughter-in-law, the *Liji*'s specific regulations in this regard are even more revealing, because the private, understood as what properly belongs to her, will also define her essentially as an outsider in the spouse's family.

> No daughter-in-law, without being told to go to her own [*si*] apartment, should venture to withdraw from that (of her parents-in-law). Whatever she is about to do, she should ask leave from them. A son and his wife should have no private goods, nor animals, nor vessels; they should not presume to borrow from, or give anything to, another person. If any one give [*sic*] the wife an article of food or dress, a piece of cloth or silk, a handkerchief for her girdle, an iris or orchid, she should receive and offer it to her parents-in-law. If they accept it, she will be glad as if she were receiving it afresh. If they return it to her, she should decline it, and if they do not allow her to do so, she will take it as if it were a second gift, and lay it by to wait till they may want it. If she want to give it to some of her own [*si*] cousins, she must ask leave to do so, and that being granted, she will give it.[11]

---

[8] Hsia, *The Classic Chinese Novel: A Critical Introduction*, pp. 290–91.

[9] *Liji xunzuan* 1: 11a, *SBBY*, my translation.

[10] See *Liji jishu* 1: 14a.

[11] *Li Chi, Book of Rites*, translated by James Legge, 1: 458; *Liji xunzuan* 12: 5b.

Such ritual prescriptions handed down from antiquity, elaborated and augmented by voluminous Family Instructions, should help the reader of *The Stone* to gauge more effectively the actions and words of various characters in the narrative. In the immediate context, they certainly disclose the bent of orthodoxy in the person of Bao-chai. Those private interests of passion, as far as Bao-yu is concerned, may focus on his relations to his immediate female companions, for the last part of the narrative takes pains to show us that he, despite his seemingly inconsolable grief for Dai-yu, is still very much the same person, susceptible to the "old weakness for the fairer sex" (chap. 98).[12] In the wider context of the narrative, those interests point to his habitual likes and dislikes, to personal tastes and activities that nonetheless may affect his, and therefore Bao-chai's, destiny. Her remark in effect raises this question: given what I know of you, can I count on you to put away personal feelings and preferences sufficiently to become a true Confucian husband, one who practices filial piety by, among other things, seriously preparing for and passing the civil service examinations? When the tension between dominant cultural ideals and individual aspirations is thus brought to the fore, not only does Bao-chai's debate with Bao-yu invite comparison with the episode in *The Scholars*, but Cao Xueqin's novel itself also presents many points of affinity with the depictions found in a text such as *Six Chapters of a Floating Life* by Shen Fu (1763–1803). It is no accident that echoes and parallels run through all three texts, for they are all preoccupied in one way or another with the issues of desire (*qing*), vocational choice, and the role of women in the effort of upholding family values and success.[13] It is in these preoccupations, in fact, that *Hongloumeng* makes its distinctive contribution, for they provide the context within which many of the most cherished activities of the literate elite are depicted and scrutinized. In ways perhaps more subtle and dramatic than those of the other two texts, *Hongloumeng* reveals how such activities may violate and challenge certain ethical, political, and social norms. With a remarkable modernist ac-

---

[12] The full-length narrative's portrayal of the male protagonist is consistent in bringing out the full implications of what Disenchantment seems to ascribe to a flaw to his character: "the lasciviousness of the mind" (chap. 5). Though Bao-yu's love for Dai-yu acquires intensity and singularity throughout the novel, reaching its zenith after her death, that love is always subject to division and distraction. In that sense, the nature of the love between the two lovers is hardly symmetrical, and it is the genius of the narrative to give full development to this difference.

[13] For Shen's text, see *Shen Fu: Six Records of a Floating Life*, translated by Leonard Pratt and Chiang Su-hui. For some pertinent studies of the three works, see Chen Yupi, "*Hongloumeng he Fusheng liuji*"; Paul S. Ropp, *Dissent in Early Modern China*, and "Women between Two Worlds"; Jonathan Hall, "Heroic Repression." The novels by Wu, Shen, and Cao hardly exhaust the group of imaginative works that portray a marriage in which the wife is more literate and talented than the husband. For a perceptive study of this important theme, see Keith McMahon, *Misers, Shrews and Polyganists*, chapter 5: "The Chaste 'Beauty-Scholar' Romance and the Superiority of the Talented Woman."

cent, Cao Xue-qin's creation suggests that a text of culture both mirrors and produces the conflicts of culture.

No reader of *Hongloumeng* will dispute the contention that one constant source of conflict between Bao-yu and his father lies in the boy's ostensible lack of self-discipline in his studies. "In traditional China," as C. T. Hsia has aptly written of *The Scholars*, "to pass the provincial and metropolitan examinations is the quickest way to attain fame, rank, and wealth."[14] Success in that endeavor, in the words of one recent scholarly study, requires "substantial investments of time, effort, and training," but success itself is also construed as the most apposite expression of filial piety on the part of the male child.[15] To repay parental nurture and sacrifice, there is no more immediately rewarding and far-reaching attainment than having one's name inscribed at the head of the list (*bang*) of successful candidates. Such accomplishment epitomizes the ideal, pithily stated in the *Three Character Classic*, to "spread your fame/ [and] make illustrious your parents."

In the case of Jia Bao-yu, the pressure for him to succeed is not generated by the yearning of an indigent household, for the Jia family is already illustrious—by reason of its ancestors' meritorious deeds that are further enhanced by a cousin recently chosen to be the imperial concubine. Bao-yu's duty, rather, entails the maintenance of the family's glory, a task rendered more imposing because he is the only surviving male heir of his immediate line. Jia Zheng's expectation for his second son and his exasperation over the latter's seeming lack of vocational commitment thus betray a deeper concern for forestalling familial decline.[16] After the Jias incur imperial disfavor by their repeated and

---

[14] *The Classic Chinese Novel*, p. 225.

[15] Benjamin A. Elman, "Political, Social, and Cultural Reproduction via Civil Service Examinations in Late Imperial China." This informative essay fully addresses the cultural implications of the system. Unfortunately, it is somewhat marred by over-reliance on Ichisada Miyazaki's *China's Examination Hell* as a source. The latter's estimate of 400 thousand characters of textual materials to be memorized for the mastery of the Four Books and Five Classics is an exaggeration, since not every character is a different word in these texts, which also contain many repetitive sections. The system itself, moreover, makes use of selected materials from these canonical texts, particularly for candidates for the first degree. See Shang Yanliu, *Qingdai keju kaoshi shulu*.

[16] Furth in her essay on "Household Instructions" has sought to attribute the formative cause of such treatises to the "perennial Confucian fears of ritual decay" ("The Patriarch's Legacy," p. 188). To dispel such fears leads to making "the creation of an instruction a testamentary act." It may be misleading to think of such instructions as largely a deathbed ritual, since even Book One of *The Great Learning* stipulates "ordering the family (*qi jia*)" as the abiding and present obligation of every Confucian. On the other hand, Furth's essay illuminates not merely historical households but also the novelistic one when she says: "In sum, for elders the gravest threat to the *chia* was not filial defiance and rebellion, but rather hedonism and irresponsibility. Patriarchal concern with their sons' choice of a vocation . . . went hand and hand with the worry that a family that succeeded in producing many sons risked seeing them living a life of idleness" (ibid., p. 198). The behavior of the young males of the Jia mansion helps explain Jia Zheng's neurosis.

flagrant flouting of the law, the father's concern deepens into an obsession. Prior to escorting the coffins of his mother, Phoenix, and Dai-yu to the south, Jia Zheng leaves the injunction that Bao-yu and his nephew Jia Lan must attend the state examinations that year. "If they can pass the examination and become Provincial Graduates," so he reasons, "it will help to redeem the family from its present disgrace" (*SS* 5:298; *HLM* 3: 1,590). In face of the explosive crisis that threatens to bring the clan to total ruin, academic success must now assume the added burden of atoning for familial transgressions (*shu zui*).

In the running battle between father and son on vocational commitment, what Jia Zheng wants Bao-yu to do is not as signficant as what he eventually prohibits him from doing. That the young boy has never taken a liking to official learning is emphasized from the beginning, when one line from two lyrics to the tune of "Moon over West River" cited by the narrator compares him with "A doltish mule, to study disinclined" (*SS* 1: 102; *HLM* 1: 50). The Chinese original of the line is far more explicit: stupid and stubborn, he dreads studying examination compositions (*wenzhang*). The son's dread is the father's anxiety, and the latter's perpetual concern is to find out whether in his progeny a modicum of learning can be salvaged from habitual sloth. That concern, as the text tells us, lies at the base of Jia Zheng's action in chapter 17, when he asks his son to supply some of the poetic inscriptions for various sites and buildings in the Prospect Garden newly built to accommodate the imperial concubine's imminent visit. "Although the boy showed no aptitude for serious study," so the boy's tutor had reported to the father, "he nevertheless possessed a certain meretricious talent for versification not underserving of commendation" (*SS* 1: 326; *HLM* 1: 225). This lengthy episode of garden-touring which details Jia Zheng's efforts in testing his son's "aptitude" ends with a negative paternal pronouncement, "that's no good" (*SS* 1: 346; *HLM* 1: 238), and a curt dismissal.[17]

A second episode much later, in which the father once more makes a trial of his son's learning, actually ups the stakes considerably for Bao-yu. In the tour of the new garden, the boy was merely asked to provide, with justification, couplets and phrases to be mounted as inscriptions, whereas in the latter instance of chapter 78, the father's rehearsal of a rather melodramatic anecdote eventuates in a demand for a full-blown elegiac poem. Rising to the challenge, Bao-yu declares that the subject of the "Winsome Colonel," an obvious variation of the celebrated theme of the Woman Warrior (Hua Mu-lan and other legendary Chinese women who proved themselves better warriors than men), requires a ballad in the Old Style (*guti*), undoubtedly because it affords greater narrative scope and rhetorical flourish than the shorter forms of regulated verse. His

---

[17] The Chinese passage, much more brusque and hostile in tone than Hawkes' rendering (*SS* 1: 348), reads: "Why aren't you gone yet? Haven't you had enough of a tour? When you've wandered off half a day, Old Grannie must worry about you. Don't you ever think of that? Get inside quickly! She has wasted her love on you!" (*HLM* 1: 240)

poem and the "Hibiscus Dirge (*Furong lei*)" which he composed almost immediately thereafter for his maid Skybright are both lengthy works (by Chinese
poetic standards) built on the general theme of the mistreatment of talented
girls—unappreciated Fourth Sister Lin in the father's story put to shame the
entire court of Prince Heng with her courageous death on the battlefield, and
chaste Skybright died as a victim of envy and slander. The two compositions
actually demonstrate the young man's considerable gifts for stylistic imitation
(as in his mimicking of Zhuangzi in chap. 21), his understanding of different
poetic genres and their capacities (superior to that of his male kin), and his
penchant for rhetorical excess in diction (thereby inviting Dai-yu's complaint
of "shop-worn" phrases in the following chapter).[18] Despite its better-than-
average quality, however, the ballad wins no greater paternal approbation than
Jia Zheng's final assessment: "Though you've written quite a few lines, they
are still not earnest enough" (*HLM* 2: 1,129).

The apparent paternal animosity toward the son's fondness for poetry and
his preference for studying and writing it cannot be attributed to the father's
self-acknowledged lack of adroitness for such activity (cf. chap. 17).[19] It must
be seen as the expression of a deeply entrenched view of what constitutes
intellectual priority and ethical obligation for a young man of Bao-yu's social
status and upbringing. When the father finally lowers the boom to compel his
son to work in earnest preparation for the examinations, his pronouncement
cannot be more succinct:

I've heard that you spend every day fooling about in the garden with your cousins.
You indulge in your antics even with the maidservants so much that your own
proper business hardly ever enters your head. So you've managed to compose a
few lines of poetry, but there's not much to them. What's so special about them?
When you go to sit for the examinations, the essays, in the last analysis, will
decide your success, and in that endeavor you're not the least bit accomplished.
I'm telling you: from today, you are not permitted to write any more poetry or
compose couplets. You must practice writing only Octopartite Compositions. I'll

---

[18] Red Inkstone's brief comment on the ballad sees it as a foil (probably in both the emotive
and linguistic sense) to the Hibiscus Dirge. This is how I understand the terms *bin* (guest) and
zhu (host) with which the scholiast talks about the two poems: as guest is to "Ballad of the
Winsome Colonel," so host is to "Hibiscus Dirge" (*Pingyu*, p. 713). The scholiast, moreover,
takes pains to point out that Jia Zheng's conflation of Fourth Sister Lin (a legendary figure of
the late Ming mentioned in *Mingshi* 119 and the writings of Wang Yuyang and Pu Songling)
with Han stories of Yellow Turbans and Red Eyebrows is for the purpose of demonstrating that
all such tales "are of the same kind" (ibid., p. 714), that is, legendary tales. Contemporary
Redologists, of course, are quick to discern possible and sensitive references to dynastic politics that the novelist may want to camouflage. See Cai Yijiang, *Hongloumeng shici qufu pingzhu*,
pp. 311–13; Zhou Ruchang, *Hongloumeng xinzheng* 1: 230–31.

[19] Cf. Bao-yu's remark to himself in chapter 82, when he is compelled by his father to spend
time strictly on the Classics and compositions: "Poems are easy, but I can't make head or tail of
this stuff!" (*SS* 4: 54; *HLM* 3: 1,177).

give you a year. If you still show no sign of progress, you needn't bother to study any more. And I will not wish to have a son like you either. (*HLM* 3: 1,172, my translation)

This speech by Jia Zheng, expressing ideas and sentiments that old Mr. Lu in *The Scholars* would have heartily approved, finds further amplification when the father thereafter commissions Jia Dai-ru, an older clansman, to become Bao-yu's tutor.

"I've myself escorted him here today," Jia Zheng said, "because I want to entrust him to you. This child is no longer young. He really has no choice but to learn to master those exam essays, for only then can he be successful in the enterprise of establishing himself and winning a name for the rest of his life. At home right now, all he does is to frolic with other children. He may know how to compose a few verses, but they are no more than doggerels and inanities. Even the better ones display no nobler expressions than those alluding to the wind and the cloud, the moon and the dew—all romantic trifles that have nothing to do with the proper business of his life."

"His looks are certainly presentable," replied Dai-ru, "and he seems intelligent enough. Why doesn't he want to study but instead only indulges in idle mischief? The way of poetry and lyrics is not a forbidden subject. It's only that after one has attained a prosperous career, there will be time enough to learn that." (*HLM* 3: 1,173, my translation)

That both the father and the tutor echo each other without premeditation in calling versification a gross hindrance to academic success may surprise those readers who know something of the premodern Chinese examination system. Although it cannot be denied that the content of the various degrees since the Tang period placed overwhelming emphasis on prose annotation and exegesis of canonical classics and histories, specifically literary writings, somewhat ignominiously classified as "Miscellaneous Compositions (*za wen*)," did have a place in the *jinshi* degree.[20] Probably instituted in 681, this degree added the requirement of composing one poem (the choice varied from a twelve-line regulated verse with six end rhymes to a longer poem known as *pailü*, with tonal metrics and rhyme scheme serially extended) and one *fu* (rhyme-prose or rhapsody; developed in the Han, this genre of *fu* by the Tang evolved further into the form of regulated rhyme-prose or *lüfu*).[21] Almost since the examination's

---

[20] On the examination system, see Miyazaki and Shang Yanliu cited above. I have also consulted Deng Siyu, *Chongguo kaoshi zhidu shi*; Chen Dongyuan, *Zhongguo jiaoyu shi*; and more recent studies of the Song examination system by John Chaffee, Theodore de Bary, and Thomas Lee.

[21] The structure of a twelve-line regulated verse, slightly longer than the accepted conventional form of eight-line regulated verse (pentasyllabic or septasyllabic), has been compared with the various sections of the Octopartite Composition by scholars since the Ming. See Chen Dongyuan, *Zhongguo jiaoyu shi*, p. 178.

inception, the practice of designated subject matter (*ti*) and end rhyme (*yun*) became standard, as evident from numerous entries in such compendia as the *Wenyuan yinghua* (Finest Flowers of the Preserve of Letters) and the *Quan Tang Shi* (Complete Tang Poems). During the reign of the Song Emperor Shenzong (1072), this part of the examination was terminated because of Wang Anshi's reform movement, but it was reinstated in 1086. Three years later, in fact, the *jinshi* degree was divided into two subdegrees, one on poetry (*shifu jinshi*) and one on the Classics (*jingyi jinshi*). In 1094, when the reform faction of the government regained power, poetry was again eliminated, only to be reinstated in 1127 "in accordance with the 1089 provisions." For almost two and a half centuries thereafter, in fact, the *jinshi* examination alternated between emphasizing elucidation or exegesis of classics (*jingyi*) and the composition of verse and *fu*, though by the end of the Southern Song, the exegetical emphasis seemed to have gained the upper hand.[22] The Ming system indeed abolished the requirement of verse and *fu* altogether.

In the Qing period, this oscillation between the two modes of examination apparently continued, although the dynasty came into being following the Ming precedent.[23] In 1705, one official's petition to reinstate the poetry examination was rejected with the following rationale from the court:

> The established curriculum for selected scholars must emphasize the ability to elucidate the meaning of the classics. If poetry and *fu* were added, then students would concentrate on poetic writings and become unfamiliar with the meaning of the classics. This goes against the national government's intention of encouraging substantive learning (*shi xue*).[24]

However, by the twenty-second year of Emperor Qianlong's reign (1757), three years after the first extant manuscript of *The Story of the Stone* had come into private circulation, the district examination added one pentasyllabic poem with eight rhymes (that is, the sixteen-line *pailü*), and thereafter, the practice extended rapidly to all levels. Even prior to this date, the special examination called by imperial decree (*boxue hongci*) requested from the candidates in 1679 the composition of one *fu* and one poem, to be read and judged by Emperor Kangxi himself.[25]

---

[22] John W. Chaffee, *The Thorny Gates of Learning in Sung China*, p. 71, 271–72.

[23] Miyazaki reports that a poem was required at every level of the examination, from the district and prefectural ones, through the qualifying examinations, to the provincial and metropolitan ones (see pp. 22–23, 27–29, 38, 45, 67). But his descriptive account does not make clear the debated principles underlying the differing practices of the examinations in different regnal periods of the Qing.

[24] Deng Siyu, p. 275, citing *Tushu jicheng*, "Xuanju dian," 70.

[25] Ibid., p. 262. It is interesting that this added requirement of poetic composition forms the basis for Yu Yue to assert in his *Xiaofumei xianhua* (1899) Gao E's proven authorship of the last forty chapters, because, according to Yu, the narrative indicated poetic activities at the examination site (*ke chang*). See *HLMJ* 2: 390–91.

In view of the longstanding, albeit intermittent and sometimes hotly contested, custom of testing for talent through such established literary forms throughout nearly fourteen hundred years of Chinese institutional history, we may justly wonder what could account for the animosity toward poetic activities on the part of novelistic characters like the Lus of *The Scholars* and the Jias of *The Stone*. Part of the answer may be found again in the history of the debate on the principles guiding the examination practice, a debate that may in turn shed light on the words and behavior of the fictive persons themselves.

Historians of Chinese education and the civil service examination system are unanimous in noting the powerful views of Wang Anshi (1019–1086), the reformer statesman who ardently objected to the use of rote memory (primarily for source identification) and of poetry and *fu*.[26] Considering his voluminous writings on sundry governmental policies and on the ideals of literary compositions (*wen*) that had been preserved, we must say that his actual pronouncement on why he thought ill of the poetic requirement is surprisingly brief. One sentence in a memorial submitted in 1069 simply states: "in order to reinstate the ancient system, . . . it is necessary that we eliminate the kind of compositions that focus on the match of parallelisms (*dui ou*) and on finding fault with tonalities (*sheng bing*), so that the student may concentrate his efforts on probing the meaning of classics."[27] In his famous so-called "Ten Thousand Character Memorial" or *Wan yan shu* submitted to Emperor Renzong in 1058, there is no explicit discussion of the poetic requirement, though a reader can infer here and there that Wang thought a candidate chosen for accomplishments in belles lettres was not thereby qualified to assume responsibility in finance, legal affairs, or the supervision of rites.[28] Throughout this extraordinarily long document, Wang's primary concern is to advise the emperor on how talent ought to be nurtured (through schools and proper education), discovered (through proper examinations), and used (by matching training and knowledge with duty).

Scattered in his letters are certain remarks that reveal his ideals for writing (*wen*). In one of them he observes, "Our contemporary men of letters distress me, for their rhetoric shows no regard for rational principles (*li*), and their principles care little for actual affairs (*shi*). They confuse accumulating clichés with learning, sculpting jargon with originality. It is like picking the blossoms of a rare flower and storing them for enjoyment. Though their brilliance and fragrance may be loveable, at bottom they are of no practical usage."[29] For a

---

[26] For brief accounts of Wang's views, see Chen Dongyuan, *Zhongguo jiaoyu shi*, pp. 244–46. For the achievement of Wang's own writings, see Liang Qichao, *Wang Anshi pingzhuan*, pp. 140–56. An overall assessment of Wang as reformer may be found in James T. C. Liu, *Reform in Sung China*.

[27] *Linchuan xiangsheng wenji, juan* 42, p. 450.

[28] See ibid., p. 419.

[29] "Shang Shao xueshi shu," ibid., p. 799.

man deeply committed to the belief that language exists for its proper utility, literary writing (*wen*) is actually equivalent to ritual learning (*lijiao*) and politics (*zhizheng*), something the fundamental purpose of which must be to succor the world (*you bu yu shi*). Rhetoric (*ci*), on the other hand, is the surface appearance (*rong*) of language, like carved or painted designs on a vessel: they may be clever and decorative but not useful.[30]

Among his 1,500 plus poems, the often cited quatrain ("Inside the Examination Hall") and the two poems of eight-line regulated verse entitled "Judging Examination Scripts" do reveal more explicitly his disdain for selecting candidates with belletristic criteria. Alluding repeatedly to the Han rhapsodist Yang Xiong (53–18 B.C.E.), who once described his youthful mastery of *fu* writing as a "trivial craft of carving insects (*diao chong xiao ji*)," Wang compares the tendency to rhetorical embroidery requisite in writing *fu*-type compositions—the skill in piling up (*duici*) ornate diction—to no more than the art of song girls.[31] In his view, it is a kind of labor inferior even to lexical annotation.[32]

Wang's low estimate of the poetic components in the examination system is thus based partly on subject (it diverts attention from the classics that purportedly have to do with historical truth and political ethics) and partly on language (as literature it attends only to its self-glorifying reflexivity).[33] His kind of objection, repeated down through the centuries, has found an echo in as recent a thinker and reformer as Kang Youwei. In his famous 1895 memorial on the *jinshi* degree that led to the reform of the examination system three years later, Kang declares, "I suspect that the reason why Wang Anshi wanted to examine candidates with the meaning of classics was that he saw how poetry and *fu* tend to display surface brilliance (*fu hua*) and lack substance."[34]

This assessment by Wang and Kang of poetry and *fu* highlights the divided views of belletristic or literary language that has been deeply entrenched in

---

[30] "Shang ren shu," ibid., p. 811.

[31] Yang Xiong, *Fayan* 2: 1a. (SPPY).

[32] For the poem to the title of "Inside the Examination Hall," see *Linchuan*, p. 336; cf. the second poem to the title of "Judging Examination Scripts," p. 238.

[33] The fifth line of the second poem on "Judging Examination Scripts" reads: "It [that is, the art of crafting the *fu*-type compositions] is lesser than a Visiting Minister because of brush and ink." The line alludes to the "Rhapsody on The Tall Poplars Palace (*Changyang Fu*)," in the preface of which Yang Xiong satirically names the brush Master of the Plume Grove (*hanlin zhuren*), and ink Visiting Minister/Chamberlain (*zimo keqing*). The important point here is that Yang considers this particular composition to have derived solely from "brush and ink (*liao yin bimo zhi cheng wenzhang*)." According to his assumption, therefore, it has no substantive raison d'être, even though his own preface assigns it a stated "purpose of swaying the emperor's opinion." See *Wen Xuan or Selections of Refined Literature*, translated by David R. Knechtges, 2: 137. Wang Anshi's line, however, would demote this kind of composition even further!

[34] Kang Youwei, "Qing fei bagu shitie kaifa gaiyong celun," cited in Wang Dezhao, *Qingdai keju zhidu yanjiu*, p. 77.

Chinese history.[35] Although these views possess such depth and complexity that they require much lengthier treatment than can be given here, the point of the debate accepted by both sides is that language may both pervert and subvert by reason of the subject it treats and the characteristics of the language itself. Jia Zheng's command to his son to stop writing poems indicates not only the academic efforts on which Bao-yu must concentrate but also the pernicious activity that he must shun at all cost. Neither the father nor the tutor, to be sure, has anything explicit to say about such perniciousness. It remains for Xue Bao-chai, the future daughter-in-law of Jia Zheng who is also the most committed orthodox Confucian of the young women in the Garden, to bring out part of the crucial implications of poetic acitivities.

CENSORSHIP AND THE CRITICS

In her famous "lecture" to Dai-yu (chap. 42) for the misconduct of quoting certain forbidden books in a drinking game, Bao-chai declares:

> "What do you take me for? I'm just as bad. At seven or eight I used to be a real little terror. Ours was reckoned to be rather a literary family. My grandfather was a bibliophile, so the house we lived in was full of books. We were a big family in those days. All my boy cousins and girl cousins on my father's side lived with us in the same house. All of us younger people hated serious books but liked reading poetry and plays. The boys had got lots and lots of plays: *The Western Chamber, The Lute-Player, A Hundred Yuan Plays*—just about everything you could think of. *They* used to read them behind *our* backs, and we girls used to read them behind theirs. Eventually the grown-ups got to know about it and then there were beatings and lectures and burning of books—and that was the end of that.
>
> "So, you see, in the case of us girls it would probably be better for us if we never learned to read in the first place. Even boys, if they gain no understanding [*ming li*] from their reading, would do better not to read at all; and if that is true of boys, it certainly holds good for girls like you and me. The little poetry-writing and calligraphy we indulge in is not really our proper business. Come to that, it isn't a boy's proper business either. A boy's proper business is to read books in order to gain an understanding of things, so that when he grows up he can play his part in governing the country.
>
> "Not that one hears of that happening much nowadays. Nowadays their reading

---

[35] Wang Anshi's use of the adjective *qiao* (crafty, clever, cunning) resonates with Confucian censure: "It is rare, indeed, for a man with cunning words (*qiao yan*) and an ingratiating face to be benevolent" (*Analects* 1. 3). For a detailed study of the pertinent debate on language—its function and use—in classical Chinese philosophy, see Lisa Raphals, *Knowing Words*. For an account of how Han *fu* helped to develop "the dramatic sense of language as play and performance" through self-conscious exploitation of its resources, see Wai-Yee Li's *Enchantment and Disenchantment*.

seems to make them even worse than they were to start with. And unfortunately it isn't merely a case of their being led astray by what they read. The books, too, are spoiled, by the false interpretations they put upon them. They would do better to leave books alone and take up business or agriculture. At least they wouldn't do so much damage.

"As for girls like you and me: spinning and sewing are *our* proper business. What do we need to be able to read for? But since we *can* read, let us confine ourselves to good, improving books; let us avoid like the plague those pernicious works of fiction, which so undermine the character that in the end it is past reclaiming." (*SS* 2: 333–34; *HLM* 2: 583–84)

This speech of Bao-chai has elicited different reactions from different audiences. Her immediate addressee, Dai-yu, seemed to be "so chastened . . . that she sat with head bowed low over her teacup and . . . her heart consented." Her meek response might have led one entry of the Red Inkstone manuscripts to assert, perhaps with a good bit of sarcasm, that "the author, with the utmost seriousness (*yi pian kuxin*), is expounding the Law on behalf of Buddha and lecturing on the Dao for sages" (*Pingyu*, p. 608). On the other hand, the nineteenth-century scholiast Zhang Xinzhi latches onto the very description of Dai-yu's behavior and fumes: "I might have consented when I was young, but I do not consent to [Bao-chai's speech] now. Moreover, I dread it like a serpent and avoid it like an arrow, if only because I'm now good at reading this book!" (*Sanjia*, 2: 671). These comments, though consistent with the contrasting attitudes of the narrative's historical readership toward Bao-chai and Dai-yu, do not pick up sufficiently the startling quality of Bao-chai's remarks.

What her words reveal first of all is the totality of her subscription to the orthodox Confucian position. Literacy, in this view, is not a good in itself, but only an instrumental good for both men and women to gain access to "serious books" (*zhengjing shu*). Men study to understand the principles of things (*dushu mingli*) so as to serve the state and govern the people. That is the "proper business" (*fen nei zhi shi*) for males, and it is an ideal to which women also must give complete assent. For a woman, by contrast, her "proper business" concerns the distaff and the needle, not poetry and calligraphy. If men and women cannot accept such a political obligation, which is also imposed as a moral one, then it is better for them to be illiterate.

The political control of literacy finds its logical corollary in literary censorship. That is the second cardinal point of Bao-chai's speech. "Serious books" are juxtaposed to writings that are obviously undesireable. What Bao-chai and her male and female cousins love to read behind each other's backs are poetry (*shi*), lyrics (*ci*), and plays, the last of which she refers to further with named works and collections. The specificity of her reference is matched only by the severity of how readers of such writings are dealt with—beatings, lectures, and periodical burnings of the books they love. This familial censorship in turn testifies to the perceived power in those "pernicious works of fiction" (an overtranslation, nevertheless unerring, of *zashu*, which literally means hetero-geneous, noncanonical, and thus heterodox books): they can "so undermine the character [*xingqing*, literally, nature-and-feeling, the composite term for human nature discussed by Chinese thinkers from the time of Mencius to the Qing] that in the end it is past reclaiming.'

When they are thus analyzed, Bao-chai's words provide readily a luminous gloss on the pronouncements by Jia Zheng and Jai Dai-ru. Whereas those two grown men may lack both the intelligence and fluency to articulate the ratio-nale for curbing Bao-yu's behavior, Bao-chai's instructions for Dai-yu ironi-cally place their male cousin's predilections and activities in the glare of the dominant cultural ideology. She has been taught exceedingly well, and her words, first of all help explain Jia Zheng's spontaneous deprecation early in the narrative when told of Bao-yu's progress in school—the boy having just finished studying Book Three of the *Poetry Classic*.

> If he read *thirty* books of the *Poetry Classic*, it would still be tomfoolery. No doubt he hopes to deceive others with this sort of thing, but he does not deceive me. Give my compliments to the Headmaster and tell him from me that I want none of this trifling with the *Poetry Classic* or any other ancient literature. It is of the utmost importance that he would thoroughly understand and learn by heart the whole *Four Books* before he attempts anything else. (*SS* 1: 204; *HLM* 1: 135–36)

The father's denunciation of the *Poetry Classic* or *Shijing* betrays his utter carelessness, if not his ignorance, about the requisite texts in Bao-yu's curric-ulum. The emphasis on the *Four Books* is not wrong, but Jia Zheng should have remembered that the volume of ancient poetry had also attained the status of a classic (hence *jing*), indeed long before his time and thus before the time of the novelistic setting. Large portions of the work have been so thoroughly assimilated, through allegorical exegesis, into the Confucian discourse on state-craft and ethics that the anthology's examination has always been considered a part of the test devoted to ascertaining the meaning of classics (*jingyi*). If Bao-yu were to succeed in the examinations, in short, he had little choice but to master much of this book's content.[36]

The irrationality of Jia Zheng's precipitous outburst is further underscored by the very poetic text slightly misquoted by an unwitting, stuttering servant:

> Hear the happy bleeding deer
> Grousing in the vagrant meads . . .

This song (Mao, 161) heading a section of the anthology titled "Calling Deer" (*lu ming*) is, in fact, the sung text that accompanies the banquet given for the

---

[36] For a sense of the importance of the *Poetry Classic* as part of the examination curriculum, see the informative charts and discussion in Benjamin A. Elman, "Changes in Confucian Civil Service Examinations from the Ming to the Ch'ing Dynasty."

successful candidates in the triennial provincial examination. Hence it is named The Banquet of the Calling Deer (*lu ming zhi yan*).[37] Had his been a more alert and agile intelligence, the father could perhaps have turned the servant's citation into an occasion to exhort his young son to strive for the honor associated with the poetic lines. As it is, his dim-witted impetuosity cannot be more bitingly displayed by the novelist.

This lapse of memory and perspective notwithstanding, Jia Zheng's declaration is perfectly consistent with his intentions throughout the narrative to wean his son from a diet of what he considers worthless and dangerous books. Why does he speak so pejoratively of the *Poetry Classic*? Was not Confucius himself represented as having spoken several times in the *Analects* in praise of the anthology? Did he not declare that one phrase could sum up the entire volume's content of some three hundred poems: never think of swerving from the right (the *Analects*, 2. 2)? Did he not also pronounce that [the notes of the] *Guanju*, the anthology's first poem, convey "pleasure but not lascivious abandonment (*yin*)" (3. 20)? Despite such grandiose reassurance from the Master, it appears that Confucian puritans down through the ages have always been nervous about the range and power of the emotions exhibited in this collection of songs. The history of their exegesis, beginning with the so-called "Great Preface" (variously dated from the fifth century B.C.E. to the second century C.E.), has more often than not attempted to reconcile provocative language with orthodox moralism.[38] Such attempts are not always successful, as a devastatingly funny scene from the famous Ming drama, *The Peony Pavilion*, reminds us. The twisted allegoresis practiced by an unctuous tutor proves completely ineffectual in stifling the stirring passion of a young girl caught up in the erotic urgency of the *Guanju* poem.[39]

Perhaps the mention of the *Poetry Classic* has triggered some such sense of unease in Jia Zheng. Whatever the cause, his words and those of Bao-chai carry an authoritative ring that in turn may remind the reader of the persistent ambivalance—and frequent hostility—of the Qing government toward a variety

---

[37] Chen Dongyuan, *Zhongguo jiaoyu shi*, p. 381; Shang Yanliu *Qingdai keju kaoshi shulu*, p. 76. What this banquet meant to many of the candidates might best be seen in a story about the eighteenth-century poet, Yuan Mei (1716–1798). When he was twenty-two (1738), he obtained the Second Degree and attended the banquet. Almost sixty years later, anticipating that he might be able to attend the banquet again as an old alumnus, he wrote a series of nine quatrains to celebrate this event in advance. See *Xiaochang shanfang shiwenji, juan* 37, 12ab (SBBY).

[38] For an informative account of how the ancient anthology became a classic (*jing*), see Zhu Ziqing, *Gudian wenxue zhuanji* 1: 185–291. Zheng Zhenduo, in "Du Maoshixu," represents the modern reaction against the practice of ethical-political exegesis. Recent studies of such canonical allegorization include Zhang Longxi, "The Letter and the Spirit"; John B. Henderson, *Scripture, Canon, and Commentary*; and Steven van Zoeren, *Poetry and Personality*. My translation of the lines from the *Analects* follows van Zoeren's discussion on pp. 25–51.

[39] See "Scene Seven: The Schoolroom," in Tang Xianzu, *The Peony Pavilion*, pp. 24–30.

of literary writings.[40] Indeed, Bao-chai's lecture virtually echoes the sentiment of an edict of Emperor Kangxi, issued in 1715 to various high governmental agencies (including commanders-in-chief of all Eight Banners, the Censorate, and the Imperial Prefecture), banning the sale of fiction and ordering the destruction of both print and block: "We have seen recently how many shops are selling works of fiction and lascivious diction (*yin ci*). Written in absurd (*huangtang*) and vulgar language, they are not works of correct principles (*zhengli*). Not only do they seduce ignorant people, but they may even cause the eyes of officials and scholars to wander and thus inveigle their minds."[41] Bao-chai's words and those of the emperor join not only to disclose for us the risk of the literary activities favored by Bao-yu and his female companions; they also confront the reader with the seditious nature of the narrative itself, for *The Story of the Stone* dares proclaim repeatedly from the beginning that "its pages are filled with absurd language (*man zhi huangtang yan*)."[42]

If poetry, drama, and fiction—indisputably three major genres that can stand for a large part, if not the whole, of pre-modern Chinese literature—all possess such parlous capacity to lead astray, it remains for us to ask one further question. How exactly is this capacity realized? Is it by means of the content or the language, the message or the medium? Although the history of Chinese literary theories and poetics presents us with several answers with differing emphases, Cao Xueqin seems to favor a view that stresses the effect of reading: that is, on the emotive arousal concomitant with the reader's imaginative participation. Grandmother Jia's disquisition ridiculing "the clichés of romantic fiction" (chap. 54), generally taken—for the wrong reason—by modern readers as represen-

---

[40] Censorship of books is a venerable practice in China. Specific actions taken against fiction and drama since the Yuan have received detailed documentation in Wang Xiaochuan (Liqi), *Yuan Ming Qing sandai jinhui xiaoshuo xiqu shiliao*. For incidents in the Qing, see accounts by L. Carrington Goodrich, *The Literary Inquisition of Ch'ien-lung*, and "On Certain Books Suppressed by Order of Ch'ien-lung during the Years 1772–1788"; André Lévy, "La Condamnation du roman en France et en Chine"; Ropp, *Dissent in Early Modern China*, pp. 47–48; Ma Tai-loi, "Novels Prohibited in the Literary Inquisition of Emperor Ch'ien-lung, 1722–1788"; and Chow Kai-wing, *The Rise of Confucian Ritualism in Late Imperial China*, chapter 1. The sporadic literary inquisitions undertaken by previous Qing emperors became much more systematic during Qianlong's reign, and the kinds of books banned are revealing. As can be seen readily in Ma Tai-loi's study, the seven novels placed on Qianlong's index librorum prohibitorum are all works treating such highly sensitive themes as patriotism, political rebellions, and military expeditions. He rightly notes at the end of his essay that "it is significant that no erotic novel is included in any *Index*" (p. 212). On the other hand, the objection to fiction and drama as vehicles for promoting lascivious language or diction (*yin ci*) seems to have begun with Emperor Shunzhi and acquires frequency and ferocity especially under Kangxi. See Wang Xiaochuan, *Yuan Ming Qing sandai*, pp. 19–26.

[41] Wang, *Yuan Ming Qing sandai*, p. 24.

[42] The 1715 edict by Kangxi is not the only locus for the adjective "absurd" or *huangtang*; it is, in fact, a favored code word for the condemnation of fiction. See Ma Tai-loi, "Novels Prohibited," p. 210.

tative of the author's point of view, clinches the censorious argument advanced by Bao-chai. Provoked by two blind ballad-singers who say that they would be telling a story titled *A Phoenix Seeks a Mate*, thereby signaling a blatant effort on their part to pander to the family's good will through the auspicious doubling of names, the matriarch pontificates:

> These stories are all the same, . . . so tedious! Always the same ideally eligible young bachelors and the same ideally beautiful and accomplished young ladies—at least, they are *supposed* to be ideal, but there's certainly nothing ideal about them at all. Invariably, we are told how well-born they are. Their father has been a Prime Minister, or a First Secretary at the very least. They are always their father's only child and the apple of his eye. They are always amazingly well-educated, a model of decorum, a regular paragon of all the virtues—that is, until the first presentable young man comes along. As soon as *he* appears on the scene—it doesn't matter who or what he is—all their book-learning and the duty they owe their parents fly out of the window and the next moment they are planning for the "great enterprise of lifelong settlement" and generally carrying on in a way that would bring blushes to the cheek of a cat-burglar—certainly not in the least like respectable, educated young ladies. You would hardly call a young woman who conducted herself like that a "paragon", however many books she might have read—any more than you would acquit a young fellow charged with highway robbery on the grounds that he was a good scholar. The people who make up these stories give themselves the lie every time they open their mouths. . . .
>
> [I]t's because the writer is envious of people so much better off than himself, or disappointed because he has tried to obtain their patronage and failed, and deliberately portrays them in this unfavourable light as a means of getting his own back on them. In other cases the writers have been corrupted by reading this sort of stuff before they begin to write any themselves, and, though totally ignorant of what life in educated, aristocratic families is really like, portray their heroines in this way simply because everyone else does so and they think it will please their readers. I ask you now, never mind *very* grand families like the ones they pretend to be writing about, even in average well-to-do families like ours when do you ever hear of such carryings-on? It's a wonder their jaws don't drop off, telling such dreadful lies! For my part, *I* have never allowed these sort of stories to be told. Even the maids here don't know about such matters. It's true that . . . I *do* once in a while listen to a snatch or two of one of these stories, when I feel in need of cheering up a bit; but as soon as the children arrive, I make the person telling it stop. (*SS* 3: 30–31, text modified; *HLM* 2: 758–59)

At last the mystery begins to unravel. Certain kinds of writing offend because they dare show the powerlessness of ritual learning (*lijiao*) in the face of desire. Young men and women, though well schooled and brought up, would at once forget books and parents to lead lives similar to "cat-burglars" and "highway robbers." Grandmother's observation merely recalls and expands colloquially a severe judgment laid down by an ancient sage: "those who bore holes in the wall to peep at one another, and climb over it to meet illicitly, waiting for neither the command of parents nor the good offices of a go-between, are despised by parents and fellow-countrymen alike" (*Mencius*, 3B, 108). The thief metaphor, intertextually generated, fully evokes the transgressive, antinomian character of desire, against the surge of which even the most elaborate and rigid code of hierarchical order may prove too fragile a rampart. Despite the frequent injunction for desire's proper regimentation, however, we have, in the long history of Chinese literature, countless monuments to oretic potency: from the spontaneous sensualism of the *Poetry Classic* to the prolonged ruminations on desire in the Han rhapsodies; from the exquisite lyrics on illicit, rebellious, or obsessive love in Tang-Song poetry to the most graphic erotic fiction such as *The Carnal Prayer Mat* and *The Plum in the Golden Vase (Jinpingmei)* in the Ming. It is no accident that mentioning dramas like *Western Wing* and *Peony Pavilion* can cause Bao-chai, only half in jest, to demand that Dai-yu demonstrate penitence by kneeling, for those two Yuan-Ming works are only too familiar in their intense celebration of furtive romance that defies orthodox boundaries. Imaginative literature, in sum, proves itself to be the most puissant means to record, transmit, and glorify the private interests begotten of passion. Tongue in cheek, the nineteenth-century scholiast Zhang Xinzhi declares at one point, "*Hongloumeng* on the surface is a dirty book. This, its author has already confessed without denial" (*Sanjia* 1: 84). One might justly wonder what Bao-chai or Grandmother would say about reading a text like *The Story of the Stone*!

Grandmother's sweeping exposition of so-called fictional clichés must therefore be assessed in terms of both its insight and its blindness. True, she has put her finger on the general weakness in the emplotment of much of the second-rate romantic fiction, the so-called novels of talented scholars and beautiful ladies (*caizi jiaren*), which were immensely popular in the late Ming and Qing periods.[43] Taking her to be speaking for the author, contemporary Redologists think that this is the way Cao Xueqin dissociates himself from the mediocre products of hack novelists crowding the shelves of Qing book shops. What these readers miss is the fact that Grandmother's verbose critique of such fiction cannot be more ironically staged, for she is, of course, totally oblivious to the possibility that the targets of her stinging remarks might well be personified or replicated by living members of her own household. Their very experience and behavior might enact the fictive courses of action she deplores. Are not her granddaughter Lin Dai-yu and grandniece Xue Bao-chai the embodiment

---

[43] The only full-length study of this genre in English is Richard C. Hessney, "Beautiful, Talented, and Brave." A perceptive account of *Hongloumeng*'s relationship to this type of fiction may be found in Huang Lixin, "Qingchu caizi jiaren xiaoshuo yu *Hongloumeng*."

of the young females she describes—their father's only child, the apple of his eye, amazingly well-educated, a model of decorum, a regular paragon of all the virtues? Is not her own grandson, Jia Bao-yu, a presentable young man that would cause at least one of these girls to think obsessively of "the great enterprise of lifelong settlement"? Little does she realize that later in the narrative, even her death-bed exhortation ("My boy, you must promise to do your very best for the family!" [SS 5: 192; HLM 3: 1,514]) cannot restrain her most beloved grandson from forsaking books and parents to lead—not a thief's life, but perhaps something even worse—a celibate's solitary existence away from the family, and all for the sake of a memory haunted by guilt and love.[44] Grandmother Jia indeed may proscribe the telling of such romantic tales before an audience of young masters and mistresses, with a zeal perhaps no less ardent than the effort of her daughter-in-law, Lady Wang, who ransacks the Prospect Garden in a later episode just to ferret out some erotic prints. But the matriarch fails, as do all agencies of authority like the elders in Bao-chai's family or governments past and present as well, to appreciate the pervasiveness of language, and therefore, the ubiquity of fiction. Her indictment amplifies that of Bao-chai in the previous episode by showing more clearly the power of desire, and of fiction as both mimesis and dissemination of desire, to decenter and destabilize hierarchical order. What she does not yet know is that such a transformation will be experienced by a young woman whom she is said to love best and care for most within the very family she tries so hard to safeguard and uphold.

If Grandmother's lengthy lecture encountered repeated endorsements from kinfolk and servants, she did not fare so well finally in the hands of the novelist. In the person of Xi-feng (Phoenix), her tart-tongued granddaughter-in-law, the elderly lady's authority is at once questioned and undermined. Urging the matriarch to drink some wine to wet her "whistle" before continuing any further, Xi-feng tells the gathered family members:

> The story you've just been listening to is called Falsehood Exposed, or The Tale of a Grandmother. It is a story which took place under the reigning dynasty, on this very day of this very month of this very year on this very spot and at this very hour. How can Grannie "with one mouth tell a double tale"? Ah, how indeed! Our tale puts forth two tails. Which tail to wag? Wig-wag. But for the time being we do not inquire which tale is false, which true. Our story turns rather to those

---

[44] The phrase zhengqi, translated as "do your best for the family," literally means the qi (the vital force or energy) of contentiousness (cf. Xunzi jijie 1. 12, p. 141). Grandmother's exhortation to Bao-yu thus says in effect: "You must strive or you won't be in any position to revive the family." The rhetorical pathos of her words cannot be fully felt until one hears how they echo, ironically, the prediction of decline sounded in chapter 5: literally, "the fate of the family and the numerical meaning of its nodal or vital forces have both reached their extremity" (yunzhong shujin). In the shu of the phrase is couched the term qishu (destiny, fortune, fate).

people in the party who were admiring the lanterns and watching the play. . . .
Just give these two kinsfolk a chance to drink a cup of wine and watch a scene or
two more of the play, Grannie, and then you can get on with your *Exposure of
Falsehood*—dynasty by dynasty. (*SS* 3: 31–32; *HLM* 2: 759)

These words of Xi-feng have justly won her the sobriquet of "Hard Mouth"
from the two professional storytellers. Not only is the expositor exposed, the
ridiculer ridiculed, but the double entendres of those cutting observations in
effect inform Grandmother that she has talked herself into fictionalizing her
family. Xi-feng's remarks once more make dazzling play of the true-false
dialectic so centrally operative in the whole narrative, helping us thereby see
ever more sharply the doubleness of fictive discourse. Grandmother's family,
the Jia family, is indeed "true" in the sense that it is very much a realistic given
of the narrative, and its very existence, as Xi-feng says, can be dated down to
the very present within the novelistic chronotope. What Xi-feng is saying, in
short, is that the Jia family is indeed "history." But Grandmother's "tale" about
her family is in truth also a story, for it is a fable of desire, fashioned continuously by her fears and hopes. She would make of her kinfolk much as those
two storytellers would of the characters in their tales—all for the pleasure and
approbation of herself and a specific audience. Such moralized and thus idealized "history" falls flat on the perceptive but cynical Xi-feng. Grandmother,
the trenchant critic of fiction, therefore, is also shown to live by a fiction hardly
different from those she so roundly criticizes.

THE FICTION OF DESIRE

If Grandmother Jia's critique of "romantic fiction" is made an instance of grand
irony in the narrative, the full force of that irony is not to be found even in Xi-
feng's counter-critique, biting as her words may be. The piquant truth of the
younger woman's sarcastic remark must be felt and seen in terms of how ready
indeed are members of the matriarch's own household, as I have argued, to
abide by the Confucian ideal of enlisting ritual to delimit desire (*fa hu qing, zi
hu li*). This last question, of course, cannot even be raised meaningfully with
respect to a vast majority of the Jia household, since so many of them have
distinguished themselves by their conspicuous failure. From those episodes
on Jia Zhen's devoting his life to pleasure (chap. 2), Qin-shi's intimated incest,
and Jia Rui's philandering (chap. 12), through the incidents of Bao-yu playing
the voyeur (chap. 19), Jia Lian's lust (chap. 21), Golden's suicide (chap. 32)
and Bao-yu's beating (chap. 33), to Jia Lian's adultery with You Er-jie (chap.
65), Moonbeam's attempted seduction of Xue Ke (chaps. 90–91) and Bao-yu's
of Fivey (chap. 109), the entire narrative is studded with accounts of unbridled
passion. Grandmother's words about "what life in educated, aristocratic families

is really like" must thus be examined in those lives supposedly most representative of the noble ideals of such families.

It is no accident that when she receives the censorious lecture by Bao-chai in chapter 42, Dai-yu is portrayed in the narrative as one assuming a "scarlet, shame-filled face and pitifully entreating voice" (*SS* 2: 333; *HLM* 2: 582). Her ostensible symptoms of a jolted conscience are attributable not merely to the fact that she has read such proscribed materials, but even more decisively, as the author cannily renders it, to the *manner* in which she has experienced those materials. In her experience is disclosed once again the power of literary fiction and the effect of its reading.

Readers of *The Story of the Stone* have not failed to notice the frequent allusions made by the narrative to two classical dramas of the Yuan-Ming periods, *The Story of the Western Wing (Xixiangji)* and *The Peony Pavilion (Mudanting)*. At least eight times—in chapters 18, 23, 26, 35, 36, 40, 42, and 51—the plays or parts thereof are named or cited.[45] Along with other dramatic materials, these two texts attest to the Jia family's love of theater characteristic of many aristocratic Qing households and the intimate knowledge of the stage's scripts and stories enjoyed by both masters and servants, mistresses and maids. Incidents, words, and emotions of various dramatic situations are readily recalled by the novelistic characters so that these texts function constantly both as the medium of communication and as gloss and commentary of actions and thoughts.

Despite the acceptance of theater as legitimate entertainment, however, some of the texts themselves, as we have gathered from Bao-chai's remarks to Dai-yu, are also regarded as licentious, and thus subversive, writings. To understand the way *Hongloumeng* "reads" certain works of traditional Chinese literature, we shall have to examine in some detail the circuitous process by which the dramatic texts are brought into the narrative and how their reading in turn affects the lives of the novelistic characters.

Although scenes of *The Peony Pavilion* were already alluded to in chapter 18 when the family was entertaining the imperial concubine, portions of the dramatic texts themselves receive sustained attention first in chapter 23, after Yuan-chun by decree installed Bao-yu to live in the garden as the solitary male among his female cousins. Out of special consideration for Lady Wang and Grandmother Jia's feelings that their beloved offspring would not be left behind, she ordered Bao-yu "to accompany the young ladies into the Garden and to continue his studies there" (*SS* 1: 455; *HLM* 1: 319). When this transfer of residence had been accomplished, however, the young hero's occupation was anything but studious. "Every day was spent in the company of his maids and cousins in the most amiable and delightful occupations, such as reading, / practising calligraphy, / strumming on the *qin*, / playing Go, / painting, / composing

---

[45] Xü Fuming, "*Xixiangji, Mudanting*, he *Hongloumeng*," p. 181; Xu's essay does not mention chapter 18.

verses, / embroidering in coloured silks, / competitive flower-collecting, / making flower-sprays, / singing, / word games and / guess fingers" (*SS* 1: 460; *HLM* 1: 322).

His life may have been "blissfully happy," as the narrator tells us, but it is also one that the Confucian perspective would consider both deplorable and conducive to mischief. Not only does it lead eventually to the kind of harsh paternal censure (chap. 81) discussed above but as its immediate consequence Bao-yu's ostensibly carefree existence also betokens a kind of corruption. The degeneration of his moral sensibility manifests itself at once in the four regulated octets on the four seasons he composes after he moves into the garden. Such language as "silk hangings," "giggling maids," "burning sandal," "the great quilt's golden bird," "Indian rugs" and the "languid master droops his raven head" would have been regarded as unmistakably ornate and sensual by traditional Chinese poetics. The young man's rhetorical excess bespeaks his indulgence, lapses that in fact are defined by the responsive readership that these poetic chronicles manage to locate. "Flippant youths [*qingbo zidi*]" outside the garden love the "flirtatious and seductive lines [*fengsao yaoyan zhi ju*]" (*HLM* 1: 324) so much that they have the poems copied "on to fans and wall-spaces and recited them on the least provocation (or none at all) at social gatherings" (*SS* 1: 461; *HLM* 1: 324).

It is in the context of such idle pleasure that Bao-yu was introduced to the dramatic texts themselves, and he in turn is the one who transmits one of the them to his cousin, Dai-yu. The entire episode in chapter 23, by focusing on certain acts of exchange and reciprocity in the handling of these texts, thus brings to light the facility and fluidity of textual migration, and with it, the traffic of certain dangerous ideals and values within the family's guarded space. Just as his own poems have been copied, transported, and circulated outside the garden, so he receives from his page Tealeaf a bundle of prohibited books, purchased in an effort to relieve him of his seemingly implacable boredom and ennui. Included in these volumes are explicitly pornographic works and also some written with more "careful observance of literary principles [*wenli ximi*]" (*HLM* 1: 324, my translation), among the latter being the drama *The Western Chamber*, or *The Story of the Western Wing*.[46]

To savor in greater measure the enormous irony wherewith the narrative has shown us the origin, the classification, and the effect this dramatic text (and later, *The Peony Pavilion* as well) had on its readers, we begin by noting the detailed anatomy of Bao-yu's psychology that functions as the formal cause of its appearance. For our young hero basking in the garden's "agreeable existence," observes the narrator,

---

[46] For the English text of the drama, I cite Wang Shifu, *The Moon and the Zither: The Story of the Western Wing* (hereafter cited as *The Western Wing*). For the Chinese text, I use Wang Shifu, *Xixiangji*, edited by Wang Jisi.

[who could have thought that such serenity would give rise to misery (*jing zhong sheng fannao*)]. He got up one day feeling out of sorts. Nothing he did brought any relief. Whether he stayed indoors or went out into the garden, he remained bored and miserable. The garden's female population were mostly still in that age of innocence when freedom from inhibition is the fruit of ignorance. Waking and sleeping they surrounded him, and their mindless giggling was constantly in his ears. How could *they* understand the restless feelings that now consumed him? In his present mood of discontent he was bored with the garden and its inmates; yet his attempts to find distraction outside it ended in the same emptiness and ennui. (*SS* 1: 462, text modified; *HLM* 1: 324)

Arguably one of the longer passages in the entire novel devoted to the description of a character's inward disposition, the passage offers us remarkable insight into Bao-yu's psychology. Those readers recalling the dialogue between the pre-incarnate Stone and the two mysterious clerics recorded in the 1754 text will at once notice the similarity of circumstance between the human protagonist here in the garden and his mythic antecedent below the Green Sickness Peak. Just as the latter's request to be transported to the "Red Dust world" after hearing of its glory and riches had been adjudged "the fated change of 'extreme repose giving rise to movement'" (1754, 4–5; *HLM* 1: 3), so Bao-yu's agitated condition is described by the narrator as "serenity giving rise to misery."[47] In both instances, the protagonist's passage from stasis to change has been induced by the stirring of desire.

Despite such correspondences in their experience, there are also significant differences. Stone's original decision to enter the human realm was based on its having overheard a narrated tale of that world's attractiveness; it is, in other words, the effect of a reported, if not a fictive, account of another kind of existence that propels it toward an encounter with human reality. The case with the human Bao-yu, on the other hand, seems an exact reverse of Stone's situation. Bao-yu's struggle with what looks almost like a bad case of acedia (if his sloth in discharging his Confucian duties may be deemed analogous to indifference in the religious devotee) causes him at this particular instance to shun human community and seek gratification, however momentary, in the world of the vicarious and the imaginary. Given his declared preference for the company of women in general, and of sisters and cousins his own age in particular, one would think that his residence in the garden would have provided him with incomparable delight. The astonishing revelation of the passage quoted from chapter 23 is that he is unhappy—especially because he holds within himself certain "affairs of the mind-and-heart [*xinshi*]" which, he thinks, they can neither know nor understand.

[47] The editors of the 1792 B text, in fact, emend the text to read: "serenity or stillness giving rise to movement/action [*jing zhong sheng dong*]."

Although the narrative tantalizes us by refusing to disclose the exact nature and cause of the young man's restlessness, there is no mystery with respect to the possible medium of his deliverance. The "cure" dreamed up by his desperate page is consonant not merely with the provider's character and experience— that he knows no better solution to his master's boredom than to buy him pornography—but with that as well of Bao-yu, the intended recipient of the proffered palliative. What this episode brings into ever sharper relief is that aspect of Bao-yu's personality which has already received prophetic delineation and caution in chapter 5: that he is most susceptible to both desire's suasion and its mimetic simulation. Bao-yu's present dealings with his page, in other words, can find revelatory glosses in antecedent parts of the narrative.

We should remember that at the beginning of chapter 19 Tealeaf's sexual dalliance with a maid was first spied upon and then interrupted by Bao-yu. How the latter chanced to discover the affair and in what terms he interpreted this voyeuristic moment are given in narration that further recalls his prior experience of erotic smell, sense, and sight.

> Finding himself alone, [Bao-yu] began thinking about a certain painting he remembered having seen in Counsin Zhen's "smaller study." It was a very lifelike portrait of a beautiful woman. While everyone was celebrating, he reflected, she was sure to have been left on her own and would perhaps be feeling lonely. He would go and have a look at her and cheer her up.
>
> But as he approached the study, he experienced a sudden thrill of fright. A gentle moaning could be heard coming from inside it.
>
> "Good gracious!" he thought. "Can the woman in the painting really have come to life?"
>
> He made a tiny hole in the paper window with his tongue and peeped through. It was no painted lady he saw, stepped down from her hanging scroll upon the wall, but Tealeaf, pressed upon the body of a girl and evidently engaged in those exercises in which Bao-yu had once been instructed by the fairy Disenchantment. (SS 1: 377; HLM 1: 262)

The reference to Disenchantment and, by implication, the entire dream tour of the Land of Illusion (chap. 5) is neither fortuitous nor derivative merely from the author's felt need for rhetorical decorum—the use of circumlocution to say that his young hero has witnessed a couple engaging in sexual intercourse. On the contrary, the whole passage here reverberates with verbal, imagistic, and motivic echoes of the earlier episode. When Bao-yu in chapter 5 was invited by Qin Shi, the young wife of his cousin-nephew, to take an afternoon nap in her living quarters, the residential furnishings therein symbolized the warring antinomies in the teenager's psyche. In "an inner room in the main building" Bao-yu, we are told, was at first exasperated by the sight of didactic painting and calligraphy strident in their exhortation to studiousness, learning, and "the skillful management of human relationships" (SS 1: 26; HLM 1: 70–

71) extolled as the substance of literary achievements (*wenzhang*).[48] Only when he was allowed to enter Qin's own bedroom and its radically different aesthetic and material environment was his aroused antipathy sufficiently appeased that he could stay and sleep. Even at this early stage of the story, then, the pattern of psychological conflict that will impress his whole life distinctly emerges. Through his reactions to his physical surroundings, the reader can see how the Confucian principle of filial duty, though only mimetically intimated by cultural artifacts, is made to compete with, and yield to, the claims of desire.

It is no surprise that in Qin's bedroom Bao-yu was inducted into the secret pleasures of sex. However the sequence of his actual experience is to be comprehended—whether he made love first to Qin and then again to his maid Aroma after he awoke from his protracted dream, or whether his first ejaculation was the sign only of an erotic dream—the point germane to my argument is that the hero's sexual initiation took place in an appropriate setting. His very presence in Qin's inner chamber and his occupation of her bed are themselves acts risking the construal of illicit contact. But further to convey the sense of assertive, unfettered sensualism that adorns this lady's lavish boudoir and how it conspires to excite and sway its temporary inhabitant, the narrator seems intent on ransacking Chinese lore for a totalizing allusiveness. Thus every object in her room (a mirror, a platter, a quince, a bed, a canopy, a coverlet, a double headrest) is made to associate with some of the most famous—and infamous—beauties in Chinese legend and history.

The extravagant description emphasizes that virtually every one of Bao-yu's senses was stimulated in this seductive atmosphere: his smell ("a subtle whiff of the most delicious perfume assailed his nostrils"), his touch (the coverlet, double headrest, and the bed itself), and above all, his sight (all the appointments in the room). All the more appositely, the place that will produce the most intense oneiric vision and mnemonic impact is one which also has plenty of attractions for his eyes. After all, the first object of the bedroom that caught his attention "was a painting by Tang Yin entitled 'Spring Slumber' depicting a beautiful woman asleep under a crab-apple tree" (*SS* 1: 127; *HLM* 1: 71).

Although the narrative says little more immediately of the effect such a painting had on Bao-yu, that it did affect him powerfully cannot be doubted. We should remember that throughout the story, the young man is portrayed as one peculiarly responsive to the vision of feminine pulchritude. More than once the narrative dwells on the discerning gaze of Bao-yu's roving eyes. A casual outing finds him "bird-dogging," even while riding a carriage, two maids by the roadside. After interrupting Tealeaf's furtive session with the maid, the young master's "eye fell upon the girl. She had a soft, white skin, to whose

---

[48] The couplet flanking a painting is made up of hackneyed aphorisms; it is not the author's original creation.

charms he could not be insensible" (*SS* 1: 377; *HLM* 1: 263). A little later, when he visited Dai-yu in her bedroom, this is what he saw:

> two young mistresses still lay fast asleep under the covers. Dai-yu was tightly cocooned in a quilt of apricot-coloured damask, the picture of tranquil repose. Xiang-yun, by contrast, lay with her hank of jet-black hair tumbled untidily beside the pillow, a white arm with its two gold bracelets thrown carelessly outside the bedding and two white shoulders exposed above the peach-pink coverlet, which barely reached her armpits. (*SS* 1: 415; *HLM* 1: 288)

Later still, when he requested to see a string of medicine-beads on Bao-chai's arm and she had difficulty at first pulling it off (for she "was inclined to plumpness"), "Bao-yu had ample opportunity to observe her snow-white arm, and a feeling rather warmer than admiration was kindled inside him." In fact, this alluring object incited in his mind a deliberate comparison and confession.

> "If that arm were growing on Cousin Lin's body," he speculated, "I might hope one day to touch it. What a pity it's hers! Now I shall never have that good fortune."
> Suddenly he thought of the curious coincidence of the gold and jade talismans and their matching inscriptions, which Dai-yu's remark had reminded him of. He looked again at Bao-chai—
>
> > that face like the full moon's argent bowl;
> > those eyes like sloes;
> > those lips whose carmine hue no Art contrived;
> > and brows by none but Nature's pencil lined.
>
> This was beauty of quite a different order from Dai-yu's. Fascinated by it, he continued to stare at her with a somewhat dazed expression. (*SS* 2: 66; *HLM* 1: 401–2)

That a moment's vision can trigger at once his urge to possession and conjure up for him the implied marital promise of their respective birth talismans ("the goodly affinity of gold and jade") measures the magnitude of his desire. Like the Mencius of antiquity acknowledging that he wanted both fish and bear paw for food (*Mencius*, 6A, 10; p. 166), Bao-yu suddenly finds himself struggling with the dilemma of competing appetites. The irony of the passage, of course, is that one day, Bao-yu's dilemma will be resolved for him and he will be able to touch Bao-chai indeed, but the circumstances then will render that physical union far from satisfactory. Nonetheless, the intensity of his present longing aroused by sight (Bao-chai's "plumpness" so impresses him that he teasingly compares her with Yang Gueifei in chapter 30) makes him already perilously close to being a vivid example of "the typically lustful man" described by the goddess Disenchantment: "a man who likes a pretty face, who is fond of singing and dancing, who is inordinately given to flirtation; one who makes love in season and out of season, and who, if he could, would like to have every pretty girl in the world at his disposal, to gratify his desires whenever he felt like it. Such a person is a stupid creature, who would expend his lust, as it were, merely in a skin-deep fashion" (*SS* 1: 146, text modified; *HLM* 1: 90).

The closing sentence of the goddess' remark cannot be more pointed and ironic, for "a stupid creature" (*chun wu*) is the precise term the mysterious clerics in chapter 1 employed to designate the preincarnate Stone of the opening myth.[49] A nineteenth-century scholiast was thus justifiably moved to comment at this point in chapter 5: "Actually, what the wielded brush had written concerned this affair and also this very creature. [The writing here] is simply a smoke screen" (*Sanjia* 1: 85). Bao-yu's explicit act of comparing the distinctive attractiveness of Xiang-yun and Dai-yu in their sleep also recalls for us what he had encountered during his dream visit to the Land of Illusion: the apparition of a fairy girl whose "rose-fresh beauty" and "delicate charm" reminded him of his two female cousins, respectively (*SS* 1: 145; *HLM* 1: 89–90). Moreover, that that fairy girl in the end was introduced to him as the goddess's younger sister, named Two-in-One or Ke-qing (in reality the "childhood name" of his niece Qin Shi) and that he dreamt of making love to her both serve to reveal the tangled web of his ambivalence.[50]

Bao-yu's lifelong susceptibility to sensual enticements, to visual adulations of the female body,[51] thus provides a good deal of the ground for the goddess's indictment of masculine hypocrisy and rationalization:

there are always any number of flippant philanderers who would use the motto, "being fond of woman's beauty without being lustful," as a subterfuge, and the motto, "having loving feelings but no lust," as a pretext. These are all phrases designed to cover up their wickedness and shame! For to be fond of woman's beauty is to be lustful, and to experience loving feelings even more so. Every act of love, every carnal congress of the sexes is brought about precisely because sensual delight in beauty has kindled the feeling of love. (*SS* 1: 145, text modified; *HLM* 1: 90)

Her pronouncement resonates with the tacit recognition by ancient philosophers that "fondness for woman's beauty" (*hao se*) is a stubborn trait of nature and,

[49] Hawkes has "absurd creature" in his translation. Cf. *SS* 1: 54; *HLM* 1: 9.

[50] This episode and one prophetic poem in the "Supplementary Register No. 1" of The Twelve Beauties of Jinling that seems to foretell the combined fate of Bao-chai and Dai-yu (*SS* 1: 133; *HLM* 1: 78), along with other minor textual details, have led the early scholiasts to think of the two female cousins sometimes as a single person with two names. See *Pingyu*, p. 606 and my discussion in Chapter 1. Shuen-fu Lin in "Chia Pao-yü's First Visit to the Land of Illusion," takes up the psychological issue of ambivalence.

[51] Even as late as chapter 109, when in his ostensibly implacable grief for Dai-yu he was sleeping in an outer room so as to facilitate any eventuality of her soul visiting him in his dreams, Bao-yu would easily succumb to the looks of a maid with a remarkable resemblance of Skybright. This bitterly ironic episode had the young man attempting a protracted seduction of the maid, all the while acting as if he were indeed waiting for Dai-yu.

at the same time, trenchantly exposes the self-serving exegesis that attempts to mask or dismiss the ubiquitous presence of desire.[52] It is, in fact, on this basis of predilection for feminine beauty and loving feelings that she not only judges Bao-yu to be "the most lustful person . . . in the whole world" but also enjoins him, ironically, to attend to the teachings of Confucius and Mencius once he has experienced, under her tutelage, the illusory nature of love.

Fortunately for the human Bao-yu, therefore, he is not merely "a stupid creature" in the eyes of Disenchantment, for it is her verdict that nature has filled the boy's being with a form of "blind, defenceless love" (*chi qing*) which she terms "the lust of the mind" (*yi yin*). That last phrase, of course, has spurred the speculation of many readers down through the ages. According to Red Inkstone, the "mental nature (*xinxing*) of Bao-yu's entire life is to be found in "empathy (*titie*)" or the ability to identify with other people's feelings (*Pingyu*, p. 135), and such an exegesis has the merit of highlighting the goddess's own assessment of Bao-yu's character: that women will find him "a kind and understanding friend" (*SS* 1: 146; *HLM* 1: 90). On the other hand, the term *yi yin* translated as "the lust of the mind" may literally mean something like aiming at or intending toward excess, and the French translation, "*luxure d'imagination*" (*PR* 1: 138), may be read as an apt though perhaps unwitting echo of Zhang Xinzhi's interlinear gloss: "*yi* is what issues from the heart-and-mind" (*Sanjia* 1: 85).[53]

However the term is to be definitively understood, the general thrust of its meaning with respect to the person it seeks to characterize seems comprehensible. By contrasting him with "the typically lustful man," the goddess' delineation of his character shows Bao-yu to be someone who does not merely care for the lure of the senses, for the bewitching beauty of form that the word *se* (Skt. *rūpa*) connotes so powerfully, especially in its usage after Buddhism's arrival. Since the meaning of "the lust of the mind," according to her, "can be grasped by the mind but not expressed, apprehended intuitively but not described in words" (*Yang* 1: 85; *HLM* 1: 90), her remark may indicate that the content of such desire Bao-yu experiences will be determined more by his own subjectivity than by its object. Intellectually and emotionally far more capacious than those worldly profligates who respond only to immediate phys-

---

[52] Cf. *The Analects*, 9. 18 (p. 98): "The Master said, 'I have yet to meet the man who is as fond of virtue as he is of beauty (*hao se*) in women" (saying repeated in 15. 13), and *Mencius*, 5A, 1: "beautiful women are something every man desires; . . . when a person is young he yearns for his parents; when he understands fondness for beauty in women (*hao se*), he yearns for the young and the beautiful."

[53] The *Shuowen* (10B, 24b–25a, p. 502) glosses *yi* with *zhi*, thus authenticating the two words' eventual combination as one term in later usage. Bernhard Karlgren (*Grammata Serica Recensa*, #957a) defines *yi* as "to think, thought, intention, will," whereas *zhi* he explains (#962e) as "aim, goal; will, purpose."

ical stimuli, he is someone who also feels the grip of desire through vicarious participation in memory or imagination.

If such an interpretation is not far off the mark, it should help us understand his motive and reaction in the episode in chapter 19. For surely, to visit a beautiful woman painted on a scroll and to "cheer her up" in her loneliness, as Bao-yu wishes to do in this part of the story, is an expression of delirious sentiment (*chi qing*). Such desire is not just "blind" or "defenceless," but literally mad in the sense of a capitulation, however fleeting, to the dictates of his fancy. To think of a painted portrait in terms befitting a real person is to turn reality entirely into a constituent of imagination and longing. Truth is subjectivity, indeed! Could this kind of make-believe exceed the vagaries of youthful whims to indicate part of his defining ethos, *yi yin* or wilfulness to excess? In recalling this "very lifelike portrait of a beautiful woman" that he had seen in his Cousin Zhen's "smaller study," could he also be thinking of another painting that he previously saw in Qin Shi's bedroom? Could both paintings form a continuous, interactive chain of represented form and desire?

Read with these questions, the episode of chapter 19 can indeed be seen as a psychological and symbolic extension of Bao-yu's initiatory experience in chapter 5. The erotic encounter that provides a kind of closure to his dream-tour of the Land of Illusion also serves as a perpetual reminder and stimulant for further encounters. Having "proceeded to follow out the instructions that Disenchantment had given him, which led him by predictable stages to that act which boys and girls perform together" (*SS* 1: 147; *HLM* 1: 91), Bao-yu would repeat the act immediately thereafter with Aroma after he had awakened from his dream (chap. 6). If the oneiric experience of sex had found embodiment as a series of "instructions" and then reenactment as a "lesson" to be shared (*SS* 1: 150; *HLM* 1: 93), the later vision of "Tealeaf pressed upon the body of a girl" (chap. 19) also returns Bao-yu the voyeur to his dream images—"those exercises in which [he] had once been instructed by the fairy Disenchantment" (*SS* 1: 377; *HLM* 1: 262). For the consciousness of Bao-yu as depicted in the narrative, desire and its symbolic representation—in word, image, and gesture—are virtually interchangeable in the sense that they are linked in a process of mutual generation. Just as desire often manifests itself in representation, so representation continually begets desire.

This complicitous link of mimesis with desire will find the most poignant confirmation in Bao-yu's relations to Dai-yu. Troubled by the sight of his young master's ostensibly groundless misery, the page Tealeaf in chapter 23 tries to cheer him up with pornography. Bao-yu's choice of a literary masterpiece rather than serializations of graphic sex as a constant companion of reading betokens not simply the refinement of his taste. His refusal to heed Tealeaf's plea for him not to bring the books into the garden makes it clear that he enjoys reading them as much as anyone. However, in the well-wrought but unambiguously romantic tale of chanced meetings, secret intrigues, and furtive seduction through specific literary media that is *The Story of the Western Wing*, Bao-yu might have found the most genial representation with which he could identify, thereby focalizing the nameless, objectless passion that afflicts him. It is, after all, during his "attentive" perusal (*xi kan*) of the book that a part of his own Prospect Garden is scenically, and thus symbolically, merged with the garden of clandestine romance realized in the dramatic text (*SS* 1: 462–23; *HLM* 1: 324–25). When Dai-yu accidentally intrudes into this highly suggestive locale strewn with fallen red petals, she will also run into unexpected turmoil born of the interactive union of art and life.[54]

Terrified at first by Dai-yu's interrogation about the book he is reading, for he knows only too well from Tealeaf's warning that this text, just like those pornographic titles, is a proscribed artifact in the garden, Bao-yu tries to pass it off as a volume of Confucian classics (*Doctrine of the Mean, The Great Learning*). Succumbing eventually to her insistent behest, he shares the book with her, and the spreading contagion of desire at once seals the fate of their reading.

For the young man, the commonality of their textual experience permits the expression of his feelings for her in the guise of provocative teasing. This will not be the only time when he speaks to her in quotations:

> How can I, full of sickness and of woe,
> Withstand that face which kingdoms could o'erthrow?
>
> (*SS* 1: 464; *HLM* 1: 325)[55]

Three chapters later, catching Dai-yu quoting from the same play, he will address her maid Cuckoo (and indirectly Dai-yu herself) by appropriating the rhetorical question of Student Zhang:

---

[54] West and Idema in their Introduction to the translation of *The Western Wing*, pp. 141–44, have called attention to the garden as a topos of "courtship and seduction" in the drama. The narrative's account of how "a little gust of wind blew over and a shower of [peach] petals suddenly rained down from the tree above" onto Bao-yu beneath as he was reading the line from the drama—"The red flowers in their hosts are falling"—reveals a conspicuous merging of the two gardens. The seemingly accidental action of nature in the narrative renders Bao-yu's lived experience a virtual imitation of the artistic text he is reading. In this highly charged setting he suddenly encounters Dai-yu, who is already assuming her famous role of a person who pities the flowers (*xi hua ren*) enough to scoop them up for burial, thus anticipating her celebrated action of flower burial later in the story (chap. 27). Rhetorically, the most significant diction in this episode is "the falling red [petals]," for *luo hong* in literary usage serves as a stock metaphor for hymeneal drops when a woman loses her virginity. The latent eroticism in both *The Western Wing* and the *Hongloumeng* is thus barely concealed, for although the falling petals in both texts may betoken the passing of spring, this imagery can also suggest the pent-up desire that ends in the loss of sexual innocence.

[55] The lines come from Play 1, Act 4. See *The Western Wing*, p. 212.

> If with your amorous mistress I should wed,
> Would I let you only make our bridal bed?
>
> (*SS* 1: 517, text modified; *HLM* 1: 36)[56]

Since one function of poetry, according to the culture's venerable tradition, is to articulate aim, wish, or intent (*shi yan zhi*) in both the private and public spheres of life, these lines cannot be more transparent in their revelation of Bao-yu's subjectivity. Indeed, throughout the narrative, the intimated declarations of one's deepest feelings by means of art and artifice remain the two lovers' privileged means of communication, whether successful or abortive. Just as Dai-yu later will try to convey her anxious affections for him through the sound of a string instrument (*qin*) in chapters 86–89, so even after she dies, his purposive recollection of her will express itself in the familiar lines of Bai Juyi's "Song of Everlasting Sorrow" (chap. 109). In the assumed voice of a Student Zhang or the Tang Emperor Xuanzong, Bao-yu asserts unmistakably what he thinks of her: as a prospective spouse in the early parts of their story and as a wedded mate after her death.

That Dai-yu greets his taunting citations from *The Western Wing* with explosive anger (chap. 23) or tearful exasperation (chap. 26) is, as I have argued already, an understandable reaction stemming from both surprise and embarrassment. Her vocal protest and castigation of the young man, however, imply that she is not so much resistant to the *idea* conveyed by those citations as she is to the manner and circumstance of its conveyance. In fact, the narrative has gone to considerable length in detailing for the reader how she, once exposed to it, has been taken total captive by the mimetic content of this famous drama.

> He handed the book to her, and Dai-yu put down her garden tools and looked. The more she read, the more she liked it, and in less time than that of a meal she had read several acts. She felt the power of the words and their lingering fragrance. Long after she had finished reading, when she had laid down the book and was sitting there rapt and silent, her mind still went over quietly the lines she had committed to memory. (*SS* 1: 464, text modified; *HLM* 1: 325)

Louder than even her vocal response to Bao-yu's query ("Is it good?"), her reactions more than confirm his enthusiastic commendation of the work ("It's a marvelous composition [*hao wenzhang*]"). Like him, she will be haunted henceforth by the verbal fragments and rhetorical traces of the text so powerfully inscribed in her consciousness. She will quote them in unguarded moments (chap. 26); she will summon them as scenic setting for her own lodging (chap. 35); and she will cite them during the casual bouts of games and chit-chat (chap. 40). Even after she has been censured by Bao-chai (chap. 42), she shows neither remorse nor hesitancy in defending another girl (chap. 51) against the

---

[56] These lines come from Play 1, Act 2, ibid., p. 190.

charge of confusing fiction with history, because the latter has incorporated *The Western Wing* and *The Peony Pavilion* into a suite of poems celebrating famous sites of the past.

These actions of Dai-yu should inform us that her's is much more than merely a detached appreciation of a literary work. Like Bao-yu and even more than he, the girl has inserted herself into the text through reading. Dai-yu's ready identification with Oriole (Cui Ying-ying), the heroine of *The Western Wing*, finds eloquent expression when lines of the play are retrieved (chap. 35) to make of her residence a synecdochic extension of her condition:

> As they entered the courtyard, the chequered shadows of the bamboos and the dew-pearled moss reminded her [Dai-yu] of two lines she had read in *The Western Chamber*:
>
>> A place remote, where footsteps seldom pass,
>> And dew still glistens on the untrodden grass.
>
> "It's all very well," she thought, as she reflected on the heroine of that play, "Ying-ying may have been poor in her fate, but at least she had a widowed mother and a little brother. The poverty of my fate, Lin Dai-yu's, is that I have no one." (*SS* 2: 174, text modified; *HLM* 1: 474)

If the melancholic solitude of the Naiad's House arouses in her a comparison of herself with the lady in the drama, is it too far-fetched for the reader to imagine that Dai-yu must also have wondered, in her reading and meditation of the text, who might turn out to be her Student Zhang who will release her from her sad fate?

As if it has already anticipated such a line of questioning from the reader, the narrative swiftly moves to dispel any needless speculation by redoubling its emphasis on the impact of drama and lyric on Dai-yu's psyche. Shortly after she is separated from Bao-yu in the garden episode of chapter 23, she is assaulted once again by the sound and text of potent literary art. This time it is *The Peony Pavilion*, a few scenes of which are rehearsed by twelve little actresses. Though her first response to the snatches of an aria she overhears dwells on her appreciation of the beauty of the play's poetry, and is thus a silent refutation of the dismissive view that dramas are mere "entertainment," the eventual effect of the text on her is shattering.

> She listened again. This time it was another voice:
>
>> "Because for you, my flowerlike fair,
>> The swift years like the waters flow—"
>
> The words moved her to the depth of her being.

> "I have sought you everywhere,
> And at last I find you here,
> In a dark room full of woe—"

It was like intoxication, a sort of delirium. Her legs would no longer support her. She collapsed on to a near-by rockery and crouched there, ruminating on the flavour of those two lines:

> "Because for you, my flowerlike fair,
> The swift years like the waters flow . . ."

Suddenly she thought of a line from an old poem she had read quite recently:

> The waters flow, the flowers fade—both pitiless!

From that her mind turned to those famous lines written in his captivity by the tragic poet-emperor of Later Tang:

> The blossoms fall, the water flows,
> And spring is gone—
> Heaven's above; here, the human world!—

and to some lines from *The Western Chamber* which she had just been reading:

> As flowers fall and the flowing stream runs red,
> A thousand sickly fancies crowd the mind.

All these different lines and verses combined into a single overpowering impression, riving her soul with a pang of such keen anguish that the tears started from her eyes. (*SS* 1: 466–67, text modified; *HLM* 1: 327–28)

It is no random detail that Dai-yu is moved to ardent longing by two dramatic texts of Chinese literary history not only most forceful in their glorification of heterosexual love, but also most daring in their portraits of young women living through their own sexual awakening. Both Oriole and Bridal Du, the heroines of the plays, have yielded to the dictates of their passion, "waiting for neither the command of parents nor the good offices of a go-between."[57] Although their transgressions may appeal to Dai-yu, much as all stolen pears may taste sweeter to a thief, the thrill of illicit action alone cannot account for all the dramatic impact.[58] As the narrative makes clear in the first place, the

---

[57] This passage from Mencius, in fact, was quoted by Bridal Du after her resurrection to forestall her lover's wish to make love to her immediately, pleading that "a ghost may be deluded by passion; a woman must pay full atention to the rites." See *The Peony Pavilion*, "Scene Thirty-Six: Elopement," p. 207.

[58] Cf. Augustine, *Confessions* 2: 6.

overheard lines that trigger the recollection of other literary texts all focus on one fundamental theme: the relentless passing of time.

We should recall that every aspect and every feature of the Prospect Garden at this point of the story is, so to speak, "brand new." Yet, what immediately arrests Dai-yu's attention and elicits her eventual approbation are lines sung by Bridal Du that depict a markedly different surrounding evoked by a different mood:

> "Here multiflorate splendour blooms forlorn
> Midst broken fountains, mouldering walls—"

and:

> "And the bright air, the brilliant morn
> Feed my despair.
> Joy and gladness have withdrawn
> To other gardens, other halls—"

(SS 1: 466; HLM 1: 327)

Through the eyes of yearning she shares with the dramatic heroine, Dai-yu is already viewing her own environment from the perspective of its incapacity to endure as any dwelling of lasting happiness. The new for her already takes on the ominous potential of the old and the dying, and in this manner her reception of the dramatic verse anticipates the eventual, fated decline of the garden. Because the particular condition of her life makes her more alert and responsive than either Bao-yu or Xi-feng, both of whom having been duly warned— through the medium of dreams—of the short-lived prosperity and impending doom of the Jia household, Dai-yu's hearing of fiction suddenly thrusts her into the terror of impermanence. As she listens to the actresses rehearsing, the rendered phenomenon of humans and flowers both inevitably fading validates the poetic indictment of the temporal flux as pitiless or unfeeling (*wu qing*). That line of regulated verse by the Tang poet Cui Tu (fl. ninth century) origi-nally opens a septasyllabic octet transcribing his "Traveling Moods in a Spring Night (*chun xi lü huai*)," but her mnemic appropriation of it conflates it conve-niently with the famous lines of the Later Tang Emperor Li Yu (937–978).[59] Even as the repetitive diction (flowing water, fading flowers) in both poetic allusions heightens for her the speed of time's motion, the respective conditions of the poets (one in mid-journey, the other an exiled ruler in confinement) no doubt deepens her own sense of loneliness and alienation.

This fusion of poetic topoi thus points to a venerable paradox: that only the person of consciousness/feelings (*you qing ren*) that qualifies all three subjects in view—Cui Tu, Li Yü, and Dai-yu—can best discern the indifference of time, its refusal to accommodate the human longing for stability and change-lessness. Yet the specific pain now afflicting Dai-yu does not derive solely

---

[59] The octet is in *QTS*, 10: 7,783.

from her awareness of nature's transitoriness. The crisis of consciousness precipitated in this young reader and listener centers rather on whether a solution can be found in a timely fashion for her problem: aging without marital prospects which is also aging without the security of home. It is this aspect of her agony that helps explain her violent response ("It was like intoxication, a sort of delirium. Her legs would no longer support her") to the passionate declamation by Liu Mengmei, the dramatic hero, to Bridal Du:

> "Because for you, my flowerlike fair,
> The swift years like the waters flow—"
>
> . . .
>
> "I have sought you everywhere,
> And at last I find you here,
> In a dark room full of woe—"

Liu's words in *The Peony Pavilion*, uttered just before he made love to Du in their dream of love, must have crystallized for Dai-yu the peculiar vexation tormenting her: a dread of time's swift passage without concrete hope of a remedy. Because Heaven seems unwilling to allow for any alternative circumstance (*naihe tian*, translated by Hawkes as "feed my despair"), she has, with Bridal Du, found "the bright air and brilliant morn" wanting and "those pleasing affairs that reward the heart-and-mind (*shangxin le shi*)"[60] retiring to "unknown halls and yards (*shui jia yuan*)." In the play, however, no sooner had the dramatic heroine uttered those lamenting words when the person of her heart's desire, her *yi zhong ren*, did appear to remedy her plight. Bridal Du's memento mori, in other words, finds redemption at once in romantic love. If Dai-yu, then, is also locked up "in a dark room full of [literally] self-pity (*you gui zilian*)," who will come looking for her to deliver her from such narcissistic anguish?[61] Could the person of her heart's desire be, as the Chinese proverb has it, one "as far as the edge of the sky or as near as what's before the eye" (*yuan zai tianbian, jin zai yanqian*)? Could he be the very teenage cousin who shared with her another equally moving text of fiction only minutes ago and teased her with its provocative message? Could those borrowed lines of *The Western Wing* proclaim in truth his secret wish? If such a line of query is permitted to reach across culture and history, could she say with Francesca da Rimini that Bao-yu "*fu 'l libro e chi lo scrisse* (was the book and he wrote it)" (Dante, "Inferno," 5. 137)?

---

[60] Contemporary editors, in fact, forthrightly interpret this phrase to mean "the affairs concerning love and a happy marriage." See note 1 in *HLM* 1: 327.

[61] The sense of self-pity in Dai-yu is intense and persistent; just as her comparison of her fate with Oriole's in chapter 35 reveals such a tendency, so the very term *zilian* will surface again in her crysanthemum poems in chapter 38.

THE FATE OF READING

The reference above to the *Commedia* will appear less far-fetched or abrupt if we perceive that Bao-yu is indeed the book and author of Dai-yu's affection as well as their go-between—in their previous existence no less than in this one. In her preincarnate form as the Crimson Pearl Plant, Dai-yu's grateful response to the Stone Page's daily ministrations itself provides a striking parallel to Francesca's alliterative delineation of the reciprocity of desire: a love that releases no loved one from loving ("Amor, ch'a nullo amato amar perdona").[62] It is precisely such an exchange—an act of solicitude exacting in turn a debt of tears—that has earned for the Chinese couple the epithet of "romantic damned souls" (*fengliu niegui*) and a painful existence on earth. The human Bao-yu and Dai-yu in the garden, to be sure, are not the wailing inmates of Hell. But like Paolo and Francesca, I would argue, this Chinese couple can also trace the first root of their human love ("la prima radice/del nostro amor") to their experience of reading—and hearing—literary fiction.

In those Buddhistlike terms that the narrative advances for adumbrating the poetics of reading, Bao-yu and Dai-yu may be said to have both begun in the respective Void (boredom, "poor fate") of their existence and "came to the contemplation of Form (which is Illusion); and from Form engendered Passion; and by communicating Passion, entered again into Form" (*SS* 1: 51; *HLM* 1: 6). Their encounter with literary fiction not only awakens their passion but drives them into a continuous act of self-dramatization, of the displacement of self-identity onto the text as a means of communicating that awakened passion. For both of them, of course, the final and crucial stage of that process—"from Form awoke to the Void (which is Truth)"—has yet to be realized, and its realization will take a different form in each of their lives. Nevertheless, their experience even at this segment of the story proffers an unforgettable example of what, in Western terms, is the infectious link of mimesis with desire. René Girard's perceptive diagnosis of the Italian lovers is thus equally applicable to the Chinese ones as well.

> The written word exercises a veritable fascination. It impels the two young lovers to act as if determined by fate; it is a mirror in which they gaze, discovering in

---

[62] This declaration is part of the triple, anaphoric definitions of *amor* in Canto 5. Usually regarded as succinct statements of the law of courtly love in their emphasis on that emotion's speed ("Amor, ch'al cor gentil ratto s'apprende"), irresistible reciprocity, and the wish for death as final union ("Amor condusse noi ad una morte"), they are also commonly condemned as the sinful parody of the principle of Christian charity. Cf. Guido Da Pisa, *Expositiones et Glose super Comediam Dantis*, p. 113; Charles Williams, *The Figure of Beatrice*, p. 118. But as Charles S. Singleton reminds us, citing I John 4:19, the notion of reciprocity in courtly love is itself derived from Christianity. See Dante Alighieri, *The Divine Comedy: Inferno*, 2. Commentary, p. 90.

themselves the semblances of their brilliant models. . . . It is the book itself, Francesca maintains, that plays the role of the diabolical go-between, the pander, in her life. The young woman curses the romance and its author. . . . Dante is not writing literary history; he is stressing that, whether written or oral, it has to be some person's word that suggests desire. . . . Paolo and Francesca are the dupes of Lancelot and the queen, who are themselves the dupes of Galleot. And the romantic readers, in their turn, are dupes of Paolo and Francesca. The malignant prompting is a process perpetually renewed without its victims' being aware of it.[63]

Unlike the Western couple who exchanged kisses when they read of Lancelot and Queen Guinevere kissing, Bao-yu and Dai-yu have seldom enjoyed amorous physical contact, let alone sexual union.[64] Nonetheless, there can be little doubt that the book Bao-yu shared with her for a few brief moments *(The Western Wing)* and the book parts of which she overheard from the rehearsing actresses (*The Peony Pavilion*) have joined to incite in her the deepest romantic longing. Bao-yu might not have been the author of those dramas, but he is the pander in her life because his action and his gift make accessible the instrument of rousing her dormant feelings. The narrative directs our attention to the shocking materiality of the texts and their potent, paradoxical impact on her physique: Dai-yu's body literally collapses under the verbal onslaught, but at the same time she finds nourishment in the power of words. While the diction and phrases *(ci ju)* of *The Western Wing* startle and excite her (*jing ren*), they also fill her mouth with their lingering fragrance (*yu xiang man kou*), just as the lines of *The Peony Pavilion* compel her to ruminate, literally to "chew finely on their flavor" (*xi zhuo . . . ziwei*). This set of eating imagery ironically confirms the verdict of her go-between, Bao-yu, who introduced her to *The Western Wing* with the unwitting but sincere observation: "Once you start reading it, you'll even stop wanting to eat" (*SS* 1: 464; *HLM* 1: 325). In her reception of the literary texts, language has displaced the claim and meaning of food.

Toward the end of her bitter struggle with fated suffering, Dai-yu will find herself compelled literally to abandon food in her suicidal attempt to end the misery of thwarted wish (chap. 89). For this early stage of the story, however, her encounter with literary fiction both precipitates and feeds her desire. The tasted, ingested, and assimilated text of *The Western Wing* will provide recurrent sustenance in the form of the "malignant prompting," as Girard says, "a process perpetually renewed without its victims being aware of it." In chapter

[63] "*To Double Business Bound*," p. 2.

[64] The fact that he could actually share her pillow during a casual moment of play and banter (chap. 19) already violates the kind of stringent strictures against physical contact between boys and girls prescribed by *The Book of Rites*. On the other hand, the narrative makes it apparent that such an action as when she tried to twist his mouth for teasing her as a little rodent spirit (*SS* 1: 397–98; *HLM* 1: 275–76) should be read as an innocent gesture.

26, her face will burn when her vocal quotation from the play ("Each day in a drowsy dream of love") is overheard by Bao-yu. Her embarrassment stems not merely from the fact that he recognizes the source of the quotation, and thus that the two emergent lovers are now bonding through the shared secrets of a proscribed work of literature; even more significantly, the line itself is sexually most suggestive, since part of it is repeated by Student Zhang in the drama just before he and Oriole have intercourse.[65]

As their story unfolds, Bao-yu and Dai-yu will have further occasions to share gifts and secrets, most tellingly in the episode (chap. 34) wherein his present of two used silk handkerchiefs elicits from her three passionate quatrains in response. Though the existence, but not the content, of those poems is known to Bao-yu—a disadvantage concordant with the tale's overall design that theirs is a madly felt but never successfully communicated affection—the narrative also makes utterly apparent the state of Dai-yu's mind and feelings when she composed those poems. If his wordless artifact aptly symbolizes both his profound appreciation of her tearful devotion and his extension of attentive consolation, her poems, as I shall argue in the chapter on tragedy, are the most unambiguous declaration of her love for him. To make sure the reader understands how Dai-yu was throwing all caution to the wind, the narrator says that "she could not even think of the obligation to avoid taboo subjects or the arousal of suspicion (*ye xiang bu qi bihui xianyi deng shi*)" (*HLM* 1: 469) when she dipped brush in ink to write her poems. One principal concern of ritual instruction, as we have seen earlier in this study, is precisely to school young men and women in the scrupulous observation of rites. For the narrator to illumine her reckless determination at this crucial moment is for him to suggest that the motivation and content of Dai-yu's writings might already have crossed the boundary of propriety. To disregard taboos, to risk suspicion, and to equate her tears for Bao-yu (as she has done in her third poem) with those immortal stains on the bamboo mythically implanted, after the ancient sage king Shun's death, by his weeping consorts is to affirm that her feelings and their expression have attained a peculiar legitimacy. She could well have said with another Western woman more explicitly entangled in an adulterous situation that what she did possesses "a consecration of its own," whatever censure she might incur from cultural dogmatics.[66] Through those original poems, even if they had been composed for her own eyes only, Dai-yu has lent assertive voice to her "tender feelings and private wish (*rou qing si yi*)," exactly that form of errant subjectivity abhorred by Confucian orthodoxy and in which Bao-chai after Dai-yu's death will accuse Bao-yu of excessive indulgence (chap. 115).

Unlike their Western counterparts (Paolo and Francesca) or even their Chinese ones (Student Zhang and Oriole, Liu Mengmei and Bridal Du), the star-crossed

---

[65] Cf. Wang Shifu, *Xixiangji*, pp. 46, 136; *The Western Wing*, pp. 221, 331.

[66] Hester Prynne in Nathaniel Hawthorne, *The Scarlet Letter*, p. 222.

lovers of this Chinese tale are not able to find fulfilment, however brief and illusory, in actual physical union. Part of the narrative's most intense poignance, paradoxically, is created by this very plight of theirs. The adherents of Confucianism may consider the desire of the lovers to have been properly held in check, since it has not impelled them into the disorder (*luan*) of sexual transgression, as it has so many other members of the clan in and out of the mansions. But the absence of any overt act of impropriety only serves to highlight with far greater brilliance the range and audaciousness of Bao-yu and Dai-yu's subjectivity and its insurgent propensity to circumvent the shackles of social authoritarianism and familial tyranny. Their affairs of the heart-and-mind (*xinshi*) will become, in the developing tragic turn of events, the illness of the heart-and-mind (*xinbing*). Just as that illness resists treatment by material medications, so *l'affaire du coeur* can never be circumscribed by either place or dogma. The lengthy course of their tortuous fortunes leaves little doubt that the lovers, in their own way, have pledged themselves to one another and consider themselves somehow affianced. In that sense, theirs is indeed a secret—and thus private—betrothal that waits for "neither the command of parents nor the good offices of a go-between." Only this recognition can enable us to feel in full the pathos of Dai-yu's dying but defiant disclosure to her maid: "My body is pure: promise me you'll ask them to bury me at home!" (chap. 98).

That deathbed request of Dai-yu is duly granted (chap. 116), for members of the Jia family have little cause for doubting the young woman's avowal of physical virginity. Could they, however, also affirm the purity of her heart-and-mind? This question leads us directly to look, finally and briefly, at the fortuitous and contradictory conjunction of character and circumstance, the result of which must eventuate in the ironic perversion of purposive action that defines the essence of literary tragedy.

The foregoing analysis has shown how extensively the narrative has made use of antecedent dramatic texts, but their contribution to the *Hongloumeng*'s making is not limited merely to their function of textual dissemination of desire, important as that may be. In constructing a garden as a latent field for erotic dalliance and rendezvous, in fashioning its male and female protagonists as characterizations that both exploit and parody the *caizi jiaren* tradition, and in crafting the romance of Bao-yu and Dai-yu as one plotted on literary courtship and intimated seduction, the narrative reveals its further indebtedness to such a text as *The Western Wing*.

In their long and informative introduction to their recent translation of that drama, Stephen West and Wilt Idema have singled out the character of Crimson (Hongniang) as an index of Wang Shifu's innovative contribution to the development of "The Story of Oriole."[67] Serving as the wily and resourceful

---

[67] See *The Western Wing*, pp. 124–41. On the evolution of Yingying's character, see Lorraine Dong, "The Many Faces of Cui Yingying."

maid of the dramatic heroine, Crimson assumes the important structural role of providing a vital, indispensable line of communication and service for the segregated lovers. What a work like *The Western Wing* makes clear is the irony of how marital prospects in imperial China often have no hope for "the commands of parents" unless "the good offices of a go-between" are first engaged. Between the unquestioned authority of Madam Cui and the dependent aspirations of the lovers, Crimson the go-between of Wang Shifu's imagination thus does much more than discharge the traditional assignments of astrological consultation (to make sure that the prospective couples' natal signs are compatible) or disclosing the scale of dowry. In the triangular structure of partisan interests dramatized in the play, Crimson must act pivotally to resolve conflicting claims; and indeed, it is her "own cunning and her deception of Madam Cui that bring the play to a satisfactory conclusion."[68]

Seen in the light of such a dramatic situation, *Hongloumeng* is a text that both follows and revises its antecedent, for the conditions for the lovers's successful union are progressively subverted, as befits the narrative's constant intimations of tragedy. As Dai-yu has said of herself in chapter 35, Oriole's fate is decidedly better than her own, because the young woman in the drama still has parents. By contrast, Dai-yu throughout her short life is haunted by the awareness that "both Father and Mother are dead, and [she has] neither home nor refuge (*fumu shuang wang, wuyi wukao*)" (*HLM* 1: 371). Orphanhood betokens total powerlessness, for with regard to marital prospects, there is no one in whom she can confide and who can "make a decision (*zuo zhu*)" for her (chap. 32). The one person on whom she can pin a large part of her hope is Bao-yu, but the circumstances they face are such that she can never disclose her feelings to him directly nor can she ever be certain either of his feelings or that he will act effectively on her behalf even if he so wishes.

As in the dramatic situation of *The Western Wing*, therefore, the fate of the lovers in *Hongloumeng* also depends greatly on the good will and action of others. Indeed, one principal device of building suspense can be found in the way the narrative uses a variety of persons as knowing or uncomprehending go-betweens for Bao-yu and Dai-yu: for example, Dai-yu's maid, Cuckoo, who seeks to ascertain Bao-yu's true feelings by falsely reporting her mistress's imminent return to the south (chap. 57), or the cynical Xi-feng, who baits the young couple frequently with innuendo and mockery. In the overall design of the plot, however, it is undoubtedly Aroma to whom is given the crucial role of a servant who attempts to manage the vested interests of her master and mistress and work toward their satisfaction.

If the Crimson of *The Western Wing*, who sees in the successful marriage of her mistress her own chance of a better life by obtaining the writ from the

---

[68] *The Western Wing*, p. 125.

husband that will "release her from indentured status,"[69] the Aroma in the narrative is similarly invested in the interests and welfare of Bao-yu, her master. She yielded her body to him at the beginning of the story with complete awareness that Grandmother Jia "intended her to belong to him in the fullest possible sense" (*SS* 1: 150; *HLM* 1: 93). Throughout their subsequent history, she has served this young man with singleminded devotion, enduring without complaint his testiness, his fickle moods, his whimsical indulgences, and even his physical abuses (such as his kicking her in chap. 30). She fusses over his health and his daily routines with a fastidiousness partly maternal and partly spouselike in intensity. Although, like Crimson, she is a person not without "bright, ambitious hopes for the future" (chap. 31), she is willing to give up redemption from her bondslave status as long as her young lord is willing to listen to her admonitions (chaps. 19–20). It is, in fact, her intelligence in speech and thought that wins Bao-chai's respect (chap. 21). Her loyalty and her levelheaded sense of responsibility also help her gain enormous trust from Lady Wang, the rather feeble and dotish mother of Bao-yu. After the Golden episode that leads to Bao-yu's savage beating by his father, it is Aroma who, like Crimson in the drama, is assigned the onerous task of vigilant watch over Bao-yu.[70]

The immediate cause for such an arrangement is again to be found in the problem of Bao-yu's relations to the opposite sex. Aroma's extended conversation with his mother (chap. 34) is a masterpiece of rhetorical and political cunning, crafted to serve the interests of herself no less than those of Lady Wang. Exploiting the latter's grief at his recent beating, her fears that he may not amount to much in his studies and thus his career, and her obvious awareness of her son's developing libido (though the mother as a matter of course places the blame entirely on the maid Golden for her attempt to corrupt Bao-yu), Aroma first concedes the necessity of Bao-yu's discipline, before diverting the mother's attention quickly to the less apparent dangers of entrapped desire. Because Bao-yu and his cousins are growing up, "the difference of sex" (*SS* 2: 164; *HLM* 1: 467) renders the garden a parlous place for the youths to live together. If Lady Wang took offense at his liberties with the maid Golden, think of what he could do with his cousins! Even if such enforced intimacy does not lead to actual transgression, there is always the risk of scandalous rumor that may well ruin Bao-yu's reputation for life, and with it any hope of security and happiness on the part of a servant like herself.

Aroma's disquisition, presented as one of passionate concern for the young master and his family, garners for her a reward far weightier than a spontaneous word of praise. Her mistress's expression of gratitude takes the form of another momentous exchange: just as Aroma's body had been given to Bao-

[69] Ibid., p. 127.
[70] Ibid., p. 129.

yu, the young man is now yielded up by the mother and entrusted entirely in her care, a declaration that, given such a social context, virtually bestows spousal privileges and responsibilities to the maid. Lady Wang's final injunctions are thus both a threat and a promise: "Be very careful with him, won't you? Remember that anything you do for him you will be doing also for me. You will find that I am not ungrateful" (*SS* 1: 165–66; *HLM* 1: 466).

Although Aroma will be the first to realize that her social status precludes the possiblity of her ever becoming Bao-yu's legitimate wife, that last sentence of Lady Wang can easily be construed as a likely pledge of a concubinage. It takes no great act of imagination on her part, or the reader's, to realize that more than ever, her own fortunes are inextricably bound with Bao-yu's. The irony created by Lady Wang's words, however, lies in how they must further aggravate the maid's concern and worry, for by the time they were uttered, Aroma already knew something that no other person in the Jia mansion knew: namely, the true object of Bao-yu's desire. When he inadvertently blurted out the innermost secrets of his heart-and-mind (chap. 32), thinking that he was speaking to Dai-yu, Aroma was the unintended auditor. It was her knowledge of those words and her dread for "an ugly scandal developing" (*SS* 1: 135; *HLM* 1: 448) that quickly prompted her to address Lady Wang.

Like Crimson of *The Western Wing*, then, Aroma is also the bearer of an unspeakable secret. Confronted by the final crisis of the lovers, however, she will be compelled to speak. With Bao-yu mysteriously sick for the loss of his birth pendant, Dai-yu deathly ill, and Grandmother anxiously urging an early marriage for her grandson even if it means overstepping the bounds of rites (chap. 96), Aroma will make desperate attempts to disclose, first to Lady Wang and then to Grandmother, what she knows of the young couple's hearts-and-minds. In her despairing effort to make the truth of their feelings avert any further disastrous consequence (*SS* 4: 330; *HLM* 3: 1,356), Aroma, in fact, fulfils the classic function of the go-between, "a single confidante who knows what her young mistress [and master are] getting up to," and whose privileged role is for that reason roundly condemned by Grandmother's severe critique of the talent-and-beauty genre of popular fiction (*SS* 3: 30–31; *HLM* 2: 759).

Indeed, Grandmother's eventual response to Aroma's courageous revelation proves entirely consistent with the outlook of her earlier critique, for she now judges her most beloved granddaughter to be little better than the "cat-burglers" inhabiting the fiction she despises.

> Ours is a decent family. We do not tolerate unseemly goings-on. And this business of the illness of the heart (*xinbing*) is absolutely forbidden! If her illness is of a respectable nature, I do not mind how much we have to spend to get her better. But if she is suffering from some form of lovesickness, no amount of medicine will cure it and she can expect no further sympathy from me either. (*SS* 4: 343, text modified; *HLM* 3: 1,363)

Grandmother's ringing declaration reiterates the venerated dogma that within the structure of familial authority, there is no place for "private" or "selfish desire (*si yu*)."[71] In accord with the cultural ideals of long standing, her words maintain that the concerns of what the Chinese name as the larger, communal "I" (*da wo*) of family or state must take precedence and priority over the solitary, little "I" (*xiao wo*). She is, moreover, a woman who, as it were, "practices what she preaches," and the narrative provides a moving account of how, in the family's darkest hour, it is Grandmother's unselfish relinquishment of her own savings and belongings that forestalls the community's total ruin (chap. 107). As the grand Confucian overtones reverberating from the first line of that chapter's titular couplet make clear, hers is an act that illustrates great righteousness (*ming da yi*), in comparison with which the romantic longings and attachments of her grandchildren may, from the perspective of traditional ritualism, diminish in scale and significance. Grandmother, in this view, may not be someone who has studied many books, to borrow Bao-chai's words when she lectured her husband, but Grandmother is someone who understands Principle (*ming li di ren*).

Does such an observation imply that the narrative is founded most fundamentally on the clash between Principle (*li*) and desire (*qing*), a clash debated by Song-Ming philosophy and made to underlie many of what modern Chinese scholars consider to be tragic dramas?[72] That, I believe, will be too pat a conclusion, for it risks robbing *Hongloumeng* of its most intensely tragic dimension: namely, that the rift sundering both familial and personal integrity comes from the irreconcilable conflict of desire itself. For the inhabitants of the novelistic world, if they reflect at all the society at large, seem to have little recognition that what they invent as the laws of nature and the principles of human rites are in actuality forms of desire. One perduring myth of Chinese civilization, in this regard, must be its affirmation of the "natural" basis for hierarchy that is said to pervade every aspect of the human cosmos. The subordination of one person to another, of one sex to another, of the individual to the social unit, which concretizes the ideals of human relations (*lun*), is thus deemed indispensable for securing and maintaining a condition supposedly reflective of the alleged harmonious order of nature. *Hongloumeng* testifies to one literary work's challenge to this form of normative understanding when it shows how such a formulation leaves little consideration for adjudicating competing, legitimate

---

[71] On the significance of the term in Neo-Confucianism, see Fung Yu-lan, *A History of Chinese Philosophy* 1: 558–62.

[72] See the "Introduction" to Wang Zisi, ed., *Zhongguo shida gudian beijuji* 1: 10–11. For a study of how the intensified emphasis of *li* (ritual, rite, propriety) underlying much of Qing thought finds focused expression in the master theoretician Ling Tingkan (1755–1809), a near contemporary of the novel's author(s), see Zhang Shouan, *Yi li dai li: Ling Tingkan yu Qing zhongye Ruxue sixiang*.

interests or coping with unacknowledged tendencies toward degeneration and self-deception. The only sure principle of Heaven *(tian li)* inexorably operative within the narrative's given cosmos is the family's predicted decline, but none of the living members of the household seems cognizant of it. In the light of such a fated certainty, every act of the clan to preserve familial stability and prosperity—by dogged espousal of threadbare orthodoxies, by reliance on royal connections and sychopancy, by blatant greed and corruption, by desperate gestures of altruism—is also an act of unenlightened desire. The words of the twelfth song in the prophetic cycle, "Dream of the Red Chamber," ring true indeed.

> The weakness in the line began with Jing;
> The blame for the decline lay first in Ning;
> But retribution all was of Love's fashioning.
>
> (*SS* 1: 144; *HLM* 1: 89)

The stark formula for causality and end in the last line is *su nie zong yin qing*—literally, predestined punishment is all because of desire. In the unavoidable finality of death or destruction, "when the tree falls and the monkeys scatter," the finely calibrated hierarchy of distinctions and preferences (note the song's puns on *jing* [reverence] and *ning* [stability/serenity/security], Confucian values all) will meet an invincible leveler.

In her critique of popular fiction earlier in the story, Grandmother is quite blind to desire's force and mobility. If it spreads and overflows like waves, as Zhu Xi's famous simile has described it, no "decent family" can erect strong enough an "Iron Door" or an "Iron Threshold" (or even an "Iron House" of Lu Xun's fame) for its effectual containment.[73] When she rules against the hopes of Dai-yu, she has also misjudged the propriety of her granddaughter's feelings or their tenacious hold on her grandson. She will destroy their love and thereby their lives in the name of her love for them. That is the tragic irony worthy of perpetual tears.

---

[73] The Song philosopher writes: "desire emanates from feelings. The mind is comparable to water, nature is comparable to the tranquillity of still water, feeling is comparable to the flow of water, and desire is comparable to its waves." For a convenient location of this selection from his *Gathered Sayings*, see *A Source Book in Chinese Philosophy*, translated and compiled by Wing-tsit Chan, p. 631. Cf. also Fung, *A History of Chinese Philosophy*, 2: 556–8. For an illuminating discussion of the important issue of nature and emotion in Zhu's philosophy and its debate with Chinese Buddhism, see Whalen W. Lai, "How the Principle Rides on the Ether: Chu Hsi's Non-Buddhist Resolution of Nature and Emotion."

For the metaphoric significance of "Iron Door" in Ming-Qing prose fiction when the control of desire for both sexes was one reigning ideology, see the thoughtful study by Keith McMahon, *Causality and Containment in Seventeenth-Century Chinese Fiction*. "Iron Door" is the name of a Confucian puritan whose daughter is eventually seduced by the philandering Vesperus. See *The Carnal Prayer Mat*, chapter 3. "Iron Threshold" is the name of a Buddhist temple in the outskirts of the capital city where the Jia families often hold their religious services. It is also here that Qin Zhong, one of Bao-yu's bosom friends, seduces a young nun (chap. 15).

CHAPTER V

Tragedy

Quid enim miserius misero non miserante se ipsum
et flente Didonis mortem. . . ?
(St. Augustine, *Confessions*)

CHOOSING THE PROTAGONIST

The Chinese literary historian and critic Wang Guowei is justly famed for his innovative and path-breaking essay, published in 1904, on *Hongloumeng*.[1] Not only has he assumed therein "a new critical attitude" and elaborated "a new method in the interpretation and criticism of Chinese literature," as one modern study of Wang's essay aptly observes, but in calling this Chinese narrative "the tragedy of tragedies (*beiju zhong zhi beiju*)," he has also summed up the common reaction of many readers of this work since its publication in the late eighteenth century.[2] Those "pages full of idle words/penned with hot and bitter tears" (*SS* 1: 51; *HLM* 1: 7) have elicited everywhere the lachrymose response of countless devoted admirers, and like the *Oresteia* of Aeschylus, during the performances of which the sight of the Erinyes was said to have shocked pregnant Athenian women into miscarriages, or *Die Leiden des jungen Werthers* of Goethe, the publication of which caused a wave of suicide in Europe, *Hongloumeng* has spawned its own sensational legend that the effect of its sympathetic reading can be lethal.[3]

There is no question that one element constituting the narrative's enduring greatness is its unflinching portrayal of human sorrow and suffering, of blighted dreams and blasted lovers, and of the finality of separation and death. This vision of the narrative, as Wang Guowei correctly perceives, is itself a radical reversal of some of the most cherished values in Chinese literary culture. In his judgment, the happy, united, and prosperous endings in work after work of drama and fiction may indicate both the "this worldliness" and "optimism" characteristic of the Chinese.[4] Whereas, for example, hero and heroine at the

[1] Wang Guowei, "*Hongloumeng* pinglun," in *Haining Wang Jing'an xiansheng yishu*, 4: 1,592–1,635.

[2] C. H. Wang, "Recognition and Anticipation in Wang Kuo-wei's Criticism of *Hung-lou meng*," p. 94; see also Joey Bonner, *Wang Kuo-wei*. Wang, "*Hongloumeng* pinglun," p. 1,614.

[3] A young man who read the novel seven times in a month was so profoundly affected that he died of melancholy shortly thereafter. Similarly, a girl died vomiting blood after a single perusal! See the amusing accounts by Chen Yong, "Shusanxuan congtan."

[4] Wang, "*Hongloumeng* Pinglun," pp. 1,609–11; for similar observations, see Zheng Zhenduo,

end of *The Story of the Western Wing (Xixiangji)* apostrophize in unison: "May lovers of the whole world all be thus united in wedlock,"[5] the *Hongloumeng* from the outset speaks of a mansion's "gilded beams" shrouded by cobwebs and "raven locks" turning white in the very midst of celebrated "perfumed elegance" (*SS* 1: 64; *HLM* 1: 13). By enclosing the central love story within a large mythic framework, by making the engrossing vicissitudes of the great Jia household a palimpsest against which the individual tales of private woe and personal triumph unfold, and by creating for the setting of this massive tale a garden of such scenic grandeur and symbolic resonance that it mirrors the sweeping totality of imperial Chinese civilization,[6] the author of the *Hongloumeng* has endowed his work with an all-encompassing magnitude that may have surpassed even the greatness of the *Plum in the Golden Vase (Jinpingmei)*, the other acknowledged masterpiece of domestic and social drama in traditional Chinese fiction.

In considering the Qing narrative as having given full and unprecedented expression to the spirit of tragedy, Wang Guowei was deeply influenced by the philosophy of Arthur Schopenhauer. Alluding specifically to Book III of *The World as Will and Idea*, Wang concluded that *Hongloumeng* belongs to the third and highest type of tragedy described by the German philosopher.[7] According to Schopenhauer, "the representation of a great misfortune is alone essential to tragedy," but how it is brought about is what distinguishes the better from the less well-made plays. In the latter, the great misfortune may be caused by a "character of extraordinary wickedness" or "blind fate," but in the best plays, it may be brought about

> by the mere position of the *dramatis personae* with regard to each other, through their relations; so that there is no need either for a tremendous error or an unheard-of accident, nor yet for a character whose wickedness reaches the limits of human possibility; but characters of ordinary morality, under circumstances such as often occur, are so situated with regard to each other that their position compels them, knowingly and with their eyes open, to do each other the greatest injury, without any one of them being entirely in the wrong. This last kind of tragedy seems . . . to surpass the other two, for it shows us the greatest misfortunate, not as an exception, not as something occasioned by rare circumstances or monstrous characters, but as arising easily and of itself out of the actions and characters of men, indeed almost as essential to them, and thus brings

---

Chatuben Zhongguo wenxueshi 2: 679; Chung-wen Shih, *The Golden Age of Chinese Drama*, pp. 75–81.

[5] Wang Shifu, *The Moon and the Zither*, p. 412.

[6] See Andrew H. Plaks, *Archetype and Allegory in the "Dream of the Red Chamber,"* especially chapters 7 and 8.

[7] Wang, "*Hongloumeng* Pinglun," pp. 1,612–14.

it terribly near to us. In the other two kinds we may look on the prodigious fate and the horrible wickedness as terrible powers which certainly threaten us, but only from afar, which we may very well escape without taking refuge in renunciation. But in the last kind of tragedy we see that those powers which destroy happiness and life are such that their path to us also is open at every moment; we see the greatest sufferings brought about by entanglements that our fate might also partake of, and through actions that perhaps we also are capable of performing, and so could not complain of injustice; then shuddering we feel ourselves already in the midst of hell.[8]

As a part of the history of Western literary criticism, this statement reveals the shrewd perception of Schopenhauer and his distance both from the dramatists of Greek antiquity and from their most influential interpreter, Aristotle. No one, of course, would quarrel with the assertion that the tragic catastrophes in fictive representations are often self-induced or self-caused by the dramatis personae, but modern students of classical tragedy and theory have stressed, even more than Aristotle, that the most paradigmatic tragic situation evident in epic and drama is one in which the heroes or heroines are paradoxically both victims and agents of the evil that befalls them. Tragic suffering, in other words, can never be simply an affair of retributive justice, the poetic enactment of crime and punishment. It is, rather, the result of certain peculiar, and often ironic, conjunctions of character and circumstance in such a way that a person of surpassing excellence (Gk., *aretê*) commits a fatal act of intellectual or moral error (as when Oedipus chooses to kill the stranger on the road or Deianeira decides to use the deadly charm in the *Trachiniae*), so that the very strength and virtue of the protagonist are transformed into the instrument of his or her destruction.[9] Though the hero is, in this sense, responsible for the fearful consequence of his action, the forces that set in motion the train of causally connected events leading to disaster are forces over which the person may have little control. The tension underlying the tragic action is thus an outgrowth of the ambiguous relation between freedom and compulsion, between the personal decision to act and necessity divinely or socially imposed, between human desire and a kind of "hostile transcendence" (to use the apt phrase of Paul Ricoeur) mythically represented in Homer and the tragedians by the dreaded god-sent *atê* that blinds, deludes, and leads astray.[10]

---

[8] Arthur Schopenhauer, *The World as Will and Idea* 1: 329.

[9] On this point, see Elder Olson, *Tragedy and the Theory of Drama*, pp. 202ff.

[10] See, for example, E. R. Dodds, *The Greeks and the Irrational*, especially, chapters 1–3; Arthur W. H. Adkins, *Merit and Responsibility*, pp. 50–57, and "Aristotle and the Best Kinds of Tragedy"; Albin Leskey, *Geschichte der griechischen Literatur*, pp. 274–82; Paul Ricoeur, *The Symbolism of Evil*, pp. 211–31; R. D. Dawe, "Some Reflections on *Atê* and *Hamartia*"; J. M. Bremer, *Hamartia*; Anthony C. Yu, "New Gods and Old Order"; T. C. W. Stinton, "*Hamartia* in Aristotle and Greek Tragedy"; and James M. Redfield, *Nature and Culture in the "Iliad."*

Whether such a view of tragedy can aid in our understanding of *Hongloumeng* remains to be seen. Certainly what appeals to Wang Guowei in Schopenhauer's theory is not the dialectics of tragedy but its didactic possibility. Since for Schopenhauer "the end of the drama in general is to show us in an example what is the nature and existence of man," and the specific end of tragedy is to hold up to the audience "the bitterness and worthlessness of life; thus the vanity of all its struggle," the function of tragic drama is to summon us to renunciation and resignation, "to rise above all the ends and good things of life" and turn toward "another kind of existence." The noblest kind of tragedy is one that gives form to such enlightened perception in the hero, to the change in his frame of mind induced by the experience of suffering, the sight of which in turn should enable the spectator to become conscious, "if only in obscure feeling, that it is better to hear his heart free from life, to turn his will from it, to love not the world nor life."[11] Tragic art, which like the other forms of art provides us entrance into a state of pure objectivity of perception, thus offers us a kind of "deliverance," if only momentarily, akin to what the great religions proffer: liberation from the blind strivings of the Will.

How attractive this theory of Schopenhauer has been for Wang may readily be seen in the latter's essay on the Chinese narrative, for what most impresses the Chinese critic is the extent to which Jia Bao-yu exemplifies in his experience the kind of tragic suffering leading to final renunciation that the German philosopher extols. Whereas the appropriateness of Bao-yu's decision at the end of the story to leave the family and thereby, ostensibly, to affirm the ideal of ultimate detachment upheld by the narrative's syncretic blend of Buddhism and Daoism has been questioned by some readers on textual and structural grounds, for Wang Guowei the hero's action signals his final victory on the path to deliverance (*jietuo zhi tujing*). Having drunk to the lees the bitter wine of existence, Bao-yu at last repudiates family, friends, and official career, and this decisive renunciation is interpreted by Wang—punning on the homophones *yu* (jade) and *yu* (desire)—to be the very rejection of the will to life. The greatness of *Hongloumeng*, like the greatness of Goethe's *Faust*, lies precisely in its powerful and intentional staging of human suffering while pointing at the same time to a way of redemption.[12]

As one of the first works of Chinese literary criticism influenced by Western thought, this essay of Wang Guowei reveals less of a comprehensive grasp of the *Hongloumeng's* depth and complexity than of his insightful appropriation of Schopenhauer. The Buddhist strands of Schopenhauer's thinking may have struck an especially responsive chord in Wang, who was himself no stranger to the major themes of Chinese Buddhism.[13] And, though Wang made no system-

---

[11] Schopenhauer, *The World as Will*, 1, 211 and 214–15.
[12] Wang, "*Hongloumeng* pinglun," pp. 1,604–9.
[13] See Dorothea Dauer, *Schopenhauer as Transmitter of Buddhist Ideas*.

atic study of German philosophy, the turbulent events of early Republican China surrounding him and his personal development no doubt served to enlarge his own "tragic sense of life" and strengthen his appreciation for philosophical pessimism.[14] What makes his interpretation of the narrative only partially satisfying is that it almost totally ignores the other central character in the narrative. Though the significance of Bao-yu's experience and action may indeed find illumination in the schematizations of Schopenhauer's philosophy, the very nature of the argument in that theory of tragedy must perforce belittle the stature and importance of Lin Dai-yu, who may be for many readers the most memorable and moving character of the narrative and without whom the story of Bao-yu cannot be told or understood.

Reading *Hongloumeng* as a monolithic story about Bao-yu also may find its odd parallel in the more recent criticism that makes use of feminist theory. Writing in 1994, Louise P. Edwards argues that

> the role given to women in the novel is . . . subsidiary. . . . Daiyu and Baochai are valorized primarily for their potential to reflect Baoyu's problems with, among other issues, the signification of gender in Chinese society. In their tumultuous relationships with Baoyu, Daiyu invokes the more feminine values and Baochai the more masculine.[15]

Although Edwards' study generally succeeds in avoiding the ascription to the novelistic representation the rigid binary opposition of masculinity and feminity, one wonders if the judgment cited here is not too reductive. Just as one may ask of Wang Guowei whether Dai-yu assumes the mere function of an instrument to her lover's enlightenment, if indeed Bao-yu attained enlightenment, so one may ask of Edwards whether Lin Dai-yu is truly "relegated to the margins as [a mirror] of his male choice."[16] The perception of desire, male or female, is a function of critical reading, and the singular focus on the male protagonist's choice or suffering necessarily belittles the character and experience of the female one. In Wang's or Edwards' terms, Lin Dai-yu seems hardly qualified to be named a tragic heroine because she, above all others in the narrative, seems to suffer with neither insight nor resignation. Brilliant, compulsive, and almost completely held captive by her emotions as much as her desires, Dai-yu remains willful to the very end, falling dead with a question

---

[14] See C. Y. Yeh Chao [Ye Jiaying], "Wang Guowei: His Character and His Scholarship."

[15] *Men and Women in Qing China*, pp. 44–45.

[16] Ibid., p. 45. This disagreement with a feminist reading of Dai-yu's fate notwithstanding, one must reckon seriously with Liao Zhaoyang's perceptive suggestion (based on the study of certain themes in Chinese Daoism by Miyakawa Hisayuki) that the causality of the Crimson Pearl Plant's incarnation in *Hongloumeng* may stem from a formula common to the tales of "banished or exiled immortals (*zexian*)." In Liao's opinion, such immortals enjoy no freedom at all in choosing their fate, whereas the mythic Stone seems to have been given a measure of choice. See his "Yiwen yu xiao wenxue," pp. 16–17.

on her lips.[17] If Bao-yu "ends the novel as a victim who escapes common morality and earthly ties by becoming an immortal," and his denouement thus may support the feminist critic's contention about the narrative's entrenched gender ideology, which tends always to privilege the male capacity for attaining liberation or transcendence, one must query all the more why the pointless pathos of Lin Dai-yu nonethless can be productive of such enduring appeal.[18]

From the mythical framework of the narrative, the fate of these star-crossed lovers is, to be sure, foreordained. As the Divine Luminescent Stone-in-Waiting at the Court of Sunset Glow, Bao-yu in his premundane existence befriended the Crimson Pearl Flower, who out of gratitude for his gift of dew vowed to become a human and repay his kindness with the tears of a lifetime. That gift indeed suggests "a proto-sexual encounter" but perhaps not necessarily as an experience "forced" by Nüwa.[19] Similarly, Crimson Pearl's tears may promise sorrow and misfortune but not, at least at this point of the narrative, the inability of the incarnate plant to marry her beloved stone.[20] Nevertheless, whatever the specific fulfilment of predicted woe, Dai-yu's miseries in the world of Red Dust are, from the point of view of celestial detachment, the unavoidable consequence of a foolish decision, the certain catastrophe brought on herself by a "romantic damned spirit (*fengliu niegui*)." When, however, she is seen in the developed plenitude of the narrative as the frail, talented, and undisputedly beautiful young woman amid the baroque opulence and worldly inhabitants of the Jia mansion, her passionate involvement with her lover is no less real, her illness no less lamentable, and her suffering no less wrenching despite our knowledge that her earthly pains amount to no more than the requisite payment of a debt incurred in a previous existence. This solitary, enigmatic girl in the narrative becomes a person who has so powerfully laid claim to the care and concern of readers down through the ages that no aetiological myth of predestined suffering can remove the authenticity stamped on her private grief and public despair.

Once the reality and appeal of the human lovers are acknowledged, the celestial perspective, in fact, becomes a powerfully ironic commentary on the events of the plot. True, the Jia Bao-yu in the story may be someone who

---

[17] I agree with C. T. Hsia's reading in his *The Classic Chinese Novel, A Criticial Introduction*, p. 292, that Dai-yu's apocope just before her death—"Bao-yu, *ni hao* . . ."—should be understood as "Bao-yu, how could you? . . ." Although the rest of this chapter argues that Lin may be understood as a tragic heroine, I do not mean to imply that that role is depicted narratively as her conscious choice. On this point, see Ann Waltner, "On Not Becoming a Heroine: Lin Dai-yu and Cui Ying-ying."

[18] Edwards, *Men and Women in Qing China*, p. 86.

[19] Ibid., p. 59.

[20] Waltner, in "On Not Becoming a Heroine," p. 64, interprets "the debt of tears" by means of the prophetic song, "The Mistaken Marriage (*zhong shen wu*)," of chapter 5. Although both items may belong to the realm of the mythic in the narrative, it should be noted that the song is definitely written from the point of view of Bao-yu and not of Dai-yu.

finally succeeds in embracing the ideal of detachment, his resolve strengthened by his lover's death (according to Wang Guowei's reading), and almost all these characters who are in any way involved in the life of love end in disaster.[21] But this does not mean that the love story of Dai-yu and him, told in such realistic and disturbing manner, should in any way have a lesser hold on the reader's imagination. On the contrary, this story of the fragile and transient nature of love is one that paradoxically succeeds in the most permanent engagement of our sympathy. The goddess Disenchantment, the Daoist and Buddhist clerics who appear as so many dei ex machina in the narrative, and even the narrator himself may warn us against taking such an *affaire du coeur* too seriously when they repeatedly mock our vulnerability to human emotions and desires. In a dramatized reader such as the Daoist Vanitas (the Kongkong Daoren of chapter 1), however, we are given a different view of what sort of experience the perusal of such a story may produce. As has been argued in chapter 3, Cao Xueqin may be seen to have contradicted Buddhist verity (and by extension, its possible appropriation by Schopenhauer) by ever so slyly suggesting that renunciation is not necessarily the only path to enlightenment, because reading the world and reading a text about the world may evoke similar or contradictory reactions. Insofar as the male protagonist is portrayed as having departed with mysterious clerics, leaving his family and worldly vocation at the story's end, the novelistic action may give the impression of a traditional religious awakening (*wu*). On the other hand, the double significance embedded in the dexterous deployment of the term *mingbai* (to comprehend, to understand, to realize) separates the reader's "enlightenment" from that of the fictive hero—whether seen as the human Bao-yu or the mythic Stone. There is no detachment or disenchantment for Vanitas, only the Augustinian misery of "weeping for Dido slain."

Although Lin Dai-yu has been a character of irresistible charm for most traditional Chinese readers, recent criticism has become discernibly more muted in its acclaim. Reacting in part to the adulation heaped upon her by earlier commentators and influenced in part by modern psychology, modern writers place greater emphasis on the neurotic and self-destructive tendencies in Dai-yu's personality. Though her intellectual brilliance, her wit, and her literary talents are acknowledged, she is also regarded as a person excessively stubborn, self-pitying, and obsessed with the uncertain question of her marriage, as someone more deserving of our pity than our admiration.[22] On the other hand, many critics of the Pepople's Republic of China who have continued to sing her praises have usually commended her and Bao-yu for their "rebellious natures (*panni xingge*)" and for their having waged a vain but heroic campaign against

[21] Wang, "*Hongloumen* Pinglun," pp. 1,608.

[22] For example, Mei Yuan, *Hongloumeng di zhongyao nüxing*, pp. 43–71; Jeanne Knoerle, "*The Dream of the Red Chamber,*" pp. 56–66.

the oppressive feudalism of old China.[23] Although this chapter has no intention of repeating outmoded encomia to Dai-yu or to deny that much of her suffering may have been caused by despotic social structures and familial intrigues, it does hold to the supposition that a character nearly devoid of nobility or self-knowledge is no more capable of commanding our sustained interest than a passive and pathetic martyr who, like the Io of Aeschylus's *Prometheus Bound*, is wholly a victim of tyranny and injustice.[24] If the paramount ethical problem posed by tragedy, as James Redfield has argued, has to do with the question of under what conditions virtue is insufficient to happiness, then surely its perennial aesthetic problem, since the time of Aristotle, has to do with the question of under what conditions the exhibition of pain and suffering is productive of pleasure.[25] These questions, to be sure, are brought by Western theorists to their examination of Western literatures, but like the issues of gender ideology, they are not irrelevant to the study of a work like *Hongloumeng*. When applied to the scrutiny of a central character like Dai-yu, however, the problem of tragedy cannot be adequately addressed without considering her development in the context of the narrative's total design.

THE ORPHANED CONTENDER

We are first introduced to the person of Lin Dai-yu in chapter 3 of the narrative as a young girl newly bereft of her mother and sent to the distant mansion of the Jia family to live with her maternal grandmother, the aged matriarch of the Jia clan.[26] By chapter 14, her father has also passed away, and Dai-yu, with neither brother nor sister, is reduced to being a solitary dependent in a large, strange household where the observance of proper etiquette toward her elders requires constant vigilance, and where even such a trivial difference as when to drink tea after meals demands from her at the beginning a conscious effort of adjustment (*SS* 1: 87, 94, 99–100; *HLM* 1: 33, 43, 48). The fact that she lost her parents at a young age is hardly unique in Chinese literature, for in her we can readily recognize similar figures that populate earlier fiction and drama— the Xie Xiao'e, the Tan Yige, and the Xiao Shulan who have not only lost one

---

[23] See, for example, the collected essays in *Hongloumeng yanjiu ziliao jikan*, and the essays of Li Xifan and Lan Ling in *Hongloumeng pinglunji*.

[24] Compare the observation on the lack of character by C. T. Hsia, *The Classic Chinese Novel*, p. 277.

[25] See Redfield's *Nature and Culture in the "Iliad,"* especially chapters 1–4.

[26] The geography of the work is a nightmare for both the translator and the critic. Regardless of whether the Jia mansion is to be thought of as being located in Peking or Nanking, and regardless of whether there were actually, one, two, or three gardens that served as models for the Daguanyuan, the important point in the narrative is that Dai-yu is consistently portrayed as having left home far behind to reach the Rongguo Fu.

or both parents, but who are also precocious youths of enormous literary talents. Even in *Hongloumeng* itself, Dai-yu is by no means the only person who is without her parents. Two other girls related to the Jia family and often viewed as her arch rivals in her relation to Bao-yu also share her plight: Xue Bao-chai, a fatherless cousin who has come from afar to live with the clan, and the vivacious Shi Xiang-yun, the orphaned great-niece of the matriarch Shi Taijun. Despite the apparent similarities of their fates, however, the narrative does suggest explicitly that much of Dai-yu's turmoil and torment stem from the isolation of her orphanhood.

Unlike Bao-chai, whose entrance into the formidable environment of the Rong-guo mansion at least benefits from the company of a mother and an elder brother of considerable wealth, Dai-yu, as the narrator tells us in chapter 3, "brought only two of her own people with her from home": an old wet nurse and a ten-year-old maid named Snowgoose (*SS* 1: 105; *HLM* 1: 53). And, unlike Shi Xiang-yun, whose "generous, open-hearted nature . . . fortunately" (*SS* 1: 141; *HLM* 1: 86) no adversity or human harshness could alter or diminish, Dai-yu's sensitivity makes her agonize over the most inconsequential incident or the merest provocation.[27] It is thus her straitened circumstance in conjunction with her temperament that serves to enhance her fundamental sense of insecurity and enlarge her fears. Given her peculiar emotional make-up, we can only guess at the kind of traumatic impact her mother's death must have had on her. To batter even further the bruised ego of this young life, the necessity for her to leave the familiar surroundings of her native home for her grandmother's house is thrust upon her within a month of her mother's death. The admonition of Lin Ru-hai,

> Your father is half a century old already, and he has no intention to remarry. What's more, your health is poor, and you are so young; but you don't have your *own* mother to rear you nor do you have any sister to look after you. If at this time you were to entrust yourself to the care of your maternal grandmother and your uncles' girls, it would greatly relieve my domestic worries. Why don't you go? (*HLM* 1: 37, my translation)

accentuates with special poignance both the dilemma of her family situation and the plight of her chronic illness, which not only accounts for a great deal of her erratic behavior and physical anguish later, but also proves to be the most direct cause of her unhappiness at the end. Small wonder that the Red Inkstone scholiast has penned in here: "How pitiable! A passage where every sentence is a drop of blood, every sentence is a drop of blood!" (*Pingyu*, p. 57).

The reception of Dai-yu in her grandmother's house is undeniably warm

---

[27] The word *xing* (luckily, fortunately), which begins the fifth line of the song, "Grief Amidst Gladness," makes it clear that it is Xiang-yun's good fortune to be endowed with such a capacious disposition.

and cordial at the beginning. The effusive compliments by Xi-feng and her breathless solicitousness (*SS* 1: 92; *HLM* 1: 42) during that first meeting no doubt betray those aggressive streaks of manipulativeness and opportunism that make her such a fascinating person as well as so formidable a member of the familial oligarchy. But the sincerity of the matriarch's affection for her granddaughter cannot be questioned, as it is evident even in so simple a gesture as her hugging the fragile girl during a party to shield her from the noice of fireworks (chap. 54). This is a love that Dai-yu not only cherishes and acknowledges (hence the pathos of her exclamation in chapter 97: "Lao Tai-tai, you have loved me in vain!"), but also clings to with a desperation equaled perhaps only by her fear of losing the love of Bao-yu (hence her sorry plea in her dream in chapter 82: "Grandmother, you are the most kind-hearted person here and you have always loved me best. How come you are not helping me now that I am in such straits?")[28]

Neither the genuine kindness of the old woman, however, nor the dutiful amity of Lady Wang, let alone the shallow and calculated friendliness of Xi-feng, is strong enough to remove in Dai-yu that gnawing sense of mistrust born of her uncertainty as to whether she is in truth an accepted member of the family. Throughout the story, she is depicted as nursing such longing for her native home in the south (in chap. 87, she borrows the famous words of Li Yu, poet and exiled last ruler of the Southern Tang, to express her grief) that the mere sight of certain local products from that region causes her to brood over her own loneliness and her dependence on others (chap. 67). Again and again, she is lacerated by the feeling that she is actually an outsider even though she has been told to treat her uncle's house as her own, that she has no one to rely upon (*wuyi wukao*) now that both her parents are dead, and that she is merely finding shelter (*yixi*) in someone's house (chap. 26). This division in her consciousness between her indisputable stature as a close kin of the family and the persistent suspicion that she does not belong ironically renders her situation almost wholly analogous to that of a new bride in a premodern Chinese household, and markedly different from that of her cousin Bao-chai (for no bride goes to the groom's residence with mother and brother in tow). Dai-yu herself, in chapter 45, delineates this difference with utmost clarity (*SS* 2: 398; *HLM* 2: 625):

> There's no comparison between us. You've got your mother and your brother for a start. You've got property and businesses. You've still got land and a home of your own back in Nanking. It's true that as marriage-relations they allow you to live here free of charge, but you provide everything for yourselves apart from the accommodation. You don't cost them a penny. And any time you feel like it, you

---

[28] The translation here is by C. T. Hsia, taken from the quotation in *The Classic Chinese Novel*, p. 273.

can just get up and go. I've got nothing at all of my own, absolutely nothing. Yet everything they give me—food, clothing, pocket-money, even the flowers and trees in my garden—are the same as they give their own girls. Can you wonder that the servants are so resentful?[29]

Abruptly and, in Dai-yu's case, irrevocably severed from the security and familiarity derived from uterine relations (to borrow the terms of anthropologists), she is thrust into a new set of relations virtually affinal in character. The ambiguity of her position in the family, she realizes, makes her particularly vulnerable to the politics of the large household, and that in turn is what makes her so sensitive to the teasing of her peers and so apprehensive of criticism by members of the domestic staff. Moved by a gift of bird's nest offered for the improvement of her health (chap. 45), Dai-yu nonetheless says to her benefactor Bao-chai:

> The bird's nest may be easy to get, but my health is not getting any better. Every year this sickness of mine, though not terribly serious, is already turning Heaven and Earth upside down with all that bustle about fetching doctors, brewing medicines, and buying ginseng and cinnamon. If I pull this new stunt now by asking for rice congee simmered with bird's nest, Lao Taitai, Taitai (Lady Wang), and Elder Sister Feng—the three of them may not object, but those old amahs and young maids below them will find it hard not to regard me as a pest. Just look at them! They even glower like tigers when they see how partial Lao Taitai is toward Bao-yu and Sister Feng, and how they talk behind their backs! How would they react if they find me in the place of favor? I am, moreover, not their rightful mistress. I came originally as a suppliant, because I had no other shelter or refuge. Those people have long despised me already. Why should I be so foolish now as to invite them to curse me? (*HLM* 2: 624–25, my translation)

Again, when her request in chapter 87 to have some rice gruel prepared at her lodge is mistaken by her maid Cuckoo to be her aversion to the general lack of cleanliness of the family kitchen, Dai-yu replies: "I'm not objecting to their filth; it's just that I've been sick for quite some time, and all my wants and needs have been supplied already by someone's family. If at this time I insist on taking soup, rice gruel, and what not, people will only consider me a

---

[29] Bao-chai's attempt to comfort her cousin hardly succeeds. On the one hand, she rightly concedes that her own situation is indeed better than Dai-yu's ("It's really only in having a mother that I can count myself a bit luckier than you"). Exploiting the worthlessness of her brother, however, she tries to slough off further difference with a bit of unctuous casuistry: "In other resepcts we have enough in common to think of ourselves as fellow-sufferers" (*SS* 2: 399; *HLM* 2: 625). "Fellow-sufferers" is the translation for *tongbing xianglian*, literally, "with the same illness we pity each other." In the context of the immediate conversation, Bao-chai's unwittingly ironic use of this cliché only serves to deconstruct her argument: on what ground could she claim to share the same "illness" with Dai-yu?

nuisance" (*HLM* 3: 1246–7, my translation). Though she lives in the Prospect Garden, as the narrator tells us in chapter 83, "by the love of the matriarch," she has been always wary of what other people might do or say. It is wholly in character, therefore, that when her health is rapidly failing, an old amah's invective outside her window intended for another maid but misconstrued by Dai-yu to be an attack on herself can precipitate her extreme response of weeping until she faints.

If the actions of Dai-yu thus strike us as overly reactive and her emotions as highly unstable, the underlying causes of such behavior should also be apparent. Her physique has been devastated early by what is, in all likelihood, pulmonary tuberculosis, and this disease has not only made her moody, irritable, chronically depressive, and continuously susceptible to fatigue, but has also severely curtailed even her enjoyment of food and drink (for example, see chapter 38).[30] Added to the enervating effects of consumption is her diffidence over her position in the household, which in turn intensifies the haunting sense of her vulnerability and powerlessness. Her remark in chapter 82 to Bao-yu's maid Aroma that "in family affairs it's either the east wind that vanquishes the west wind, or the west wind that crushes the east wind," articulates with striking clarity her grasp of power politics and its fearful implications in a large and complex household. The immediate occasion of her statement is the maid's mention of You Er-gu-niang, one of Jia Lian's concubines tricked by Xi-feng into taking up residence in the Garden, only to be driven to suicide finally by the jealous wife's vicious tactics. By pointing out how easily a person may be destroyed by the capricious whims or calculated venom of familial intrigues, Dai-yu's words may have provided unintentionally a gnomic warning to Aroma (so Wang Guowei seems to think) and prompted her to side later with Xi-feng's interests.[31] Quite apart from whatever ironic consequence these words may have wrought, however, they themselves reveal the speaker's perception and, in the context of the narrative, alert us to the mental and emotional cost such awareness entails.

Wholly lacking what might have been the stabilizing influence of parental authority and affirmation, Dai-yu often has difficulty in knowing how to respond to the praise and blame, whether open or veiled, from those who surround her. And as she goes through adolescence, a time when the smallest disappointment

---

[30] Detailed descriptions of Dai-yu's illness are given in chapters 82–83, when her maids first discover "a thick wriggling strand of dark blood" in the phelgm she coughed up (*SS* 4: 68; *HLM* 3: 1,186). Imagistically, her spitting of blood provides a realistic counterpoint to her nightmare when she dreamt that Bao-yu cut open his chest and "blood came spurting out." For historical and modern discussions of traditional Chinese medical views of consumption and pulmonary disorders, see Shen Jin'ao, *Zhongyi fuke xue*, pp. 170–79; *Jianming Zhongyi neike xue*, compiled by Nanjing Zhongyiyuan, 281–84; *Zhongyi neike xue*, pp. 258–65; Nathan Sivin, *Traditional Medicine in Contemporary China*, pp. 294, 408.

[31] Wang, Guowei "*Hongloumen* Pinglun," pp. 1,613–14.

may seem a disaster or the most insignificant incident betoken extravagant hope and promise, she again has neither the cushioning support of parental comfort nor the steadying guidance of experienced wisdom. Endowed with intelligence, sensitivity, and literary talents, she has to grow up in a society where the aphorism, "a woman's virtue is her lack of talent," is its unchallenged watchword.[32] Throughout the span of her brief life, therefore, a great deal of her vexation is attributable to her inability to resolve the conflict between duty and desire, between the need to acquire the traditional social virtues of self-restraint and deference to others and the self-assertive impulse to compete, to achieve, and to excel. Within the vast Jia mansion, the two persons known for their quick wit and sharp tongue are Dai-yu and Xi-feng. Whereas the latter uses her skillful volubility to ingratiate, to placate, and to manipulate, Dai-yu's penetrating intelligence fired by her impassioned nature allows for little caution or compromise: her quick-wittedness and biting remarks serve primarily as instruments of self-expression. This is the reason why she seems almost always to be the first to lampoon and ridicule even those whom she considers her friends, winning for herself the reputation that "Miss Lin's tongue is sharper than a knife!" And yet, during those endless rounds of chit-chat or formal festivity in and out of the Garden, any similar teasing on the part of her companions, especially when they touch on her feelings for Bao-yu or the subject of her future marriage, almost invariably sends her into fits of rage and tears.

That she appears to be small-minded and self-centered, that she finds it difficult to face with equanimity the jostling life among her peers are not merely signs of youth or pettiness; they are actually symptoms of the seething turmoil inside her. It has been the impression of many readers that Lin Dai-yu seems indeed a striking picture of what the narrator has said of her in chapter 5: a gifted girl who nonetheless affects the "air of lofty self-sufficiency and total

[32] The citation of this maxim is first made in the narrative in connection with the introduction of Li Wan, the widow of Bao-yu's deceased elder brother, at the beginning of chapter 4. Significantly, it is cited again by Bao-chai in chapter 64 when she and Bao-yu ask to see five poems on famous beauties of Chinese history newly composed by Dai-yu. The request is couched in another lecture for Dai-yu on Confucian values, re-enforcing Bao-chai's previous remarks made in chapter 42. "A girl's first concern is to be virtuous," Bao-chai says in the present instance, "her second is to be industrious in women's work. She may write poetry if she likes as a diversion, but it is an accomplishment she could just as well do without. The last thing girls of a good family such as ours need is a literary reputation" (SS 3: 64, text modified; HLM 2: 913). From a near-contemporary moralist like Zhang Xuecheng, who asserted that "ancient women's learning (fuxue) perforce comprehends poetry through ritual, whereas present women's learning destroys ritual through poetry" (Wenshi tongyi, juan 5, 31b; SBBY), Bao-chai's sentiment would have met hearty approval. Chen Dongyuan in Zhongguo funü shenghuoshi, traces to the Ming the origin of the saying that a woman's lack of talent is virtue. For further discussion of the saying and its shaping of cultural ideology, see K'ang-i Sun Chang, "Ming-Qing Women Poets and the Notions of 'Talent' and 'Morality.'"

obliviousness to all who did not move on the same exalted level as herself."
Her deep love for poetry, drama, music, and even the style of her life at the
Naiad's House have been taken by many to be indicative of her elegance and
refinement. She herself can sing, with ardent lyricism, of the noble ideal of
philosophic detachment when she pays poetic tributes to the chrysanthemum
by praising its unattended and unsullied beauty (chap. 38), but Tao Qian's
lofty, reclusive spirit, of which this flower has by association long been a symbol, remains for her more a conceit of poetic exercise than a cherished model
for imitation. In contrast to the verse of the Jin poet, in which the solitary
chrysanthemum thriving along "the eastern fences" is homologous to his serene
existence at one with nature, Dai-yu's three poems present the flowers as expressive of her projected self-esteem no less than her anxiety. Witness those
agitated queries, for example, posed in the second poem, "Questioning the
Chrysanthemum":

> Peerless and arrogant, with whom can you abide?
> You, too, have flowers, but why bloom so late?
> Do garden dew and courtyard frost make you forlorn?
> When wild geese leave and crickets grieve, would you
>   then mourn?

(*HLM* 1: 526, my translation)

These questions show us her poetic daring and ingenuity, justly praised by Shi
Xiang-yun, as much as her own turbulent emotions. The flower in the third
poem, "Chrysanthemum Dream," would chase after the wild geese longingly
even in its dream (line 5) and take offense at the crickets for disturbing its
sleep (line 6). Its solitary condition is not a source of joy, as it would be in a
genuine poem of reclusion, for solitude here only intensifies its loneliness because there is no one to whom the flower can disclose its secret sorrow during
the moments of consciousness (line 7). Read in this manner, these poems tell
us something of the fundamental make-up of Dai-yu. Though she may be able
to write part of a gāthā as transcendently indifferent to human affairs and sentiments as any composed by a Zen master (chap. 22; *SS* 1: 442; *HLM* 1: 307),
she writes on that occasion only to demonstrate a point. The literal paradox
asserted by her gāthā is that "that which is beyond proof (*wu ke yun zheng*)"
constitutes the best ground on which to stand (*shi lizhu jing*), but her composition actually functions as both ground and proof of her superiority over Bao-
yu. The "insight" of her rhetoric is thus controverted by her desire, and hers is
in reality a life of passionate involvement. Even as she is about to speak of the
chrysanthemum's "chaste yearning" in her first poem of that series, she
confesses at the same time that she is filling the page with self-pity (*manzhi
zilian*), and she ends her questions to this flower in the second poem with the
insistent plea:

Let not speech from your silent world be banned;
Converse with me, since me you understand!

(SS 2: 252; *HLM* 1: 526)*

Companionship, communication, and communion—these are the paramount concerns of this young girl, who is in many ways the most isolated person in the Garden's lively society. Because of the affection of matriarch and Bao-yu, she might have been included in most of the family's activities, but her own insecurity only aggravates her continuous craving for attention. She may not feel as free as Shi Xiang-yun in flouting conventional manners by eating fresh venison and drinking with abandon while composing poetry (chaps. 49–50), or by falling asleep in a drunken stupor openly on a garden bench during the height of a party (chap. 62), but Dai-yu herself is not immune to the heady elation of public recognition. When the imperial concubine Yuan-chun returns home for a visit in chapter 18, and all her young kin are asked to submit poems in celebration of various aspects of the newly constructed Garden, this is what we see of Dai-yu:

> She had confidently expected that this night would give her an opportunity of deploying her talents to the full and amazing everyone with her genius. It was very disappointing that no more had been required of her than a single little poem and an inscription; and though she was obliged to confine herself to what the Imperial Concubine had commanded, she had composed her octet without enthusiasm and in a very perfunctory manner. (*SS* 1: 367; *HLM* 1: 253)

A few moments later, she is moved to lend a little assistance to the perspiring Bao-yu, who is still struggling to finish his composition, but her motivation is as much a part of her care for him as her own "dissatisfaction because her talent had been underemployed." Still later, in another poetic contest held by the girls and Bao-yu (chap. 37), which requires that each person compose a poem to the begonia before one stick of Sweet Dream Incense—merely three inches in length—burns down, Dai-yu takes unmistakable delight in showing how vastly superior her poetic skill is to that of everyone else. While Bao-yu frets about his own deliberation and struggle to compose, Dai-yu remains calm and indifferent. Only after three persons have presented their poems and after several urgings does she finally respond.

> "Oh! Have you all finished?"
> She picked up a brush and proceeded, writing rapidly and without a pause, to set down the poem that was already completed in her mind. She wrote on the first sheet of paper that came to hand, and having finished, threw it nonchalantly across the table for the others to inspect. (*SS* 2: 224; *HLM* 1: 506)

When her companions began reading the poem on crab-blossoms, she was, of course, greeted by repeated praise.

Dai-yu's histrionic display may certainly be interpreted as part of the narcissism of youth, but it may also be viewed as the self's longing to be known, to be desired, and to be affirmed. The episode of the imperial concubine arguably satirizes the received notion of male candidates being examined for their poetic talents before the Throne, much as the poetic club activities in the narrative parody the real-life activities of men and women in writing clubs and poetic societies that had begun to flourish since the Yuan period.[33] In all these episodes, Dai-yu's behavior betrays a consistent streak of competitiveness and a deep need for recognition to which even the solitary declamation of the elegiac Flower Burial Song (chap. 27) bears witness. Her repeated protests in that lengthy poem against the cruel retreat of spring that irrevocably confirms the transience of both floral and human life rise to the vehement outburst at the end:

> Can I, that these flowers' obsequies attend,
> Divine how soon or late *my* life will end?
> Let others laugh flower-burial to see:
> Another year who will be burying me?
>
> As petals drop and spring begins to fail,
> The bloom of youth, too, sickens and turns pale,
> One day, when spring has gone and youth has fled,
> The Maiden and the flowers will both be dead.
>
> (*SS* 2: 39; *HLM* 1: 383)

The last phrase of the song literally has the meaning: "neither of them will know anything or be known (*liang bu zhi*)," and it reveals that the poetic speaker's darkest fear is that she, like the petals she buries, will be forgotten and consigned to oblivion.

THE THWARTED COMMUNION

This aspect of Dai-yu's character sheds further light on the tragic nature of the love between her and Bao-yu. It is not without reason that the tortuous path of

---

[33] Hence Bao-chai's sarcastic remark to Bao-yu when he was struggling to remember the proper source for the metaphor "green waxen": "If this is what you are like tonight, Heaven knows what you'll be like in a few years' time when you come to answer questions on policy in the Imperial Palace. Probably you'll find you have forgotten even the *Child's First Primer of Rhyming Names*" (*SS* 1: 368, text modified; *HLM* 1: 253). The Ming poet and calligrapher Li Dongyuan (1446–1516) has an entry in *Lutang shihua* that mentions the fondness of literati in the southeast for poetic societies. The rules and contests were modeled after the civil service examination, complete with a published list of successful candidates. See *Lidai shihua xubian* 3: 1,380. For further descriptions of activities of the participants by one such society (*Yuequan yinshe* or The Moon Spring Poetry Society) flourishing in 1286/87 and its convenor Wu Wei, see the prefaces to *Yuequan yinshe shi* in *Congshu jicheng chubian*, ed. Wang Yunwu, vol. 80.

their encounter is marked from beginning to end by a series of halting questions, disguised disclosures, deliberate provocations, unintended ironies, and misunderstood remarks. "Don't you know my feelings about you?" is a question that Bao-yu asks again and again in the course of the story, and the word *xin* translated by David Hawkes in chapter 20 as "feelings" is, as we know, the familiar word for heart-and-mind. Together with those common compounds of the vernacular built upon the graph, such as suspicion (*duo xin*), intention (*yongxin*), earnestness (*kuxin*), relief (*fangxin*), matter of the heart (*xinshi*), and sickness of the heart (*xinbing*), this word and its network of associative meanings reverberate like a letimotif structured throughout the narrative, climaxing in that shattering scene of Dai-yu's dream in chapter 82, when Bao-yu is driven to self-immolation by his lover's quest for knowledge of his heart. The significance of that episode goes beyond the realism in the portrayal of Dai-yu's subconscious terror and desire; it arises even more from the thematic and structural extension of an earlier segment of the narrative which dwells on the difficulty, both circumstantially induced and self-imposed, which the lovers find in making their true feelings known to each other. In chapter 32, Bao-yu has come close to giving full revelation of his love for Dai-yu, who is visibly moved also by the young man's earnest plea for her to be less anxious (*fangxin*) so that she will not further jeopardize her precarious health. Instead of waiting for any additional word from him, however, Dai-yu walks away after an awkward silence during which they stare dumbly at each other. At that moment, Aroma the maid catches up with her young master but, still lost in his own thoughts (*chuliao shen*) and no doubt overwhelmed at the same time by the surge of emotion he senses both in himself and in the girl he so passionately loves, Bao-yu blurts out:

> Dearest coz! I've never before dared disclose this affair of my heart (*xinshi*). Now at last I'm brave enough to tell you, and even if I have to die for it I'm willing (*ganxin*). Because of you I, too, have made my self completely sick, but I haven't dared tell anyone. I've just covered it up. Only when your illness is cured, I'm afraid, will I get any better. In sleep or dream I can never forget you. (*HLM* 1: 447–48, my translation)

As she is already in the distance, Dai-yu never knows the joy and comfort, however momentary, such words might have brought to her; they are overheard only by a startled and embarrassed Aroma, the unintended audience.

A few years later, this difficulty of communion continues to plague the two lovers. Going to her residence to try to offer his well wishes for the improvement of her health, his apocope—"If you end up by undermining your health, I . . ."—is symbolic of their dilemma, a heartfelt but unutterable desire. As the narrator explains,

> The realization that what he was about to say was probably something that ought not to be said caused the words to stick in his throat. For although, from the fact

that he and Dai-yu had grown up together, there existed a most perfect sympathy between them, although there was nothing in the world that either of them wanted more than to live and die in each other's company, such an understanding was only intuited by the heart (*xin zhong linghui*). They never spoke about the matter face to face. (*SS* 3: 254–55, text modified; *HLM* 2: 912)

Still later in chapter 97, the word *xin* is heard again in that pathetic scene when the ailing Bao-yu, unaware of the treacherous plot of Xi-feng to provide him with a substitute bride, says to his interviewer: "I have a heart, but I have already given it to Cousin Lin." Had he made such a remark earlier to someone like the grandmother during the moments of his lucidity and not during what appears to be an incoherent spell of his illness, things might have been quite different. As it is, the meaning of his utterance is not lost on the alert Xi-feng nor, for that matter, on the matriarch who has been eavesdropping on the two of them, but his words at that time can only spur the two older women on to execute their plan. After Dai-yu's death, the agony that haunts Bao-yu (chap. 104) and causes him to break down and weep uncontrollably (chap. 108) comes not only from his remembrance of her, but even more intensely from his self-examination of whether he has been truly heartless (*fuxin*) or not. In one last desperate effort to justify himself (chap. 113), he seeks to speak to the maid of Dai-yu, Nightingale, who has, however, nothing but scorn for him. Frustrated in his every attempt, Bao-yu cries in despair: "Finished! Finished! In this life I'll never be able to lay bare my heart! Only old Heaven knows it!" (*HLM* 3: 1,559, my translation). When at last he resolves to leave the family, ostensibly to embrace the life of renunciation, he says pointedly to Aroma, referring to the piece of jade that has accompanied him since his birth and the sudden, mysterious loss of which has been one cause of his misery, "I won't be sick anymore. I have already found my heart. What further use do I have for the jade?"

In a similar manner, the question so haunting Dai-yu's consciousness that it finds vocal expression more than once is: "Do I have a discerning friend?" The object of her quest in Chinese is *zhiyin*, meaning literally one who knows or understands the sound, the melody, or the notes, and it originates from the familiar story recorded in numerous ancient texts, including the *Lüshi chunqiu* and the *Liezi*. The friends Zhong Ziqi and Bo Ya enjoy such extraordinary oneness of spirit that when the latter plays his lute, the former can divine at once his thoughts by the musical notes. Whether it is a tall mountain or flowing water that Bo Ya happens to think of as he plays, Ziqi shows such unerring discernment of his intent that after he dies, Bo Ya breaks the strings and refuses to touch his instrument again.[34]

---

[34] See *Lüshi chunqiu, juan* 14, 4a (*SBBY*); *The Book of Lieh-tzu: A Classic of Tao*, translated by A. C. Graham, pp. 109–10.

The term *zhiyin*, in the evolved history of its usage, thus comes to mean not only an intimate friend but also one who recognizes and apprecaites the friend's hidden ability and true worth. As Dai-yu employs it in the text, it is unmistakably laced with amorous overtones, though the musical background may have led the author to devise that fairly extended episode, running through chapters 86–89, on her taking up the *qin* and on her attempt to teach Bao-yu something of the theory and technique of playing that stringed instrument. The situation, in fact, is a parody of the classic love story chronicled in the *Shiji, juan* 117, where the newly widowed Zhuo Wenjun is moved to elope with Sima Xiangru because of his marvelous performance of the lute. In the narrative, however, Dai-yu's effort to elicit some form of assurance from her lover is met, as in so many other occasions, by a disappointing and unthinking response from Bao-yu: "It's a pity that I don't recognize the notes (*wo bu zhi yin*), and I've listened in vain for all this time."

All the difficulties that the two lovers face in communicating their feelings form part of the larger tragic pattern that has, from the very beginning, compelled us to see both the distance and the intimacy that exist between them. When they meet for the first time in chapter 3, their shock of recognition (both feeling as if they might have met somewhere before) is meant to indicate, within the mythic frame of the narrative, their common celestial origin underlying the living bond of the spirit that will soon develop between them. As the objects of their grandmother's partiality, so the narrator tells us in chapter 5, they "began to feel an affection for each other which far exceeded what they felt for any of the rest. Sharing each other's company every minute of the day and sleeping in the same room at night, they developed an understanding so intense that it was almost as if they had grown into a single person" (*SS* 1: 124; *HLM* 1: 69).

For Bao-yu, of course, his deepest attachment to Dai-yu stems from his realization that among all his acquaintances known from youth, whether they are old or young, of high rank or low in the family, Dai-yu is the only girl who has never tried to persuade him "to establish himself and acquire a name" (chap. 36)—in other words, to seek success in a civil service career. Dai-yu's support for him in his resistance to such vocational aspiration cannot be interpreted as merely an immature form of youthful rebellion, although Bao-yu's own lack of zeal for his studies and mental lethargy have been the repeated targets of the narrator's lament and satire. When we have seen, as in the previous chapter, how crucial the mastery of designated canonical classics and the "eight-legged" essay is to the passing of official examinations at their various levels, and how important the success of an official career is to the establishment and survival of an illustrious family like the Jia's, we begin to comprehend as well the momentousness of the issues. Given the tendency to reckless profligacy and unbridled waste pervasive in the entire clan, the male heir's vocational—and thus, academic and political—attainment becomes virtually the only antidote for the family's destructive economics. That is why the matter of Bao-yu's schooling has provoked such anxious concern for Jia Zheng, and why the son's patent insouciance and incorrigible sloth have been such a continuous source of friction between father and offspring. And it is in regard to this issue that Dai-yu's attitude reveals her greatest distance from all the other girls that come into the life of Bao-yu.

Unlike Shi Xiang-yun and Xue Bao-chai, who both have attempted to admonish Bao-yu to be more diligent in his formal education, Dai-yu has hardly ever encouraged him in this endeavor. The one exception may be her remark recorded in chapter 82, but her assertion that Bao-yu may want to pursue "merit and fame (*gongming*)" should be taken in the context of her repudiation of his outlandish and sweeping generalization that all books and all learning are worthless.[35] After his savage beating by his father in chapter 34, Dai-yu cries until her eyes resemble "two walnuts," and her stammering words to him when he regains consciousness are: "You'd better change!" Later in the story, she even helps to provide him with the daily quota of calligraphic exercises he is charged to produce (chap. 70), and from time to time, she has given him gentle urgings to study. But her promptings are motivated by her concern to prevent his suffering from any further outbreak of paternal wrath and not necessarily by her desire to see him succeed in officialdom at some later date. This enormous contrast between her attitude and that of the two other girls cannot be accounted for by the rather glib assertion that Dai-yu happens to be less worldly minded (*su*) than her cousins. Whereas the other girls have, despite their own undeniable attractiveness and intelligence, conceived of their relations to someone like Bao-yu as a part of their basic obligation to uphold the priority of the family, of its structures and values, Dai-yu's love of Bao-yu reflects her unconditional affirmation of him as an individual. That is the fundamental difference, and it is a difference that cannot easily accommodate any binary schematization that seeks to categorize, whether by means of yin-yang, five phases, or *Yijing* theories (as in nineteenth-century commentaries) or the notions of masculinity and feminity (as in more recent criticism), the contrast and complementarity obtaining between Dai-yu and Bao-chai.[36]

Bao-chai's reluctant consent to go along with Xi-feng's fraud to deceive Bao-yu and marry him during the height of his illness does not represent a momentary lapse of integrity; it points to a decision consistent with all that we have seen of her as a young woman with "a generous, accommodating disposition which greatly endeared her to subordinates" (chap. 5), as someone who

[35] For critics who dislike the content of the last forty chapters, Dai-yu's remark becomes an early sample of inconsistent characterization.

[36] See the brief discussion of these issues in Edwards, *Men and Women in Qing China*, pp. 46–49.

"saw in conformity/the means of guarding her simplicity" (chap. 8). Through the spoken and unspoken thoughts of the domestic staff, particularly the private musings of Aroma (chap. 96), we are given the impression that Bao-chai is a person who can put in order and unite the family, for it is clear that she has learned at an early age to subordinate her personal dislikes and preferences, her dreams and desires, to the larger collective interest of the group.

Faced with a weak mother and a hopelessly spoiled and unruly elder brother, Bao-chai is forced to acquire the disciplined taciturnity and cultivated tactfulness so necessary to the management of household affairs. In the previous chapter, we have seen how she can lecture Dai-yu, sternly and with complete conviction, on the dangers of perverting one's nature through the reading of vernacular literature, despite her own obvious knowledge and enjoyment of romantic but proscribed works. Her final debate with Bao-yu in chapter 118, as we have also seen, actually ends with her plea that he conform to his parental wishes, to take at least one degree so that he, assuming so pivotal a role in the family, can duly repay "Imperial kindness and ancestral benevolence." It need hardly be said that Bao-chai's words are indeed words of rectitude, but her emergence as an articulate and eloquent champion of Confucian values does not take effect only after she has married her cousin. Predicted by poetic oracles from the beginning, her development has been consistent throughout the narrative, and chapter 56, for example, compellingly portrays her as a learned reader of Zhu Xi no less than a thoughtful and efficient administrator in familial economics.

To say that of Bao-chai is to aver that as a constructed subject she, like Dai-yu, resists reductive typology, for both of these novelistic persons, as do so many finely wrought characters of the narrative, bear the authentic stamp of individuality, of difference in subjectivity despite the surface semblance that they are equally attractive and well-educated. The difference between Bao-chai and Dai-yu in turn continues to fuel their smoldering sense of rivalry, despite certain episodes that seem to celebrate their attainment of "sisterly understanding" (chap. 45) or that depict Dai-yu as the recipient of Aunty Xue's "words of loving kindness" (chap. 57). When Dai-yu revives the Peach-Flower Poetry Club in chapter 70, not only do Bao-chai's own competitiveness and ambition unmistakably imprint her lyric on the catkin or willow-floss, but her lyric virtually challenges point by point Dai-yu's poem on the same subject.

Characteristic of her deepening sense of mortality and impermanence, Dai-yu's *Tangduoling* (*HLM* 2: 996) sounds an insistent motif of "falling pollen (*fenduo*)," "fading fragrance (*xiangcan*)," youthful bloom turning hoary white, and the floss's rootlessness and tendency to drift as comparable to an ill-fated human (*ren ming bo*). Her anxious unconscious perhaps finds its most ironic expression in line 1 of the second part, for "even grasses and plants know of grief" recalls for us her mythic preincarnate identity, echoing, as Wong Kam-ming aptly reminds us, another instant of such unwitting self-designation in chapter 28: "I'm just a common person like any grass or plant (*buguo shi caomu zhi ren*)" (*HLM* 1: 401).[37] The specific source of the floss's grief in the poem is that even if it is "wedded" to the "east wind," it would but receive from it a completely indifferent treatment. In the hands of Dai-yu, a phrase borrowed from a Tang poet has received rueful transformation, for the east wind as a traditional literary topos has the assigned role of revivifying floral life.[38] Hence its name, the protector of flowers (*huhua*), which gendered diction also uses to designate the male lover, and such meaning is clearly present in Li Shangyin's familiar opening of his untitled, regulated octet: "To meet is difficult; to leave, too, is hard./The east wind's powerless, and a hundred flowers fade."[39] Dai-yu's representation makes the floss completely a victim of the east wind's whim and the conspiratorial indifference of spring.

By great contrast, Bao-chai's poem to the tune of "Immortal by the River" celebrates from beginning to end the enabling potency of the east wind, for throughout the lyric, the floss is never allowed to drift, scatter, or drop to the ground (*HLM* 2: 997). Thanks to the whirling east wind, the dance of the willows is made harmonious and orderly (*junyun*). Despite chaotic swarms of bees and butterflies, a none-too-subtle allusion to male suitors in gendered rhetoric, it is the poetic speaker's contention that the floss has never (rhetorical interrogative *ji ceng*) perished in the water, nor is it necessary (rhetorical interrogative *qi bi*) that it die in the dust. Because the willow's ten thousand strands or filaments will never change, the floss does not fear union or separation, a pointed reply to the last three lines of Dai-yu's lyric. Indeed, Bao-chai's reaction to both Bao-qin and Dai-yu in this episode is to criticize the "defeatism (*sangbai*)" she discerns in their poems. Whether her own composition represents "optimism" deriving from her confidence that she will definitely wed Bao-yu is debatable, but the east wind is named "good (*hao feng*)" in the penultimate line.[40] And her exultation in its strength to lift the poem's speaking subject (notice the striking invocation of the first person *wo* in the last line, which serves to unite both subject and author) to the height (*qing yun*, literally green clouds or sunny sky) of success plainly announces her aspiration, her *zhi* or desire.

Dai-yu, as we have seen already, is hardly a person without personal ambition, but her obsessive passion lies elsewhere. Her love for Bao-yu is extraordinary

---

[37] Wong Kam-ming, "Point of View and Feminism," p. 47.

[38] The phrase "wed to the east wind (*jia yu dongfeng*)" directly refers to poem 1 of a series of thirteen quatrains on the South Garden (Nan Yuan) by the Tang poet Li He (791–817). See *QTS, juan* 390; 6: 4,401. The last two lines of Li's poem reads: "Loveable's the delicate scent that drops at dusk; / It's wed to the east wind, without go-betweens." Despite the falling scent, the poem's mood is not at all melancholy, for the scent may benefit from the wind in its further dissemination.

[39] See "Wuti" in *QTS, juan* 539; 8: 6,168–69.

[40] This is the reading of Wong Kam-ming, "Point of View and Feminism," p. 57.

precisely because she places his freedom for self-affirmation above his obligatory allegiance to the family. A love that has the potential to challenge some
of the most cherished values of a culture must appear, for that very reason,
perverse and anarchic, for it threatens to repudiate or revise the long-accepted
norms of that tradition. But a love of such quality, I suspect, is also what en-
dears her to readers traditional and modern, because it registers the most
eloquent intimation of tragic nobility. She has never demanded that her lover
be anything other than what he is; all she has ever hoped from him is the
unambiguous assurance of his love. And her love for him deepens when she
accidentally overhears a conversation between Bao-yu, Xiang-yun, and Aroma,
during which she comes to the realization that his regard for her is based
squarely on her attitude toward his future career (chap. 32). Offended by his
cousin's words that he should at least talk business and government with some
of the family's official friends for the sake of the future, Bao-yu begins to
address her with unfeigned sarcasm; and when the maid frantically attempts
to placate Xiang-yun by an undiscriminating remark linking Xiang-yun and
Dai-yu together, the boy angrily replies, "Has Miss Lin ever mouthed such
ridiculous nonsense? If she had, I would have broken up with her long ago."
The effect of Bao-yu's brief outburst on the eavesdropping girl outside is
revealing:

> When Dai-yu heard this statement, she became both startled and happy, both sad
> and dejected. She was happy for the fact that her perception had not failed her. "I
> have always regarded you as my discerning friend (*zhiji* [literally, one who knows
> the self])," she thought to herself, "and indeed you prove to be such a friend.
> And what startles me is the way you publicly praise me before others; your warmth
> and affection seem to have overridden any fear of violating taboo or arousing
> suspicion. But I have cause for dejection. If you can be my discerning friend, I
> can, of course, be yours too; but if you are indeed such a friend, then why must
> we be faced with that theory of gold-and-jade? Even if there had to be such a
> theory, why couldn't it be one applicable only to you and me? Why must there be
> also a Bao-chai? And I have cause for sadness, too! Since my parents have died
> early, there is no one who can assume responsibility on my behalf to make known
> those thoughts of mine engraved on my heart and bones. Moreover, my spirit
> these days seems so dissipated and low, a sign no doubt of my illness taking
> hold. Even the physician says, 'Her vital breath is weak and she's anemic. I fear
> that she's stricken with consumption.' I may be your discerning friend, but I'm
> afraid I can't last. And you may be my discerning friend, but what can you do
> with my poor fate?" (*HLM* 1: 446, my translation)

This moving passage offers us a glimpse of Dai-yu's deepest feelings and
all the inexorable causes of her tragedy. To the plights of her orphanhood and
physical malady is added a third form of menace and one equally threatening
to Dai-yu, the folk theory of gold-and-jade affinity. As the dreaded but resisted

element which nonetheless powerfully determines the heroine's final destiny, the theory functions in a manner similar to the oracle confronting Oedipus or the witches' announcement to Macbeth: it both affects the humans involved and in turn receives their manipulation. In this theory of affinity the mythic and the realistic strands of the story converge, not merely rendering the ordeal of Dai-yu a struggle against the perfidy of ungenial family elders but also elevating it to a protracted, if ultimately self-defeating, conflict with fate itself.

What Dai-yu refers to in her silent reflection is the fact that Bao-yu carries at birth in his mouth a piece of jade that has on it certain inscriptions (chap. 8), a curious phenomenon that has not failed to remind those who come into contact with him of "the goodly affinity of gold-and-jade (*jinyu liangyuan*)," a traditional metaphor for a happy and well-matched marriage. Since, however, Bao-chai is supposed to have been given a golden locket by a monk with the instruction, reported by her mother to Lady Wang, that she is to marry only someone with a corresponding piece of jade (chap. 28), it is not surprising that she is soon considered by Dai-yu to be the arch-rival and a threat to her desired happiness. What further heightens Dai-yu's insecurity is that Shi Xiang-yun is known also to possess a golden unicorn, and this is a young woman whose beauty and intelligence are obviously not lost on Bao-yu. Understandably, Dai-yu would lash out at them, particularly in the presence of Bao-yu, at almost every opportunity, and attack by sardonic insinuation or forthright criticism the idea of the gold-and-jade affinity. Her alarm, moreover, is heightened by too active an imagination. She who can listen, silent and transfixed, to the melancholy arias of the *Western Wing* and be moved to tears (chap. 23) can also fantasize about her lover meeting his preordained mate because of the contrived affinity made to exist between certain delicate, small objects just like those of countless heroes and heroines of the scholar-and-beauty (*caizi jiaren*) stories she has heard and read. This fear, in fact, has driven her to spy on Xiang-yun and Bao-yu at one time (chap. 32), although that occasion provides for her the unexpected but happy discovery of Bao-yu's genuine appreciation of her.

The myth of gold-and-jade affinity, whether it is consciously believed or not by the rest of family, indisputably exerts enormous pressure on these three persons who make up the so-called love triangle. Bao-chai is certainly not impervious to the implications of the object in her possession, as the narrator makes plain in his passing remark in chapter 28, and Bao-yu stubbornly denies that it has any significance for him whenever the subject is broached by Dai-yu. From the moment of their first meeting in chapter 3, when he flings the jade away in a tantrum as soon as he hears that Dai-yu owns no such similar object, to the time (chap. 36) when he talks in his sleep, to an eavesdropping Bao-chai ("These are the words of Daoists and Buddhists! How could we believe them? What's this gold-and-jade marriage? I insist on the marriage of wood and stone!"

HLM 1: 492, my translation), he fights, often vehemently but vainly, to dispel her fears. For Dai-yu, however, denial can appear as affirmation, and this talk of special affinity amounts to a "perverse discourse (*xieshuo*)," and her anguish is fanned by her burning desire to find out whether her lover would value the myth more than the person (chap. 29). The more furiously Bao-yu denies her charges, according to the remarkably astute analysis of her psyche by the narrator in chapter 29, the more she thinks that he is subscribing to the claim of the myth.

The ominous presence of the myth thus sorely exercizes, if it does not poison, the relation of the two lovers, causing their times together in the Prospect Garden to end more often than not in tearful dispute or surly silence. Their rancorous arguments at one point even provoke the grandmother to quote the proverb: "'Tis Fate brings foes and lo'es tegither" (chap. 29). Since this familiar saying is commonly used to describe a married couple, its ironic suggestion of predestined union and discord is itself a poignant reminder of the sort of vexation predicted of the lovers in the second lyric of the song cycle, "A Dream of Golden Days," which the goddess Disenchantment shares with Bao-yu in his dream in chapter 5:

> One was a flower from paradise.
> One a pure jade without a spot or stain.
> If each for the other one was not intended,
> Then why in this life did they meet again?
> And yet if fate had meant them for each other,
> Why was their earthly meeting all in vain?
>
> (*SS* 1: 140; *HLM* 1: 85)

This painful ambiguity of the lovers' uncertain destiny reflected in their occasional ambivalence finds consistent development in a series of artfully juxtaposed images that alert the reader to the foreboding causes of their misery as well as to the touching intimations of their happiness.[41] If Bao-yu and Dai-yu frequently clash in heated and acrimonious words, there are also moments of lighthearted banter and tender exchange. His teasing her with the story of the little rodent (chap. 20), her concern for him when his face is burnt (chap. 25), her jocular reference to him as "a gawping goose" (chap. 28), his draining the wine cup for her, knowing that she cannot drink (chap. 54), and her simple request for her maid to brew a good cup of tea for him (chap. 82)—these are

---

[41] The phrase "foes and lo'es" used by David Hawkes to translate the term *yuanjia* has the meaning of "sweet foe" or, as Qian Zhongshu expands the oxymoronic definition, *dolce mia guerriera, la ma cara nemica, ma douce guerriere*. See his *Guanzhuibian* 3: 1,058–59 for a fine discussion of the various possible semantic shadings of the term, all of which elaborate the suggestion of ambivalence.

small but unerring signs of their affection. Similarly, their violent reactions in chapter 57 betray the awesome intensity of their love, when a deliberate lie of Nightingale sends him into fits of paroxysm, thinking that Dai-yu has been sent away to be married, and the subsequent erroneous news of his death drives Dai-yu to ask to be strangled by the rope.

Perhaps the most memorable episode in this regard is when Bao-yu, after he has been severely beaten by his father, sends two used silk handkerchiefs to Dai-yu subsequent to her tearful visit of him (chap. 34). Puzzled at first by his gesture, she soon comes to the ecstatic realization that they actually betoken the most telling expression of his love and understanding. Unbeknownst to her, her proclivity to tears had already elicited his declared concern at the time when she accompanied her father's cortège to Soochow for burial.[42] She who has spent a good part of her young life shedding tears for him is now presented with a gift so appropriate for those sorrowful symptoms of love, and once she perceives his intention, she pours out her feelings in three spontaneous poems, which she writes on the handkerchiefs (*SS* 2: 168; *HLM* 1: 469). As lyric poetry, these heptasyllabic quatrains are not particularly subtle or refined if measured by the canons of traditional Chinese poetics. As statements of love, however, they are the most revealing of Dai-yu's complete devotion to her beloved. Like the youthful poetic speaker in Adalbert von Chamiso's "Frauenliebe und -Leben" who confesses:

> Sonst ist licht- und farblos
> Alles um mich her,
> Nach der Schwestern Spiele
> Nicht begehr' ich mehr,
> Möchte lieber weinen,
> Still im Kämmerlein; . . .

> But all is dark and pallid around me;
> With my sisters I'd play no more.
> I'd rather weep in silence in my little room.

Dai-yu with equal candor and ardor makes explicit the meaning of her weeping.

Defying the established artistic ideals of reticence and suggestiveness that she herself commends when she discusses poetics with Caltrop in chapter 48, her handkerchief poems are the most unreserved and passionate declarations that she weeps—and therefore she lives—solely for him. The direct cause of her weeping on this occasion is presumably the sight of his wretched condition after the beating, but the more immediate reason for fresh tears comes, paradox-

---

[42] "'Poor thing!' said Bao-yu. 'How she must have cried and cried during this past week or so!' The thought of her crying made him knit his brows and sigh" (*SS* 1: 281; *HLM* 1: 193).

ically, from the sorrow (*shangbei*, poem 1) renewed by his gift. The implied answer to the rhetorical question posed in line 2—"For whom are they idly and secretly shed?"—makes it clear that Bao-yu has always been the object of her tears that so frequently spot her pillows and sleeves that the stains cannot be wiped away (poem 2). In the climactic third poem, her perpetual tears that the colorful silk cannot easily preserve are metonymically conflated with the stains on the mottled bamboos outside her residence. By invoking the myth of the two imperial consorts who wept unconsolably to their suicidal death for the sage King Shun, Dai-yu has ironically made her poems answerable to her fate. The comparison of her experience to the consorts', as I have argued in the previous chapter, makes a bold claim for the status and nature of her love.

In this abortive exchange of gifts, wherein her love for him is verbalized and inscribed on his material present but never successfully conveyed, the entire episode both recalls the primordial experience of exchange between the Stone and the Plant and amplifies its meaning in human terms. If the golden locket of Bao-chai and the jade of Bao-yu may be taken as symbols of what is beyond their ken or control, which nonetheless affects their destinies, these handkerchiefs so inscribed represent the realistic counterpart of those mythic objects, for they are the concrete mementos of human sentiments and the deepest spiritual union. The effect on Dai-yu of writing these poems, moreover, may offer one final clue to their full meaning:

> [She] was preparing to write another quatrain, when she became aware that her whole body was burning hot all over and her cheeks were afire. Going over to the dressing-table, she removed the brocade cover from the mirror and peered into it.
>
> "Hmm! 'Brighter than the peach-flower's hue,'" she murmured complacently to the flushed face that stared out at her from the glass, and, little imagining that what she had been witnessing was the first symptom of a serious illness, . . . (*SS* 2: 168; *HLM* 1: 470)

It may be obvious that the "serious illness" refers to the physical malady which has plagued her from the beginning (chap. 3), for which she has been placed on permanent medication (chap. 28), and which ultimately claims her life. Given the allusiveness and intricacy of infratextual rhetoric in this narrative, however, one may perhaps also read this illness more appositely as metaphor for that illness of the heart (*xinbing*), for the guilt of which Dai-yu receives in chapter 97 grandmother's unqualified condemnation (*SS* 4: 343; *HLM* 3: 1,363). The fatal symptom of an incurable disease thus tropes the irrevocable expression of love, much as toward her life's end, her bloody fits of coughing will poignantly recall her preincarnate name of Crimson Pearl. The suggestive color of her countenance ("brighter than the peach-flower's hue") gives a clue as to why Dai-yu considers the burning of her handkerchief manuscript before she dies an absolute necessity, for only the elimination of Bao-yu's gift and its textualized evidence of her delirious desire (*chi qing*) can fully sustain her claim to a pure body, and this is why their destruction evokes such indescribable desolation and grief.[43]

BETWEEN DELUSION AND HOPE

"Unless we have the death of Dai-yu," writes one modern Chinese critic, "the subject matter of *Hongloumeng* is not fully established."[44] She no more dies, however, simply to illustrate how the embodied Wood of Lin Dai-yu's name would be inevitably superceded by the Metal of Xue Bao-chai's as in a reading by correlative cosmology, than to validate a thesis of contemporary theory: "when the Other is no longer required to represent Bao-yu's dilemma, it ceases to exist."[45] The problem with an interpretation like that advanced by Louise Edwards is that it construes Dai-yu to be providing for Bao-yu the only "link to the feminine," a link "that was the essence of" their relationship. I should think, however, that the narrative portrays "the feminine" with far greater complexity than this, and for Bao-yu at least, his two beloved cousins represent in actuality two kinds of "the feminine": one that openly subscribes to the norms of the Confucian discourse and an emergent one that reflects a more resistant and skeptical attitude. Bao-yu's dilemma with the Other, therefore, by no means resolves itself when Dai-yu dies; in a real sense, it has only just begun.

The overwhelming power of her death can perhaps best be seen in the numerous imitations of the narrative and its spurious sequels wherein their authors, like the eighteenth-century editors of *King Lear*, attempt to modify its devastating impact by giving the story of Bao-yu and Dai-yu a happy ending. The reason this event leaves so indelible an impression is not merely that her death casts so absolute a shadow and creates in readers such a sense of irreparable loss; its overpowering effect arises also from the way her death, and thus her final separation from her lover, is anticipated and prepared for in the narrative. Through a series of incidents in the last forty chapters, we are made to see how Dai-yu, in the face of mounting despair, strives to keep alive her hopes, and this spectacle of her painful struggle is what intensifies our pity and fear.

---

[43] Even the comparison of a woman's face to the color of peach blossoms may not be merely a hackneyed, innocuous description when one recalls a story in popular fiction. It concerns the famous detective and just magistrate, Bao Gong or Judge Bao, who unmasked a reputedly chaste widow's adulterous affair with an ape because he noticed how her face bore the hues of peach blossoms (*lian dai taohua zhi se*). See *Bao Longtu pan baijia gongan*, chapter 2, p. 1,532. What an ironic gloss of the Mencian maxim: "When one has something within, it necessarily shows itself without" (*Mencius*, 6B, 6).

[44] Song Jing, *Hongloumeng renwu lun*, p. 271.

[45] The argument on Wood and Metal is Zhang Xinzhi's in "*Hongloumeng* du fa," p. 156. See Edwards, *Men and Women in Qing China*, p. 47.

The first of these incidents is her dream in chapter 82. Since C. T. Hsia has already made such a fine analysis of this entire episode, I shall confine my discussion to Dai-yu's mental preoccupation and emotional disquietude just before the onset of the dream.

> In the quietness of the dusk, a multitude of worries and vexations assailed her heart. Her health was getting worse, she thought, and she was not getting any younger. From the look of things, though Bao-yu did not care for any one else, his grandmother and mother apparently were making no move to bring about her union with him. How wonderful it would have been if, when they were still alive, her parents had arranged the marriage for her! But, on the other hand, she thought, her parents could have very well matched her with someone else, and that person could not possibly have stood up to Bao-yu for talent, character, and tenderness. As things stood now, she could still plan for her happiness. Preoccupied with these thoughts, her heart went up and down like a pulley. (*HLM* 3: 1,182)[46]

Dai-yu's attempt to convince herself that there is still a chance for her to realize her fondest hope astonishes us by her desperate rationalization, for she is even willing to entertain the implausible notion that her parents' death might have been an advantage for her after all. Has not she always lamented the fact that, because she has lost both parents, she has lost the only way that her own preference in marriage might have been taken into consideration?[47] Now that they are gone, is she not wholly subject to the will of the elders in this family with whom she has never been fully at ease? What, then, could possibly be the basis of her speculation that "she could still plan for her happiness"?

The answer to this last question may point to several factors. The cited passage makes it clear that she is, at the moment, somewhat more assured of Bao-yu's devotion, and since her ostensible acceptance of Bao-chai's friendship in chapter 45 (though she has never succumbed to the latter's suasion to give up poetry and literature), the threat of the gold-and-jade affinity seems to have receded from her consciousness. As for her feelings for Bao-yu, she may not have told anyone explicitly, but they are not unknown—so she may have

---

[46] The translation is by Hsia in *The Classic Chinese Novel*, p. 272.

[47] If this suggestion that filial consent or preference may play a nominal role in the whole marital transaction seems itself implausible, it should be remembered that in the narrative, Aunty Xue does twice seek the opinion of her daughter (chaps. 95 and 97) concerning the proposal of marriage to Bao-yu. Bao-chai's response, of course, is a model of filial obedience and modesty: "This affair concerning a girl should be decided by the parents. Since my father has passed away, Mama should decide for me. If not, you should at least consult with Elder Brother. Why bring up the question with me?" That by mid-Qing children's opinion might affect some marriage arrangement can also be seen in chapter 1 of Shen Fu's *Fusheng liuji* (*Six Chapters of "A Floating Life"*). The ready consent of Shen Fu's mother to his request to marry Chen Yun, his cousin, makes it all the more understandable that Dai-yu's pins all her hope on Bao-yu's explicit choice.

reasoned—to the important members of the family. Has not Xi-feng herself indulged in a little cruel baiting in chapter 25, when she says to Dai-yu, "If you have drunk the tea of our family, why don't you become one of our daughters-in-law?" And did not Aunty Xue, Bao-chai's mother, also mention specifically, though half in jest, that it would please the matriarch to give Dai-yu rather than someone "outside the family" to her grandson (chap. 57)? Would these people not take her interest to heart and speak to the grandmother, especially when she is known to be so fond of Dai-yu?

Though the narrative has made no explicit report of Dai-yu's thinking in this manner, I do not believe the foregoing speculation to be far-fetched. Certainly, the entire dream episode reveals not only the terror and desire of the heroine but also the pitiful illusion of her hope. Several of the incidents following the dream are designed to sustain this tension generated by her expectancy and despair. Shortly after the dream episode, the matter of Bao-yu's marriage, unknown to the two young persons, is indeed taken up by the grandmother with his father, whose proposal to marry Bao-yu into a certain Zhang family is immediately rejected by the doting matriarch ("Our Bao-yu can't even take care of himself when he has all those people serving him. How could we ask him to manage the affairs of another household?"). When she reports her conversation to Xi-feng (chap. 84), this sly woman at once raises archly the question: "When we have right here a marriage ordained by Heaven, why look elsewhere? We have a precious jade and a golden locket! How could Lao Tai-tai have forgotten this?" How deeply this reminder has penetrated the matriarch's consciousness may be gathered from her decisive instruction to her son later in chapter 96. "As long as our two families are willing, and the children are bound by the principle of gold-and-jade," she says, the marriage of Bao-yu (then gravely ill) and Bao-chai must be concluded without further delay. The apprehension of Dai-yu about the myth is justified after all, although she fails to realize that the persons who have the power to exploit the myth are the ones truly to be feared, and not only the individuals to whom these gold and jade oddities are given.

When Jia Zheng's small promotion is announced soon after his initial conversation with his mother, several members of the family make a point to congratulate Bao-yu for his father's elevation. As he is about to tender his own compliment to his seniors, Bao-yu is further congratulated by Jia Yun for the "double happiness" of an imminent betrothal (*SS* 4: 126; *HLM* 3: 1,224). Though the remark at once embarrasses Bao-yu, it also explains why he is depicted as so "overjoyed that he could hardly speak (*xi de wuhua ke shuo*)" (*HLM* 3: 1,224) when he enters the matriarch's quarters moments later. For what strikes his immediate vision are Dai-yu and Xiang-yun sitting to grandmother's left, while Bao-chai is conspicuously absent. His elated and elaborate acts of congratulating senior family members—Grandmother Jia, Lady Wang, Lady Xing—are motivated no doubt by misconstruing his own betrothal to Dai-yu as a fait accompli, a bitter irony if ever there was one, and not by his father's promotion.[48] Thus Xi-feng's teasing words to the lovers in this gathering ("The two of you are together all the time, and yet you treat each other deferentially like guests") reinforce the lovers' public embarrassment and private pleasure because her offhanded remark contains the common reference to the ideal conduct of a wedded couple.

After Dai-yu's vain attempt to elicit some specific response from Bao-yu through her discourse on music theory and instruments, and alarmed by her maids' conversation on Bao-yu's marital prospect that she overhears, Dai-yu is overcome all at once by the sinister prophecy of her dream, and seeks to die by fasting and deliberate abuse of her body (chap. 89). Once more, however, the furtive exchange between one of her maids and another page intervenes, for as her condition deteriorates drastically, Dai-yu accidentally learns that the future mate of Bao-yu is likely to be found right in the Garden because the matriarch's wish is to join kin to kin. Her spirit buoyed by this unexpected discovery, though she has no way of knowing that the identification of her as the selected candidate of the matriarch is an erroneous inference of the servants, Dai-yu's health takes a turn for the better.

The suddenness of her ostensible recovery has received severe criticism, for her health's oscillation has been taken as another indication of the author or redactor's uncertain hand in the last forty chapters of the narrative.[49] It should be pointed out, however, that its place in the action itself is not illogically plotted, for Dai-yu's dramatic sense of betterment in chapter 90 may be interpreted as that period of brief remission before the final collapse which is one of the classic symptoms of the advanced state of pulmonary tuberculosis.[50] What is most damaging to Dai-yu's cause is that these abrupt changes in her condition have at last impressed upon the grandmother that this girl is too weak to live very long. Hence her final resolution: let Bao-yu marry first, then propose marriage on behalf of Dai-yu to someone else.

Wholly ignorant of the fact that her future is already determined, Dai-yu in those last days of her life presents a pathetic figure who could clutch at anything

---

[48] Unable or unwilling to detect the irony of the narrative's rendering of this marvelous scene, Redologists consider it to be another testimony to the inferior quality of the last forty chapters, for Bao-yu is now said to be depicted as one lustful of career success and advancement in officialdom, a damning inconsistency in the representation of his character. See *HLMZP*, p. 430. What the modern commentators fail to notice is that not once did the narrative actually report the content of Bao-yu's words of congratulation; his action was simply narrated (*dao xi*). He was never allowed to say directly that he was pleased by his father's advancement.

[49] See Lin Yiliang, "*Hongloumeng* xin lun," pp. 196–97.

[50] See Sir William Osler, *The Principles and Practice of Medicine*, p. 249; Russell L. Cecil, *A Textbook of Medicine*, p. 214. I have deliberately consulted standard medical texts published prior to the widespread use of modern antibiotics. For an astonishing portrayal of the mental and physical feats of which a dying TB patient is capable, see Albert Camus, *A Happy Death*.

to keep alive her hope. The capitulation of her intelligence to her desperate longing becomes most apparent in the episode of a begonia tree suddenly bloom- ing in late autumn (chaps. 94–5). When various members of the family puzzle over this curious omen and speculate on what sort of meaning it may portend, the suggestion by Li Wan that it is likely a herald of some happy tidings con- cerning Bao-yu strikes the fancy of Dai-yu at once.

> She spoke jubilantly: "One of our farmers long ago also had a bramble bush. Because the three sons in that family decided to divide up their inheritance, the plant withered. Later, when the three brothers were moved to live in harmony again in one place, the plant revived and bloomed. We can see from this that even grasses and plants follow human affairs. Now that Second Elder Brother (that is, Bao-yu) is truly working hard in his studies, Uncle must be very pleased, and that's why the tree blossoms." When the grandmother and Lady Wang heard this, they, too, were pleased, saying, "Miss Lin's comparison is very reasonable, very interesting!" (*HLM* 3: 1,330, my translation)

This statement of Dai-yu probably represents the closest attempt she has ever made to ingratiate herself with the elders of the family. The reference to Bao-yu's diligence and all that pandering to superstition seem so entirely out of character with what we have seen of her previously that one would wonder if the writer knew what he was doing here, were it not for the pathos and irony that her words also reveal. Unwitting of her own preincarnate iden- tity, she does not realize either that "grasses and plants [that] follow human affairs," from the point of view of the framing myth of her story, make for the originating seed of woe. Though she succeeds for a fleeting moment in elicit- ing a favorable reaction from the grandmother and mother of her lover, she has no means to stop the floodtide of disaster that is about to strike. Immedi- ately thereafter, Bao-yu goes crazy because he has mysteriously lost his birth stone; his illness, the death of his sister Yuan-chun, and the necessity of his father going abroad for official business descend on the family in rapid succession, the cumulative effect of which is to hasten the elders' desire to conclude a quick marriage for the young man. When at last the choice of Bao- chai becomes known to Aroma, her loyalty to Bao-yu and his feelings over- rides her approbation of Bao-chai, as we have seen, but her valiant attempt to plead his cause before the matriarch and Lady Wang (chap. 96) only precipi- tates Xi-feng's ultimate scheme of a substitute bride.

Throughout these events in the Jia household, Dai-yu remains mostly by herself, her doubt and bewilderment also intensifying to such an extent that she would now interpret everything according to her own wishes (chap. 95).

> She even grew happy when she recalled the old myth of gold-and-jade, thinking to herself: "Truly one can't believe the words of Buddhists and Daoists. For if gold and jade indeed had affinity, then how could Bao-yu have lost that piece of jade? Perhaps it's because of me their affair of gold-and-jade has been broken

up. Who knows?" After reflecting like this for a long time, she felt even more relieved, so much so that the fatigue of the day seemed to have worn off by itself and she began to read again. Nightingale, on the other hand, felt very tired and repeatedly urged Dai-yu to sleep. When she lay down, her thoughts drifted once more to the begonia tree. "This piece of jade," she thought, "has been brought from the womb; it's no ordinary thing. Its appearance and disappearance must have some significance. If the begonia blossoms point to a happy event, then he shouldn't have lost the piece of jade. Come to think of it, these flowers must be unlucky. Could it be that he would have to face something unfortunate?" As she pondered thus, she began to grieve once more. As soon as she thought of the possibility of their marriage, however, she felt that this flower was predestined to bloom just as the piece of jade was predestined to disappear. Her feelings thus alternating between sadness and gladness, she did not fall asleep until the hour of the fifth watch. (*HLM* 3: 1,342, my translation)

The primitive concept of *atê*, according to T. C. W. Stinton, a modern classicist, "whereby gods achieve their ends by perverting human action and making use of human error," is not only central to Greek tragedy but also may be understood as having much in common with the Aristotelian notion of *hamartia*, flaw or missing the mark. For the gods, "from another point of view (which may have been Aristotle's), . . . are simply a projection of the unaccountable in human action and human suffering." In the language of early Greek poetry of both epic and drama, the characteristic workings of *atê* may thus be described: "the god induces a malfunction of the *phrenes* (intelligence, mind) resulting in *apatê* (delusion, self-deception)."[51]

Although the self-deceiving optimism of Dai-yu may not quite evince the weightiness of a tragic error, her behavior does bring to mind the terrifying truth of the choral observation in Sophocles' *Antigone*:

If evil good appear
To any, Fate is near.[52]

Dai-yu's emotional vacillation does not have to last very long. Thunderstruck by the chanced revelation of a nameless maid in the garden that Bao-yu will indeed take Bao-chai as his bride while she herself will be married off to someone else, Dai-yu makes one last effort to see him (chap. 96). The effect of this inadvertent disclosure, according to the narrative, assaults her emotions and her body with a ferocity surpassing even the potent strains of *The Peony Pavilion* that captured her imagination long ago (chap. 23).[53] In that shattering encounter

---

[51] T. C. W. Stinton, "*Hamartia* in Aristotle and Greek Tragedy," pp. 172, 173.

[52] F. Storr's translation of lines 621–23. See the Loeb edition of Sophocles, 1: 363.

[53] "Dai-yu's heart felt as though oil, soy-sauce, sugar and vinegar had all been poured into it at once. She could not tell which flavour predominated, the sweet, the sour, the bitter or the salty. . . . Her body felt as though it weighed a hundred tons, her feet were as wobbly as if she

with fictive representation of human transience, the young girl collapsed on a nearby rockery as if "intoxicated or delirious (*ru zui ru chi*)." Here, the revelation of her unalterable fate in this life makes her deranged or, as the titular couplet asserts, "lose her original nature (*mi ben xing*)." The final interview with Bao-yu, too desolate for tears, presents the sorry sight of two hapless lovers "staring into each other's faces and smiling like a pair of half-wits" (*SS* 4: 338; *HLM* 3: 1,361).

In depicting Dai-yu's experience from the time of her dream to her death as governed by several incidents that incite her false hopes yielding in turn to greater despair, the action of this part of *Hongloumeng* is not unworthy of comparison with that of *The Trojan Women* by Euripides. As D. J. Conacher has written so perceptively of this play,

> a mere sequence of disaster . . . does not make a drama, and in default of real action on the part of Hecuba there appears a faint outline of policy and even of a curious intermittent hope which punctuates the sufferings. Again and again, this hope is stamped out and gives way to desolation, only to flicker forth in some new place until its final quenching at the end of the play. Thus a certain rhythm is introduced in what would otherwise be a mere chain of woeful experiences, and it is this rhythm which informs the structure of the play.[54]

After Troy's occupation, Hecuba must face, in addition to the total defeat and ruination of her city, the progressive destruction of her family and heirs—the enslavement of Cassandra and Andromache no less than the cruel death decreed for her grandson, Astyanax. Any hope she has for some form of refuge for the Trojan women and for the future revival of their race is steadily extinguished. In a similar way, Dai-yu must journey from her uncertain speculations just prior to her dream, through the heightened delusion induced by the incidents of the begonia tree and the loss of Bao-yu's jade, to the terminal fulfilment of her greatest fear. Unlike Hecuba, however, who at least survives, confirmed in the outrageous knowledge that the gods are cruel and utterly indifferent to human misery but also somewhat consoled by the dim awareness that Trojan suffering will win for her race indestructible poetic vindication (see lines 1,240–50; 1,280–82), Dai-yu expires in the agony of doubt. Her unfinished accusation, hanging on her lips as she dies, expresses her final but futile effort to determine how Bao-yu could be so cruel as to have given consent to the marriage and thereby reject her.[55]

In this sense, Dai-yu's death is indeed the saddest of all the many deaths of

---

were walking on cotton-floss. She could only manage one step at a time" (*SS* 4: 356; *HLM* 3: 1,359–60).

[54] *Euripidean Drama*, p. 139.

[55] Her apocope may perhaps be best completed as *"Bao-yu, ni hao renxin?"* or "Bao-yu, how could you be so cruel?"

women portrayed in the narrative. Even the maid Skybright has the comfort of a tender visit by Bao-yu before she dies, but Dai-yu goes to the grave alone and unattended, except by her maids; not one of the senior members of the Jia household comes to see her during the final hours. Her solitude justifies the bitter thought of Nightingale—"Why are these people so hard-hearted and cold?"—and recapitulates her essential condition when she first enters the Jia mansion: she comes and departs in complete isolation. If the representative greatness of the *Odyssey* is to be seen in the experience of one lonely voyager's homecoming made to articulate the universal longing of all wayfarers to return to father, wife, son, and domestic felicity, then the profound and perduring appeal of Dai-yu's story perhaps may be explained by the way it dramatizes the fears and frustrations of the women of an entire culture. An orphan and a suppliant, Dai-yu seeks refuge in a distant household and succeeds in gaining the affection of both its aged matriarch and young master but, alas, she is no match for the fateful working of ill health, human deceit, and mythic beliefs. "The girl's upset:/Not knowing how the future's to be met." So sings one of the girls during a party in chapter 28, and the question of marital future, which is *the* question of destiny, is not the obsession of Dai-yu alone. Virtually all the young women of the Garden, be they ladies, concubines, or servants, have asked this question at one time or another. When the matriarch decides against making Dai-yu her granddaughter-in-law, her decision is based not on the sudden hostility she feels toward the girl but on her love for her grandson, who must have a healthy wife better able to give him an heir. As the story draws to its denouement, Bao-chai is indeed carrying the child of Bao-yu, though he will soon be leaving the family forever and the child will grow up fatherless, just like the mother. All the goodwill of the matriarch cannot prevent the tragic and ironic perversion of purposive action, and Dai-yu dies as much a victim of human duplicity as of human good intention, since the deep love between her and Bao-yu is sacrificed by the family's concern for biological perpetuation. Mark van Doren is quite right when he says in his preface to Wang Chi-chen's translation of the work:

> The whole society is doubtless what seems most interesting in the end. It is a human organism that must obey the laws of its own survival; and it does so no matter what individual gets in its way. To certain of its members it now and then seems heartless. But to say this is to suggest how far *Dream of the Red Chamber* transcends the ordinary novel of manners. It transcends it, indeed, to the point of tragedy.[56]

The full tragic stature of Dai-yu, however, is not to be measured merely by the depth of her suffering, as sustained and excruciating a portrayal as that may be, comparable to any in world literature, but also by the strenuousness of

---

[56] Tsao Hsueh-chin, *Dream of the Red Chamber*, pp. v–vi.

her struggle—in her words, her poems, her tears, and even her dreams—against impossible constraints and overwhelming odds. She has fought and won the love of Bao-yu, but she is powerless to bring their love to its desired consummation. In her very attempt to do so, when she exploits the meager means available to her, she also encounters adverse circumstances that, as James Redfield has said of tragic plots, "seem to give evidence of a hidden pattern hostile to man."[57]

In classical Greek tragedy, the heroic men and women learn from their confrontation with necessity (*anangkê, moira*), be it embodied in fate or the gods, and their coming to knowledge or recognition usually coincides with their destruction. When Oedipus tears out his eyes with his own hands, he discovers both his innocence and the gods' complicity.[58] If Lin Dai-yu was obsessively concerned with how the absence of parents had rendered her powerless, the presence of other loving kin—grandmother, Bao-yu, the friendly Bao-chai, the kindly spoken Aunty Xue—never improved her lot. Her heart-rending question to the matriarch in her dream (chap. 82)—"Lao Tai-tai, you have always been merciful, the one who loves me most. How could you not care for me at all in my hour of need?"—bespeaks a knowledge that is both truthful (that she was indeed the apple of grandmother's eye) and uncomprehending (that even the grandmother's affection cannot transgress patriarchy's central desire of preserving the family line). In this sense, I agree in great part with Andrew Plaks, who has written in his fine study of the Garden's archetypical structure and signficance that in this narrative, "it is a block in perception rather than a failure of action or a weakness of will that gives rise to the tragic situation."[59]

Plaks' observant comment finds confirmation, in fact, in the poetic prophecy of the final section of the song cycle, "A Dream of Golden Days" (chap. 5):

> The disillusioned to their convents fly,
> The still deluded miserably die.
>
> (*SS* 1: 144; *HLM* 1: 89)

The word translated as "disillusioned" here has the literal meaning of one who has seen through everything (*kanpo di*), and Dai-yu, unlike Bao-yu and his cousin Xi-chun, who both seek ultimate refuge at the Gate of Emptiness, has not been capable of attaining such perspicacity of vision. Xi-chun's assessment of her (chap. 82), in fact, has the authority of a final verdict because its language echoes the prophetic oracle: "Cousin Lin is such an intelligent person, but I view her as someone who can't quite see through it all (*qiao bu po*)" (*HLM* 3: 1,187, my translation). From the perspective of disillusionment or

---

[57] Redfield, *Nature and Culture in the "Iliad,"* p. 86.
[58] See lines 1,329–33 of *Oedipus Rex* (Loeb edition).
[59] Plaks, *Archetype and Allegory*, p. 78.

disenchantment, hope is but another form of delusion. A modern scholar's verdict is likewise on the mark when she declares: "the problems raised by human passion in the novel are not merely social. In a world where passion is the product of illusion, there can be no happy love stories."[60] But if delusion could create so captivating a life as Lin Dai-yu's, and madness so memorable a love, who would want for *her* enlightenment?

[60] Waltner, "On Not Becoming a Heroine," p. 78.

Conclusion

> Poetry, to be
> Poetry truly, must be more than poetry;
> in perfection
> It is never fiction,
> It never falsifies.
>
> (Elder Olson, "A Valentine for Marianne Moore")

IN ITS CONVERSATION with Vanitas, the dramatized reader, at the beginning of the novel, the stone already bearing the inscribed narrative of its own worldly experience has fashioned and proclaimed an apology for its story that is based on opposition to the convention of miming history and the enlistment of personal experience.[1] Although the reference by Stone as narrator to "a number of females" whom he has spent "half a lifetime studying with [its] own eyes and ears" (*SS* 1: 50; *HLM* 1: 5) has undoubtedly helped to feed the critical reception of the novel as an autobiographical account, the importance of the account itself according to Stone, however, is that its perusal may help stimulate in the readers "the contemplation of [the women's] actions and motives." As I have pointed out in Chapter III, this seemingly casual statement actually brings into view one of the most audacious and enduring claims of the writer of fiction: namely, the capacity of knowing the mind and feelings of another person, whether contemporary with the writer or inhabiting a different space and time. And it is this alleged capacity that enables the writer in the West frequently to assume the "godlike privileges of unhampered vision, penetration to the innermost recesses of the [fictive] agents' minds, free movement in time and space, and knowledge of past and future."[2] In China, such privileges were readily thought to be part of the prerogative and authority of the historian.

We might recall here the words of Zhang Xuecheng, the eighteenth-century scholar and philosopher of history, that I cited in Chapter I. Discussing the unavoidable necessity of adding or subtracting details in an account of the

---

[1] Miming history: "All the romances ever written have an artificial period setting—Han or Tang for the most part" (*SS* 1: 49; *HLM* 1: 4–5). Stone's remark at this point in the 1982 edition is collated with the 1754 text, and there is thus a signficant difference in the opening sentences between the Chinese text cited here and the English translation. Personal experience: "Surely my 'number of females,' whom I spent half a lifetime studying with my own eyes and ears, are preferable to this kind of stuff" (*SS* 1: 50; *HLM* 1: 5).

[2] Meir Sternberg, *Expositional Modes and Temporal Ordering in Fiction*, p. 257.

past, Zhang sought to establish a normative principle of stability amidst the vicissitudes of recorded history and language (*wenshi*). The proper guidance for the historical author (*zuo zhe*), when attempting to set down the words or speeches of past persons, resides in "what he [the historian] desires to be the case (*suo yu ran*), so that he would infer [the content of past utterances] only from the intentionality of the past speaker."[3] This remark of Zhang not only highlights his unquestioning reliance on the possibility of ascertaining with accuracy the intentionality of historical subjects, perhaps an understandable assumption on his part but a difficult, if not impossible, undertaking in our view of the matter today. More significantly, it reveals that the "truth" or "meaning" of history is dependent on the subjectivity of the historian, on what he or she "desires to be the case." It is such a desire that impels the historian to "add" or "delete" (*zeng, sun*) words or events, or to "invent (*chuang*) that which is deemed appropriate to the words and events" to be recorded.[4]

As astute as Zhang was on matters of history and historiography, he offered no solution to the perplexing issue that surfaces in his writings: namely, how could the historian's propriety of desire—his or her virtuous intentionality—effectively produce proper history? If pressed on this issue, Zhang might resort to the answer that the rectitude of disposition borne of arduous moral self-cultivation would guarantee accuracy in both inference and record. A formulation like this would, in fact, comport with the Confucian discourse on desire that only an educated and disciplined nature could produce the politically—and thus also morally—desirable artifacts of culture.

Whether the historical writings preserved in the long course of Chinese civilization have managed to fulfil this prescribed ideal is not at issue here. The products of literary history, however, provide luxriant examples of "unofficial" or "unorthodox" histories (*yeshi*) existing alongside the voluminous specimens of official histories (*zhengshi*). The question of reliability, accuracy, and scope aside, what this mixture of history and pseudo history reveals is surely the widespread though not often declared conviction that there cannot be merely one view or one account of an event, a person, or a recorded statement. The differences of history exist, in other words, not only because of the differences among historiographical objects, but supremely because of the possible differences in knowledge and representation resulting from differences in the intentionality of the historiographer.

These presumed differences, in fact, help clarify the significance of the term *yanyi*, traditionally but misleadingly translated as "romance," which denominates a large body of fictive and near-fictive writings in premodern China. Because the word *yan* can mean both to popularize and to expound in a detailed and exhaustive manner, *yanyi* is hardly a "baseless story with exaggerated and

---

[3] "Yu Chen Guanmin gongpu lun shixue," p. 14.
[4] Zhang Xuecheng, *Wenshi tongyi*, p. 290 (Zhonghua edition).

fanciful details" or "an account of heroic exploits in an imaginary setting," which constitutes a part of our contemporary dictionary definition of romance.[5] The Chinese term is better thought of as a story that purports to provide an alternative perspective or propound a systematic development of hidden meanings, and that takes on the semblance of an extended allegory.[6]

So understood, *yanyi* encompasses not only a large quantity of prose writings of the medieval and late imperial periods, the content of which has to do with fictionalized or embroidered history. Arguably, its spirit and character also pervade the large genre of "singing about history (*yong shi*)" that includes within itself countless titles of the lyric tradition (both *shi* and *ci*) and numerous works of traditional drama that purport to give new or different meaning to known events and recognized persons of the past.

That such an understanding is shared by the author of *Hongloumeng* may readily be seen in the episode of chapter 64 in which Lin Dai-yu composes five poems celebrating five famous beauties of history. The praise that Bao-chai ostensibly lavishes on her cousin actually articulates a brief poetics of *yong shi*.

> Regardless of whatever subject one chooses for a poem, the composition must be adept in overturning the meaning of the ancients. Merely plodding along the footsteps of others will turn the poem into a second-rate composition. The diction and lines may be refined, but it cannot be considered a good poem. Thus the many poets who had previously taken Lady Bright [Wang Zhao-jun] as their theme have variously emphasized the sad fate of Lady Bright herself, the wickedness of the painter Mao Yan-shou, or the frivolousness of the Han emperor who employed him to paint portraits of court ladies rather than portraits of distinguished statesmen and soldiers, and so on. Later, new twists were given to this theme by Wang An-shi:
>
>> What brush could ever capture a beauty's breathing grace?
>> The painter did not merit death who botched that lovely face.
>
> and by Ou-yang Xiu:
>
>> A prince so ill able to control what went on under his nose
>> Must hope in vain to impose his rule on remote barbarian foes.

[5] *Random House Unabridged Dictionary*, second edition, s. v.

[6] Such is, in fact, the claim made by the nineteenth-century commentator Zhang Xinzhi, when he uses a vast network of neo-Confucian and *Yijing* terminologies to expound the meaning of *Hongloumeng*. See *Sanjia, passim*. For an earlier example of the term *yanyi*'s association with literary and religious allegory, one may consult the novel by Pan Jingruo around 1615 entitled *Sanjiao kaimi guizheng yanyi* (A Dilation of the Meaning of How the Three Religions Expose Delusions and Return to the Truth). The manuscript, preserved in Tenri University Library, is now reprinted in a three-volume edition. See bibliography.

Both these two poems were able to present the poets' own views that differed from those of other people. Today these five poems by Cousin Lin can also substantiate the claim of presenting each of her subjects in a novel and interesting light. (*SS* 3: 258, text modified; *HLM* 2: 916)

Bao-chai's remark about "overturning the meaning of the ancients" and about presenting one's own views may strike a reader familiar with contemporary literary theory as quaintly evocative of the agonistic poetics of Harold Bloom, but what is germane to the present discussion is not the ostensible emphasis on originality. Rather, it concerns what her comment does not deal with explicitly: namely, the epistemological issue of truth. How could Wang An-shi know that the painter did not truly merit death? On what evidence, apart from the wisdom of folk idiom, could Ou-yang Xiu justify the a fortiori charge against the emperor's incompetence?

Questions of this kind, in fact, may be extended to the five poems authored by Dai-yu. How did the young poet know that she had accurately expressed Yu Ji's point of view when she wrote: "Let the others wait for the hangman, to be hacked and quartered and rent; / Better the taste of one's own steel in the decent dark of a tent" (*SS* 3: 257; *HLM* 2: 914). Was it in truth Li Jing's manner (meeting the powerful Yang Shu in plain clothes and refusing to bow) and confident speech that irrevocably caught Red Duster's eye of favor (*SS* 3: 258; *HLM* 2: 915)? If Dai-yu's treatment of her poetic subjects are adjudged "novel and interesting" by her cousin, much as the poetic lines by historical figures like Wang An-shi and Ou-yang Xiu are praised for their originality, does that mean that their compositions have in some way fully satisfied the requisite of historical truth—of proper desire and inference—set forth by Zhang Xuecheng? Does not Zhang's reference to the historian's own desire no less than the kind of verdict laid down by Bao-chai also expose the possibility of multiple versions or interpretations of the same person or event? Even more importantly, is not the very possibility of that multiplicity ensured by the unavoidable difference of desire among different writers who may envision another scenario, entertain a novel motive, or encourage a new explanation?

To answer in the affirmative these last three questions is to acknowledge that the constraints determining the activities of the historian and the poet or the writer of fiction are often very similar. The historian may insist on the "factuality" of his data and depiction, but to get at those "facts," he or she must often infer (*tui*) or invent (*chuang*) what is probable or plausible. By contrast, the poet may be free to represent something ultimately as insubstantial or unreal as "airy nothing," but the privilege to give to this nothing "a local habitation and a name" necessarily entails the weighing of probability or plausibility, including even "the contemplation of actions and motives."

The Tang poet Du Fu in his familiar poem, "Thinking about My Brother in a Moonlit Night," asserts that

> The dew from tonight will turn white;
> The moon only at home shines bright.[7]

If one is to question how the poet could know that such a condition existed in his distant home, the answer apparent to virtually all readers is to be found in his *qing*, his feelings of sadness induced by war, distance, and separation—all plainly evoked in the entire poem. The "truth" he ascribes to *his* moon is thus one fashioned by his own disposition and desire; it is not a condition or quality that can be verified by historical research (was the nocturnal atmosphere at the Jingzhao Prefecture, commonly identified by scholars as Du's real ancestral home, somehow clearer than that in the rest of the country around 759 when the poem was thought to have been written?) or by the canons of modern physics. In a similar manner, the three poems on the chrysanthemum by the fictive Lin Dai-yu (chap. 38) not only make constant use of the familiar literary device of prosopopoeia, the imaginary personfication of inanimate objects. Transforming the plant into her conversation partner, Dai-yu's lines disclose as well her readiness to put herself in the place of the plant so as to articulate its melancholy and vexation. In her third poem on "The Dream of the Chrysanthemum," for example, Dai-yu writes:

> Following the wild goose, into sleep I slid;
> From which now, startled by the cricket's cry,
> Midst cold and fog and dying leaves I wake,
> With no one by to tell of my heart's ache.
>
> (*SS* 2: 252; *HLM* 1: 528)

The poet's impersonation of a flower here is, of course, a commonplace device of rhetoric, long recognized and utilized not only in Chinese versification but also in many poetic traditions the world over. What the lines by Du Fu and Lin Dai-yu illustrate is the dialectic of literary composition that underlies much of traditional Chinese poetic practice. On the one hand, the language of both Du and Lin reveals the projective and shaping power of their own desire. Their poems are instances of "thinking by the spirit (*shensi*)" formulated by Liu Xie that I cited in Chapter II as an example of pathocentric understanding of literary language: "ascending mountains, one's disposition (*qing*) will fill the mountains, and viewing the seas, one's intent will overflow the seas."[8] On the other hand, the representations that give voice to Du's and Lin's sentiments cannot be regarded as literal transcriptions of the poets' conditions. The moon that shines brightly only at home and the chrysanthemum that can fall asleep chasing wild geese and wake up chafing at chirping crickets are inventions of

---

[7] See *QTS, juan* 225; 4: 249.
[8] *Wenxin dialong zhu, juan* 6, 26: 1a.

desire as well. They are in truth fictions that, nonetheless, have a claim to being truthful, in the sense that poets are presumed to be able to know and to render—appositely and plausibly—the situations, the circumstances, and the inner dispositions of selected subjects (*zhiqing, zhi qi qing*).

Although such a conception of fiction may not find frequent and explicit formulation in traditional poetics, this does not mean that its utility is seldom recognized or exploited. Quite the contrary, the lengthy history of lyric poetry in China is replete with examples of ingenious inventions that are nothing if not also wondrous fiction. One striking instance of such poetic license may be found in Bai Juyi's three poems written on behalf of a dead woman. Moved by the several elegies that his best friend Yuan Zhen had penned in the memory of his deceased wife, Bai wrote in her supposed voice to reply to her husband's poetic tribute.[9] Characteristic of the lucid style for which this Tang poet was famous, Bai's unadorned diction and simple syntax make it abundantly clear that the poetic speaker in the three lyrics acted as someone addressing her husband from the grave.

She praised his spousal virtue:

> I had married a Liang Hong for six, seven years.
> . . .
> I forgot we were poor for my husband was good.

(Poem One)

She teased him about his addictive indolence:

> He loved books and wines, sleeping till high noon.
> Our spring yard, rain-wrecked, grew only grass;
> Our kitchen, snow-packed, had not even smoke.

(Poem One)

She worried about their young daughter:

> Worries came to my illness for our daughter was young.

(Poem One)

> The widower still is tied to his post;
> A young girl has yet to conquer her grief.

(Poem Two)

She took note of their unbridgeable separation:

> When you go to the empty terrace,
> You leave at dawn but return at night.

---

[9] See "Gan Yuan Jiu daowangshi yin wei daida sanshou," in *Bai xiangshan shiji* 14: 8a–b (*SBBY*).

> When I entered the terrace of the springs,
> The gates by the springs won't open again.

(Poem Two)

And she reminded him of their familiar haunts:

> Forget not the spots where we used to sit and walk—
> Beneath the steps of rear hall, before the bamboos.

(Poem Three)

In a poetic tradition in which male poets have presumed to speak in the voice of women for over three thousand years, Bai's rhetoric and poetic gesture here should hardly occasion surprise or even notice. And yet Bai's brief compositions (one heptasyllabic octet, one pentasyllabic octet, one heptasyllabic quatrain) surely merit attention, if only because they may serve to clarify the complex relations between poetry, autobiobiography, and fiction. Modern critcism often refers to these complex relations as the decisive difference dividing premodern Chinese verse from its Western counterpart, and they also bear directly upon our consideration of *Hongloumeng*.

It is commonly alleged that because China lacks "concepts comparable to Aristotelian mimesis or Christian figura," Chinese poetry is concerned with neither "the representation of action in time" nor fictionality. "Rather, the object of representation is mood at a point in time and correspondences between mind and state of the surrounding world, . . . [and] the literary work is generally understood by the critic as if it were personal history."[10] Because China has not developed a concept of either creation or a transcendent creator, not only must the circumambiant world be reckoned as uncreated but even the poet himself must be disassociated from any creative activity. Thus, according to Stephen Owen, "in the uncreated world such willful fabrication [as that by Western poets] is perverse, a mere deception: the poet is concerned with the authentic presentation of 'what is,' either interior experience or exterior percept. The *shih* poet's function is to see the order in the world, the pattern behind its infinite division; like Confucius, he 'transmits but does not create.'"[11]

Since internal experience or subjectivity is always expected to find "authentic presentation," the poem is quite properly received as ultimately autobiographical. Drawing on a discussion of the Confucian exegesis of the *Poetry Classic*, Pauline Yu also contends that "a poem is generally read as a literal comment on an actual historical situation." What such a commentarial tradition bequeaths to the culture are not only "moralizing, topically allusive readings" but also the persistent notion of a poem "not as a work of fiction but as what Barbara Smith has called a 'natural utterance.' . . . In the traditional Chinese view, poetry

---

[10] Craig Fisk, "Literary Criticism," p. 49.
[11] *Traditional Chinese Poetry and Poetics,* p. 84.

chronicles the life of an individual as naturally as it does the fate of a feudal state, and the reading process becomes one of contextualization rather than the attribution of some referential otherness."[12]

Such generalizations about traditional Chinese poetry and poetics are all observant and accurate—up to a point. Certainly they are consistent with that part of contemporary Chinese criticism that continues to read Lin Dai-yu's chrysanthemum poems as revealing not only the fictive woman's character but also of the disposition of Cao Xue-qin, putatively the real author.[13] How well such a perspective helps us perceive what is going on in Bai Juyi's poems is another matter. No doubt a dear friend's elegies for a deceased wife provided the real stimulus to Bai's compositions, as the title plainly tells us, and the poet's mood was the state of his being moved (*gan*) by those linguistic mementos of grief and desire. The indisputable context of the writings also had to be located in the known and well-recorded friendship that existed between Bai and Yuan Zhen. All of these facts are thus firmly historical.

Can Bai's three poems, however, be properly construed as an authentic presentation of "what is" his "interior experience"? Can they be read merely as "a literal comment on an actual historical situation," as "natural utterances" chronicling "the life of a [real] individual"? My reply to these last two questions must be a resounding No. The poems may be contextualized, indeed, by Bai's historical experience, but the poems themselves are representations of a dead woman speaking to her still-living husband—in the acts of praise, consolation, mild rebuke, shared remembrance, and mutual lament. As such, they produce a small but well-wrought and moving fiction. And the fiction exists not simply because the speaking woman is a dead woman, but first and foremost because a man purports to speak as a female subject.

Contemporary criticism of Chinese poetry, informed by feminist concerns, may justifiably protest this agelong, transgressive habit of male poets. But acceptance of this critique should not prevent our recognition that the act of impersonation—when an actor or a poet speaks in the guise and voice of another—is one of the most universal devices of artifice and one of the most fundamental feats of creative freedom. Drama and stage performances may be relatively late in development in Chinese history, and as we have been reminded repeatedly, Chinese critical vocabulary does not readily include notions of creation or creator. This does not mean, however, that Chinese poets have been impervious to the possibility of rhetorical and linguistic ventriloquism, or have lacked a sense of the dramatic. Although the Confucian discourse on desire persists in grounding a stimulus-response aesthetics upon the insistence that all expressions are inescapably and finally self-expressions, the poets themselves at every opportunity have been eager to indulge in the license to chant

---

[12] "Alienation Effects: Comparative Literature and the Chinese Tradition," pp. 172, 173.

[13] See, for example, Cai Yijiang, *Hongloumeng shici qufu pingzhu*, pp. 208–9.

and write in the voice of another—an abandoned wife, a failing official, an aged recluse, an innocent youth, a warrior of a distant past, a heroic martyr of a different state, a ghost in search of lost love, an illiterate bond-servant meeting again his former lord, even an exulting flower or a grieving insect. Each time that the poet writes from the point of view of imagined identity and simulated subjectivity, the lyric in fact turns dramatic because the poet purports to assume—however obliquely or fleetingly—the consciousness and personality of someone else (remember Xue Bao-cai's use of the first person pronoun in her catkins lyric discussed in Chapter v). Drama is feigning, and feigning is fiction; "referential otherness" cannot be avoided in all such "willful fabrications." There may be endless reasons why poets want to write in this manner, and their writings under critical analysis may yield all sorts of revelation about the poet's life and condition. But the poem as the poetic fiction a writer has invented need never be identical with autobiography, because the manner and means of representation can generate a difference in perceived intention and reception. In this regard, traditional Chinese poetics and the commentarial tradition are often blind to the practice of their own poets.

It is, however, the acute awareness of the possibility of impersonation and its fictive implications that led ironically the Confucian tradition to its cardinal emphasis in exegesis: namely, representations of sexual desire are really about something else. Once more, in the words of Zhang Xuecheng I cited in Chapter II, "the ancients, when thinking of the ruler or yearning for their friends, frequently entrust such feelings to the depiction of ardent sentiments between men and women."[14] To legitimate erotic expressions of one variety or another, Zhang and his like down through the centuries would resort to allegoresis by coopting both words and sentiments (*tuoyan, tuoqing*) of an other for a supposedly more noble purpose. What Zhang fails to mention, of course, is that allegories, too, are fictions. When a man yearns for his ruler but chooses to represent his experience—in verse or narrative—as a woman longing for her lover, the literal referent of such a story cannot be real. The unreality of the referent, so goes this line of thinking, would render the erotic elements innocuous by making them metaphors of desire that is acceptable to Confucian morality and politics. In the kind of criticism Zhang advocates, therefore, fictions are continuously created by his desire to save the appearances of autobiographies from illicit desire.

This observation about the eighteenth-century scholar may return us to a few final remarks about *Hongloumeng*. In the famous self-exegesis passage that opens the narrative and is part of Stone's apologia for its story, we have witnessed what appears to be strong hints of autobiography as the basis for the writing. There are repeated allusions to the girls and women of the narrator's acquaintance whom he admires and reveres; there is the explicit confession of

[14] *Wenshi tongyi, juan* 5, 29a (*SBBY*).

past and present faults; and there is the expression of the desire to redeem personal failures through the making of a narrative. Understandably, therefore, Hu Shi and a host of other modern Chinese critics have sought to read the story as a thinly veiled account of a historical author's life.

The autobiographical reading, however, is virtually oblivious to the implication of fiction couched in the Stone's apology that claims the authoritative knowledge and representation of other minds and lives. To delineate the full import of such a claim, I can do no better than borrow the opening words of Wayne Booth in a book that has now become a classic in the study of fiction:

> One of the most obviously artificial devices of the storyteller is the trick of going beneath the surface of the action to obtain a reliable view of a character's mind and heart. Whatever our ideas may be about the natural way to tell a story, artifice is unmistakably present whenever the author tells us what no one in so-called real life could possibly know. In life we never know anyone but ourselves by thoroughly reliable internal signs, and most of us achieve an all too partial view even of ourselves. It is in a way strange, then, that in literature from the very beginning we have been told motives directly and authoritatively without being forced to rely on those shaky inferences about other men which we cannot avoid in our own lives.[15]

To stress authorial omniscience as an indication of fictive narration is not to deny the writer's privilege of using historical materials. Of course, he or she is utterly free to draw on all kinds of data from both personal and larger histories for incorporation into the story being fashioned. What, however, such rhetorical prerogative provides for the writer of fiction, as Booth's remark and the rest of his study make clear, concerns the nature and scope of representation, the extent of control, and the internal mechanisms for verification (that is, what counts for narrative reliability). *Hongloumeng* emerges in its generic character as fiction mainly because, responding to the words and actions of different allegorical figures in the work's framing episodes and to the narrator's promptings, a reader will choose to read it in the light of certain functions and codes of narrative embedded therein. Even if scholarly research continues to enlarge our knowledge of Cao Xue-qin's life and household to the extent that we may identify with relative certainty the historical figures on whom the characterizations of several novelistic personages are based (an aunt for Lin Dai-yu, a cousin for Xue Bao-chai, as some critics have speculated), the text as we have it cannot properly be read as a transcript of actual events and experiences.

The autobiographical reading, moreover, conveniently ignores or slights the complex and sophisticated system of rhetoric that the text constantly uses

---

[15] Wayne C. Booth, *The Rhetoric of Fiction,* p. 3.

to call attention to its own fictiveness. Unlike the compact economy of the Chinese lyric, which permits the creation of fiction on only a limited scale and scope, a prose narrative of *Hongloumeng*'s magnitude and vintage (coming so late in the line of monumental novels produced by Chinese literary culture) has at its disposal a vast array of rhetorical devices to serve its inventive purpose. Impersonation is only one major medium, but it is an important one because the narrative's indebtedness to traditional Chinese drama has been widely acknowledged. Moreover, other means as compendiously recorded by another contemporary theorist may also be in view.

> Signs pointing to the fictionality of fiction are many and well known. The list is extensive: authors' intrusions; narrators' intrusions; multiple narrators; humorous narrative that acts as a representation of the author or of a narrator or that suggests an outsider's viewpoint without fully intruding; metalanguage glossing narrative language; generic markers in the titles and subtitles, in prefaces, and in postfaces; emblematic names for characters and places; incompatibilities between narrative voice and viewpoint and characters' voices and viewpoints; incompatibilities between viewpoint and verisimilitude, especially omniscient narrative; signs modifying the narrative's pace and altering the sequence of events (backtracking and anticipation, significant gaps, prolepsis and analepsis); mimetic excesses, such as unlikely recordings of unimportant speech or thought (unimportant but suggestive of actual happenings, of a live presence, creating atmosphere or characterizing persons); and, finally, diegetic overkill, such as the representation of ostensibly insignificant details, the very insignificance of which is significant in a story as a feature of realism. Narratology seems to have neglected the constant coincidence between textual features declaring the fictionality of a story and a reassertion of the truth of that story.[16]

The terminologies of this pointillistic survey may bear the difference of culture and time, but the features and functions of fictional narrative so enumerated are not irrelevant for studying a work like *Hongloumeng*. Virtually all of these signs make their appearance in the Chinese text.

To document fully such appearances would take another tome of comparable length. I have decided in my study to concentrate deliberately on some of the features suggested by the text. Since the opening episodes mention the phenomena of dream (*meng*), mirror (*jian*), and fantasy or invention (*huan*), I have made them part of the discussion. Since its "first" reader declares that its "principal theme is about *qing*," that theme has been given a fairly lengthy investigation. The crucial parts of my interpretation often place enormous weight on paronomastic play and emblematic names, for I agree with Riffaterre that they are "especially blatant indices of fictionality."[17] And if the narrator

---

[16] Michael Riffaterre, *Fictional Truth*, pp. 29–30.

[17] Ibid., p. 33. See also J. Hillis Miller, who has pointed out in his "Introduction" to Charles

invokes early in the narrative what seems like Buddhist wisdom in describing the experience of readerly reception, I have sought to follow his lead to explore how the process of religious enlightenment may parallel aesthetic discovery and act as a trope of literary effect.[18] All in all, I have tried not to neglect what is surely one of the most notable features of *Hongloumeng*—"the constant coincidence between textual features declaring the fictionality of a story and a reassertion of the truth of that story." Thus those readers past and present who want to insist on "there really being such persons and there really being such events (*zhen you qi ren; zhen you qi shi*)" may get to see only a partial picture. Better to read with the "first" reader Vanitas, whose final assessment declares the story of Stone to be

> Uncanny and not uncanny (*qi er bu qi*);
> Vulgar and not vulgar (*su er bu su*);
> Real and not real (*zhen er bu zhen*);
> False and not false (*jia er bu jia*).

(*HLM* 3: 1,646)

Such, indeed, is fiction that does not falsify!

Dickens' *Bleak House*, pp. 22–23, that "the names of so many characters in the novel are either openly metaphorical (Dedlock, Bucket, . . . Krook, . . .) or seem tantalizingly to contain some covert metaphor lying almost on the surface of the word (Tulkinghorn, Turveydrop, Chadband, . . .)." This textual feature, for Miller, betokens Dickens's "implicit recognition that the characters to which he gives such emblematic names are linguistic fictions. The metaphors in their names reveal the fact that they are not real people or even copies of real people. They exist only in language. This overt fictionality is Dickens's way of demystifying the belief, affirmed in Plato's *Cratylus*, that the right name gives the essence of the name." If Miller's reading persuades, what shall we say of Cao Xue-qin's narrative and the Confucian rectification of names? For an interesting study of the significance of personal naming in Chinese culture, see Viviane Alleton, *Les chinous et la passion des noms*.

[18] The utilization of certain familiar Buddhist concepts and terms as aesthetic categories was not an esoteric device peculiar to the author of *Hongloumeng*. Apparently it was enough of a common practice that the fictive Lin Dai-yu could routinely deploy such notions as form (*se*) and appearance (*xiang*) to describe the creature in her poem on the crab in chapter 38. See *HLM* 1: 530. Sun Yunfeng (1764–1814), a celebrated poet and student of Yuan Mei, wrote in her lyric to the tune of "Washing Sand Silk (*Huan xi sha*)" on "My Own Inscription for Painted Plums": "Snap with the moon what seems like emptiness or form (*si se si kong he yue zhe*)." The invocation here of the venerable contrast between emptiness and form has little to do with Buddhist metaphysics. Rather, the two terms seem to function as an apt metaphor for the "ontology" of painted plum flowers. See *Xiangyun guan ci*, 2: 7a, in the *Xiao tanluanshi huike guixiu ci*. My translation of this brief lyric will appear in *An Anthology of Chinese Women Poets: From Ancient Times to 1911*, edited by K'ang-i Sun Chang and Haun Saussy, forthcoming from Stanford University Press.

aimu zhi qing　愛慕之情

aiqing　愛情

anshen leye　安身樂業

baiguan zhe, yuyan ye　稗官者，寓言也

baishi　稗史

bang　榜

bao　報

baobian　褒貶

bei　碑

beiju zhong zhi beiju　悲劇中之悲劇

ben　奔

benxing　本性

bian　變

biao　標

bin　賓

bizhan　筆戰

boxing　薄倖

boxue hongci　博學鴻詞

bu　補

bu ke mian　不可免

bu lei　不類

bu shen mingbai　不甚明白

bu yu wo hao　不與我好

buguo shi caomu zhi ren　不過是草木之人

bujie　不解

butian jishi zhi cai　補天濟世之材

buzhi　不知

cai　才／材

caizi jiaren　才子佳人

cao mu you qing　草木有情

chaodai nianji　朝代年紀

cheng'e er quanshan　懲惡而勸善

chenyu　讖語

chi　痴／笞

Ch'i Hsiang-erh (Qi Xianger)　齊香兒

chi qing　痴情

chi ren shuo meng　痴人說夢

chia (jia)　家

ch'i-chia (qijia)　齊家

chuan shi　傳詩

chuang　創

chuanqi　傳奇

chuanzuo　穿鑿

chuanzuo fuhui　穿鑿附會

chujia　出家

chuliao shen　出了神

chun　蠢

chun wu　蠢物

chun xi lü huai　春夕旅懷

chushi liqun　出世離群

ci　詞／刺

ci ju　辭句

ci shu　此書

ci shu cong he er lai　此書從何而來

cun　村／存

da huang　大荒

da shi fo fa　大施佛法

da wo　大我

da yue he xing　答曰何姓

da yue heguo ren　答曰何國人

da zhi　大旨

dai　呆

dai yu　帶欲

dang　蕩

dao　道

dao xi　道喜

dayi　大一

dian　點

diao chong xiao ji　雕蟲小技

diben　底本

dong　動

dong er zhong li　動而中禮
dongqing　動情
dongxin　動心
du fa　讀法
du zhe　讀者
du ziji wu cai, bu de ru xuan　獨
　自己無才，不得入選
duan　端
duan ju　斷句
dui chiren shuo meng　對痴人說
　夢
dui ou　對偶
duiqi　堆砌
duo xin　多心
dushu mingli　讀書明理
er　兒
er wen ming　而文明
ernü qing　兒女情
ernü si qing　兒女私情
erye　二爺
fa　發
fa hu qing, zhi hu li　發乎情，止
　乎禮
fan ben huan yuan　返本還原
fan xin　凡心
fangxin　放心
fanli　凡例
fanxin yi chi　凡心已熾
fei qing mo qu, fei jun mo jia　非
　卿莫娶，非君莫嫁
fen nei zhi shi　分內之事
fenduo　粉墮
feng　風／瘋
fengchen　風塵
fenghua　風化
fengliu niegui　風流孽鬼
fengsao yaoyan zhi ju　風騷妖豔
　之句
fengsu renqing　風俗人情
fengying zhi tan　風影之談
fengyue baojian　風月寶鑑
fu　賦
fu bi　伏筆

fu hua　浮華
fumu shuang wang, wuyi wukao
　父母雙亡，無依無靠
fusheng liuji　浮生六記
fuxin　負心
fuxue　婦學
ganqing　感情
ganxin　甘心
ganying　感應
ge fan qi suo shi ye　各返其所是
　也
ge wu　格物
ge zhong ren　個中人
gongan　公案
gongming　功名
guan　觀
guan qi xing shi　觀其行事
guanji　官妓
gui gen　歸根
gui gen yue jing　歸根曰靜
guige tingwei zhi juan　閨閣庭闈
　之卷
guiqing　閨情
guisheng　貴生
guiyuan　閨怨
guolai ren　過來人
guti　古體
hanlin zhuren　翰林主人
hao　好
hao feng　好風
hao se　好色
hao wenzhang　好文章
haofang　豪放
he　何
he guo ren　何國人
hongxue　紅學
hongxuejia　紅學家
hua　化／畫
huai　懷
huan　幻
huan xing　幻形
huan yu　還玉／欲
huanbi　幻筆

huang zao yi shi   謊造一事
huangtang   荒唐
huangtang yan   荒唐言
huanhua   幻化
huanqing   幻情
huhua   護花
hulu   葫蘆
huo   惑
ji ceng   幾曾
J/jia   賈 / 假 / 價
jia er bu jia   假而不假
jia nie yi ren   假捏一人
jia yu dongfeng   嫁與東風
jia zhong you zhen   假中有眞
jiaguo dashi   家國大事
jian   見 / 賤
Jian Mei   兼美
jiao   敎
jiashi   家史
jiaxun   家訓
jiayu cun   假語存
jiayu cunyan   假語村言
jie   解 / 節
jie yong yu yu   節用馭欲
jietuo zhi tujing   解脫之途徑
jin hu   近乎
jing   經 / 敬
jing ji sheng dong   靜極生動
jing ren   驚人
jing zhong sheng dong   靜中生
　動
jing zhong sheng fannao   靜中生
　煩惱
jingliguo zhe   經歷過者
jingqi chiwan   警其痴頑
jingyi   經義
jinyu liangyuan   金玉良緣
jishi   記事
jiyan   記言
jue   覺
jun   君
junzi   君子
junyun   均勻

kanpo di   看破的
ke chang   科場
ke you ke wu   可有可無
kong   空
kongyan   空言
kongzhong louge, jinghua shuiyue
　空中樓閣，鏡花水月
kuxin   苦心
laili   來歷
le er bu yin   樂而不淫
le ji sheng bei   樂極生悲
leiying   類應
li   曆 / 禮 / 理
lian dai taohua zhi se   臉帶桃花
　之色
liang bu zhi   兩不知
liao yin bimo zhi cheng wenzhang
　聊因筆墨之成文章
lijiao   禮敎
ling   靈
ling qi   靈氣
lingxing yi tong   靈性已通
liu   流
liu qing   六情
liu sheng   流聲
lixin   離心
lü   律
lu ming   鹿鳴
lu ming zhi yan   鹿鳴之宴
luan   亂
lüfu   律賦
lun   倫
luo hong   落紅
man zhi huangtang yan   滿紙荒
　唐言
manzhi zilian   滿紙自憐
mei yi zhengyan quanjie   每以正
　言勸解
meiren xiangcao   美人香草
meng   夢
mi   迷
mi benxing   迷本性
miao   妙

min zhi xing 民之性
ming 命 / 冥 / 明
ming da yi 明大義
ming li 明理
ming li di ren 明理的人
mingbai 明白
mingqing 冥情
M/mo 莫 / 磨
mudu 目睹
mushi wuqing, caomu wuqing 木石無情，草木無情
naihe tian 奈何天
nannü qing 男女情
nannü yinqing 男女殷情
nei 內
ni hao renxin 你好忍心
ning 寧
nüer bei 女兒悲
nüyao 女妖
pailü 排律
panni xingge 叛逆性格
pi 批
ping 評
pingdian 評點
piyue 批閱
qi 氣 / 綦
qi bi 豈必
qi er bu qi 奇而不奇
qi jia 齊家
qi wu 奇物
qi yan bu rang 其言不讓
qian wang hou di 前王後帝
qianyin houguo 前因後果
qiao 巧
qiao bu po 瞧不破
qiao yan 巧言
qichuan 奇傳
qigui 奇貴
qin 琴
qin li qi jing 親歷其境
qin zhe shu 親者疏
qing 情 / 卿
qing buqing 情不情

qing dong 情動
qing dong yu zhong 情動於中
qing shen 情深
qing yun 青雲
qing zhi dong 情之動
qing zhi suo ying ye 情之所應也
qing zhi suo yu 情之所欲
qing zhi zhi 情之至
qingbo zidi 輕薄子弟
qinggen 情根
qingjiao 情教
qingjing 情境
qingqing 情情
qingren 情人
qingwen 情文
qingxing 情性
qingye 情業
qingyu 情欲
qingyu zhi si 情欲之私
qingyuan 情緣
qingzhong 情種
qinwen 親聞
qiqing 七情
qishu 氣數
quandian 圈點
quwei 趣味
ren 仁
ren fei cao mu 人非草木
ren ming bo 人命薄
ren zhi da lun 人之大倫
ren zhi qing 人之情
renqing 人情
rensheng ru meng 人生如夢
rong 容
rou qing si yi 柔情私意
ru 如
ru he xing 汝何姓
ru zui ru chi 如醉如痴
san gang wu lun 三綱五倫
sangbai 喪敗
se 色
sha 傻

shan jia 善價
shang jia 上賈／價
shangbei 傷悲
shangxin le shi 賞心樂事
shanshu 善書
shanzhi 善質
shen 身
shen fei mu shi 身非木石
Shen Fu 沈復
shen qian shen hou shi 身前身
　後事
sheng 聲
sheng bing 聲病
sheng bu feng shi 生不逢時
shensi 神思
shezhan 舌戰
shi 事／識／詩／時
shi he yisi 是何意思
shi lizhu jing 是立足境
shi neng yan 石能言
shi yan zhi, yan qing 詩言志，
　言情
shi yuan qing er qimi 詩緣情而
　綺靡
shi yuezhe liaoran buhuo 使閱者
　了然不惑
shi(h) 詩／史／實／事
shihua 詩話
shili jie 十里街／勢利街
shiren zhi suo yu zhi shi 詩人志
　〔＝誌〕所欲之事
shishi 史事／實事
shixue 實學
shizai di haochu 實在地好處
shu 疏／述
shu wang shi, si lai zhe 述往
　事，思來者
shu zhe qin 疏者親
shu zui 贖罪
shuai er 率爾
shui jia yuan 誰家院
shujihu shi 庶幾乎史
shuqing 抒情

shuqing chuantong 抒情傳統
shuqing di daotong 抒情的道統
si 私
si fan 思凡
si se si kong he yue zhe 似色似
　空和月折
si wu xie 思無邪
si xie zhi xian 私褻之嫌
si yu 私欲
su 俗
su er bu su 俗而不俗
su nie zong yin qing 宿孽總因
　情
suo yu ran 所欲然
suoyin 索隱
tan qing 談情
ti 題
tian li 天理
tianfen 天分
Tiechu 鐵杵
Tiejiu 鐵臼
titie 體貼
tong xing 同姓
tong yu 同欲
tongbian 通變
tongbing xianglian 同病相憐
tongling 通靈
tongling baoyu 通靈寶玉
tu 途
tui 推
tuoqing 托情
tuoyan 托言
wai 外
wang 枉
wang qing 忘情
wanghua 王化
wanshi 頑石
wanshi dian tou 頑石點頭
wanyue 婉約
wei 僞
wei qing zuo wen 爲情作文
wei wen zuo qing 爲文作情
weiqing 僞情

wen　文
wenli ximi　文理細密
wenshi　文史
wenshi chuanqi　問世傳奇
wenxue　文學
wenzhang　文章
wo bu zhi yin　我不知音
wo suoxing bu mingbai liao　我
　索性不明白了
wu　無 / 悟
wu chaodai nianji ke kao　無朝代
　年紀可考
wu ji　無稽
wu jing　五經
wu ke yun zheng　無可云證
wu qing　無情
wu zhen　悟眞
wu zhong sheng you　無中生有
wude　五德
wuhua　物化
wuji　無稽
wuming　無明
wuqing　無情
wuqing di ren　無情的人
wuqing shuo fa　無情說法
wuqing zhe　無情者
wuxing　五行
wuyi wukao　無依無靠
wuzhi　五至
xi an　細案
xi de wuhua ke shuo　喜得無話
　可說
xi hua ren　惜花人
xi jue . . . ziwei　細嚼 . . . 滋味
xi kan　細看
xiang　象
xiangke　相克
xiao tan　笑談
xiao wo　小我
xiaoshuo　小說
xie　邪
xieshuo　邪說
xieyin　邪淫
xiezi　楔子

xin　心
xin dong　心動
xin fei mu shi　心非木石
xin zhong linghui　心中領會
xinbing　心病
xing　性 / 形 / 醒
xing zhi dong　性之動
xingneng　性能
xingqing　性情
xingzhe　行者
xinli que ye mingbai　心裡卻也
　明白
xinli zao youxie mingbai liao　心
　裡早有些明白了
xinshi　心事
xinxing　心性
xiong　兄
xiong huai da zhi　胸懷大志
xitang saohua xingzhe　西堂掃花
　行者
xiu　修
xiu xiao shiren chi　休笑世人痴
yan　言
yan bu jin yi　言不盡意
yan qi shu yuanshi kongxu huanshe
　言其書原是空虛幻設
yan zhi　言志
yanfa　演法
yang　陽 / 養
yang bing　養病
yang qing　養情
yang shen　養神
yanshi　豔詩
yanyi　演義
yaodang xingqing　搖盪性情
ye　業
ye xiang bu qi bihui xianyi deng
　shi　也想不起避諱嫌疑等事
yeshi　野史
yi　義 / 易 / 意
yi jia wei zhen　以假爲眞
yi pian kuxin　一片苦心
yi qing dai shi　以情待實
yi shi lun wen　以事論文

yi wen lun wen　以文論文

yi wen sheng shi　以文生事

yi wen yun shi　以文運事

yi yin　意淫

yi zai yan wai　意在言外

yi zhi　意旨

yi zhong ren　意中人

yin　因／陰／音／淫

yin ci　音詞／淫詞

yinben　淫奔

ying　應

yinshi　淫詩

yinxin　淫心

yinyong　吟詠

yiqi lai yan fa　一齊來演法

yiwu zhi qing　異物之情

yixi　依棲

yong shi　詠史

yongxin　用心

you　有

you bu yu shi　有補於世

you gui zilian　幽閨自憐

you liao xin　有了心

you qing　有情

you qing ren　有情人

you quwei　有趣味

you ren ye　有人也

you sheng yu wu　有生於無

you yu　憂鬱

Youzhou　幽州

yu　欲／玉／愚／御

yu xiang man kou　餘香滿口

yu you qing, qing you jie　欲有情，情有節

yu yu　馭欲

yuan zai tianbian, jin zai yanqian　遠在天邊，近在眼前

yuanjia　冤家

yuanqing　怨情

yuanwei　原委

yuanxing　原形

yun　運／韻

yun yong　運用

yunzhong shujin　運終數盡

yuyan di xianming　語言的鮮明

zaijia　在家

zashu　雜書

zawen　雜文

zeng, sun　增、損

zhang　杖

zhen　眞

zhen er bu zhen　眞而不眞

zhen er you zhen　眞而又眞

zhen you qi ren, zhen you qi shi　眞有其人，眞有其事

zhenbian　鍼砭

zhengjing shu　正經書

zhengshi　正史

zhenzhen jiajia　眞眞假假

zheng　證

zheng li　正理

zheng si　正思

zhengqi　爭氣

zhexian　謫仙

zhi　之／志／止／至／質

zhi qing　治情

zhiguai　志怪

zhiji　知己

zhiqi　志氣

zhiqing, zhi qi qing　知情，知其情

zhizheng　治政

zhongliu　中流

zhongshen dashi　終身大事

zhongxin　忠心

zhu　注／主

zhuan　傳

zhuming laili　注明來歷

zi　子

zike　自克

zilian　自憐

zimo keqing　字墨客卿

ziran　自然

zhongzhong xiang　種種相

zun xing er jian qing　尊性而賤情

zuo　作

zuo zhe　作者

zuozhu　作主

Bibliography

Works in Chinese and Japanese

Aixinjueluo (Asin Gioro) Yurui 愛新覺羅裕瑞. *Zaochuang xianbi* 棗窗閒筆. Shanghai: Wenxue guji kanxingshe, 1957.

An Pingqiu 安平秋 and Zhang Peiheng 章培恆, eds. *Zhongguo jinshu daguan* 中國禁書大觀. Shanghai: Wenhua, 1988.

Ayin 阿印. *Lin Daiyu di beiju* 林黛玉的悲劇. Hong Kong: Qiandai, 1948.

Aying 阿英. *Xiaoshuo sitan* 小說四談. Shanghai: Guji, 1981.

Ba Jin 巴金 et al. *Wo du Hongloumeng* 我讀紅樓夢. Tianjin: Renmin, 1982.

Bai Juyi 白居易. *Bai Xiangshan shiji* 白香山詩集. *SBBY*.

Ban Zhao 班昭. *Nüjie* 女誡. Facsimile of 1580 edition. Shanghai: Dazhong, 1931.

Bao Zhao 鮑照. "Ni Xinglu'nan 擬行路難." In *Gushi xuan* 古詩選 2: *juan* 2, 10a–11a. *SBBY*.

Beifang luncong bianjibu 北方論叢編輯部, ed. *Hongloumeng zhuzuoquan lunzhen ji* 紅樓夢著作權論爭集. Xi'an: Shanxi renmin, 1985.

Beijing daxue wenxue yanjiusuo 北京大學文學研究所, ed. *Wenxue yanjiu jikan* 文學研究集刊. Beijing: Renmin wenxue, 1956.

Bi Wanchen 畢萬忱. "Yanzhi yuanqing shuo manyi 言志緣情說漫議." *GDWXLLYJ* 6 (1982): 57–69.

Bohu tongde lun 白虎通德論. *SBCK*.

Cai Bingkun 蔡炳焜. *Manshuo Honglou* 漫說紅樓. Taipei: Sanmin, 1984.

Cai Renhou 蔡仁厚. *Songming lixue nan Song pian: xinti yu xingti yizhi shuyin* 宋明理學南宋篇：心體與性體義旨述引. Taipei: Xuesheng, 1980.

Cai Yijiang 蔡義江. "Cao Xueqin bixia di Lin Daiyu zhi si 曹雪芹筆下的林黛玉之死." *HLMXK* 1 (1981): 39–74.

———. *Hongloumeng shici qufu pingzhu* 紅樓夢詩詞曲賦評注. Beijing: Beijing, 1979.

Cai Yingjun 蔡英俊. *Bixing wuse yu qingjing jiaorong* 比興物色與情景交融. Taipei: Daan, 1990.

Cai Yuanpei 蔡元培, ed. *Shitouji suoyin* 石頭記索引. Shanghai: Shangwu, 1922.

Cao Juren 曹聚仁. *Xin Hongxue congwei* 新紅學叢微. Hong Kong: Chuangken, 1955.

Cao Xueqin 曹雪芹 and Gao E 高鶚. *Hongloumeng* 紅樓夢. 3 vols. Beijing: Renmin wenxue, 1982.

Cao Zhaolan 曹兆蘭, ed. *Lidai funü shici xuan* 歷代婦女詩詞選. Wuchang: Hubei renmin, 1983.

Cen Jiazhuo 岑佳卓. *Hongloumeng pinglun* 紅樓夢評論. Taizhong: self-printed, 1985.

Chan Hingho (Chen Qinghao) 陳慶浩. *Xinbian Shitouji Zhiyanzhai pingyu jijiao* 新編石頭記脂硯齋評語輯校. Revised edition. Taipei: Lianjing, 1986.

Chang K(uang) C(hih) 張光直. "Zhongguo chuangshi shenhua zhi fenxi yu gushi yanjiu 中國創世神話之分析與故事研究." *Zhongyang yanjiuyuan minzuxue yanjiusuo jikan* 中央研究院民族學研究所集刊 8 (Autumn 1959): 47–76.

Chen Dongyuan 陳東原. *Zhongguo funü shenghuo shi* 中國婦女生活史. Shanghai: Shangwu, 1928. Reprinted in Taiwan, 1977; in Shanghai, 1990.

———. *Zhongguo jiaoyu shi* 中國教育史. Shanghai: Shangwu, 1931.

———. *Zhongguo keju shidai zhi jiaoyu* 中國科舉時代之教育. Shanghai: Shangwu, 1934.

Chen Hang 陳沆. *Shi bi xing jian* 詩比興箋. Hong Kong: Zhonghua, 1962.

Chen Hao 陳澔. *Liji ji shuo* 禮記集說. Taipei: Taiwan Shangwu, 1979.

Chen Qingzhi 陳青之. *Zhongguo jiaoyu shi* 中國教育史. Shanghai: Shangwu, 1936.

Chen Qitai 陳其泰. *Tonghua fengge ping Hongloumeng ji lu* 桐花鳳閣評紅樓夢輯錄. Edited by Liu Caonan 劉操南. Tianjin: Renmin, 1981.

Chen Shixiang 陳世驤. *Chen Shixiang wencun* 陳世驤文存. Edited by Yang Mu 楊牧. Taipei: Zhiwen, 1973.

Chen Shiyuan 陳士元. *Mengzhan yizhi* 夢占逸旨. Shanghai: Shangwu, 1939.

Chen Xizhong 陳熙中. "Shuo 'zhen you shi shi'—du Zhipi suizha 說眞有是事——讀脂批隨札." *Beijing daxue xuebao* 北京大學學報 5 (1980): 85–86. Reprinted in Liu Mengxi 劉夢溪, ed., *Hongxue sanshinian lunwen xuanbian* 紅學三十年論文選編, 3: 384–87, Tianjin: Baihua wenyi,1984.

Chen Ying 陳瑛 et al. *Zhongguo lunli sixiangshi* 中國倫理思想史. Guiyang: Guizhou renmin, 1985.

Chen Yinque 陳寅恪. *Yuan Bai shi jianzheng gao* 元白詩箋證稿. Shanghai: Guji, 1978.

Chen Yong 陳鏞. "Chusanxuan congtan 樗散軒叢談," *juan* 2. In *HLMJ* 2: 349–50.

Chen Yupi 陳毓羆. "*Hongloumeng* he *Fusheng liuji* 紅樓夢和浮生六記." *HLMXK* 4 (1980): 211–30.

———. "*Hongloumeng* shi zenyang kaitou di 紅樓夢是怎樣開頭的?" *Wenshi* 文史 3 (1963): 333–338.

———, Liu Shide 劉世德, and Deng Shaoji 鄧紹基. *Hongloumeng luncong* 紅樓夢論叢. Shanghai: Guji, 1979.

Chen Zhao 陳詔. *Hongloumeng tanyilu* 紅樓夢談藝錄. Yinchuan:Ningxia remin, 1985.

———. *Hongloumeng xiaokao* 紅樓夢小考. Shanghai: Guji, 1985.

Chen Zizhan 陳子展. *Shijing zhijie* 詩經直解. 2 vols.Shanghai: Fudan daxue, 1983.

Cheng Peng 程鵬. "Cao Xueqin 'butian' sixiang zai tantao 曹雪芹補天思想再探討." *Hongloumeng yanjiu* 紅樓夢研究 10 (1981): 9–16.

Chow Tse-chung 周策縱. "*Honglou* sanwen 紅樓三問." *Zhongguoshibao* 中國時報 (China Times), June 7 and 8, 1987, p. 8. Reprinted in Feng Qiyong 馮其庸 et al., eds., *Hongloumeng daguan: guoji Hongloumeng yantaohui lunwenji* 紅樓夢大觀: 國際紅樓夢研討會論文集, pp. i–xv. Hong Kong: Baixing banyuekan, 1987.

———. "*Hongloumeng* yu *Xiyoubu* 紅樓夢與西遊補." *HLMYJJK* 5 (1980):135–42.

Cui Rongche 崔溶澈. "*Hongloumeng* di wenxue beijing yanjiu 紅樓夢的文學背景研究." Master's thesis, National Taiwan University, 1983.

Da Qing huidian 大清會典. Compiled by Kun Gang 崑崗 et al. Beijing: Beijing huidianguan, 1899 (Guangxu 光緒 25).

Deng Siyu 鄧嗣禹. *Zhongguo kaoshi zhidushi* 中國考試制度史. Taipei: Xuesheng, 1967.

Deng Yunxiang 鄧雲鄉. *Honglou fengsu tan* 紅樓風俗譚. Beijing:Zhonghua, 1987.

———. *Honglou zhi xiao lu* 紅樓識小錄. Taiyuan: Shanxi renmin,1984.

Ding Guanghui 丁廣惠. *Hongloumeng shici pingzhu* 紅樓夢詩詞評注. Haerbin: Heilongjiang renmin, 1980.

Dipingxian chubanshe 地平線出版社, ed. *Cao Xueqin di yisheng* 曹雪芹的一生. Taipei: Dipingxian, 1975.

Dong Yue 董說. *Xiyoubu* 西遊補. Shanghai: Beixin, 1929.

Dong Zhongshu 董仲舒, ed. *Chunqiu fanlu* 春秋繁露. *SBBY*.

Du Shijie 杜世傑. *Hongloumeng beijin daoyu shikao* 紅樓夢悲金悼玉實考. Taizhong: self-printed, 1971.

———. *Hongloumeng kaoshi* 紅樓夢考釋. Taizhong: self-printed,1977.

Du Weiyun 杜維運 et al., eds. *Zhongguo shixueshi lunwenxuanji* 中國史學史論文選集. Vol. 3. Taipei: Huashi, 1980.

Feng Chuan 馮川. *Mengzhao yu shenhua* 夢兆與神話. Chengdu: Sichuan renmin, 1993.

Feng Erkang 馮爾康. *Fengjian shehui di yimian jingzi:Hongloumeng* 封建社會的一面鏡子——紅樓夢. Beijing:Zhonghua, 1974.

Feng Menglong 馮夢龍, comp. *Qingshi leilüe* 情史類略. Beijing: Ziqiang, 1911.

Feng Minghui 馮明惠. "Tang chuanqi zhong aiqing gushi zhi pouxi 唐傳奇中愛情故事之剖析." In *Zhongguo gudian xiaoshuolunji* 中國古典小說論集, pp. 111–51. Edited by Lin Yiliang 林以亮 et al. Taipei: Youshi wenhua, 1975.

Feng Qiyong 馮其庸, ed. *Cao Xueqin jiashi Hongloumeng wenwutulu* 曹雪芹家世紅樓夢文物圖錄. Hong Kong: Sanlian, 1983.

———. *Cao Xueqin jiashi xinkao* 曹雪芹家世新考. Shanghai: Guji,1980.

———. *Lun gengchen ben* 論庚辰本. Shanghai: Wenyi, 1978.

———. *Mengbian ji* 夢邊集. Xi'an: Shanxi renmin, 1982.

——— et al., comp. *Hongloumeng daguan: guoji Hongloumeng yantaohui lunwenji* 紅樓夢大觀:國際紅樓夢研討會論文集. Hong Kong: Baixing banyuekan,1987.

Fu Sheng 浮生. *Ping Hongloumeng wenyi* 評紅樓夢文藝. N.p., n.d.

Fu Tianzhen 傅天正. "Fojiao dui Zhongguo huanshu di yingxiang chutan 佛教對中國幻術的影響初探." In Zhang Mantao 張曼濤, ed., *Fojiao yu Zhongguo wenhua* 佛教與中國文化, pp. 237–50. Taipei: Dasheng wenhua, 1978.

Fu Zhenggu 傅正谷. *Zhongguo meng wenhua* 中國夢文化. Beijing: Zhongguo shehui kexue, 1993.

Gao Boyu 高伯雨. *Du xiaoshuo zhaji* 讀小說劄記. Hong Kong: Shanghai, 1957.

Gao Yang 高陽. *Gao Yang shuo Cao Xueqin* 高陽說曹雪芹. Taipei: Lianjing, 1973.

———. *Honglou yijia yan* 紅樓一家言. Taipei: Lianjing, 1977.

Gao Yougong (Yu-kung Kao) 高友工. "Wenxue yanjiu di meixue wenti 文學研究的美學問題." Part 2. *CWLM* 7/12 (1979):4–51.

Ge Lianxiang 葛連詳. *Zhongguo shilun* 中國詩論. Taipei: self-printed, 1961.

Gengchen ben Shitouji 庚辰本石頭記. Reprint of 1955 edition by Beijing wenxue guji kanxingshe. 6 vols. Taipei: Guangwen, 1977.

Gong Juzhong 龔居中, ed. *Honglu dianxue* 紅爐點雪. Shanghai: Kexue jishu, 1959.

Gu Pingdan 顧平旦, ed. *Daguanyuan* 大觀園. Beijing: Wenhuayishu, 1981.

———, ed. *Daguanyuan yanjiu ziliao huibian* 大觀園研究資料匯編. Beijing: Wenhuabu wenxue yishu yanjiuyuan, 1979.

———, ed. *Hongloumeng yanjiu lunwen ziliao suoyin (1874–1982)* 紅樓夢研究論文資料索引. Beijing: Shumu wenxian, 1982.

Guan Huashan 關華山. *Hongloumeng zhong di jianzhu yanjiu* 紅樓夢中的建築研究. Taizhong: Jingyuxiang, 1984.

Guangdongsheng wenxue yishu gongzuo zhe lianhehui and Guangzhoushi wenxue yishujie lianhehui 廣東省文學藝術工作者聯合會、廣州市文學藝術界聯合會, eds. *Dui Hongloumeng yanjiu zhong cuowu guandian di pipan* 對紅樓夢研究中錯誤觀點的批判. N.p., n.d

Gugong bowuyuan Ming Qing dang'anbu 故宮博物院明清檔案部, ed. *Guanyu jiangning zhizao Caojia dang'an shiliao* 關於江寧織造曹家檔案史料. Beijing: Zhonghua, 1975.

Guizhousheng *Hongloumeng* xuehui 貴州省紅樓夢學會, ed. *Hongloutanyi: Hongloumeng lunji* 紅樓探藝：紅樓夢論集. Vol. 2. Guiyang: Guizhou renmin, 1983.

Guo Shaoyu 郭紹虞. *Zhaoyu shi gudian wenxue lunji* 照隅室古典文學論集. 2 vols. Shanghai: Guji, 1983.

Guo Yushi 郭豫適. *Honglou yanjiu xiao shi xugao (wusi shiqi yihou)* 紅樓研究小史續稿 (五四時期以後). Shanghai: Wenyi,1981.

———. *Hongloumeng wenti pinglunji* 紅樓夢問題評論集. Shanghai: Guji, 1981.

———. *Zhongguo gudai xiaoshuo lunji* 中國古代小說論集. Shanghai: Huadong shifan daxue, 1985.

Guoyu 國語. *SBBY*.

Ha Sibao 哈斯寶. *Xinyi Hongloumeng huipi* 新譯紅樓夢回批. Translated by Yi Linzhen 亦鄰眞. Huhehaote:Neimenggu renmin, 1979.

Han Jinlian 韓進廉. *Hongxue shigao* 紅學史稿. Shijiazhuang: Hebei renmin, 1981.

Han Yu 韓愈. *Han Changli quanji* 韓昌黎全集. 2 vols. *SBBY*.

Heilongjiang renmin chubanshe 黑龍江人民出版社, ed. *Yibu Hongloumeng wanjia xieleishi* 一部紅樓夢萬家血淚史. Haerbin: Heilongjiang renmin, 1975.

Hong Guangsi 洪廣思. *Jieji douzheng di xingxiang lishi—ping Hongloumeng* 階級鬥爭的形象歷史——評紅樓夢. Beijing: Renmin wenxue, 1974.

Hong Pimo 洪丕謨. *Meng yu shenghuo* 夢與生活. Beijing: Zhongguo wenlian, 1993.

Hong Qiufan 洪秋蕃. *Hongloumeng kaozheng* 紅樓夢考證. Shanghai: Shanghai yinshuguan, 1935.

Hongloumeng renmin cidian 紅樓夢人名詞典. Hong Kong: Guangzhi, n.d.

Hongloumeng sanjia pingben 紅樓夢三家評本. 4 vols. Shanghai: Guji, 1988.

Hongloumeng wenti taolun ji 紅樓夢問題討論集. Vols. 1–4. Beijing: Zuojia, 1955.

Hongloumeng yanjiu xiaozu 紅樓夢研究小組, ed. *Hongloumeng yanjiu zhuankan* 紅樓夢研究專刊. 11 vols. Hong Kong: Xinya shuyuan, 1967–1974.

Hongloumeng yanjiu ziliao jikan 紅樓夢研究資料集刊. Shanghai: Huadong zuojia xiehui ziliaoshi, 1954.

Hongloumeng ziliao ji 紅樓夢資料集. 5 vols. Hong Kong: The Sinological Center, 1983.

Hu Jingzhi 胡經之. "Wangru hongchen ruoxu nian 枉入紅塵若許年." *HLMYJJK* 6 (1981): 143–57.

Hu Shi(h) 胡適. "*Hongloumeng* kaozheng 紅樓夢考證." In *HSWC* 1:575–620.

———. *Hu Shi(h) wencun* 胡適文存. 4 vols. Taipei: Yuandong, 1961.

———. "Kaozheng *Hongloumeng* di xin cailiao 考證紅樓夢的新材料." In *HSWC* 3: 373–403.

———. "Qing banxing xinshi biaodian fuhao yian 請頒行新式標點符號議案." In *HSWC* 2: 115–28.

———, ed. *Shenhui heshang yiji* 神會和尚遺集. Shanghai: Yadong,1930.

Hu Wenbin 胡文彬. *Hongbian cuoyu* 紅邊脞語. Shenyang: Liaoning renmin, 1986.

————, ed. *Hongloumeng xulu* 紅樓夢敘錄. Jilin: Jilin renmin,1980.

———— et al., eds. *Haiwai Hongxue lunji* 海外紅學論集. Shanghai: Guji, 1982.

———— et al., eds. *Hongxue congtan* 紅學叢譚. Taiyuan: Shanxi renmin, 1983.

———— et al., eds. *Hongxue shijie* 紅學世界. Beijing: Beijing, 1984.

———— et al., eds. *Xianggang Hongxue lunwenxuan* 香港紅學論文選. Tianjin: Baihua wenyi, 1982.

Hu Wenkai 胡文楷. *Lidai funü zhuzuo kao* 歷代婦女著作考. Revised edition. Shanghai: Guji, 1985.

Huang Boyin 黃砵隱, ed. *Hongxue congchao* 紅學叢鈔. Hangzhou: Hangzhou tushuguan, 1984.

Huang Gongwei 黃公偉. *Foxue yuanli daoshi* 佛學原理道釋. Banqiao: Xiandai wenyi, 1966.

————. *Zhongguo fojiao sixiang chuantong shi* 中國佛敎思想傳統史. Taipei: Shizihou zazhishe, 1972.

Huang Huajie 黃華節. *Funü fengsu shihua* 婦女風俗史話. Shanghai: Shangwu, 1933.

Huang Lixin 黃立新. "Qingchu caizi jiaren xiaoshuo yu *Hongloumeng* 清初才子佳人小說與紅樓夢." *HLMYJJK* 10 (1983):259–80.

Huang Zongxi 黃宗羲, comp. *Mingru xuean* 明儒學案. Shanghai: Shangwu, 1935.

———— et al., comps. *Sung-Yuan xuean* 宋元學案. Shanghai: Shangwu, 1934.

Huiyin 慧印, ed. *Yunzhou dongshan Wuben chanshi yulu* 筠州洞山悟本禪師語錄. In *T.* 47:507–19.

Huiyuan 慧遠. "Ming baoying lun 明報應論." In Kimura Eiichi 木村英一, ed., *Eon Kenkyū: Ibun-hen* 慧遠研究：遺文篇, pp. 76–78. Tokyo: Sōbunsha, 1960.

————. "Shamen bujing wangzhe lun 沙門不敬王者論." In Kimura Eiichi 木村英一, ed., *Eon Kenkyū: Ibun-hen* 慧遠研究：遺文篇, pp. 84–90. Tokyo: Sōbunsha, 1960.

Ishida Mikinosuke 石田幹之助. "Chōan no kagi 長安の歌妓." In *Zōtei Chōan no haru* 增訂長安の春, pp. 100–125. Tokyo: Sōgensha, 1967.

Ishigawa Tadahisa 石川忠久, ed. *Chūgoku bungaku no joseizo* 中国文学の女性像. Tokyo: Kyūko Shoin, 1982.

Itō Sōhei 伊藤漱平, trans. *Kōrōmu* 紅樓夢. 3 vols. In *Chūgoku koten bungaku taikei* 中国古典文学大系. Tokyo: Heibonsha,1969.

————. "*Kōrōmu* shukai, botto bubun no hissha ni tsuite no gimon 紅樓夢首回，冒頭部分の筆者に就いての疑問." *Tokyo Shina gakuhō* 東京支那学報 4/4 (June 1958): 99–108; (*zoku*) 8 (June 1962): 43–59.

Izuishi Yoshihiko 出石誠彥. *Shina shinwa densetsu no kenkyū* 支那神話伝說の研究. Tokyo: Chuo Koronsha, 1973.

Jian Bozan 翦伯贊. "Lun shiba shiji shangbanqi Zhongguo shehui jingji di xingzhi 論十八世紀上半期中國社會經濟的性質." In *Lishi wenti luncong* 歷史問題論叢, pp. 188–252. Revised edition. Beijing: Sanlian, 1957; reprinted in Liu Mengxi 劉夢溪,ed., *Hongxue sanshinian lunwen xuan bian* 紅學三十年論文選編, 1: 26–92, Tianjin: Baihua wenyi, 1983.

Jiang Daqi 蔣大器. "Xu 序." In Luo Guanzhong 羅貫中, *Sanguozhi tongsu yanyi* 三國志通俗演義, 1: 1a–5b. Hongzhi 弘治 edition (1494).

Jiang Hesen 蔣和森. *Hongloumeng gaishuo* 紅樓夢概說. Shanghai: Guji, 1979.

————. *Hongloumeng lungao* 紅樓夢論稿. Beijing: Renmin wenxue,1959.

Jiangxi daxue zhongwenxi 江西大學中文系. *Hongloumeng shici yishi* 紅樓夢詩詞 譯釋. Nanchang: Jiangxi renmin, 1979.

Jin Rujie 金儒杰, ed. *Hongloumeng pinglun* 紅樓夢評論. Hong Kong: Shenzhou, 1974.

Jin Shengtan 金聖嘆. "Du Diwu caizishu fa 讀第五才子書法." In Shi Naian 施耐 庵, *Shuihuzhuan* 水滸傳, 1: 90–107. Taipei: Wenyuan, 1970.

———. "Dufa 讀法." In *Yuanben Sanguozhi yanyi* 原本三國志演義, 1: 4–24. Taipei: Wenyuan, 1969.

Jin Yufu 金毓黻. *Zhongguo shixue shi* 中國史學史. Shanghai: Shangwu, 1957.

Jingsan luyue caoshe jushi 晶三蘆月草舍居士. *Hongloumeng oushuo* 紅樓夢偶 說. N.p.: Kuifu shanfang, 1876.

"Jinpingmei yuyishuo 金瓶梅寓意說." In *Liangzhong Zhupo pingdian ben hekan Tianxia diyi qishu* 兩種竹波評點本合刊天下第一奇書, pp. 1a–7a. Hong Kong: Huiwen ge, 1975.

Kan Duo 闞鐸. *Hongloumeng juewei* 紅樓夢抉微. Tianjin: Tianjin dagong baoguan, 1925.

Kang Laixin 康來新. *Shitou duhai—Hongloumeng sanlun* 石頭渡海——紅樓夢散 論. Taipei: Hanguang, 1985.

Kang Zhengguo 康正果. *Chongshen fengyue jian: xing yu Zhongguo gudian wenxue* 重審風月鑑：性與中國古典文學. Taipei: Maitian, 1996.

———. *Fengsao yu yanqing* 風騷與豔情. Taipei: Yunlong, 1991.

Kishibi Shigeo 岸辺成雄. "Gikan no katsudō 妓館の活動." In *Tōdai ongaku no rekishi teki kenkyū: Gakusei hen* 唐代音楽の歴史的研究：楽制篇, 1: 95–106. Tokyo: Tokyo Daigaku,1960.

Kongzi jiayu 孔子家語. *SBBY*.

"Kongzi xianju 孔子閒居." In *Liji xun zuan* 禮記訓纂. *SBBY*.

Koyannagi Shikita 小柳司氣太. *Daojiao gailun* 道教概論. Translated by Chen Binhe 陳彬龢. Shanghai: Shangwu, 1930.

Kumarajiva (Jiumoluoshi 鳩摩羅什), trans. *Jingang jing* 金剛經. In *T*. 8: 748–752.

Lan Dingyuan 藍鼎元. *Nüxue* 女學. Yonghe: Wenhai, 1977.

Lan Yanzhou 藍豔周. "Zhongguo shanggu shenhua di zhexue beijing 中國上古神話 的哲學背景." Master's thesis, Zhongguo wenhua xueyuan, 1968.

Lei Jin 雷瑨, comp. *Qingren shuohui* 清人說薈. 2 vols. Reprint of Saoye shanfang 掃 葉山房 edition (Shanghai, 1928). Numbers 142–143 of *Zhonghua wenshi congshu* 中華文史叢書. Taipei: Huawen, 1969.

Lengzhai yehua 冷齋夜話. In *Congshu jicheng* 叢書集成 (1939), 2: 549.

Li Ao 李翱. *Li Wengong ji shiba juan* 李文公集十八卷. *SBCK*.

Li Chendong 李辰冬. *Hongloumeng yanjiu* 紅樓夢研究. 1958. Reprinted Taipei: Zhengzhong, 1977.

Li Chuanlong 李傳龍. *Cao Xueqin meixue sixiang* 曹雪芹美學思想. Xi'an: Shanxi renmin jiaoyu, 1987.

Li Fang 李昉 et al., comps. *Taiping guangji* 太平廣記. Reprint of Cuiwen tang 粹文 堂 edition. 5 vols. Tainan: Minglun, 1987.

Li Jiafu 李甲孚. *Zhongguo gudai di nüxing* 中國古代的女性. Taipei: Liming, 1973.

Li Shuangqing 李霜青. *Cong Lin Yutang toufa shuoqi* 從林語堂頭髮說起. Taipei: Zhezhi, 1969.

Li Waiyee (Huiyi) 李惠儀. "Jinghuan yu yi qing wu dao 警幻與以情悟道." *CWLM* 22/2 (1993): 46–66.

Li Xifan 李希凡 and Lan Ling 藍翎. *Cao Xueqin han ta di Hongloumeng* 曹雪芹和他的紅樓夢. Hong Kong: Zhonghua, 1973.

———. *Hongloumeng pinglunji* 紅樓夢評論集. Beijing: Zuojia, 1973.

Li Yu 李漁. *Li Liweng quhua* 李笠翁曲話. Shanghai: Qizhi, 1933.

Li Zhi 李贄. *Chutan ji* 初潭集. Vol. 1. Beijing: Zhonghua, 1974.

———. *Fen Shu* 焚書. Beijing: Zhonghua, 1961.

———. *Li Wenling ji* 李溫陵集. 2 vols. Taipei: Wenshizhe, 1971.

Liang Guizhi 梁歸智. *Shitouji tanyi* 石頭記探佚. Taiyuan: Shanxi renmin, 1983.

Liang Qichao 梁啓超. "Fanyi wenxue yu fojiao 翻譯文學與佛教." In *Foxue yanjiu shiba pian* 佛學研究十八篇, n.p. Taipei: Zhonghua, 1966.

———. *Wang Anshi pingzhuan* 王安石評傳. Hong Kong: Guangzhi, n.d.

Liang Qixiong 梁啓雄. *Xunzi jianshi* 荀子簡釋. Beijing: Renmin, 1956.

Liang Shaoren 梁紹壬. *Liangban qiuyu'an suibi* 兩般秋雨盫隨筆. Shanghai: Guji, 1982.

Liang Xiao 梁效 et al. *Hongloumeng pinglunji* 紅樓夢評論集. Shanghai: Renming, 1975.

Liang Yizhen 梁乙眞, ed. *Qingdai funü wenxueshi* 清代婦女文學史. Shanghai: Zhonghua, 1932.

Liao Zhaoyang 廖朝陽. "Yiwen yu xiao wenxue? Cong hou zhimin lilun yu minzu xushi di guandian kan *Hongloumeng* 異文與小文學？從後殖民理論與民族敘事的觀點看紅樓夢." *CWLM* 22/2(1993):6–45.

Lidai shihua 歷代詩話. Edited by He Wenhuan 何文煥. 2 vols. Beijing: Zhonghua, 1981.

Lidai shihua xubian 歷代詩話續編. Edited by Ding Fubao 丁福保. 3 vols. Beijing: Zhonghua, 1983.

Liezi 列子. *SBBY*.

Liji xunzuan 禮記訓纂. 2 vols. *SBBY*.

Lin Guanfu 林冠夫. *Hongloumeng zongheng tan* 紅樓夢縱橫談. Nanning: Guangxi renmin, 1985.

Lin Ketang 林科棠. *Songru yu fojiao* 宋儒與佛教. Shanghai: Shangwu, 1930.

Lin Mingde 林明德. *Wan Qing xiaoshuo yanjiu* 晚清小說研究. Taipei: Lianjing, 1985.

Lin Xingren 林興仁. *Hongloumeng di xiuci yishu* 紅樓夢的修辭藝術. Fuzhou: Fujian jiaoyu, 1984.

Lin Yiliang 林以亮 (Song Qi 宋淇). "*Hongloumeng* xinlun 紅樓夢新論." In Youshi yuekan bianjishi 幼獅月刊編輯室, ed., *Hongloumeng yanjiuji* 紅樓夢研究集, pp. 183–215. Taipei: Youshi yuekan, 1972.

———. *Hongloumeng xiyouji: xiping Hongloumeng xin yingyi* 紅樓夢西遊記: 細評紅樓夢新英譯. Taipei: Lianjing, 1976.

Lin Yu-t'ang (Yutang) 林語堂. *Pingxin lun Gao E* 平心論高鶚. Taipei: Zhuanji wenxue, 1969.

Liu Chenghuai 劉城淮. *Zhongguo shanggu shenhua* 中國上古神話. Shanghai: Wenyi, 1988.

Liu Dajie 劉大杰. *Hongloumeng di sixiang yu renwu* 紅樓夢的思想與人物. Shanghai: Gudian wenxue, 1956.

Liu Hengjing 劉蘅靜. *Funü wenti wenji* 婦女問題文集. Nanjing: Funü yuekanshe, 1947.

Liu Mengxi 劉夢溪. *Hongloumeng xinlun* 紅樓夢新論. Beijing: Zhongguo shehui kexue, 1982.

———, ed. *Hongxue sanshinian lunwen xuanbian* 紅學三十年論文選編. 3 vols. Tianjin: Baihua wenyi, 1983–1984.

Liu Wenying 劉文英. *Meng di mixin yu meng di tansuo* 夢的迷信與夢的探索. Beijing: Zhongguo shehui kexue, 1989.

———. "Zhongguo gudai dui meng di tansuo 中國古代對夢的探索." *Shehui kexue zhanxian* 社會科學戰線 4 (1983): 32–39.

Liu Xiang 劉向. *Lienü zhuan* 列女傳. *SBBY*.

Liu Xie 劉勰. *Wenxin diaolong [zhu]* 文心雕龍 [注]. Annotated by Huang Shulin 黃叔琳. Taipei: Kaiming, 1958.

Liu Zaifu 劉載福, ed. *Lingshengui yu zongjiao* 靈神鬼與宗教. Tainan: Zonghe, 1976.

Liu Zhiji 劉知幾. *Shitong tongshi* 史通通釋. 2 vols. *SBBY*.

Liu Ziqing 劉子清. *Zhongguo lidai xianneng funü pingzhuan* 中國歷代賢能婦女評傳. Taipei: Liming, 1978.

Lü Buwei 呂不韋. *Lüshi chunqiu* 呂氏春秋. *SBBY*.

Lü Chengzhi 呂誠之. *Zhongguo zongzu zhidu xiaoshi* 中國宗族制度小史. Shanghai: Longhu, 1935.

Lu Ji 陸機. *Lu Shiheng ji* 陸士衡集. Shanghai: Shangwu, 1936.

———. "Wenfu 文賦." *SBBY*.

Lü Qixiang 呂啓祥. *Hongloumeng kaijuan lu* 紅樓夢開卷錄. Xi'an: Shanxi renmin, 1987.

Lu Xingji 盧興基 and Gao Mingluan 高鳴鸞, eds. *Hongloumeng di yuyan yishu* 紅樓夢的語言藝術. Beijing: Yuwen, 1985.

Lü Zhenghui 呂正惠. *Shuqing chuantong yu zhengzhi xianshi* 抒情傳統與政治現實. Taipei: Daan, 1989.

Lunyu zhushu ji buzheng 論語注疏及補正. Taipei: Shijie, 1963.

Luo Dezhan 羅德湛. *Hongloumeng di wenxue jiazhi* 紅樓夢的文學價值. Taipei: Dongda, 1979.

Luo Guanzhong 羅貫中. *Sanguozhi tongsu yanyi* 三國志通俗演義. Hongzhi 弘治 edition (1494).

Machii Yōko 町井洋子. "Sindai no josei seikatsu: Shōsetsu no chusin to shite 清代の女性生活：小說の中心として." *Rekishi kyōiku* 歷史教育. Second series (1958): 37–43.

Mao Debiao 毛德彪 et al., eds. and comps. *Hongloumeng zhuping* 紅樓夢注評. Nanning: Guangxi renmin, 1981. (Also published as *Hongloumeng zhujie* 紅樓夢注解 by the same publisher in the same year.)

Mao Dun 茅盾. *Shenhua yanjiu* 神話研究. Tianjin: Xinhua, 1981.

Mao Pengji 毛鵬基. *Yimeng xuanbian* 異夢選編. Taipei: n.p., 1972.

Mao Qiling 毛奇齡. *Bailuzhou zhuke shuoshi* 白鷺洲主客說詩. Changsha: Shangwu, 1939.

Mao Xiaotong 毛效同, comp. *Tang Xianzu yanjiu ziliao huibian* 湯顯祖研究資料彙編. 2 vols. Shanghai: Guji, 1986.

Maoshi zhengjian 毛詩鄭箋. *SBBY*.

Masaru Mitarai 洗手御勝. *Kodai Chūgoku no kamigami: kodai no densetsu kenkyū* 古代中国の神タ——古代の伝説研究. Tokyo: Sōbunsha, 1984.

Mei Yuan 梅苑. *Hongloumeng di zhongyao nüxing* 紅樓夢的重要女性. Taipei: Taiwan shangwu, 1967.

Moren 墨人. *Hongloumeng di xiezuo jiqiao* 紅樓夢的寫作技巧. Taipei: Taiwan shangwu, 1966.

Mori Mikisaburō 森三樹三郎. *Shina kodai shinwa* 支那古代神話. Kyoto: Taigado, 1944.

Mou Zongsan 牟宗三. *Xinti yu xingti* 心體與性體. 2 vols. Taipei: Zhengzhong, 1968–1969.

Na Zhongxun (Tsung-hsün) 那宗訓. *Hongloumeng tansuo* 紅樓夢探索. Taipei: Xinwenfeng, 1982.

Nanjing shifan xueyuan Zhongwenxi ziliaoshi 南京師範學院中文系資料室. *Hongloumeng banben luncong* 紅樓夢版本論叢. Nanjing: Nanjing shifan xueyuan Zhongwenxi ziliaoshi, 1976.

Nanjing Zhongyiyuan 南京中醫院, comp. *Jianming Zhongyi neikexue* 簡明中醫內科學. Kowloon: Minglang, 1970.

Neijing suwen 內經素問. Annotated by Wang Bing 王冰. 2 vols. *SBBY*.

Ouyang Xiu 歐陽修. "Liuyi shihua 六一詩話." In He Wenhuan 何文煥, ed., *Lidai shihua* 歷代詩話, 1: 263–72. Beijing: Zhonghua, 1981.

———. *Shibenyi* 詩本義. *SBCK*.

Pan Jingruo 潘鏡若. *Sanjiao kaimi guizheng yanyi* 三教開迷歸正演義. 3 vols. Shanghai: Guji, 1990.

Pan Mingshen 潘銘燊. *Hongloumeng renwu suoyin* 紅樓夢人物索引. Hong Kong: Longmen, 1983.

Pan Zhonggui 潘重規. "Gao E buzuo *Hongloumeng* hou sishi hui di shangque 高鶚補作紅樓夢後四十回的商榷." *Xinya xuebao* 新亞學報 8/1 (1967): 367–82.

———. *Hongloumeng xinbian* 紅樓夢新辯. Taipei: Wenshizhe, 1974.

———. *Hongloumeng xinjie* 紅樓夢新解. Singapore: Qingnian, 1959.

———. *Hongxue wushi nian* 紅學五十年. Hong Kong: Zhongwen daxue xinya shuyuan zhongwenxi, 1966.

Pei Songzhi 裴松之. *Sanguo zhi zhu* 三國志注. Beijing: Zhonghua, 1959.

Pei Ziye 裴子野. "Diaochonglun 雕蟲論." In *QuanLiangwen* 全梁文, juan 53. *SGLCW*.

Pi Shumin 皮述民. *Hongloumeng kaolunji* 紅樓夢考論集. Taipei: Lianjing, 1984.

Qian Zhongshu 錢鍾書. *Guanzhuibian* 管錐編. 4 vols. Beijing: Zhonghua, 1982.

Qianlong Chaoben bainian hui Hongloumeng gao 乾隆抄本百廿回紅樓夢稿. Reprint of 1963 facsimile edition. Shanghai: Guji, 1984.

Qianlong Jiaxuben Zhiyanzhai chongping Shitouji 乾隆甲戌本脂硯齋重評石頭記. Taipei: Hu Shi(h) jinianguan, 1961.

Qinghuilou zhuren 清暉樓主人, comp. *Qingdai guixiu shichao* 清代閨秀詩鈔. 4 vols. Shanghai: Zhonghua xin jiaoyushe,1922.

Qiu Shiliang 邱世亮. *Hongloumeng lun* 紅樓夢論. Taipei: self-printed, 1981.

Qu Wanli 屈萬里. *Shangshu jishi* 尚書集釋. Taipei: Liangjing, 1983.

Quan Tang shi 全唐詩. 12 vols. Beijing: Zhonghua, 1960. Reprinted Tainan: Minglun, 1974.

Ren Jiyu 任繼愈. *Han Tang Fojiao sixiang lunji* 漢唐佛教思想論集. Beijing: Sanlian, 1963.

———, ed. *Zhongguo Daojiao shi* 中國道教史. Shanghai: Renmin, 1990.

Renmin chubanshe 人民出版社, ed. *Hongloumeng pinglunji* 紅樓夢評論集. Shanghai: Renmin, 1975.

Renmin wenxue chubanshe bianjibu 人民文學出版社編輯部, ed. *Hongloumeng yanjiu lunwenji* 紅樓夢研究論文集. Beijing: Remin wenxue, 1959.

Rong Zhaozu 容肇祖. *Mingdai sixiangshi* 明代思想史. Taipei: Kaiming, 1962.

Ruan Yuan 阮元. *Shisanjing zhushu [ji buzhen]* 十三經注疏 [及補正]. 16 vols. Taipei: Shijie, 1963–1969.

Rumeng 如夢 and Liu Min 劉敏. *Guaimeng yu yuce* 怪夢與預測. Xiamen: Xiamen daxue, 1993.

Sa Mengwu 薩孟武. *Hongloumeng yu Zhongguo jiu jiating* 紅樓夢與中國舊家庭. Taipei: Dongda, 1977.

———. *Zhongguo fazhi sixiang shi* 中國法制思想史. Taipei: Yanbo, 1978.

Sa Dula 薩都拉. *Yanmen ji* 雁門集. Shanghai: Guji, 1982.

Sawada Mizuho 澤田瑞穗. *Bukkyō to Chūgoku bungaku* 佛教と中国文学. Tokyo: Kokusho, 1975.

Shang Daxiang 尚達翔. *Gao E shici jianzhu* 高鶚詩詞箋注. Zhengzhou: Zhongzhou shuhuashe, 1983.

Shang Yanliu 商衍鎏. *Qingdai keju kaoshi shulu* 淸代科舉考試述錄. Beijing: Sanlian, 1958.

Shanghai shifan daxue Zhongwenxi qisanji *Hongloumeng* xuanxi bianxiezu 上海師範大學中文系七三級紅樓夢選析編寫組. *Fengjian moshi di xingxiang tuhua—Hongloumeng xuanxi* 封建末世的形象圖畫——紅樓夢選析. Shanghai: Renmin, 1975.

Shanghai wenyi chubanshe 上海文藝出版社, ed. *Zhongguo gudian beiju xiju lunji* 中國古典悲劇喜劇論集. Shanghai: Wenyi, 1983.

Shehui kexue zhanxian bianjibu 社會科學戰線編輯部, ed. *Hongloumeng yanjiu luncong* 紅樓夢研究論叢. Jilin: Jilin Renmin, 1980.

Shen Gangbo xiansheng bazhi rongqing lunwenji 沈剛伯先生八秩榮慶論文集. Taipei: Lianjing, 1976.

Shen Jin'ao 沈金鰲. *Zhongyi fuke xue* 中醫婦科學. Taipei: Wuzhou, 1969.

Shi Daqing 施達青. *Hongloumeng yu Qingdai fengjian shehui* 紅樓夢與淸代封建社會. Beijing: Renmin, 1976.

Shi Huiyue 釋慧嶽, ed. *Tiantai jiaoxue shi* 天台教學史. Xindian: Zhonghua Fojiao wenxian bianzhuanshe, 1974.

Shi Lei 石壘. *Wenxin diaolong yu Fo Ru erjiao yili lunji* 文心雕龍與佛儒二敎義理論集. Hong Kong: Yunzai shuwu, 1977.

Shi Naian 施耐庵. *Shuihuzhuan* 水滸傳. 3 vols. Taipei: Wenyuan, 1970.

Shi Renyuan 史任遠, ed. *Hongloumeng xinlun* 紅樓夢新論. Hong Kong: Dayuan, 1961.

Shimizu Eikichi 淸水榮吉. "Chūgoku no setsuwa to shōsetsu ni okeru yume 中国の說話と小說における夢." *Tenri daigaku gakuhō* 天理大学学報 7/3 (1956): 81–89.

Shitouji 石頭記. Facsimile edition of a handwritten manuscript kept in the Leningrad branch of The Institute of Oriental Studies, Soviet Academy of Sciences. 6 vols. Beijing: Zhonghua, 1986.

Shixi sanren 石溪散人. *Hongloumeng mingjia tikao* 紅樓夢名家題考. Taipei: Peiwen shushe, 1961.

Shou Pengfei 壽鵬飛. *Hongloumeng benshi bianzheng* 紅樓夢本事辨證. Shanghai: Shangwu, 1927.

Shu Chengxun 舒成勛. *Cao Xueqin zai xishan* 曹雪芹在西山. Edited by Hu Deping 胡德平. Beijing: Wenhua yishu, 1982.

Shujing 書經. *SBBY*.

Sishu duben 四書讀本. Annotated by Xie Bingyin 謝冰瑩 et al. Revised edition. Taipei: Sanmin, 1988.

Song Jing 松菁. *Hongloumeng renwu lun* 紅樓夢人物論. Taipei: Xinxing, 1966.

Song Longfa 宋隆發, ed. *Hongloumeng yanjiu wenxian mulu* 紅樓夢研究文獻目錄. Taipei: Xuesheng, 1982.

Su Hongchang 蘇鴻昌. *Lun Cao Xueqin di meixue sixiang* 論曹雪芹的美學思想. Edited by Long Yunyu 龍雲喬. Chongqin: Chongqing, 1984.

―――. "Lun Cao Xueqin zai *Hongloumeng* chuangzuo zhong di 'dazhi tan qing' 論曹雪芹在紅樓夢創作中的大旨談情." *HLMYJJK* 11 (1983): 39–58.

Su Wu 蘇蕪. *Shuomeng lu* 說夢錄. Shanghai: Guji, 1982.

Sun Kekuan 孫克寬. *Hanyuan daolun* 寒原道論. Taipei: Lianjing, 1977.

Sun Xun 孫遜. *Hongloumeng Zhiping chutan* 紅樓夢脂評初探. Shanghai: Guji, 1981.

――― and Chen Zhao 陳詔. *Hongloumeng yu Jinpingmei* 紅樓夢與金瓶梅. Yinchuan: Ningxia renmin, 1982.

Sun Zhengxin 孫正心. "Tiantai sixiang di yuanyuan yu qi tezhi 天台思想的淵源與其特質." In Zhang Mantao 張曼濤, ed., *Tiantai xue gailun* 天台學概論, 1: 291–351. Taipei: Dasheng, 1978.

Taiping yulan 太平御覽. Compiled by Li Fang 李昉 et al. 4 vols. Beijing: Zhonghua, 1960.

Taiyu 太愚. *Hongloumeng renwu lun* 紅樓夢人物論. Shanghai: Guoji wenhua fuwushe, 1948.

Tan Zhengbi 譚正璧. *Nüxing cihua* 女性詞話. Hong Kong: Baixin, 1958.

―――. *Zhongguo nüxing wenxueshi* 中國女性文學史. 2 vols. Shanghai: Guangming, 1935.

Tang Guizhang 唐圭璋, ed. *Quan Song ci* 全宋詞. 5 vols. Beijing: Zhonghua, 1965. Reprinted Tainan: Minglun, 1975.

Tang Junyi 唐君毅. *Zhongguo zhexue yuanlun (yuanjiao pian)* 中國哲學原論 (原教篇). Hong Kong: Xinya, 1975.

―――. *Zhongguo zhexue yuanlun (yuanxing pian)—Zhongguo zhexue zhong renxing sixiang zhi fazhan* 中國哲學原論 (原性篇)――中國哲學中人性思想之發展. Hong Kong: Xinya, 1968.

Tang Yongtong 湯用彤. "Yi yan zhi bian 意言之辯." In *Tang Yongtong xueshu lunwenji* 湯用彤學術論文集, pp. 214–32. Beijing: Zhonghua, 1983.

Tao Qiuying 陶秋英. *Hanfu zhi shi di yanjiu* 漢賦之史的研究. Kunming: Zhonghua, 1939.

Tian Yu 田于. *Hongloumeng xulu* 紅樓夢敘錄. Taipei: Dipingxian, 1976.

Tian Yuying 田毓英. *Zhongxi xiaoshuo shang di liangge fengdian renwu* 中西小說上的兩個瘋顛人物. Taipei: Wentanshe, 1971.

Tomita Ichiro 富田一郎, ed. *Hongloumeng yuhuisuoyin* 紅樓夢語彙索引. N.p.: Caihua shulin, 1973.

Tong Xue 佟雪. *Hongloumeng zhuti lun* 紅樓夢主題論. Nanchang: Jiangxi renmin, 1979.

Uchida Michio 內田道夫. "Tōdai shōsetsu ni okeru yume to genesetsu 唐代小說に
おける夢と幻設." *Toyogaku* 東洋学 1 (1959): 2–212.

Uchiyama Tomaya 內山知也. "Tōdai shōsetsu no yume ni tsuite 唐代小說の夢につ
いて." *Chūgoku bunka kenkyūkai kaihō* 中国文化研究会会報 5/1 (1956): 63–70.

Wang Anshi 王安石. *Linchuan xiansheng wenji* 臨川先生文集. Beijing: Zhonghua,
1959.

———. *Wang Anshi shiwen xuanzhu* 王安石詩文選注. Annotated by Guangzhou
tieluju Guangzhou fenju 廣州鐵路局廣州分局 et al. Guangzhou: Guangdong
renmin, 1975.

Wang Bohang 王伯沆. *Wang Bohang Hongloumeng piyu huihui* 王伯沆紅樓夢批
語匯彙. 2 vols. Nanjing: Jiangsu guji, 1985.

Wang Changding 王昌定. *Hongloumeng yishu tan* 紅樓夢藝術探. Hangzhou: Zhe-
jiang wenyi, 1985.

Wang Chong 王充. *Lunheng* 論衡. *SBBY.*

Wang Daolun 汪道倫. "Zhongguo chuantong wenhua zhong di qingxue yu *Hongloumeng* 中國傳統文化中的情學與紅樓夢." *HLMXK* 1 (1990): 105–30.

Wang Dewei (David Der-wei) 王德威. *Cong Liu E dao Wang Zhenhe* 從劉鶚到王禎
和. Taipei: Shibao, 1986.

Wang Dezhao 王德昭. *Qingdai keju zhidu yanjiu* 清代科舉制度研究. Hong Kong:
Chinese University Press, 1982.

Wang Fuzhi 王夫之. *Du sishu daquan shuo* 讀四書大全說. Beijing: Zhonghua,
1975.

———. *Zhouyi neizhuan* 周易內傳. In *Chuanshan yishu [quanji]* 船山遺書 [全集],
box 1, vols. 1–7. Reprint of Taipingyang 太平洋 edition (Shanghai, 1935). Taipei:
Zhongguo Chuanshan xuehui, 1972.

Wang Guanshi 王關仕. *Hongloumeng yanjiu* 紅樓夢研究. Taipei: Wenfang, 1979.

Wang Guowei 王國維. *Haining Wang Jing'an xiansheng yishu* 海寧王靜安先生遺
書. 14 vols. 1940. Reprinted Taipei: Taiwan Shangwu, 1976.

Wang Jisi 王季思 et al., eds. *Zhongguo shida gudian beiju ji* 中國十大古典悲劇集.
2 vols. Shanghai: Wenyi, 1982.

Wang Kunlun 王昆侖. *Hongloumeng renwulun* 紅樓夢人物論. Beijing: Sanlian,
1983.

Wang Mengruan 王夢阮 and Shen Ping'an 沈瓶庵. *Hongloumeng suoyin* 紅樓夢索
隱. Shanghai: Zhonghua, 1916.

Wang Peiqin 汪佩琴. *Honglou yihua* 紅樓醫話. Shanghai: Xuelin, 1987.

Wang Sanqing 王三慶. *Hongloumeng banben yanjiu* 紅樓夢版本研究. Taipei: Shi-
men, 1981.

Wang Shifu 王實甫. *Xixiangji* 西廂記. Edited by Wang Jisi 王季思. Shanghai: Guji,
1984.

Wang Shunu 王書奴. *Zhongguo changjishi* 中國娼妓史. Shanghai: Shenghuo, 1935.

Wang Weimin 王衛民, ed. *Hongloumeng Liu Lüfeng piyu jilu* 紅樓夢劉履芬批語
輯錄. Beijing: Shumu wenxian, 1987.

Wang Xianqian 王先謙. *Xunzi jijie* 荀子集解. Taipei: Shijie, 1987.

Wang Xiaochuan 王曉傳 (Liqi 利器). *Li Shizhen Li Xu fuzi shoupu* 李士楨李煦父
子手譜. Beijing: Beijing, 1983.

———. *Yuan Ming Qing sandai jinhui xiaoshuo xiqu shiliao* 元明清三代禁毀小說
戲曲史料. Beijing: Zuojia, 1958.

Wang Xiaolian 王孝廉. *Shenhua yu xiaoshuo* 神話與小說. Taipei: Lianjing, 1977.
————. *Zhongguo di shenhua shijie* 中國的神話世界. 2 vols. Taipei: Shibao, 1987.
Wang Xiling 王錫齡. "Qianlong chaoben baiershi hui *Hongloumeng* gao yanjiu 乾隆抄本百二十回紅樓夢稿研究."Master's thesis, Zhongguo wenhua xueyuan, 1976.
Wang Yangming 王陽明. *Chuanxilu* 傳習錄. Shanghai: Shangwu,1933.
Wang Yi 王易. *Ciqushi* 詞曲史. 2 vols. N. p.: Guangwen, n.d.
Wang Yunwu 王雲五, comp. *Mengzi zhengyi* 孟子正義. Shanghai: Shangwu, 1935.
Wang Zhaowen 王朝聞. *Lun Fengjie* 論鳳姐. Tianjin: Baihua wenyi, 1980.
Wang Zhiwu 王志武. *Hongloumeng renwu chongtu lun* 紅樓夢人物衝突論. Xi'an: Shanxi renmin, 1985.
Wei Shaochang 魏紹昌. *Hongloumeng banben xiaokao* 紅樓夢版本小考. Beijing: Zhongguo shehui kexue, 1982.
Wei Zhengtong 韋政通. *Dong Zhongshu* 董仲舒. Taipei: Dongda, 1986.
Wen Bing 文冰, ed. *Hongloumeng shici shizhu* 紅樓夢詩詞釋注. Hong Kong: Zhonghua, 1977.
Wen Long 文龍. "Wen Long *Jinpingmei* huiping 文龍金瓶梅彙評." In Huang Lin 黃霖, ed., *Jinpingmei ziliao huibian* 金瓶梅資料彙編, pp. 411–512. Beijing: Zhonghua, 1987.
Wen Yiduo 聞一多. "Fuxi kao 伏羲考." In *Wen Yiduo quanji* 聞一多全集, 1: 3–68. Shanghai: Kaiming, 1948.
————. "Gaotang shennü chuanshuo zhi fenxi 高唐神女傳說之分析." In *Wen Yiduo quanji*, 1: 81–116. Shanghai: Kaiming, 1948.
————. *Wen Yiduo quanji*. 4 vols. Shanghai: Kaiming, 1948.
Wenhuabu wenxue yishu yanjiuyuan Hongloumeng yanjiushi 文化部文學藝術研究院紅樓夢研究室, ed. *Daguanyuan yanjiu ziliao huibian* 大觀園研究資料匯編. Beijing: Wenhuabu wenxue yishu yanjiuyuan Hongloumeng yanjiushi, 1979.
Wenshushiliwen jing 文殊師利問經. In *T.* 14:492–509.
Wong, K(am-ming) 汪鑑明. *Hongloumeng di xushu yishu* 紅樓夢的敘述藝術. Translated by Li Dengxin 黎登鑫. Taipei: Chengwen, 1977.
Wu Enyu 吳恩裕. *Cao Xueqin congkao* 曹雪芹叢考. Shanghai: Guji, 1980.
————. *Cao Xueqin di gushi* 曹雪芹的故事. Hong Kong: Zhonghua, 1978.
————. *Cao Xueqin yizhu qiantan* 曹雪芹佚著淺探. Tainjin: Renmin, 1979.
————. *Kaobai xiaoji: Cao Xueqin Hongloumeng suoji* 考稗小記：曹雪芹紅樓夢瑣記. Hong Kong: Zhonghua, 1979.
————. *Youguan Cao Xueqin ba zhong* 有關曹雪芹八種. Shanghai: Gudian wenxue, 1958.
————. *Youguan Cao Xueqin shi zhong* 有關曹雪芹十種. Shanghai: Zhonghua, 1963.
Wu Hongyi 吳宏一, ed. *Hongloumeng yanjiu ziliao huibian* 紅樓夢研究資料彙編. Taipei: Julang, 1974.
Wu Lie 吳烈. *Zhongguo yunwen yanbianshi* 中國韻文演變史. Shanghai: Shijie, 1940.
Wu Shichang (Shih-ch'ang) 吳世昌. *Hongloumeng tanyuan waibian* 紅樓夢探源外編. Shanghai: Guji, 1980.
———— et al. *Sanlun Hongloumeng* 散論紅樓夢. Hong Kong: Jianwen, 1963.
Wu Xiaonan 吳曉南. *Chai Dai heyi xinlun* 釵黛合一新論. Hong Kong: Sanlian, 1985.

Wu Xinlei 吳新雷. *Cao Xueqin* 曹雪芹. Nanjing: Jiangsu guji, 1983.

───── and Huang Jinde 黃進德. *Cao Xueqin jiangnan jiashi kao* 曹雪芹江南家世考. Fuzhou: Fujian renmin, 1983.

Wu Ying 吳穎. *Hongloumeng renwu xinxi* 紅樓夢人物新析. Guangzhou: Guangdong renmin, 1987.

Wu Zisu 吳自甦. *Zhongguo jiating zhidu* 中國家庭制度. Taipei: Taiwan Shangwu, 1968.

Wuhan daxue Zhongwenxi qierji ping Hong zu 武漢大學中文系七二級評紅組. *Women shi zenyang du Hongloumeng di* 我們是怎樣讀紅樓夢的. Beijing: Renmin jiaoyu, 1975.

Xi Kang 稽康. "Nan Zhang Liaoshu ziran haoxue lun 難張遼叔自然好學論." In *QuanSanguowen* 全三國文, *juan* 50. *SGLCW*.

───── . "Xi Shuye yangsheng lun 稽叔夜養生論." In Xiao Tong 蕭統, comp., *Wenxuan* 文選 2: 1137–1141 (*juan* 53). Reprint of the 1936 edition. Hong Kong: Shangwu, 1974.

Xiang Xiu 向秀. "Nan Xi Shuye yangsheng lun 難稽叔夜養生論." In *QuanJinwen* 全晉文, *juan* 72. *SGLCW*.

Xianggang Zhongwen daxue Xinya shuyuan Zhongwen xi Hongloumeng yanjiu xiaozu 香港中文大學新亞書院紅樓夢研究小組, ed. *Xianggang suojian Hongloumeng yanjiu ziliao zhanlan* 香港所見紅樓夢研究資料展覽. Hong Kong: Zhongwen daxue, 1972.

Xiao Gang 蕭綱. "Yu Xiangdongwang shu 與湘東王書." In *QuanLiangwen* 全梁文, *juan* 11. *SGLCW*.

Xiao Huarong 蕭華榮. "'Yinyong qingxing'—Zhong Rong shige pingpan di lilun jichu 吟詠情性──鍾榮詩歌評判的理論基礎." *GDWXLLYJ* 7 (1982): 160–75.

Xiao Tong 蕭統, comp. *Wenxuan* 文選. Reprint of the 1936 edition. 2 vols. Hong Kong: Shangwu, 1974.

Xiaoxiang 瀟湘 (Liu Guoxiang 劉國香). *Hongloumeng yu chan* 紅樓夢與禪. Taipei: Shizihou zazhishe, 1970.

Xici zhuan 繫辭傳. In *Zhouyi Wang-Han zhu* 周易王韓注. Taipei: Xinxing, 1964.

Xie Guozhen 謝國楨. *Ming Qing zhi ji dangshe yundong kao* 明清之際黨社運動考. Banchao: Hanyuan, 1975.

───── . *Mingmo Qingchu di xuefeng* 明末清初的學風. Beijing: Renmin, 1982.

Xie Wuliang 謝無量. *Zhongguo funü wenxueshi* 中國婦女文學史. Taipei: Zhonghua, 1973.

Xie Zhaozhe 謝肇淛, comp. *Wu Zazu* 五雜俎. Shanghai: Zhonghua, 1959.

Xing Zhiping 邢治平. *Hongloumeng shijiang* 紅樓夢十講. Zhengzhou: Zhongzhou, 1983.

Xinkan jing ben tongsu yanyi zengxiang Bao Longtu pan baijia gongan 新刊京本通俗演義增像包龍圖判百家公案. In *Guben xiaoshuo congkan* 古本小說叢刊, 2/4: 1493–2012. Beijing: Zhonghua, 1990.

Xinyi Xunzi duben 新譯荀子讀本. Annotated by Wang Zhonglin 王忠林. Taipei: Sanmin, 1977.

Xu Chi 徐遲. *Hongloumeng yishu lun* 紅樓夢藝術論. Shanghai: Wenyi, 1980.

Xu Fuchu 徐復初. *Hongloumeng fuji shier zhong* 紅樓夢附集十二種. Shanghai: Fanggu, 1936.

Xu Fuguan 徐復觀. *Liang Han sixiang shi* 兩漢思想史. Revised edition. Taipei: Xuesheng, 1976.

———. "Zhao Gang *Hongloumeng xintan* di tupodian 趙岡紅樓夢新探的突破點." In *Zhongguo wenxue lunji* 中國文學論集. Taipei: Xuesheng, 1974.

Xu Fuming 徐扶明. *Hongloumeng yu xiqu bijiao yanjiu* 紅樓夢與戲曲比較研究. Shanghai: Guji, 1984.

———. "*Xixiangji, Mudanting* he *Hongloumeng* 西廂記、牡丹亭和紅樓夢." *HLMYJJK* 6 (1981): 181–204.

Xu Rencun 徐仁存 and Xu Youwei 徐有爲. *Cheng keben Hongloumeng xinkao* 程刻本紅樓夢新考. Taipei: Guoli bianyiguan, 1982.

Xu Shen 許愼. *Shuowen jiezi [zhu]* 說文解字 [注]. Annotated by Duan Yucai 段玉裁. *SBBY.*

Xu Shichang 徐世昌. *Qingru xuean* 清儒學案. N.p., 1938.

Xu Shuofang 徐朔方, ed. *Tang Xianzu ji* 湯顯祖集. 2 vols. Shanghai: Renmin, 1973.

Xu Tianxiao 徐天嘯. *Shenzhou nüzi xinshi zhengxubian* 神州女子新史正續編. 1913. Reprinted Taipei: Shihuo, 1978.

Xu Zhen'e 徐震堮. *Han Wei Liuchao xiaoshuo xuan* 漢魏六朝小說選. Shanghai: Guji, 1956.

Xu Zhonglin 許仲琳. *Fengshen yanyi* 封神演義. 2 vols. Hong Kong: Zhonghua, 1970.

Xue Ruisheng 薛瑞生. *Honglou caizhu* 紅樓采珠. Tianjin: Baihua wenyi, 1986.

Yamakawa Urara 山川麗. *Chūgoku josei shi* 中国女性史. Tokyo: Kasama shoin, 1977.

Yan Kejun 嚴可均, comp. *Quan shanggu sandai Qin Han Sanguo Liuchao wen* 全上古三代秦漢三國六朝文. 5 vols. Shanghai: Zhonghua, 1965.

Yan Rongli 顏榮利. *Hongloumeng zhong shici tiyong zhi yanjiu* 紅樓夢中詩詞題詠之研究. N.p., n.d.

Yang Wanli 楊萬里. *Chengzhai shihua* 誠齋詩話. In Ding Fubao 丁福保, ed., *Lidai shihua xubian* 歷代詩話續編, 1: 135–60. Beijing: Zhonghua, 1983.

Yang Weizhen 楊爲珍 and Guo Rongguang 郭榮光, eds. *Hongloumeng cidian* 紅樓夢辭典. Ji'nan: Shangdong wenyi, 1986.

Yang Xiong 楊雄. *Fayan* 法言. *SBBY.*

Yi Su 一粟, comp. *Hongloumeng juan* 紅樓夢卷. 2 vols. Beijing: Zhonghua, 1963.

———, ed. *Hongloumeng shulu* 紅樓夢書錄. Shanghai: Gudian wenxue, 1958.

Ying Bicheng 應必誠. *Lun Shitouji gengchen ben* 論石頭記庚辰本. Shanghai: Guji, 1983.

Youshi yuekan bianjishi 幼獅月刊編輯室, ed. *Hongloumeng yanjiuji* 紅樓夢研究集. Taipei: Youshi yuekan, 1972.

Yu Guangzhong 余光中. "Shi yu yinyue 詩與音樂." *Zhongguo shibao* 中國時報 (China Times), December 5, 1993, p. 39.

Yu Pingbo 俞平伯. *Hongloumeng bian* 紅樓夢辨. Shanghai: Yadong, 1929.

———. *Hongloumeng yanjiu* 紅樓夢研究. Shanghai: Changfeng, 1953.

———. *Hongloumeng yanjiu cankao ziliao xuanji: Yu Pingbo zhuanji* 紅樓夢研究參考資料選輯: 俞平伯專輯. Beijing: Renmin wenxue, 1973.

Yu Yingshi (Yü Ying-shih) 余英時. "Cao Xueqing di fan chuantong sixiang 曹雪芹的反傳統思想." *HLMYJJK* 5 (1980): 153–70.

———. "Guanyu *Hongloumeng* di zuozhe he sixiang wenti 關於紅樓夢的作者和

思想問題." In *Hongloumeng di liangge shijie* 紅樓夢的兩個世界, pp. 183–97. Taipei: Lianjing, 1978.

———. *Hongloumeng di liangge shijie* 紅樓夢的兩個世界. Taipei: Lianjing, 1978.

———. *Lun Dai Zhen yu Zhang Xuecheng: Qingdai zhongqi xueshu sixiangshi yanjiu* 論戴震與章學誠：清代中期學術思想史研究. Hong Kong: Longmen (Lung Men Press), 1976.

Yu Yue 俞樾. "Xiaofumei xianhua 小浮梅閒話." In *HLMJ* 2: 390–91.

Yu Zengwei 郁增偉. *Weilun Hongloumeng* 微論紅樓夢. Hong Kong: Tianyuan shuwu, 1982.

Yu Zhou 于舟 and Niu Wu 牛武. *Hongloumeng shici lianyu pingzhu* 紅樓夢詩詞聯語評注. Taiyuan: Shanxi renmin, 1980.

Yuan Jian 袁健 et al. *Wan Qing xiaoshuo gaishuo* 晚清小說概說. Tianjin: Jiaoyu, 1989.

Yuan Ke 袁軻. *Zhongguo gudai shenhua* 中國古代神話. Revised edition. Shanghai: Shangwu, 1957.

Yuan Mei 袁枚. *Xiaocang shanfang shiwenji* 小倉山房詩文集. *SBBY*.

Yuasa Yukihiko 湯淺幸孫. "Shindai ni okeru fujin kaihōron 清代における婦人解放論." *Nippon Chūgokugakkai hō* 日本中国学會報 4 (1952): 111–25.

Yue Hengjun 樂蘅軍. "Zhongguo yuanshi bianxing shenhua shitan 中國原始變形神話試探." In Chen Huihua 陳慧樺 and Gu Tianhong 古添洪, eds., *Cong bijiao shenhua dao wenxue* 從比較神話到文學, pp. 150–85. Taipei: Dongda, 1977.

Yuequan yinshe shi 月泉吟社詩. In Wang Yunwu 王雲五, ed., *Congshu jicheng chubian* 叢書集成初編, 80: 33–39. Shanghai: Shangwu, 1926.

Zeng Fankang 曾繁康. *Zhongguo zhengzhi sixiangshi* 中國政治思想史. Taipei: Dazhongguo, 1959.

Zeng Minzhi 曾敏之. *Tan Hongloumeng* 談紅樓夢. Guangzhou: Guangdong renmin, 1957.

Zhai Hao 翟灝, comp. *Tongsubian* 通俗編. Beijing: Shangwu, 1958.

Zhang Ailing 張愛玲. *Honglou mengyan* 紅樓夢魘. Taipei: Huangguan, 1977.

Zhang Bilai 張畢來. *Honglou Foying* 紅樓佛影. Shanghai: Wenyi, 1979.

———. *Jiafu shusheng* 賈府書聲. Shanghai: Wenyi, 1983.

———. *Manshuo Honglou* 漫說紅樓. Beijing: Renmin wenxue, 1978.

Zhang Chengqiu 張成秋. *Xian Qin Daojiao sixiang yanjiu* 先秦道教思想研究. Taipei: Zhonghua, 1971.

Zhang Cuo 張錯. *Ernü siqing* 兒女私情. Taipei: Huangguan, 1993.

Zhang Jinchi 張錦池. *Honglou shier lun* 紅樓十二論. Tianjin: Baihua wenyi, 1982.

Zhang Jinjian 張金鑑. *Zhongguo lizhi zhidushi gaiyao* 中國吏治制度史概要. Taipei: Sanmin, 1981.

Zhang Mantao 張曼濤, ed. *Fojiao yu Zhongguo wenhua* 佛教與中國文化. Taipei: Dasheng, 1978.

———, ed. *Fojiao zhexue sixiang lunji* 佛教哲學思想論集. Vol. 1. Taipei: Dasheng, 1978.

———, ed. *Tiantai xue gailun* 天台學概論. 3 vols. Taipei: Dasheng, 1978.

Zhang Qitai 張其泰. *Tonghua fengge ping Hongloumeng* 桐花鳳閣評紅樓夢. Edited by Liu Caonan 劉操南. Tianjin: Renmin, 1981.

Zhang Shouan 張壽安. *Yi li dai li: Ling Tingkan yu Qing zhongye Ruxue sixiang zhi zhuanbian* 以禮代理：凌廷堪與清中葉儒學思想之轉變. Taipei: Zhongyang yanjiuyuan jindaishi yanjiushuo, 1994.

Zhang Shuxiang 張淑香. *Shuqing chuantong di shensi yu tansuo* 抒情傳統的深思與探索. Taipei: Daan, 1992.

Zhang Xinzhi 張新之. "*Hongloumeng du fa* 紅樓夢讀法." *HLMJ* 2: 153–58.

Zhang Xuecheng 章學誠. *Wenshi tongyi* 文史通義. *SBBY*.

———. *Wenshi tongyi* 文史通義. Beijing: Zhonghua, 1957.

———. "Yu Chen Guanmin gongbu lun shixue 與陳觀民工部論史學." In *Zhangshi yishu* 章氏遺書, *juan* 14, pp. 23b–30a. N.p.: Jiayetang, 1922.

Zhang Yufa 張玉法 et al. *Zhongguo funüshi lunwenji* 中國婦女史論文集. Taipei: Taiwan Shangwu, 1981.

Zhang Zai 張載. *Zhangzi quanshu* 張子全書. Shanghai: Shangwu, 1935.

———. *Zhangzi yulu* 張子語錄. *SBCK*.

Zhanran 湛然. "Jingangbei 金剛錍." In *T.* 46: 781–86.

Zhao Cong 趙聰. *Yu Pingbo yu Hongloumeng shijian* 俞平伯與紅樓夢事件. Hong Kong: Youlian, 1955.

Zhao Gang 趙岡. *Hongloumeng kaozheng shiyi* 紅樓夢考證拾遺. Hong Kong: Gaoyuan, 1963.

———. *Hongloumeng lunji* 紅樓夢論集. Taipei: Zhiwen, 1975.

———. *Huaxiang tongchou du Honglou* 花香銅臭讀紅樓. Taipei: Shibao wenhua, 1978.

———. *Mantan Hongloumeng* 漫談紅樓夢. Taipei: Jingshi, 1981.

——— and Chen Zhongyi 陳鍾毅. *Hongloumeng xintan* 紅樓夢新探. 2 vols. Hong Kong: Wenyi, 1970.

———. *Hongloumeng yanjiu xinbian* 紅樓夢研究新編. Taipei: Lianjing, 1975.

Zhen Jun 震鈞, comp. "Baqiren zhushu chunmu 八旗人著述存目." In Lei Jin 雷瑨, comp., *Qingren shuohui* 清人說薈, 1: 534–44. Reprint of Saoye shanfang 掃葉山房 edition (Shanghai, 1928). No. 143 of *Zhonghua wenshi congshu* 中華文史叢書. Taipei: Huawen, 1969.

Zheng Guangyi 鄭光儀, ed. *Zhongguo lidai cainü shige jianshang cidian* 中國歷代才女詩歌鑒賞辭典. Beijing: Zhongguo gongren, 1991.

Zheng Xuan 鄭玄. *Maoshi zhengjian* 毛詩鄭箋. *SBBY*.

Zheng Zhenduo 鄭振鐸. *Chatuben Zhongguo wenxueshi* 插圖本中國文學史. 2 vols. Hong Kong: Shangwu, 1961.

———. "Du Maoshixu 讀毛詩序." In Gu Jiegang 顧頡剛, ed., *Gushi bian* 古史辨 3: 382–401. Beijing: Pushe, 1926.

Zhiyanzhai chongping Shitouji 脂硯齋重評石頭記. Facsimile edition of the Jimao (1759) manuscript kept in Beijing Library. 2 vols. Shanghai: Guji, 1981.

Zhong Huiling 鍾慧玲. "Qing dai nü shiren 清代女詩人." Ph.D. dissertation, Zhengzhi daxue, 1981.

Zhong Rong 鍾嶸. *Shipin* 詩品. *SBBY*.

Zhong Sicheng 鍾嗣成 and Jia Zhongming 賈仲明. *Lu gui bu [xin jiaozhu]*, *Xu lu gui bu [xin jiaozhu]* 錄鬼簿 [新校注]、續錄鬼簿 [新校注]. Annotated by Ma Lian 馬廉. Taipei: Shijie, 1960.

Zhongguo gudai xiaoshuo lilun yanjiu 中國古代小說理論研究. Wuchang: Huazhong gongxueyuan, 1985.

Zhongguo Hongloumeng xuehui mishuchu 中國紅樓夢學會祕書處, ed. *Hong-loumeng yishu lun* 紅樓夢藝術論. Ji'nan: Qilu, 1983.

Zhongguo xueshu ziliaoshe 中國學術資料社, ed. *Hongloumeng ziliao* 紅樓夢資料. Vols. 3–5. Hong Kong: Zhongguo xueshu ziliaoshe, 1983.

Zhongguo yuwen xueshe 中國語文學社, ed. *Zhongguo wenxuepiping yanjiu lunwenji: Wenxin diaolong yanjiu lunwenji* 中國文學批評研究論文集：文心雕龍研究論文集. N.p.: Zhongguo yuwen xueshe, 1969.

Zhongguo zuojia xiehui Guizhou fenhui *Hongloumeng* yanjiuzu 中國作家協會貴州分會紅樓夢研究組, ed. *Hongloumeng lunji* 紅樓夢論集. Guiyang: Guizhou renmin, 1983.

Zhonghua renmin gongheguo wenhuabu 中華人民共和國文化部 et al. *Cao Xueqin shishi erbai zhounian jinian zhanlanhui jianyao shuoming* 曹雪芹逝世二百周年紀念展覽會簡要說明. N.p.: n.p., 1963.

Zongmi 宗密. *Yulanpen jing shu* 于蘭盆經疏. *T.* 39: 505–12.

Zhongyi neikexue jiangyi 中醫內科學講義. Shanghai: Yiyao weisheng, 1969.

Zhou Guanhua 周冠華. *Daguanyuan jiushi Ziyiyuan* 大觀園就是自怡園. Taipei: Fuxin yinshuachang, 1974.

Zhou Guansheng 周冠生. *Meng zhi mi tansuo* 夢之謎探索. Beijing: Kexue, 1990.

Zhou Ruchang 周汝昌. *Cao Xueqin* 曹雪芹. Beijing: Zuojia,1964.

———. *Cao Xueqin xiao zhuan* 曹雪芹小傳. Tianjin: Baihua wenyi, n.d.

———. *Gongwang fu kao: Hongloumeng beijing sucai tantao* 恭王府考——紅樓夢背景素材探討. Shanghai: Guji, 1980.

———, ed. *Hongloumeng cidian* 紅樓夢辭典. Guangzhou: Guangdong renmin, 1987.

———. *Hongloumeng xinzheng* 紅樓夢新證. 2 vols. Revised edition. Beijing: Renmin wenxue, 1976.

———. *Hongloumeng yu Zhongguo wenhua* 紅樓夢與中國文化. Taipei: Dongda, 1989.

Zhou Shaoliang 周紹良. *Hongloumeng yanjiu lunji* 紅樓夢研究論集. Taiyuan: Shanxi renmin, 1983.

Zhou Shuwen 周書文. *Hongloumeng renwu suzao di bianzheng yishu* 紅樓夢人物塑造的辯證藝術. Nanchang: Jiangxi renmin, 1986.

Zhou Tai 周泰. *Yue Hongloumeng suibi* 閱紅樓夢隨筆. Shanghai: Zhonghua, 1958.

Zhou Zhongming 周中明. *Hongloumeng di yuyan yishu* 紅樓夢的語言藝術. Guilin: Lijiang, 1982.

Zhouli Zheng zhu 周禮鄭注. *SBBY.*

Zhouyi jinzhu jinyi 周易今注今譯. Annotated and translated by Nan Huaijin 南懷瑾 and Xu Qinting 徐芹庭. Revised edition. Taipei: Taiwan Shangwu, 1984.

Zhu Fengyu 朱鳳玉. "*Hongloumeng* Zhiyanzhai pingyu xintan 紅樓夢脂硯齋評語新探." Master's thesis, Zhongguo wenhua xueyuan, 1979.

Zhu Meishu 朱眉叔. *Hongloumeng di beijing yu renwu* 紅樓夢的背景與人物. Shenyang: Liaoning daxue, 1986.

Zhu Xi 朱熹, comp. *Er Cheng yulu* 二程語錄. Shanghai: Shangwu, 1937.

———. *Jinsilu* 近思錄. *SBBY.*

———. *Shi jizhuan* 詩集傳. *SBCK.*

———. *Zhu Wengong wenji* 朱文公文集. *SBCK.*

Zhu Xubai 朱虛白. *Hongloumeng renwu pingzhuan* 紅樓夢人物評傳. 2 vols. Taipei: self-printed, 1960.

Zhu Yixuan 朱一玄, ed. *Hongloumeng ziliao huibian* 紅樓夢資料匯編. Tianjin: Nankai daxue, 1985.

———. *Hongloumeng Zhiping jiaolu* 紅樓夢脂評校錄. Ji'nan: Qilu, 1986.

Zhu Ziqing 朱自清. "Shi yan zhi bian 詩言志辨." In *Gudian wenxue zhuanji* 古典文學專集, 1: 183–335. Shanghai: Guji, 1981.

Zhuangzi [*jijie*] 莊子 [集解]. Annotated by Wang Xianqian 王先謙. Taipei: Sanmin, 1963.

Zuihongsheng 醉紅生, ed. *Hongloumeng tanxie* 紅樓夢譚屑. N.p.: Minyoushe, 1917.

Zuojia chubanshe bianjishi 作家出版社編輯室, ed. *Hongloumeng wenti taolunji* 紅樓夢問題討論集. Vol. 4. Beijing: Zuojia, 1955.

Works in Western Languages

Adkins, Arthur W. H. "Aristotle and the Best Kinds of Tragedy." *Classical Quarterly* n.s. 16 (1966): 78–102.

———. *Merit and Responsibility: A Study in Greek Values*. Oxford: Clarendon Press, 1960.

Alleton, Viviane. *Les Chinois et la passion des noms*. Paris: Aubier, 1993.

Arbuckle, Gary. "Some Remarks on a New Translation of the *Chunqiu fanlu*." A review of *Tung Chung-shu Ch'un-ch'iufan-lu: Üppiger Tau des Frühling-und-Herbst-Klassikers*, by Robert H. Gassmann (Bern:PeterLang, 1988). *Early China* 17 (1992): 215–38.

Aristotle. *The Complete Works of Aristotle*. 2 vols. Edited by Jonathan Barnes. Princeton: Princeton University Press,1984.

Augustine. *Confessiones*. opera et studio Monachorum S. Benedicti a Congregatione S. Mauri, Paris, 1679. Reprinted in J.-P. Migne, *Patrologia Latina*, vol. 32. Paris: Garnier frères, 1845.

Baker, Hugh D. *Chinese Family and Kinship*. New York: Columbia University Press, 1979.

Barbour, John D. *The Conscience of the Autobiographer: Ethical and Religious Dimensions of Autobiography*. New York: St. Martin's Press, 1992.

Baynes, Cary F., trans. *The I Ching or Book of Changes*. Princeton: Princeton University Press, 1950.

Beasley, W. G., and E. G. Pulleyblank, eds. *Historians of China and Japan*. London: Oxford University Press, 1961.

Benstock, Shari, ed. *Feminist Issues in Literary Scholarship*. Bloomington: Indiana University Press, 1987.

Bodde, Derk. "Myths of Ancient China." In Charles Le Blanc and Dorothy Borei, eds., *Essays on Chinese Civilization*, pp. 45–84. Princeton: Princeton University Press, 1981.

Bol, Peter. *"This Culture of Ours": Intellectual Transitions in T'ang and Sung China*. Stanford: Stanford University Press, 1992.

Boltz, William G. "Kung Kung and the Flood: Reverse Euhemerism in the *Yao Tien*." *T'oung Pao* 67 (1981): 141–53.

Bonner, Joey. *Wang Kuo-wei: An Intellectual Biography*. Cambridge: Harvard University Press, 1986.

Booth, Wayne C. *The Rhetoric of Fiction*. Chicago: University of Chicago Press, 1961.

Boyarin, Daniel. *Intertextuality and the Reading of Midrash.* Bloomington: Indiana University Press, 1990.

————. "Voices in the Text: Midrash and the Inner Tension of Biblical Narrative." *Revue Biblique* 93 (1986): 581–97.

Brandauer, Frederick P. *Tung Yüeh.* Boston: Twayne, 1978.

Braudel, Fernand. *On History.* Translated by Sarah Matthews. Chicago: University of Chicago Press, 1980.

Bremer, J. M. *Hamartia: Tragic Error in the "Poetics" of Aristotle and in Greek Tragedy.* Amsterdam: Adolf M. Hakkert,1969.

Brown, Carolyn T., ed. *Psycho-Sinology: The Universe of Dreams in Chinese Culture.* Lanham, Md.: University Press of America, 1988.

Bruns, Gerald L. "Midrash and Allegory: The Beginnings of Scriptural Interpretation." In Robert Alter and Frank Kermode, eds., *The Literary Guide to the Bible*, pp. 625–46. Cambridge: Belknap Press of Harvard University Press, 1987.

Bynner, Witter, trans. *The Jade Mountain: A Chinese Anthology.* New York: Random House, 1929.

Calinescu, Matei. *Rereading.* New Haven: Yale University Press, 1993.

Camus, Albert. *A Happy Death.* Translated by Richard Howard. New York: Knopf, 1972.

Cao Xueqin and Gao E. *The Story of the Stone.* Translated by David Hawkes and John Minford. 5 vols. Harmondsworth: Penguin, 1973–1986.

Carlitz, Katherine. *The Rhetoric of "Chin P'ing Mei."* Bloomington: Indiana University Press, 1986.

Cecil, Russell L. *A Textbook of Medicine.* Philadelphia and London: W. B. Saunders, 1927.

Chaffee, John W. *The Thorny Gates of Learning in Sung China.* New York: Cambridge University Press, 1985.

Chan, Bing C. *The Authorship of "The Dream of the Red Chamber": Based on a Computerized Statistical Study of Its Vocabulary.* Hong Kong: Joint, 1986.

————. "A Computerized Statistical Approach to the Disputed Authorship Problem of *The Dream of the Red Chamber.*" *Tamkang Review* 16/3 (1986): 247–78.

Chan, Hing-ho (Chen Qinghao). *Le "Hongloumeng" et les commentaires de Zhiyanzhai.* Paris: Presses Universitaires de France, 1982.

Chan, Hok-lam. *Legitimation in Imperial China: Discussions under the Jurchen-Chin Dynasty (1115–1234).* Seattle: University of Washington Press, 1984.

Chan, Wing-tsit, ed., *Chu Hsi and Neo-Confucianism.* Honolulu: University of Hawaii Press, 1986.

————, trans. and ed. *Neo-Confucian Terms Explained: (The Pei-hsi tzu-i) by Ch'en Ch'un, 1159–1223.* New York: Columbia University Press, 1986.

————, trans. *The Platform Scripture.* New York: St. John's University Press, 1963.

————, trans. *Reflections on Things at Hand: The Neo-Confucian Anthology Compiled by Chu Hsi and Lü Tsu-ch'ien.* New York: Columbia University Press, 1967.

————, trans. and comp. *A Source Book in Chinese Philosophy.* Princeton: Princeton University Press, 1963.

Chang, K. C. "A Classification of Shang and Chou Myths." In *Early Chinese Civilization: Anthropological Perspectives*, pp. 149–73. Cambridge: Harvard University Press,1976.

Chang, Kang-i Sun. *The Late Ming Poet Ch'en Tzu-lung: Cries of Love and Loyalism.* New Haven: Yale University Press,1990.

———. "Ming-Qing Women Poets and the Notions of 'Talent' and 'Morality.'" In R. Bin Wong, Theodore Huters, and Pauline Yu, eds., *Culture and State in Chinese History: Conventions, Conflicts and Accommodations.* Stanford: Stanford University Press, forthcoming.

———, and Haun Saussy, eds. *An Anthology of Chinese Women Poets: From Ancient Times to 1911.* Stanford: Stanford University Press, forthcoming.

Chao, C. Y. Yeh (Ye Jiaying). "Wang Guowei: His Character and His Scholarship." *Journal of the Chinese University of Hong Kong* 1 (1973): 61–96.

Chao, Paul. *Chinese Kinship.* London: Kegan Paul International, 1983.

Ch'en, Kenneth. *Buddhism in China, A Historical Survey.* Princeton: Princeton University Press, 1964.

———. *The Chinese Transformation of Buddhism.* Princeton: Princeton University Press, 1973.

Chow Kai-wing. *The Rise of Confucian Ritualism in Late Imperial China: Ethics, Classics, and Lineage Discourse.* Stanford: Stanford University Press, 1994.

Collingwood, R. G. *The Idea of History.* Oxford: Oxford University Press, 1943.

Conacher, D. J. *Euripidean Drama: Myth, Theme and Structure.* Toronto: University of Toronto Press, 1967.

Crites, Stephen. "The Narrative Quality of Experience." *JAAR* 39/3 (1971): 291–311.

Culler, Jonathan. *On Deconstructionism: Theory and Criticism after Structuralism.* Ithaca: Cornell University Press, 1982.

———, ed. *On Puns: The Foundation of Letters.* Oxford and New York: Basil Blackwell, 1988.

da Pisa, Guido. *Expositiones et Glose super Comediam Dantis.* Edited by Vincenzio Cioffari. Albany: State University of New York Press, 1974.

Dante Alighieri. *La divina commedia.* Milano: Arnoldo Mondadori, 1985.

———. *The Divine Comedy.* Translated with a commentary by Charles S. Singleton. 6 vols. Princeton: Princeton University Press, 1970.

Dauer, Dorothea. *Schopenhauer as Transmitter of Buddhist Ideas.* Berne: Long, 1969.

Dawe, R. D. "Some Reflections on *Atê* and *Hamartia.*" *Harvard Study in Classical Philology* 72 (1967): 89–123.

de Bary, Wm. Theodore, and John W. Chaffee, eds. *Neo-Confucian Education: The Formative Stage.* Berkeley: University of California Press, 1985.

de Certeau, Michel. *The Writing of History.* Translated by Tom Conley. New York: Columbia University Press, 1988.

de Man, Paul. *Allegories of Reading: Figural Language in Rousseau, Nietzsche, Rilke, and Proust.* New Haven: Yale University Press, 1979.

———. *Blindness and Insight: Essays in the Rhetoric of Contemporary Criticism.* 2nd ed. Minneapolis: University of Minnesota Press, 1983.

de Voe, Sally C. "Historical Event and Literary Effect: The Concept of History in the *Tso-chuan.*" *The Stone Lion* 7 (1981): 45–58.

Demiéville, Paul. "Chang Hsüeh-ch'eng and His Historiography." In *Choix d'études sinologiques (1921–1970),* pp. 178–82. Leiden: E. J. Brill,1973.

———. "Le miroir spirituel." In *Choix d'études bouddhiques (1929–1970),* pp. 131–

56. Leiden: E. J. Brill, 1973. Reprinted as "The Mirror of the Mind" in Peter N. Gregory, ed., *Sudden and Gradual: Approaches to Enlightenment in Chinese Thought*, pp. 13–40. Honolulu: University of Hawaii Press, 1987.

Derrida, Jacques. *Of Grammatology*. Translated by Gayatri Chakravotry Spivak. Baltimore: Johns Hopkins University Press, 1976.

———. *Positions*. Paris: Les Editions de Minuit, 1972.

Dodds, E. R. *The Greeks and the Irrational*. Berkeley and Los Angeles: University of California Press, 1964.

Dong, Lorraine. "The Many Faces of Cui Yingying." In Richard Guisso and Stanley Johannesen, eds., *Women in China*, pp. 75–98. Youngstown: Philo Press, 1981.

Dubs, Homer H. "The Reliability of Chinese Histories." *Far Eastern Quarterly* 6 (1946): 23–43.

Ebrey, Patricia. *The Aristocratic Families of Early Imperial China: A Case Study of the Po-ling Ts'ui Family*. Cambridge: Cambridge University Press, 1978.

———. "Concepts of the Family in the Sung Dynasty." *JAS* 43 (1984): 219–45.

———. "Women, Marriage, and the Family in Chinese History." In Paul S. Ropp, ed, *Heritage of China: Contemporary Perspectives on Chinese Civilization*, pp. 197–223. Berkeley and Los Angeles: University of California Press, 1990.

———, and James L. Watson, eds. *Kinship Organization in Late Imperial China 1000–1940*. Berkeley and Los Angeles: University of California Press, 1986.

Eco, Umberto. *Semiotics and the Philosophy of Language*. Bloomington: Indiana University Press, 1986.

Edwards, Louise P. *Men and Women in Qing China: Gender in "The Red Chamber Dream."* New York: E. J. Brill, 1994.

Egan, Ronald C. "Narratives in *Tso Chuan*." *HJAS* 37/2 (1977): 323–52.

———. *Word, Image, and Deed in the Life of Su Shi*. Cambridge: Harvard University Press, 1994.

Eggert, Marion. *Rede vom Traum: Traumauffasungen der Literatenschicht im späten kaiserlichen China*. Stuttgart: F. Steiner, 1993.

Eliot, T. S. *On Poetry and Poets*. New York: Noonday Press, 1961.

———. *Selected Essays*. New York: Brace, 1932.

Elman, Benjamin A. "Changes in Confucian Civil Service Examinations from the Ming to the Ch'ing Dynasty." In Benjamin A. Elman and Alexander Woodside, eds., *Education and Society in Late Imperial China*, pp. 111–49. Berkeley and Los Angeles: University of California Press, 1994.

———. "Political, Social, and Cultural Reproduction via Civil Service Examinations in Late Imperial China." *JAS* 50/1 (February 1991): 7–28.

Elvin, Mark. "Female Virtue and the State in China." *Past and Present* 104 (1984): 111–152.

Englert, Siegfried. *Materialien zur Stellung der Frau und zur Sexualität im vormodernen und modernen China*. Frankfurt: Haag und Herchen Verlag, 1980.

Fehl, Noah. *Rites and Propriety in Literature and Life: A Perspective for a Cultural History of Ancient China*. Hong Kong: Chinese University Press, 1971.

Fei, Hsiao-tung. *China's Gentry: Essays in Rural-Urban Relations*. Revised and edited by Margaret Park Redfield. Chicago: University of Chicago Press, 1953.

Finley, Moses I. *Ancient Slavery and Modern Ideology*. New York: Viking Press, 1980.

Fisk, Craig. "Literary Criticism." In William H. Nienhauser, Jr., ed., *The Indiana Com-*

panion to Traditional Chinese Literature, pp. 49–58. Bloomington: Indiana University Press, 1986.

Foucault, Michel. *The Archaeology of Knowledge and The Discourse on Language*. Translated by A. M. Sheridan Smith. New York: Pantheon Book, 1972.

Fraser, J. T., et al., eds. *Time, Science, and Society in China and the West*. Amherst: University of Massachusetts Press, 1986.

Freedman, Maurice, ed. *Family and Kinship in Chinese Society*.Stanford: Stanford University Press, 1970.

————. *The Study of Chinese Society*. Stanford: Stanford University Press, 1979.

Fung, Yu-lan. *History of Chinese Philosophy*. Translated by Derk Bodde. 2 vols. Princeton: Princeton University Press, 1952–1953.

Furth, Charlotte. "Concepts of Pregnancy, Childbirth, and Infancy in Ch'ing China." *JAS* 46/1 (February 1987): 7–36.

————. "The Patriarch's Legacy: Household Instructions and the Transmission of Orthodox Values." In K. C. Liu, ed., *Orthodoxy in Late Imperial China*, pp. 187–211. Berkeley and Los Angeles: University of California Press, 1990.

Gardiner, H. M., et al. *Feeling and Emotion: A History of Theories*. New York: American Book Company, 1937.

Gernet, Jacques. "Écrit et histoire." In his *L'intelligence de la Chine: les social et le mental*, pp. 351–60. Paris: Editions Gallimard, 1994.

————. "Sur la notion de changement." In his *L'intelligence de la Chine: les social et le mental*, pp. 323–34. Paris: Editions Gallimard, 1994.

Gerstlacher, Anna, et al., eds, *Women and Literature in China*. Bochum: Studien Verlag, 1985.

Girard, René. *"To Double Business Bound": Essays on Literature, Mimesis, and Anthropology*. Baltimore: Johns Hopkins University Press, 1978.

Goodrich, L. Carrington. *The Literary Inquisition of Ch'ien-lung*. New York: Paragon Book Reprint Corp., 1966.

————. "On Certain Books Suppressed by Order of Ch'ien-lung during the Years 1772–1778." In *Proceedings of the XXV International Congress of Orientalists* 5 (1963): 71–77.

Graham, A. C. "'Being' in Western Philosophy Compared with *Shih/Fei* and *Yu/Wu* in Chinese Philosophy." *Asia Major* n.s. 7 (1959): 79–111. Reprinted in his *Studies in Chinese Philosophy and Philosophical Literature*, pp. 322–59, Singapore: National University of Singapore Press, 1986; and his *Disputers of the Tao: Philosophical Argument in Ancient China*, pp. 410–14, La Salle, Ill.: Open Court, 1989.

————, trans. *The Book of Lieh-tzu: A Classic of the Tao*. New York: Columbia University Press, 1990.

————, trans. *The Book of Lieh-tzu*, A New Translation. London: John Murray, 1960.

————, trans. *Chuang-tzu: The Seven Inner Chapters and Other Writings from the Book "Chuang-tzu."* London and Boston: Allen & Unwin, 1981.

————. *Disputers of the Tao: Philosophical Argument in Ancient China*. La Salle, Ill.: Open Court, 1989.

————. *Later Mohist Logic, Ethics and Science*. Hong Kong: Chinese University Press, 1978.

————. "The Meaning of *Ch'ing* [*qing*]." First appeared as a section in "The Background of the Mencian Theory of Human Nature," *Tsing Hua Journal of Chinese*

Studies 6/1, 2 (1967): 259–65. Reprinted in his *Studies in Chinese Philosophy and Philosophical Literature*, pp. 59–65, Singapore: National University of Singapore Press, 1986.

———. *Studies in Chinese Philosophy and Philosophical Literature*. Singapore: National University of Singapore Press, 1986.

Granet, Marcel. *Danses et légendes de la Chine ancienne*. Paris: Paris: F. Alcan, 1926.

Gregory, Peter N., ed. *Sudden and Gradual: Approaches to Enlightenment in Chinese Thought*. Honolulu: University of Hawaii Press, 1987.

Grisar, Elizabeth. *La femme en Chine*. Paris: Buchet/Chastel, 1957.

Guisso, Richard W. "Thunder over the Lake: The Five Classics and the Perception of Woman in Early China." In Richard W. Guisso and Stanley Johannesen, eds., *Women in China: Current Directions in Historical Scholarship*, pp. 47–62. Youngstown: Philo Press, 1981.

———, and Stanley Johannesen, eds. *Women in China: Current Directions in Historical Scholarship*. Youngstown: Philo Press, 1981.

Guy, R. Kent. *The Emperor's Four Treasuries: Scholars and the State in the Late Ch'ien-lung Era*. Cambridge: Harvard University Press, 1987.

Hall, David L., and Roger T. Ames. *Thinking through Confucius*. Albany: State University of New York Press,1987.

Hall, Jonathan. "Heroic Repression: Narrative and Aesthetics in Shen Fu's *Six Records of a Floating Life*." *Comparative Criticism* 9 (1987): 155–72.

Hanan, Patrick, trans. *The Carnal Prayer Mat*. By Li Yu. New York: Ballantine Books, 1990.

———. *The Chinese Vernacular Story*. Cambridge: Harvard University Press, 1981.

Handlin, Joanna F. *Action in Late Ming Thought: The Reorientation of Lü K'un and Other Scholar-Officials*. Berkeley and Los Angeles: University of California Press, 1983.

———. "Lü K'un's New Audience: The Influence of Women's Literacy on Sixteenth-Century Thought." In Margery Wolf and Roxane Witke, eds., *Women in Chinese Society*, pp. 13–18. Stanford: Stanford University Press, 1975.

Hansen, Chad. *A Daoist Theory of Chinese Thought: A Philosophical Interpretation*. New York: Oxford University Press, 1992.

———. *Language and Logic in Ancient China*. Ann Arbor: University of Michigan Press, 1983.

———. "Language in the Heart-Mind." In Robert E. Allinson, ed., *Understanding the Chinese Mind: Philosophical Roots*, pp. 75–123. New York: Oxford University Press, 1989.

———. "*Qing* (Emotions) in Pre-Buddhist Chinese Thought." In Joel Marks and Roger T. Ames, *Emotions in Asian Thought: A Dialogue in Comparative Philosophy*, pp. 181–211. Albany: State University of New York Press, 1995.

———. "A Tao of Tao in *Chuang-tzu*." In Victor H. Mair, ed., *Experimental Essays on Chuang-tzu*, pp. 24–55. Honolulu: University of Hawaii Press, 1983.

Hartman, Geoffrey H. "Midrash as Law and Literature." *Journal of Religion* 74/3 (1994): 338–55.

———, and Sanford Budick, eds. *Midrash and Literature*. New Haven: Yale University Press, 1986.

Hawkes, David. "*The Story of the Stone*: A Symbolist Novel." *Renditions* 25 (Spring 1986): 6–17.

Hawthorne, Nathaniel. *The Scarlet Letter: A Romance*. New York: Modern Library, 1950.

Hegel, Robert E. *The Novel in Seventeenth-Century China*. New York: Columbia University Press, 1980.

Heller, Thomas C., et al., eds. *Reconstructing Individualism, Autonomy, Individuality and the Self in Western Thought*. Stanford: Stanford University Press, 1986.

Henderson, John B. *Development and Decline of Chinese Cosmology*. New York: Columbia University Press, 1984.

————. *Scripture, Canon, and Commentary: A Comparison of Confucian and Western Exegesis*. Princeton: Princeton University Press, 1991.

Hessney, Richard C. "Beautiful, Talented, and Brave: Seventeenth-Century Chinese Scholar-Beauty Romances." Ph.D. dissertation, Columbia University, 1978.

Hirsch, E. D., Jr. "Transhistorical Intentions and the Persistence of Allegory." *NLH* 25/3 (Summer 1994): 549–67.

————. *Validity in Interpretation*. New Haven: Yale University Press, 1967.

Holland, Norman. "Unity Identity Text Self." In Jane P. Tompkins, ed., *Reader-Response Criticism: From Formalism to Post-Structuralism*, pp. 118–33. Baltimore: Johns Hopkins University Press, 1980.

Hsia, C. T. *The Classic Chinese Novel: A Critical Introduction*. New York: Columbia University Press, 1968.

Hsieh, Jih-chang, and Chuang Ying-Chang, eds. *Chinese Family and Ritual Behavior*. Taipei: Institute of Ethnology, Academia Sinica, 1985.

Huang, Martin W. "Author(ity) and Reader in Traditional Chinese *Xiaoshuo* Commentary." *CLEAR* 16 (1994): 41–67.

————. *Literati and Self-Re/Presentation: Autobiographical Sensibility in the Eighteenth-Century Chinese Novel*. Stanford: Stanford University Press, 1995.

Hung, Eva, ed. *Paradoxes of Traditional Chinese Literature*. Hong Kong: Chinese University Press, 1994.

Huntington, C. W., Jr., with Geshé Namgyal Wangchen. *The Emptiness of Emptiness: An Introduction to Early Indian Madhyamika*. Honolulu: University of Hawaii Press, 1989.

Hurvitz, Leon. "Render unto Caesar in Early Chinese Buddhism." Liebenthal Festschrift, *Sino-Indian Studies* 5: 3–4 (1957): 80–114.

Hu-Sterk, Florence. "Miroir connaissance dans la poésie des Tang." *Études Chinoises* 6/1 (1987): 29–58.

Jaggar, Alison M., and Susan R. Bordo, eds. *Gender/Body/Knowledge: Feminist Reconstructions of Being and Knowing*. New Brunswick: Rutgers University Press, 1989.

Jameson, Fredric. "Third-World Literature in the Era of Multinational Capitalism." *Social Text* 15 (1986): 65–88.

Jones, Andrew. "The Poetics of Uncertainty in Early Chinese Literature." *Sino-Platonic Papers* 2 (February 1987): 1–45.

K'ang Hsi. *The Sacred Edict*. Translated by F. W. Baller. 2nd edition. Shanghai: American Presbyterian Mission Press, 1907.

Kao, Yu-kung (Gao Yougong). "Lyric Vision in Chinese Narrative: A Reading of *Hung-lou Meng* and *Ju-lin Wai-shih*." In Andrew H. Plaks, ed., *Chinese Narrative: Critical and Theoretical Essays*, pp. 227–43. Princeton: Princeton University Press, 1977.

Karlgren, Bernhard., trans. *The Book of Odes*. Stockholm: Museum of Far Eastern Antiquities, 1950.

———. "The Early History of the *Chou Li* and *Tso Chuan* Texts." *Bulletin of the Museum of Far Eastern Antiquities* 28 (1931): 1–58.

———. *Grammata Serica Recensa*. Originally No. 29 of the *Bulletin of the Museum of Far Eastern Antiquities*, 1957; reprinted Stockholm: Museum of Far Eastern Antiquities, 1972.

Kauffman, Linda, ed. *Gender and Theory: Dialogues on Feminist Criticism*. Oxford: Basil Blackwell, 1989.

Kermode, Frank. *The Art of Telling: Essays on Fiction*. Cambridge: Harvard University Press, 1983.

King, Ambrose Y. C. "The Individual and Group in Confucianism: A Relational Perspective." In Donald Munro, ed., *Individualism and Holism: Studies in Confucian and Taosit Values*, pp. 57–70. Ann Arbor: University of Michigan, 1985.

Knechtges, David R. "Dream Adventure Stories in Europe and T'ang China." *Tamkang Review* 4/2 (1973): 101–21.

———, trans. *Wen Xuan or Selections of Refined Literature*. Vols. 1–3. Princeton: Princeton University Press, 1982–1996.

Knoblock, John. *Xunzi: A Translation and Study of the Complete Works*. 3 vols. Stanford: Stanford University Press, 1988–1994.

Knoerle, Jeanne. *"The Dream of the Red Chamber": A Critical Study*. Bloomington: Indiana University Press, n.d.

LaCapra, Dominick. *History and Criticism*. Ithaca: Cornell University Press, 1985.

Lackner, Michael. *Der chinesische Traumwelt: Traditionelle Theorien des Traumes und seiner Deutung im Spiegelder Meng-lin hsüan-chieh*. Frankfurt am Main: Peter Lang, 1985.

LaFleur, William R. *The Karma of Words: Buddhism and the Literary Arts in Medieval Japan*. Berkeley and Los Angeles: University of California Press, 1983.

———. "Saigyo and the Buddhist Value of Nature." Part I and Part II. *History of Religions* 13/2 (1973):93–128; 13/3 (1974): 227–48.

Lai, Whalen. "How the Principle Rides on the Ether: Chu Hsi's Non-Buddhist Resolution of Nature and Emotion." *JCP* 11/1 (1984): 31–66.

———. "Tao-sheng's Theory of Sudden Enlightenment Re-Examined." In Peter N. Gregory, ed., *Sudden and Gradual: Approaches to Enlightenment in Chinese Thought*, pp. 169–200. Honolulu: University of Hawaii Press, 1987.

Langer, Susanne K. *Feeling and Form: A Theory of Art*. New York: Charles Scribner's Sons, 1953.

———. *Philosophy in a New Key: A Study in the Symbolism of Reason, Rite, and Art*. New York: New American Library, 1942.

Laniciotti, Lionello, ed. *La donna nella Cina imperiale e nella Cina repubblicana*. Florence: L. S. Olschki, 1980.

Lau, D. C., trans. *The Analects*. New York: Penguin, 1979.

———, trans. "The Doctrine of Kuei Sheng in the *Lü-shih ch'un-ch'iu*." *Bulletin of the Institute of Chinese Literature and Philosophy*, Academia Sinica 2 (March 1992):51–90.

———. *Mencius*. Harmondsworth: Penguin, 1970.

―――. "The Treatment of Opposites in Lao Tzu." *Bulletin of the School of Oriental and African Studies* 21 (1958): 349–50; 352–57.

Le Goff, Jacques. *History and Memory*. Translated by Steven Rendall and Elizabeth Claman. New York: Columbia University Press, 1992.

Lee, Thomas H. C. *Government Education and Examinations in Sung China*. Hong Kong: Chinese University Press, 1985.

Legge, James, trans. *The Chinese Classics*. Originally printed in 7 volumes by Oxford University Press, 1892; reprinted in 5 volumes, Taipei: Wenshizhe, 1972. (Volume number used in this book corresponds to the reprinted edition only.)

―――, trans. *Li Chi, Book of Rites*. 2 vols. New Hyde Park: University Books, 1967.

Leskey, Albin. *Geschichte der Griechischen Literatur*. Bern: Francke, 1957.

Lévi-Strauss, Claude. *The Savage Mind*. Chicago: University of Chicago Press, 1966.

Lévy, André. "La Condamnation du roman en France et en Chine." In his *Études sur le conte et le roman Chinois*, pp. 1–13. Paris: École française d'Extrême-Orient, 1971.

Lewis, Ida Belle. *The Education of Girls in China*. New York: Teachers College, Columbia University, 1919.

Lewis, Lancaster. "Buddhist Literature: Its Canons, Scribes, and Editors." In Wendy Doniger O'Flaherty, ed., *The Critical Study of Sacred Texts*, pp. 215–29. Berkeley and Los Angeles: Graduate Theological Union, 1979.

Li, Tche-houa, and Jacqueline Alézaïs, trans. *Le rêve dans le pavillon rouge*. 2 vols. Paris: Gallimard, 1981.

Li, Wai-yee. *Enchantment and Disenchantment: Love and Illusion in Chinese Literature*. Princeton: Princeton University Press, 1993.

―――. "The Idea of Authority in the *Shih Chi* (Records of the Historian)." *HJAS* 54 (1994): 345–406.

Lin, Shuen-fu. "Chia Pao-yü's First Visit to the Land of Illusion: An Analysis of a Literary Dream in an Interdisciplinary Perspective." *CLEAR* 14 (1992): 77–106.

―――. "The Formation of a Distinctive Generic Identity for *Tz'u*." In Pauline Yu, ed., *Voices of the Song Lyric in China*, pp. 3–29. Berkeley and Los Angeles: University of California Press, 1994.

―――, and Stephen Owen, eds. *The Vitality of the Lyric Voice: Shih Poetry from the Late Han to the T'ang*. Princeton: Princeton University Press, 1986.

Lin Yutang. "Feminist Thought in Ancient China." *T'ien Hsia Monthly* 1/2 (1935): 127–50.

Lipking, Lawrence. *Abandoned Women and Poetic Tradition*. Chicago: University of Chicago Press, 1988.

Liu, Hui-chen (Wong). *The Traditional Chinese Clan Rules*. Locust Valley, N.Y.: J. J. Augustin, 1959.

Liu, James J. Y. *Chinese Theories of Literature*. Chicago: University of Chicago Press, 1975.

―――. *The Interlingual Critic: Interpreting Chinese Poetry*. Bloomington: Indiana University Press, 1982.

Liu, James T. C. *Reform in Sung China: Wang An-shih (1021–1086) and His Policies*. Cambridge: Harvard University Press, 1959.

Liu, K. C., ed. *Orthodoxy in Late Imperial China*. Berkeley and Los Angeles: University of California Press, 1990.

Llewellyn, Bernard. *China's Courts and Concubines*. London: George Allen & Unwin, 1956.

Lu, Sheldon Hsiao-peng. *From Historicity to Fictionality: The Chinese Poetics of Narrative*. Stanford: Stanford University Press, 1994.

Lu Tonglin. *Rose and Lotus: Narrative of Desire in France and China*. Albany: State University of New York Press, 1991.

Lynn, Richard John. "Chu Hsi as Literary Theorist and Critic." In Wing-tsit Chan, ed., *Chu Hsi and Neo-Confucianism*, pp. 337–54. Honolulu: University of Hawaii Press, 1986.

Ma Tai-loi. "Novels Prohibited in the Literary Inquisition of Emperor Ch'ien-lung, 1722–1788." In Winston L. Y. Yang and Curtis Adkins, eds., *Critical Essays on Chinese Fiction*, pp. 201–12. Hong Kong: Chinese University Press, 1980.

Ma, Y. W. "The Chinese Historical Novel: An Outline of Themes and Contexts." *JAS* 34/2 (1975): 277–94.

———. "Fact and Fantasy in T'ang Tales." *CLEAR* 2 (1980): 167–81.

———, and Joseph S. M. Lau, eds. *Traditional Chinese Stories: Themes and Variations*. New York: Columbia University Press, 1978.

Mair, Victor H., ed. *Experimental Essays on Chuang-tzu*. Honolulu: University of Hawaii Press, 1983.

———. *Tun-huang Popular Narratives*. New York: Cambridge University Press, 1983.

Major, John S. "A Note on the Translation of Two Technical Terms in Chinese Science: *Wu-hsing* and *Hsiu*." *Early China* 2 (1976): 1–3.

Mann, Susan. "The Education of Daughters in the Mid-Ch'ing Period." In Benjamin A. Elman and Alexander Woodside, eds., *Education and Society in Late Imperial China, 1600–1900*, pp. 19–49. Berkeley and Los Angeles: University of California Press, 1994.

———. "'Fuxue' (Women's Learning) by Zhang Xuecheng (1738–1801): China's First History of Women's Culture." *Late Imperial China* 13/1 (1992): 40–62.

———. "Widows in the Kinship, Class, and Community Structures of Qing Dynasty China." *JAS* 46/1 (February 1987):37–56.

Mather, Richard B., trans. *Shih-shuo Hsin-yü: A New Account of the Tales of the World*. By Liu I-ching. Minneapolis: University of Minnesota Press, 1976.

McMahon, Keith. *Causality and Containment in Seventeenth-Century Chinese Fiction*. Leiden and New York: E. J. Brill, 1988.

———. *Misers, Shrews, and Polygamists: Sexuality and Male-Female Relations in Eighteenth-century Chinese Fiction*. Durham and London: Duke University Press, 1995.

McRae, John R. *The Northern School and the Formation of Early Ch'an Buddhism*. Honolulu: University of Hawaii Press, 1986.

Miller, J. Hillis. *The Ethics of Reading: Kant, de Man, Eliot, Trollope, James and Benjamin*. New York: Columbia University Press, 1987.

———. "Introduction" to Charles Dickens, *Bleak House*. Harmondsworth: Penguin, 1985.

———. "Literature and History: The Example of Hawthorne's 'The Minister's Black Veil.'" *Bulletin of the American Academy of Arts and Sciences* 41 (1988): 15–31.

Miller, Lucien. *Masks of Fiction in "Dream of the Red Chamber": Myth, Mimesis, and Persona*. Tucson: University of Arizona Press, 1975.

Miner, Earl. *Comparative Poetics: An Intercultural Essay on Theories of Literature.* Princeton: Princeton University Press, 1990.

Minford, John. "The Last Forty Chapters of *The Story of the Stone*: A Literary Appraisal." Ph.D. dissertation, Australian National University, 1980.

———. "'Pieces of Eight': Reflections on Translating *The Story of the Stone*." In Eugene Eoyang and Lin Yao-fu, eds., *Translating Chinese Literature*, pp. 178–203. Bloomington: Indiana University Press, 1995.

Mink, Louis O. "History as Modes of Comprehension." *NLH* 1/3 (1970): 227–39.

Mitchell, W. J. T. *Iconology: Image, Text, Ideology.* Chicago: University of Chicago Press, 1986.

Miyazaki, Ichisada. *China's Examination Hell: The Civil Service Examinations of Imperial China.* Translated by Conrad Schirokauer. New Haven: Yale University Press, 1976.

Momigliano, Arnaldo. "Ancient History and the Antiquarian." In *Contributo alla Storia degli Studi classici*, pp. 67–106. Roma: Edizioni di Storia e letteratura, 1955.

———. "Biblical Studies and Classical Studies: Simple Reflections about Historical Method." *Biblical Archaeologist* 45/4 (Fall 1982): 224–28.

———. *Essays in Ancient and Modern Historiography.* Middletown, Conn.: Wesleyan University Press, 1977.

Munro, Donald, ed. *Individualism and Holism: Studies in Confucian and Taoist Values.* Ann Arbor: University of Michigan, 1985.

Na, Tsung-hsün (Na Zhongxun), ed. *Studies on "Dream of the Red Chamber": A Selected and Classified Bibliography.* 1979; Hong Kong: Lung Men (Longmen) Press, 1981.

Needham, Joseph. *Science and Civilisation in China.* 13 vols. Cambridge: Cambridge University Press, 1954–.

———. "Time and Knowledge in China and the West." In J. T. Fraser, ed., *The Voices of Time: A Cooperative Survey of Man's Views of Time as Understood and Described by the Sciences and the Humanities.* New York: G. Braziller, 1966.

Nienhauser, William, Jr. "Female Sexuality and the Double Standard in T'ang Narratives: A Preliminary Survey." In Eva Hung, ed., *Paradoxes of Traditional Chinese Literature*, pp. 1–20. Hong Kong: Chinese University Press, 1994.

———, ed. *The Indiana Companion to Traditional Chinese Literature.* Bloomington: Indiana University Press, 1986.

Nivison, David S. "The Philosophy of Chang Hsüeh-ch'eng." In *Occasional Papers* 3, pp. 22–34. Kyoto: Kansai Asiatic Society, 1955.

———. "The Problem of 'Knowledge' and 'Action' in Chinese Thought since Wang Yang-ming." *Studies in Chinese Thought, The American Anthropologist* 55/5, pt. 2 (1953): 126–34.

———, and Arthur F. Wright, eds. *Confucianism in Action.* Stanford: Stanford University Press, 1959.

Norman, Jerry. *Chinese.* New York: Cambridge University Press, 1988.

Nussbaum, Martha. *The Fragility of Goodness: Luck and Ethics in Greek Tragedy and Philosophy.* Cambridge: Cambridge University Press, 1986.

Oakley, Justin. *Morality and the Emotions.* London and New York: Routledge, 1992.

O'Flaherty, Wendy Doniger, ed. *The Critical Study of Sacred Text.* Berkeley and Los Angeles: Graduate Theological Union, 1979.

————. *Dreams, Illusions, and Other Realities*. Chicago: University of Chicago Press, 1984.

O'Hara, Albert Richard. *The Position of Woman in Early China According to the "Lieh nü chuan," The Biographies of Chinese Women*. 1945. Reprinted Hong Kong: Orient, 1955.

Olson, Elder. *Tragedy and the Theory of Drama*. Detroit:Wayne State University Press, 1961.

Ong, Roberto K. "Image and Meaning: The Hermeneutics of Traditional Chinese Dream Interpretation." In Carolyn T. Brown, ed., *Psycho-Sinology: The Universe of Dreams in Chinese Culture*, pp. 47–53. Lanham, Md.: University Press of America, 1988.

————. *The Interpretation of Dreams in Ancient China*. Bochum: Brockmeyer, 1985.

Osler, Sir William. *The Principles and Practice of Medicine*. 2nd edition. New York: D. Appleton, 1895.

Owen, Stephen. *Readings in Chinese Literary Thought*. Cambridge: Harvard University Press, 1992.

————. "The Self's Perfect Mirror: Poetry as Autobiography." In Shuen-fu Lin and Stephen Owen, eds., *The Vitality of the Lyric Voice: Shih Poetry from the Late Han to the T'ang*, pp. 71–102. Princeton: Princeton University Press, 1986.

————. *Traditional Chinese Poetry and Poetics: Omen of the World*. Madison: University of Wisconsin Press, 1977.

Palandri, Angela Tieug. "Women in Dream of the Red Chamber." *Literature East and West* 12/ 2, 3, 4 (1968): 226–38.

Plaks, Andrew H. "After the Fall: *Hsing-shih yin-yüan chuan* and the Seventeenth-Century Chinese Novel." *HJAS* 45/2 (1985): 543–80.

————. *Archetype and Allegory in "The Dream of the Red Chamber."* Princeton: Princeton University Press, 1976.

————, ed. *Chinese Narrative: Critical and Theoretical Essays*. Princeton: Princeton University Press, 1977.

————. *The Four Masterworks of the Ming Novel*. Princeton: Princeton University Press, 1987.

————. "Towards a Critical Theory of Chinese Narrative." In his *Chinese Narrative: Critical and Theoretical Essays*, pp. 309–52. Princeton: Princeton University Press, 1977.

Porter, Deborah. "Setting the Tone: Aesthetic Implications of Linguistic Patterns in the Opening Section of *Shui-hu chuan*." *CLEAR* 14 (1992): 51–75.

Powell, William F., trans. *The Record of Tung-shan*. Honolulu: University of Hawaii Press, 1986.

Powers, Martin J. *Art and Political Expression in Early China*. New Haven: Yale University Press, 1991.

Pratt, Leonard, and Chiang Su-hui, trans. *Shen Fu: Six Records of a Floating Life*. Harmondsworth: Penguin, 1983.

Pritchard, Earl H. "Traditional Chinese Historiography and Local Histories." In Hayden V. White et al., comps. and eds., *The Uses of History: Essays in Intellectual and Social History Presented to William J. Bossenbrook*, pp. 187–219. Detroit: Wayne State University Press, 1968.

Random House Unabridged Dictionary. Edited by Stuart Berg Flexner. 2nd revised edition. New York: Random House, 1993.

Raphals, Lisa. *Knowing Words: Wisdom and Cunning in the Classical Traditions of China and Greece*. Ithaca: Cornell University Press, 1992.

Redfern, Walter. *Puns*. Oxford: Basil Blackwell, 1984.

Redfield, James M. *Nature and Culture in the "Iliad": The Tragedy of Hector*. Chicago: University of Chicago Press, 1975.

Resnik, Salomon. *The Theatre of the Dream*. Translated by Alan Sheridon. London: Tavistock, 1987.

Ricoeur, Paul. *The Symbolism of Evil*. Translated by Emerson Buchanan. Boston: Beacon Press, 1972.

————. *Temps et récit*. 3 vols. Paris: Seuil, 1983–1985.

————. *Time and Narrative*. Translated by Kathleen McLaughlin and David Pellauer. 3 vols. Chicago: University of Chicago Press, 1984–1988.

Riffaterre, Michael. *Fictional Truth*. Baltimore: Johns Hopkins University Press, 1990.

Roberts, Moss, trans. *The Three Kingdoms, A Historical Novel*. Berkeley and Los Angeles: University of California Press; and Beijing: Foreign Languages Press, 1991.

Robertson, Maureen. "Voicing the Feminine: Constructions of the Gendered Subject in Lyrical Poetry by Women of Medieval and Late Imperial China." *Late Imperial China* 13/1(1992): 63–110.

Roetz, Heiner. *Confucian Ethics of the Axial Age*. Albany: State University of New York Press, 1993.

Rolston, David L., ed. *How to Read the Chinese Novel*. Princeton: Princeton University Press, 1990.

————. *Reading and Writing between the Lines: Traditional Chinese Fiction Commentary and Premodern Chinese Fiction*. Stanford: Stanford University Press, 1977.

Ropp, Paul S. "A Confucian View of Women in the Ch'ing Period—Literati Laments for Women in the *Ch'ing Shi tuo*." *Chinese Studies* 10/2 (1992): 399–435.

————. *Dissent in Early Modern China: Ju-lin wai-shih and Ch'ing Social Criticism*. Ann Arbor: University of Michigan Press, 1981.

————, ed. *Heritage of China: Contemporary Perspective on Chinese Civilization*. Berkeley and Los Angeles: University of California Press, 1990.

————. "Love, Literacy, and Laments: Themes of Women Writers in Late Imperial China." *Women's History Review* 2/1 (1993): 107–41.

————. "The Seeds of Change: Reflections on the Condition of Women in the Early and Mid Ch'ing." *Signs* 2/1 (1976): 5–23.

————. "Women between Two Worlds: Women in Shen Fu's *Six Chapters of a Floating Life*." In Anna Gerstlacher et al., eds, *Women and Literature in China*, pp. 98–140. Bochum: Studien Verlag, 1985.

Rosenmeyer, T. G. "History or Poetry? The Example of Herodotus." *Clio* 11 (1982): 239–59.

Rousell, Erwin. "Die Frau in Gesellschaft und Mythos der Chinesen." *Sinica* 16 (1941): 130–51.

Roy, David Tod, trans. *The Plum in the Golden Vase, or Chin P'ing Mei*. Vol. 1. Princeton: Princeton University Press, 1993.

Rubin, Vitaly A. "Ancient Chinese Cosmology and Fa-chia Theory." In Henry Rosemont, Jr., ed., *Explorations in Early Chinese Cosmology, JAAR Thematic Studies* 50/2 (1976): 95–104.

Said, Edward. *Beginnings: Intention and Method*. Baltimore: Johns Hopkins University Press, 1975.

Sartre, Jean-Paul. *Qu'est-ce que la littérature?* Paris: Gallimard, 1984.

Saussy, Haun. *The Problem of a Chinese Aesthetic*. Stanford: Stanford University Press, 1993.

———. "Reading and Folly in *Dream of the Red Chamber.*" *CLEAR* 9 (1987): 25–48.

Schleiermacher, Fr. D. E. *Hermeneutik*. Edited by Heinz Kimmerle. Heidelberg: Carl Winter, Univesitätsverlag, 1959.

Scholes, Robert, and Robert Kellogg. *The Nature of Narrative*. New York: Oxford University Press, 1966.

Schopenhauer, Arthur. *The World as Will and Idea*. Translated by R. B. Haldane and J. Kemp. 3 vols. 6th edition. London: K. Paul, Trench, Trubner, 1907–1909.

Schwartz, Benjamin I. *The World of Thought in Ancient China*. Cambridge: Harvard University Press, 1985.

Scott, Mary Elizabeth. "Azure to Indigo: *Hongloumeng*'s Debt to *Jing P'ing Mei.*" Ph.D. dissertation, Princeton University, 1989.

Shih, Chung-wen. *The Golden Age of Chinese Drama: Yüan "Tsa-chü."* Princeton: Princeton University Press, 1976.

Shils, Edward. *Tradition*. Chicago: University of Chicago Press, 1981.

Sivin, Nathan. "Change and Continuity in Early Cosmology." In *Chūgoku Kodai kagaku shiron (Zoku)*, pp. 3–43. Kyoto: Institute for Research in Humanities, 1991.

———. *Cosmos and Computation in Early Chinese Mathematical Astronomy*. Leiden: E. J. Brill, 1969.

———. "On the Limits of Empirical Knowledge in the Traditional Chinese Sciences." In J. T. Fraser et al., eds., *Time, Science, and Society in China and the West*, pp. 151–69. Amherst: University of Massachusetts Press, 1986.

———. *Traditional Medicine in Contemporary China: A Partial Translation of Revised Outline of Chinese Medicine*. Ann Arbor: University of Michigan Press, 1987.

Smith, Jonathan Z. *To Take Place: Toward Theory in Ritual*. Chicago: University of Chicago Press, 1987.

Sophocles. *Oedipus Rex and Antigone*. In F. Storr, trans., *Sophocles* I. Loeb edition. Cambridge: Harvard University Press, 1912.

Spence, Jonathan D. *Ts'ao Yin and the K'ang-hsi Emperor: Bondservant and Master*. New Haven: Yale University Press, 1966.

Sternberg, Meir. *Expositional Modes and Temporal Ordering in Fiction*. Baltimore: Johns Hopkins University Press, 1978.

Stinton, T. C. W. "*Hamartia* in Aristotle and Greek Tragedy." 1975. Reprinted in his *Collected Papers on Greek Tragedy*, pp. 143–85. Oxford: Clarendon Press, 1990.

Streng, Frederick J. *Emptiness: A Study in Religious Meaning*. Nashville, Tenn.: Abingdon Press, 1967.

Strickman, Michel. "Dreamwork of Psycho-Sinologists: Doctors, Taoists, Monks." In Carolyn T. Brown, ed., *Psycho-Sinology: The Universe of Dreams in Chinese Culture*, pp. 25–46. Lanham, Md.: University Press of America, 1988.

Suzuki, D. T., trans. *The Laṅkāvatāra Sūtra: A Mahayāna Text*. London: Routledge and Sons, 1932.

———. *Studies in the Laṅkāvatāra Sūtra*. London: Routledge and Sons, 1930.

Tang Xianzu. *The Peony Pavilion*. Translated by Cyril Birch. Bloomington: Indiana University Press, 1980.

Tatlow, Antony. "Problems with Comparative Poetics." *Canadian Review of Comparative Literature* (March–June 1993): 9–28.

Taylor, Rodney Leon. *The Cultivation of Sagehood as a Religious Goal in Neo-Confucianism: A Study of Selected Writings of Kao P'an-lung, 1562–1626.* Missoula, Mont.: Scholars Press, 1978.

Teiser, Stephen F. *Ghost Festival in Medieval China.* Princeton: Princeton University Press, 1988.

Thomson, Garrett. *Needs.* London: Routledge & Kegan Paul, 1987.

Treip, Mindele Anne. *Allegorical Poetics and the Epic: The Renaissance Tradition to "Paradise Lost."* Lexington: University Press of Kentucky, 1994.

Tsao Hsueh-chin. *Dream of the Red Chamber.* Translated by Chi-chen Wang. New York: Twayne, 1958.

Tsao Hsueh-chin and Kao Ngo. *A Dream of Red Mansions.* Translated by Yang Hsien-yi and Gladys Yang. 3 vols. Beijing: Foreign Languages Press, 1978.

Tu Wei-ming. *Confucian Thought: Self-hood as Creative Transformation.* Albany: State University of New York Press, 1995.

———. *Humanity and Self-Cultivation: Essays in Confucian Thought.* Berkeley and Los Angeles: Asian Humanities Press, 1979.

van der Loon, P. "The Ancient Chinese Chronicles and the Growth of Historical Ideals." In *HCJ*, pp. 24–30.

van Dyke, Carolynn. *The Fiction of Truth: Structures of Meaning in Narrative and Dramatic Allegory.* Ithaca : Cornell University Press, 1985.

van Zoeren, Steven Jay. *Poetry and Personality: Reading, Exegesis, and Hermeneutics in Traditional China.* Stanford: Stanford University Press, 1991.

Vasubandhu. *Wei Shih Er Shih Lun.* Translated by Clarence H. Hamilton. New Haven: American Oriental Society, 1938.

Wagner, Marsha L. "Maids and Servants in *Dream of the Red Chamber*: Individuality and the Social Other." In Robert E. Hegel and Richard C. Hessney, eds., *Expressions of Self in Chinese Literature*, pp. 251–81. New York: Columbia University Press, 1985.

Waltner, Ann. "On Not Becoming a Heroine: Lin Dai-yu and Cui Ying-ying." *Signs* 15/1 (Autumn 1989): 61–78.

Wang, C. H. "Recognition and Anticipation in Wang Kuo-wei's Criticism of *Hung-lou meng*." *Tsing Hua Journal of Chinese Studies* n.s. 10/2 (July 1974): 91–112.

Wang, David Der-wei. "Fictional History/Historical Fiction." *Studies in Language and Literature* 1 (March 1985): 64–76.

Wang Gungwu. "Some Comments on the Later Standard Histories." In Donald D. Leslie, Colin Mackerras, and Wang Gungwu, eds., *Essays on Sources for Chinese History*, pp. 50–67. Columbia: University of South Carolina Press, 1973.

Wang, Jing. *The Story of Stone: Intertextuality, Ancient Chinese Stone Lore and the Stone Symbolism in "Dream of the Red Chamber."* Durham, N.C.: Duke University Press, 1992.

Wang, John C. Y. "The Chih-yen-chai Commentary and the *Dream of the Red Chamber*: A Literary Study." In Adele Rickett, ed., *Chinese Approaches to Literature*, pp. 189–200. Princeton: Princeton University Press, 1978.

———. "Early Chinese Narrative: The *Tso-chuan* as Example." In Andrew H. Plaks, ed., *Chinese Narrative: Critical and Theoretical Essays*, pp. 3–20. Princeton: Princeton University Press, 1977.

————. "The Nature of Chinese Narrative: A Preliminary Statement of Methodology." *Tamkang Review* 6/2–7/1 (1975–1976): 229–46.

Wang, Richard G. "The Cult of *Qing*: Romanticism in the Late Ming Period and in the Novel *Jiaohongji.*" *Ming Studies* 33 (August 1994): 12–55.

Wang, Shifu. *The Moon and the Zither: The Story of the Western Wing.* Edited and translated by Stephen H. West and Wilt L. Idema. Berkeley and Los Angeles: University of California Press, 1991.

Watson, Burton, trans. *Hsün Tzu: Basic Writings.* New York: Columbia University Press, 1963.

————, trans. *Ssu-ma Ch'ien: Grand Historian of China.* 3 vols. New York: Columbia University Press, 1993.

Watson, Rubie S. and Patricia Buckley Ebrey. *Marriage and Inequality in Chinese Society.* Berkeley and Los Angeles: University of California Press, 1991.

Wayman, Alex. *Buddhist Insight: Essays.* Edited by George Elder. Delhi: Motilal Banarsidass, 1984.

————. "The Mirror as a Pan-Buddhist Metaphor-Simile." *History of Religions* 13/4 (1974): 251–269.

————. "The Mirror-like Knowledge in Mahayana Buddhist Literature." *Asiatische Studien* 25 (1971): 353–63.

White, Hayden (V.). *The Content of the Form: Narrative Discourse and Historical Representation.* Baltimore: Johns Hopkins University Press, 1987.

————. *Tropics of Discourse: Essays in Cultural Criticism.* Baltimore: Johns Hopkins University Press, 1978.

————, comp. and ed. *The Uses of History: Essays in Intellectual and Social History Presented to William J. Bossenbrook.* Detroit: Wayne State University Press, 1968.

Widmer, Ellen. *The Margins of Utopia: Shui-hu hou-chuan and the Literature of Ming Loyalism.* Cambridge: Harvard University Press, 1987.

Williams, Charles. *The Figure of Beatrice: A Study in Dante.* New York: Octagon Books, 1972.

Wolf, Margery, and Roxane Witke, eds. *Women in Chinese Society.* Stanford: Stanford University Press, 1975.

Wong, Kam-ming. "Point of View and Feminism: Images of Women in *Hongloumeng.*" In Anna Gerstlacher et al., eds., *Woman and Literature in China,* pp. 29–97. Bochum: Brockmeyer, 1985.

————. "Point of View, Norms, and Structure: *Hung-lou Meng* and Lyrical Fiction." In Andrew H. Plaks. ed., *Chinese Narrative: Critical and Theoretical Essays,* pp. 203–26. Princeton: Princeton University Press, 1977.

Wong, Sau-ling Cynthia. *Reading Asian American Literature: From Necessity to Extravagance.* Princeton: Princeton University Press, 1993.

Wong, Siu-kit. "*Ch'ing in Chinese Literary Criticism.*" Ph.D. dissertation, Oxford University, 1969.

Wu Ching-tzu. *The Scholars.* Translated by Yang Hsien-yi and Gladys Yang. New York: Grosset and Dunlap, 1972.

Wu Hung. *The Wu Liang Shrine: The Ideology of Early Chinese Pictorial Art.* Stanford: Stanford University Press, 1989.

Wu Pei-yi. *The Confucian's Progress: Autobiographical Writings in Traditional China.* Princeton: Princeton University Press, 1990.

Wu, Shih-ch'ang (Shichang). *On the Red Chamber Dream: A Critical Study of Two Annotated Manuscripts of the XVIIIth Century*. Oxford: Clarendon Press, 1961.

Yang, Lien-sheng. "The Organization of Chinese Official Historiography: Principles and Methods of the Standard Histories from the T'ang through the Ming Dynasty." In *HCJ*, pp. 44–59.

Yang, Winston L. Y., and Curtis Adkins, eds. *Critical Essays on Chinese Fiction*. Hong Kong: Chinese University Press, 1980.

Yu, Anthony C., trans. *The Journey to the West*. 4 vols. Chicago: University of Chicago Press, 1977–1984.

———. "New Gods and Old Order: Tragic Theology in the *Prometheus Bound*." *JAAR* 39 (1971): 19–42.

———. "'Rest, Rest, Perturbed Spirit!' Ghosts in Traditional Chinese Prose Fiction." *HJAS* 7/2 (1987): 397–434.

Yu, Pauline. "Alienation Effects: Comparative Literature and the Chinese Tradition." In Clayton Koelb and Susan Noakes, eds., *The Comparative Perspective on Literature: Approaches to Theory and Practice*, pp. 162–78. Ithaca: Cornell University Press, 1988.

——— et al., eds. *Culture and State in Chinese History: Conventions, Conflicts, and Accommodations*. Stanford: Stanford University Press, forthcoming.

———. *The Reading of Imagery in the Chinese Poetic Tradition*. Princeton: Princeton University Press, 1987.

———, ed. *Voices of the Song Lyric in China*. Berkeley and Los Angeles: University of California Press, 1994.

Yü, Ying-shih (Yu Yingshi). "Individualism and the Neo-Taoist Movement in Wei-Chin China." In Donald Munro, ed., *Individualism and Holism: Studies in Confucian and Taoist Values*, pp. 121–56. Ann Arbor: University of Michigan Press, 1985.

———. "The Seating Order at the Hung Men Banquet." Translated by T. C. Tang. *Renditions* (Special Issue on Chinese History and Historiography) 15 (1981): 49–61.

Zhang, Longxi. "The Letter and the Spirit: *The Song of Songs*, Allegoresis, and the *Book of Poetry*." *Comparative Literature* 39/3 (1987): 193–217.

Index

Adamantina, 125
Aeschylus: *Oresteia* and Erinyes, 219;
    Prometheus Bound and Io, 226
allegory and allegoresis, 4, 4–5n, 9, 12n, 16–
    17n, 27n, 50, 93–95, 97, 102–103, 105,
    114, 141, 153, 168–169n, 188, 258, 264–
    265
Aristotle, 34, 56, 58, 72, 85n, 95, 221, 226,
    251, 261
Aroma, 129, 131–132, 143, 148, 154, 203,
    214–216, 230, 235–236, 239, 241, 250;
    as go-between, 216
Asanga, 145
Atê, 221, 251
Augustine, 4n, 7, 51, 207n, 219, 225
Aunty Xue, 239, 247n, 248, 254
Auroras of Autumn, xi

Bai Juyi, 205, 261–263
Bailiff Wu, 18
Ban Zhao (*Nüjie or Commandments for
    Women*), 71
Bao Gong (Judge Bao), 246n
Bao Zhao, 134
Barthes, Roland, 12n, 24n
begonia-tree omen, 250–251
Benveniste, Emile, 51
Bian He, 161n
Bible, 43; David, 39; Saul, 39; Yahweh, 39
Blake, William, 43
Bloom, Harold, 259
Bo Ya, 236–37
Bodde, Derk, 111, 150n
Bodhidarma, 122
Bohu tong de lun, 67n, 70, 97n
Booth, Wayne C., 95, 265
Brother Amor (Passionate Monk), 150, 169–
    70; as reader, 171. *See also* Vanitas
Buddhism. *See* Buddhist themes; Zen
    Buddhism
Buddhist myth of stone, 120, 149, 158–159,
    162–163
Buddhist themes: *chujia* (leaving one's
    family), 122–123, 154, 169; deliverance
    (*jietuo*), 137, 149, 164, 222; dream, xii,
    10, 14, 25, 48–49, 115–116, 122, 137ff,

170, 266; enlightenment, 50, 121ff, 125,
    136, 141, 143, 147, 156, 162–163, 170,
    223, 225, 255, 266; four delusions, 137;
    huan (illusion, *māyā, māyopama*), 48–49,
    66, 121, 125, 137, 140–145, 150, 152,
    157–158, 166–170, 210, 255; Mahayana
    Buddhism, 49, 162, 170; mirror, 48, 115,
    121–122, 137, 141, 145ff, 266; monastic
    vocation, xii, 156; *nirvāna*, 141, 150, 167;
    samsāra (transmigration), 134, 143, 167;
    se (form, matter, *rūpa*), 149–150, 166–
    168, 171, 202, 210, 267n; sea of suffering,
    124; supreme (perfect) wisdom, 141, 145,
    150, 166–167; *upāya* (skillful means),
    169; Void (emptiness, *kong, śunyatā*),
    141, 149, 151, 166–169, 267n; *ye* (*kama*),
    121, 133–134, 162; *you qing* (sentiency),
    135ff. See also *mu shi wu qing*

cai, 113,119
caizi jiaren (scholar and beauty), 192, 213,
    216, 242
calendrical systems, 38
Calinescu, Matei, 26
Caltrop, 244
Camus, Albert (*A Happy Death*), 249
Cao Cao, 17
Cao Fu, 11n, 17
Cao Jie, 45
Cao Tangcun, 6n
Cao Xueqin, 5–6n, 11–12n, 14–16, 26, 49–
    50, 105, 114n, 118, 130, 135n, 136, 141,
    143, 145, 149, 168–169, 178–179, 190,
    192, 225, 263, 265, 267n; as author of
    Hongloumeng, 52, 114n, 168; his family
    and its relationship with *Hongloumeng*,
    18 (see also *Hongloumeng*: as autobiog-
    raphy and family history); as "I," 16; as
    original text, 16; as two Bao-yus of the
    novel, 16
Cao Yin, 11, 17
Cao Zhi, 105
Catastrophe of Nanjing, 11
Cervantes, Miguel de (*Don Quixote de la
    Mancha*), xi, 172
Chan Hing-ho (Chen Qinghao), 5n, 6n, 7, 11n

About the Author

ANTHONY C. YU is the Carl Darling Buck Distinguished Service Professor in the Humanities at the University of Chicago, where he teaches in the Divinity School and in the departments of East Asian Languages and Civilizations, English, and Comparative Literature, and serves on the Committee on Social Thought. An editor and author of three other books and numerous scholarly essays, he is best known for his complete, annotated translation of *The Journey to the West*.